The Hungry Empire

The Hungry Empire

How Britain's Quest for Food Shaped
the Modern World

LIZZIE COLLINGHAM

THE BODLEY HEAD
LONDON

1 3 5 7 9 10 8 6 4 2

The Bodley Head, an imprint of Vintage Publishing,
20 Vauxhall Bridge Road,
London SW1V 2SA

The Bodley Head is part of the Penguin Random House group of companies
whose addresses can be found at global.penguinrandomhouse.com.

Penguin
Random House
UK

First published by The Bodley Head in 2017

www.penguin.co.uk/vintage

A CIP catalogue record for this book is available from the British Library

ISBN 9781847922700

Typeset in India by Integra Software Services Pvt. Ltd, Pondicherry

Printed and bound by Clays Ltd, St Ives plc

Penguin Random House is committed to a sustainable future for
our business, our readers and our planet. This book is made
from Forest Stewardship Council® certified paper

FSC
www.fsc.org

MIX
Paper from
responsible sources
FSC® C018179

For Partha Mitter
and in memory of
Chris Bayly

Contents

PART III

PART IV

List of Illustrations

'A view of a stage as also of the manner of fishing and drying cod at Newfoundland', in Hermann Moll, *A New and correct map of the world, laid down according to the newest discoveries* (Canada, 1709–1720). Bridgeman Images.

Detail from 'The Kingdom of Ireland', in John Speed, *The Theatre of the Empire of Great Britain* (Thomas Basset and Richard Chiswell, London, 1676). Cambridge University Library.

The Seal for the Massachusetts Society for Promoting Agriculture, 1802. Photo © Granger/Bridgeman Images.

'Sugar refinery', in Jean Baptiste Du Tertre, *Histoire Générale des Antilles Habitées par le Français* (1667). Library of Congress, Washington DC.

John Raphael Smith after George Morland, 'The Slave Trade', 1791. Yale Center for British Art, Paul Mellon Collection.

Richard Houston, 'Morning', 1758. Yale Center for British Art, Paul Mellon Collection.

'Glaud and Peggy or The Gentle Shepherd', after David Allan, 1808. Yale Center for British Art; gift of Janet and James Sale, Yale.

Trade card of Hodson, tea dealer. The Trustees of the British Museum.

Alice F. Huger Smith, 'The sheaves are beaten with flails', 'Her little log cottage was as clean as possible', 'Gibbie and the oxen', 'A rice field "flowed"', 'The girls shuffled the rice about with their feet', 'Pounding rice' and 'Fanning and pounding rice for household use', in Elizabeth Allston Pringle, *A Woman Rice Planter* (Macmillan, New York, 1913).

George Sala, 'A Life on the Ocean Wave', undated. Yale Center for British Art; transfer from the Yale University Library and the Yale University Art Gallery.

John Lewis Krimmel, bar room dancing. Library of Congress, Washington DC.

The Indo-Chinese opium trade: the stacking room at an opium factory at Patna. Private collection/photo © Liszt Collection/Bridgeman Images.

James Ward, 'Cottage and farm buildings', undated. Yale Center for British Art, Paul Mellon Collection.

'Man outside a hut in the gum fields, holding loaves of bread', Northwood brothers, photographs of Northland. Alexander Turnbull Library, Wellington, New Zealand.

Frank Cyril Swannell, 'Oil claim Survey camp at Kishe-neh-na Creek: cook frying venison', East Kootenay region, British Columbia, 1904. Courtesy of Royal British Columbia Museum, British Columbia Archives, Canada.

Sir Charles D'Oyly, 'A punca bearer', undated. Yale Center for British Art, Paul Mellon Collection.

George Baxter, 'The Reception of the Reverend J. Williams at Tanna the Day Before He Was Massacred', 1841. Yale Center for British Art, Paul Mellon Collection.

'Tea Leaf Rolling' trade card for Nectar Tea Co., nineteenth century. Private collection/© Look and Learn/Bridgeman Images.

'The Old Room in Slumland', nineteenth century. Private collection/Bridgeman Images.

'Victims of the Madras Famine', 1877, photograph by Willoughby Wallace Hooper. Private collection/Bridgeman Images.

A River Plate Meat Company butcher's shop. Private collection.

Margaret Trowell, 'The African countryside as it is today and as it might be', in A. R. Paterson, *The Book of Civilization*, Part II (Longmans, Green and Company, London, 1935).

Colour plates

'Coolies. Demerara', Photographs and Clippings of the West Indies, 1890. Houghton Library, Harvard University.

'Coolies on board ship. Recently arrived in Demerara', Photographs and Clippings of the West Indies, 1890. Houghton Library, Harvard University.

Labels from tins of meat made by the James Gear Co., Wellington, New Zealand, 1890s. Alexander Turnbull Library, Wellington, New Zealand.

Introduction

'Bring food!' shouted the small boy who had taken on the role of the white district officer.

In a village in north-eastern Rhodesia, a group of Bemba boys were playing at being Europeans – one of their very favourite games. The main actor was lounging in a tangle of branches and bark rope, which stood in for a chair. During the course of the game he repeatedly called out for food until one of his playmates – who was acting as a servant – objected.

'You can't ask for food again,' he whispered, aghast. 'We've only just brought it to you.'

'You know nothing about Europeans!' his 'master' immediately replied. 'That is just what they do all day – just sit and call, "Boy! Bring me food."'[1]

The Bemba, who ate only one meal at the end of the day, regarded as childish the European habit of constantly breaking off from an activity to take tea or some other refreshment. This scene, witnessed by Audrey Richards, an anthropologist who lived among the Bemba for several years in the early 1930s, stands as a metaphor for the relationship of Britain to its empire. 'Bring me food' became a persistent demand.

This book tells the story of how Britain's quest for foodstuffs gave rise to the British Empire. Each chapter opens with a particular meal and then explores the history that made it possible. Why were a Frenchman and a glamorous Afro-Portuguese woman sharing a pineapple in West Africa in 1698? How did a team of surveyors prospecting for copper in British Columbia in 1901 come to be eating Australian rabbit? What configuration of circumstances led a group of Afro-Guyanese diamond miners to be cooking an iguana curry in 1993? Every chapter tells an individual story, but they all link up in a narrative that reveals food as a driving force of empire.

From the sixteenth century, when the British started to venture out across the oceans, they went in search of food. West Country fishermen began bringing cargoes of salt cod back from Newfoundland in the 1570s, and in the next century East India Company carracks unloaded millions of pounds of pepper and spices at London's East India docks. Before then, food imports had catered for the wealthy, who drank Burgundy wines with their heavily spiced meals and poured Italian olive oil on their salad greens. In the sixteenth century, the dried figs and currants, citrus fruits, almonds and spices that English merchants acquired in Antwerp in exchange for woollens accounted for only a tenth of all England's imports. But over the following centuries foodstuffs went from playing a negligible role in England's trade to centre stage. By 1775, half (by value) of all the goods Britain imported were foodstuffs, and West Indian sugar had ousted linen from first place as the most valuable of all the country's imports. In fact, with a value of over £2.3 million, West Indian sugar was worth more than all the manufactured goods arriving on Britain's shores.[2]

By now, food imports were no longer just for the rich. In fact colonial groceries had been thoroughly integrated into the diet of the entire population. Caribbean rum was the favourite Irish tipple, and everyone from street sweepers to gentlewomen enjoyed an afternoon cup of China tea sweetened with West Indian sugar. Britain sat at the centre of an impressive trading empire, and foodstuffs helped to turn the wheels of commerce. The Atlantic slave trade relied on supplies of maize and manioc grown in West Africa; the slaves working on South Carolina's plantations grew rice that the British traded with northern Europe for the timber and pitch needed by the shipbuilding industry. Trade and sea power were mutually dependent.[3] The merchant marine was an invaluable source of experienced seamen in time of war, and the Royal Navy protected the trade routes. The tax revenue generated by the import of commodities from around the globe in turn financed the building of warships.

The empire that grew out of this trade is often referred to as Britain's First Empire. It encompassed a wide variety of types of settlement – from fishing enterprises on Newfoundland's shores and agro-industrial sugar plantations on West Indian islands to neat English farms in southern Ireland and forts manned by a handful of soldiers dotted along the West African coastline. The Atlantic trade dominated, although the East India Company, with its factories in India and China, was growing in power and importance. What brought these disparate entities together in a common framework under the umbrella of Britain's empire was not the manner in which they were governed but how trade with them was regulated. The Navigation Acts stipulated that only British ships could carry their goods. For most of the eighteenth century the term 'empire' did not denote the possession of territory but the power to dominate trade. The first British Empire was an 'empire of the seas'.[4]

Britain's Second Empire emerged in the nineteenth century after the loss in 1783 of the thirteen mainland American colonies. This dealt the Empire a blow but in 1815 Britain emerged triumphant from the Revolutionary and Napoleonic wars with France as the world's pre-eminent maritime power.[5] The old closed mercantilist system was swept away by a fervent belief in the benefits of free trade.[6] British territories expanded into India, Africa and even as far afield as Australasia, and a mixture of military force and financial investment ensured that Britain's economic hegemony extended the nation's power into China and South America. Even the United States was reintegrated into this informal empire until the 1870s, when its own process of industrialisation allowed it to pull away from the British sphere of influence. This restless expansion allowed Britain to harness the world's resources.

The steamship and the railway moved unprecedented numbers of both people and goods across vast distances. Food was only one among the many commodities – textiles, dyestuffs, tin, rubber and timber – that flowed into Britain. But food imports from the commercial empire played an extremely important role as they became vital to the diet of the working classes upon whose labour the Industrial Revolution depended. By the 1930s, the wheat to make the working man's loaf was supplied by Canada and his Sunday leg of lamb had been fattened on New Zealand's grasslands.

In the tropics adventurers established plantation agriculture and imported slaves from West Africa and indentured labourers from India to provide a workforce. British migrants settled in the temperate zones and grew European foodstuffs on the land they appropriated from the indigenous inhabitants. In the process, the British eradicated entire native populations; they changed landscapes and agricultural systems, often destabilising other people's access to food; they facilitated the exchange of crops between the Old and New World, reshaping their own and other people's tastes in the process.[7] The food web that was woven by these developments created a truly global system that connected all five inhabited continents, drawing in even the most isolated and far-flung corners of the planet. *The Hungry Empire* reveals the intricate interdependence of the Empire and its role in shaping the eating habits of the modern world.

PART

·1·

CHAPTER
1

In which it is fish day on the Mary Rose, anchored in Portsmouth harbour (Saturday 18 July 1545)

How the trade in Newfoundland salt cod laid the foundations of the Empire

Saturday 18 July 1545 was a fish day on the *Mary Rose*. The crew ate on the cramped gun deck, sitting wherever they could find room. Fish days were not popular; sailors referred to salt cod as 'poor John'. But on this Saturday, the meal provided a welcome break from frantic activity as all 185 soldiers, 30 gunners and 200 mariners on board were busy readying the ship for war. That morning Nicholas Cooper and a couple of fellow cooks had climbed up to the sterncastle, passing crew members busy festooning the decks with anti-boarding netting. They had come to fetch the salt cod, which had been steeping in large vats of fresh water for the last 24 hours.[1] The ship's crew was divided into messes of six to eight men who ate together. Those men whose turn it was to prepare the food for their mess that day gathered on deck to collect their share of the fish. Each man was entitled to one quarter of a 24-inch salt cod.[2] They tied the fish into cloth bags and secured them with a peg bearing the mark of their particular mess. The bags ensured that even though the fish disintegrated into flakes as it cooked, every mess received their fair share. The men piled the bags of cod into wooden buckets and the cooks carried them down the steep companionways to the galley, a pocket of light and warmth in the dank darkness of the hold.[3]

The depths of the ship soon filled with the smell of cooking fish as the bags were set to simmer in the larger of the galley's two cauldrons. When it was ready, it was carried back up to the hungry crew on the gun deck. In each mess the fish was doled out in equal portions into the men's wooden bowls and they set to eating with wooden or horn spoons.[4] On fish days, every man was allowed four ounces of cheese and two of butter, and as the ship was in port, every man was also given a loaf of bread. This made a welcome change from the hard and worm-eaten ship's biscuit that they had to make do with when they were at sea.[5] They washed down the salty fish with gulps of beer. Their wooden drinking bowls were filled by a cook boy moving around the gun deck giving each man a portion of his daily allowance of a gallon of beer.

While the crew ate, their superiors discussed their fate. Anchored alongside the *Mary Rose* in Portsmouth harbour was the flagship, the *Henry Grace à Dieu*. Here the king, Henry VIII, was in council with the Lord Admiral of the Fleet, Viscount Lisle, and the *Mary Rose*'s commander, Vice Admiral George Carew. A French fleet had set sail for England 12 days previously and was expected to engage the English in battle the next day. As the three men schemed, Lisle sketched a battle plan on the back of a document that happened to be lying on the table. It placed the *Mary Rose*, one of the fleet's bigger warships, at the centre of the coming engagement.[6]

By the end of the following day, almost all of the crew of the *Mary Rose* were dead, drowned when she sank only a few minutes after going into battle. The gunners had just fired a round of cannon when a chance gust of wind caused the ship, overloaded with ordnance, to simultaneously turn and heel over. A Flemish survivor described how water flooded in through the open gun ports as the *Mary Rose* tipped beneath the waves.[7] Most of the men were on the upper decks, where they were caught in the web of anti-boarding netting and taken down as she sank. At most 40 survived, perhaps only as many as 25, out of a crew of 415.[8]

The wreck has bequeathed to us one of the best collections of Tudor artefacts, including shoes and tunics, medicine vials and bandage rolls, carpentry tools, guns, bows and arrows, and the skeletons of 179 men, a rat and a dog. Six of the skeletons were found in the galley.[9] Nicholas Cooper and his fellow cooks appear to have been busy preparing a tongue and some fresh beef when the ship went down. They were probably making a meal for the officers. Scattered across the galley floor were ten pewter plates belonging to the ship's commander, on which the food was meant to be served.[10] Divers found wooden bowls on the gun decks. It is from one of these that we know Nicholas Cooper's name, because he had inscribed it on his bowl. On the orlop deck and in the hold below it, archaeologists recovered the vertebrae of cattle and pigs, as well as thousands of fish spines amid the remains of the casks and wicker baskets that once held them. These were the residue of the ship's store of beef, pork and cod.[11] Salt meat and fish, biscuit, beer, cheese and butter were cheap, durable foodstuffs that could be stored for long periods and transported over great distances without becoming (completely) inedible.

The Tudor military ration drew mainly on local food sources: under Henry VIII, England was self-sufficient in staple foodstuffs. The pork and beef on the *Mary Rose* would have come from English herds of swine and cattle; the cheese from Gloucester or Cheshire; and the butter would have been made locally from the milk of Hampshire's dairy herds. But the fish was not a local product. Genetic analysis of some of the thousands of fish bones found in the wreck indicates that the cod had been caught in the northern North Sea and around Iceland. But one of the bones analysed was from a fish that came from much further afield, belonging to a genetic cluster of cod that lived off the north-eastern coast of the American continent.[12] By the middle of the sixteenth century, the Tudors were clearly venturing thousands of miles across the Atlantic Ocean in order to secure a staple foodstuff. This reliance on faraway places to supply England (and later Britain) with food was to become a hallmark of empire.

The importance of the Newfoundland fish trade in laying the foundations of the British Empire is frequently overlooked. The focus is usually on the story of maritime exploration and the quest for spices. But it was cod fishermen from the West Country who were the first Englishmen to acquire knowledge of the Atlantic currents and winds that later helped those explorers who went in search of a sea route to the Spice Islands.[13]

The medieval Christian practice of abstaining from meat on fast days had given rise to thriving European fisheries. In the fourteenth century, the Dutch mastered the art of pickling their North Sea herring catch in salt, which enabled even those devout northern Europeans living far inland to forgo meat on Fridays.[14] In the fifteenth century, pickled herring was eclipsed by Norwegian stockfish, air-dried cod that was distributed throughout northern Europe by the Hanseatic League.[15] The League's attempts to monopolise the North Sea catch drove the English to seek new fishing grounds. They found one on the continental shelf just off Iceland. The Danish authorities soon complained that the English who set up camp there in the summer months treated the island as though it were their own, digging ditches, putting up tents, even building houses, and assaulting competing Icelandic fishermen.[16] While the Icelanders wind-dried their catch, the English at first simply salted the cod before piling it in the holds of their boats. But over time, they combined these two preservation methods, lightly salting the fish before allowing it to dry in the air. The end product was both tastier than Norwegian stockfish and could be kept longer.[17]

A substantial share of the English fishermen's Icelandic catch was bought by Bristol merchants. Indeed, in the second half of the fifteenth century, Bristol emerged as England's major fish entrepôt.[18] This was because the city dominated England's wine trade at the time. The Englishman's tipple of choice was sweet 'sack' from the Iberian peninsula.[19] The Spanish and Portuguese had little use for England's staple export of woollen cloth: they preferred to exchange their wine for salt cod, which they regarded as a tasty and affordable alternative to meat.[20] Thus Bristol ships would sail to Iceland to buy up salt cod, and then continue to southern Europe and as far afield as the Spanish Canary Islands and the Azores, to exchange the fish for wine.[21] The city's place at the heart of this trade in fish for wine made Bristol a centre of knowledge about Atlantic navigation.

It was therefore no coincidence that the Venetian Zuan Caboto (better known by his anglicised name John Cabot) set sail from Bristol when in 1497 he went in search of a northern sea route to the Spice Islands. A group of Bristol merchants had already funded at least three western voyages to search for the mythical land of Hy-Brasil, said to lie beyond Ireland. They certainly knew that the seas in this part of the ocean were thick with cod. Moreover, some of these expeditions had almost certainly found land: they returned to Bristol laden down with salted and dried cod that it would have been impossible to dry on board ship.[22] Cabot would have drawn on this local knowledge, and after only 35 days at sea, his expedition arrived on the north-eastern coast of Canada. He had 'discovered' not the hoped-for sea route to the Indies but the land the Vikings had called Helluland and that Henry VII now christened Newfoundland.[23]

Cabot's discovery was much celebrated. The parsimonious king granted him a generous pension of £20 a year, to be paid from Bristol's customs receipts. The Duke of Milan's envoy in London wrote of sailors' reports of seas 'swarming with fish'.[24] The cod were supposedly so abundant that they could be caught without fishing nets or lines by simply lowering weighted baskets into the water. The envoy claimed that there was talk that England would 'have no further need of Iceland'.[25] But the king was not particularly interested in the shoals of fish. His imagination was caught by Cabot's claim that he would be able to follow the Newfoundland coastline until he reached Cipango (Japan), which he claimed was a source of spices and jewels. Henry was entranced by a vision of London as Europe's new spice entrepôt.[26]

The king's and Cabot's dreams were not to be realised for another century. In the meantime, the Bristol merchants quietly got on with making the most of the riches that had been discovered.[27] In 1501, Hugh Elyot sailed into Bristol harbour with the first recorded cargo of cod to arrive in Europe from North America. The 36 tons of salt cod were worth £180, which was equal to the annual income of a prosperous landed estate.[28] However, despite the evidence of such bounty, in the early years of the sixteenth century only a handful of West Country fishermen ventured to Newfoundland. The low level of domestic demand – due to the fact that the English lacked the southern Europeans' ability to transform the board-like fish into tasty dishes – meant that there was little incentive for English fishermen to choose the longer and stormier voyage across the Atlantic rather than the familiar journey to Iceland.[29] The seas off Newfoundland were instead dominated by the Bretons and the Basques, whose home markets were greedy for salt cod.[30]

THE WAY TO DRESS POOR JOHN, TO MAKE IT VERY TENDER AND GOOD MEAT

Put it in a Kettle of cold Water, and so hang it over the Fire, and let it soak and stew without boiling for three hours, but the Water must be very hot; then make it boil two or three walms [rolling boils]: By this time it will be very tender, and swelled up; then take out the Back-bone, and put it to fry with Onions, if you put it first into hot water … or being boyled if you let it cool, and heat it again, it will be tough and hard.[31]

The reasons for English fishermen to participate in the Newfoundland venture became more compelling over the course of the century. When Henry VIII inherited the throne from his father in 1509, he was determined to recover the territory England had once held in France and began enlarging the English navy: the *Mary Rose*, completed in 1511, was part of his ambitious shipbuilding programme.[32] The Anthony Roll, an illustrated inventory of his navy, records that by 1545 the king had used the wealth he had confiscated from the monasteries to build up a fleet of 58 ships from the five that he had inherited from his father. These were the beginnings of the navy that eventually played an important role in creating Britain's seaborne empire.

The expansion of the Tudor armada substantially increased the demand for salt cod. The Anthony Roll suggests that at full strength, Henry's navy would have employed about 7,700 men. If each of these was given a quarter of a salt cod on each of the two weekly fish days, then the annual naval demand in the 1540s would have amounted to over 200,000 salt fish.[33] At the end of every summer, naval purchasing agents would wait impatiently for the return of the fishing fleets, eager to secure their cargoes for the king's military forces. Indeed, the demands of naval provisioners expanded the English market to such an extent that by 1529, French fishermen were landing their Newfoundland catch at England's southern ports.[34]

A series of cold winters and poor harvests after Henry VIII's death in 1547 meant that England was beset by food shortages. In the face of rising food prices, naval victuallers on a tight budget struggled to supply the ships of the line with sufficient food.[35] In 1558, Elizabeth I's Secretary of State, Lord Burghley, calculated that when the cheese and butter that formed part of the sailors' salt cod ration was factored into the price, a fish day for a mess of four men cost the navy 8d – half the cost of a meat day. As part of an economy drive, he increased the number of fish days to three and replaced one of the remaining beef days with the less expensive pork and pease.[36] The suppression of rebellion in Ireland further increased demand for salt cod, in order to feed the 15,200 English soldiers who were stationed there by the end of Elizabeth's reign.[37] The soldiers liked fish days little better than the sailors. In his request for provisions in May 1599, the Earl of Essex pleaded with the Privy Council not to send his garrison any more 'Newland fish [as] … it neither keepeth well, nor pleaseth the soldier, who by such victuals hath so much to provoke his thirst and no provision to quench it'.[38] The fish's unpopularity notwithstanding, the demand for salt cod outstripped supply, and in 1595, army suppliers were forced to specially commission two fishing vessels to sail to Newfoundland to acquire salt cod provisions for the forces in Ireland.[39]

With growing demand, and an uncomfortable situation in Iceland, where the Danish authorities were demanding licence fees from the English, West Country fishermen began to sail in greater numbers to Newfoundland. By now the Basques had begun to disappear from the fishing grounds in the New World. Catholic Spain was embroiled in conflict with Protestant northern Europe, and the Spanish Crown had decimated the Basque fishing fleet by requisitioning men and ships to fight the Dutch. By the end of the sixteenth century, only about half a dozen Basque fishermen were still competing with the English, who now dominated Newfoundland's shores.[40]

Each spring, a flotilla of about a hundred ships set sail to Newfoundland from the West Country.[41] Most sailed via France, Portugal or West Africa to buy salt, and then turned west to cross the Atlantic. The first ships to arrive in Newfoundland had the pick of the best harbours.[42] Once the captain had chosen a good spot for a base camp, the ship was unrigged and 'in the snow and cold all the men go into the woods to cut timber, fir, spruce, and birch' to build landing stages and racks on which to dry the catch. They constructed makeshift sleeping huts and a cook room out of branches and turf, after which they re-assembled the skiffs and longboats they had brought out with them in pieces on the ship.[43] Once the camp was established, the fishing could begin.

In the early morning, the boats would row out to sea. Each held five men, three to catch the fish and two to stow it away in the bottom of the skiff. The cod were so 'thicke by the shoare' that one visitor to Newfoundland described how he was 'hardlie … able to row a Boate through them'.[44] Towards the afternoon the boats would return, laden down with as many as a thousand cod. As soon as they reached the shore, the foreshipman would hurry off to 'boil their kettle' and prepare a meal while the others threw their catch up to the shore men.[45]

The scale of the fishery was industrial, with hundreds of thousands of fish being caught, salted and dried every year. Newfoundland's beaches were transformed into open-air factories. Rather than each man preparing one fish

'A view of a stage as also of the manner of fishing and drying cod at Newfoundland'.
The scene shows a Newfoundland beach transformed into an industrial food-
processing factory. The men gathered round the table on the stage are beheading
and splitting the fish while to the left are the salters. In the foreground is a large
trough containing the cod liver oil; next to it men are washing the salted cod
before laying it out to air dry on the racks on the beach.

from beginning to end, the shore men were organised into efficient production
lines that enabled them to process hundreds of fish in an hour. Every man
performed a discrete task. James Yonge, a Plymouth-born ship's surgeon who
accompanied a group of fishermen to Newfoundland in 1662, described how as
the fish were thrown out of the boat a boy would pick them up and lay them on
a table on either side of which stood two men. The first, known as the 'header', dextrously opened the belly of each fish and took out the liver, which he
dropped into a tub under the table.[46] He then twisted off the head, which, along
with the guts, fell back into the sea through the slats in the landing stage. The
header then thrust the fish across the table to the second man, known as the
'splitter', 'who with a strong knife splits it abroad, and with a back stroke cuts
off the bone'. They worked so rapidly that they could process as many as 480
fish in just half an hour.

The split fish were thrown into a barrow and passed on to the 'salter', whose job was delicate and required more care. 'Too much salt burns the fish and makes it break and wet, too little makes it redshanks, that is, look red when dried, and so … not merchantable', Yonge observed.[47] The fish were left in the salt for a few days before being washed in seawater and piled up to dry on the stony beach. A day or so later, they were spread out on racks to dry in the wind – a technique the English had perfected in Iceland. At night, or if the weather was inclement, they had to be gathered into 'faggots' of four or five fish, with the skin upward. Once dried, they were piled up and pressed to make the salt sweat out of the flesh, a process known as 'corning', during which the cod turned white. Once they were finished, the fish were stored in 'dry piles', which by the end of the season were as large as haystacks.[48]

Since the Middle Ages, England had relied on its cloth industry to fund the purchase of almost all its luxury food imports. In the fifteenth century, English merchants sold woollens in Antwerp and used the profits to buy wine, spices, olive oil, and such large quantities of currants and raisins that the Italians assumed that rather than consuming them, the English must be extracting dye from the dried fruit. The economic depression of the 1550s and 1560s led to the collapse of the European market for English woollens. English demand for luxury foodstuffs did not, however, suffer a similar collapse, and wine, oil and currants became something of a drain on the country's stocks of bullion.[49] The privateer and explorer Sir Richard Hawkins complained that in order to obtain Spanish sack, which he thought caused 'hot burning Feavers, the Stone, the Dropsie, and infinite other Diseases … there is no yeare, in which [England] wasteth not two millions of Crownes of our substance by conveyance into forraine Countries'.[50] In Newfoundland cod the English now discovered a commodity that helped to remedy this trade imbalance.[51] From the late sixteenth century, Dutch, French and even a few Spanish-owned vessels would arrive in Newfoundland each year towards the end of the spring, laden with cargoes of wine, which they exchanged for salt fish. As a result, by 1620, only about 10 per cent of the Newfoundland catch was actually brought back to England, with most of it being packed into the holds of the sack ships and taken to southern Europe.[52] In September, the West Country fishermen sailed home, their ships loaded with barrels of wine as well as salt fish to sell on to military provisioning officers.

The Newfoundland fishery thus grew into a thriving branch of English commerce. Increasing numbers of investors and merchants (some from as far afield as London) began to participate in the trade, funding and commissioning voyages. The number of ships sailing to Newfoundland each spring more than doubled, until by 1615, 250 ships took part in the enterprise. The economies of the West Country ports were dominated by the Newfoundland fisheries, with at least 6,000 landlubbers employed in supporting trades such as shipbuilding, rope- and sail-making.[53] For West Country mariners, long-range travel across the Atlantic Ocean had become a routine activity.[54]

In the seventeenth century, English merchant ships joined the fishing fleet.[55] James Yonge made his third voyage to Newfoundland in 1664 on the *Robert Bonadventure*, a small ship that acted as both a fishing boat and a merchant trader. She sailed from Plymouth to Newfoundland via Bonavista, an island near Cape Verde, where she picked up a cargo of salt. After a couple of months fishing and trading in Newfoundland, she sailed for the Straits of Gibraltar and entered the Mediterranean. In Genoa, the captain handed over the cargo of salt cod to the factor acting for the merchant who had commissioned the voyage.[56] Yonge did not mention what goods made up the return cargo, but it is likely that the *Robert Bonadventure*'s hold was packed with wine, olive oil and currants before she sailed back to Plymouth. A 250-ton freighter that made a voyage from Newfoundland to southern Europe in the 1630s could expect to earn something like £465 from its cargo of cod. This was a 14 per cent return on an investment of £3,300. The sale of the return cargo, bought with the proceeds of the sale of the fish in the Mediterranean, could double this profit.[57]

Newfoundland salt cod injected the English trading economy with cash.[58] The southern Europeans' continuing appetite for salt cod eventually outweighed the English demand for southern European comestibles. This allowed England to gain access to New World specie as the Spanish were forced to pay for some of the fish in silver. The English mercantilist economist Charles Davenant criticised Spain for allowing the riches of the New World to pass through its economy undigested. The Spanish, he pointed out, failed to gain 'spirits, strength, or nourishment' from their bullion. Not so the English, who possessed a much healthier economic constitution. English merchants pumped the silver back into the economy by using it to fund further trading exploits.[59]

Before the economic downturn in the 1550s, England had played a largely passive role in global commerce. Most of its trade had been channelled through Antwerp, and the English had relied on European contacts with commodity markets further afield to access their share of exotic goods from around the world. But when Antwerp failed to recover in the 1570s, English merchants began to seek direct contact with distant markets and they put the Spanish silver acquired from the sale of salt cod to good use funding trading ventures to the Levant, Muscovy and East India.

The British Empire was born on Newfoundland's stony beaches. The fishermen living in temporary shacks on the edge of a vast continent, their leather aprons covered with fish scales and blood, conquered distance with their innovative food-processing techniques and laid down the foundations of empire. The expanding merchant marine drew on the pool of well-travelled and competent fishermen to man its ships, and in this way the Newfoundland fishery helped to fund, crew and sustain the voyages of both the maritime explorers and the merchant seamen who followed in their wake.[60] Between 1570 and 1689, the tonnage of English shipping grew sevenfold and England emerged as a major European sea power.[61] The nation's first venture into food processing on an industrial scale played an important part in enabling it to take an active and independent role in world trade.[62] Both as a portable foodstuff and as a trading commodity, 'poor John' was one of the building blocks of the British Empire.

·2·

In which John Dunton eats oatcake and hare boiled in butter in a Connaught cabin (1698)

How Ireland was planted with English, became a centre of the provisions trade and fed the emerging Empire

Supper was ready in the small cabin in Connaught where John Dunton was staying. His landlady drew a long stool in front of his bench of rushes, then pulled the linen kerchief from her head and smoothed it over the stool to act as a warm and slightly odorous tablecloth. She set before Dunton an oatcake and a 'greate roll of fresh butter' (3 lb at least) as well as a wooden vessel full of milk and water. Her daughter then brought in the hare that Dunton and his host had caught earlier that day, 'swimming in a wooden boul full of oyl of butter', in which it had been boiled. Yet, having watched the women of the household prepare the meal, Dunton found that he could not swallow a morsel and asked instead for an egg.[1]

An eccentric London bookseller and publisher, Dunton had travelled to Ireland in 1698 to escape his quarrelsome second wife. Without the help of a guide, it would have been impossible for him to venture into the rough county of Connaught, 'for in these mountains there are no inns, nor indeed any roads'. At the beginning of the letter describing his adventures in this part of Ireland, Dunton commented that he was about to proceed into a part of the country where all 'the barbarities ... under which it so long laboured, and with which it was soe miserably infected, are all accumulated'.[2]

That afternoon, however, he had been received with greater humanity than he had expected from 'persons appearing so barbarous'. His guide's relatives welcomed him to their home with a syllabub made of a mix of sour and fresh milk that Dunton admitted was 'pleasing' to the taste. They then set about preparing him a meal. The 'woman of the house' sat on an old horse's hide on the floor and, with a quern between her naked legs, lustily ground three pecks of oats. Dunton, who was no shrinking violet, claimed that he did not know where to look as she was exposed 'to the bottom of her belly'. The oats ground, she mixed them with a little water to form a dough and fashioned it into a flat cake. This was propped against a tripod to bake before the turf fire. The woman's mother was deputed to watch the cake which she did 'while … sneezing into her nose or wipeing away the snivel with the same hands that she turn'd my oaten cake'. The performance made Dunton's 'gutts wamble'. Any remaining appetite he had for the food waned when the woman brought a wooden churn over to the fire and, gripping it in the same manner as the quern between her naked legs, set to work, using her right arm instead of a churn staff to turn the fresh milk into butter. With her left hand she wiped off any flecks of milk that splashed onto her thighs and put them back in the pot. Dunton remarked that it was no wonder Irish butter smelt 'rank and strong … for surely the heate which this labour put the good wife in must unavoidably have made some of the essence of arms pitts tricle down her arm into the churn'. It was in this butter that the hare had been boiled.[3]

While the family devoured the food, Dunton ate his egg and drank his milk. Closing his eyes 'for fear of making any ungrateful discoveries in my liquor', he put the bowl to his lips. As he swallowed the last of it, he discovered a long straw between his teeth. 'You may guess', he wrote, 'at what it almost occasion'd.' His guide told him there was no hurt in it as it was 'nothing but a piece of the strainer', and they showed him the conical piece of birch bark stuffed with straw and grass that they used to strain out any hairs or dirt from the fresh milk. Countless English visitors before Dunton had complained that Irish milk was full of dirty specks due to the fact that the Irish had the unsavoury habit of straining it through 'none of the cleanest' straw. His experience confirmed Dunton in his belief that Connaught was a last bastion of the old Irish ways, which had been successfully eradicated from the rest of Ireland by the 'planting of English among them'.[4]

When John Dunton arrived at the cabin in Connaught,
the 'woman of the house' took a wooden bowl of sour
milk and dipping into it her 'nasty fingers twice or thrice
to pick out some dirt' carried it over to the family's cow
that was standing before the door of their cabin, milking
it straight into the bowl to produce the syllabub.[5] These
instructions from an eighteenth-century cookbook show
that obtaining the milk straight from the cow was considered the best way to make such a concoction.

TO MAKE A SYLLABUB FROM THE COW

Make your syllabub of either cyder or wine, sweeten it
pretty sweet, and grate nutmeg in; then milk into the
liquor: when this is done, pour over the top half a pint
or a pint of cream, according to the quantity of syllabub
you make. You may make this syllabub at home, only
have new milk; make it as hot as milk from the cow, and
out of a teapot, or any such thing, pour it in, holding
your hand very high, and strew over some currants well
washed and picked, and plumped before the fire.[6]

Henry VII had little to do other than name Newfoundland in order to incorporate it within the Crown's sphere of influence. The English went there
simply to exploit the seas and had barely any contact with the indigenous
Beothuk, who shied away from the strangers and withdrew inland.[7] In contrast, the attempt to unite the Irish lords in a 'commonwealth' held together by
a (preferably English) common law and loyal to the English Crown was a far
more challenging undertaking.[8] In 1545, a small area around Dublin known
as the Pale was governed directly by England. The northern and western up-

lands were dominated by Gaelic chieftains who spoke their own language and lived according to their own customs and law. Fynes Moryson, personal secretary to Lord Mountjoy, commander-in-chief of the English army in the early 1600s, complained that the 'O' or 'Mac' that the Gaelic lords placed before their clan names gave the impression that Ireland was peopled by 'devouring giants [rather] than Christian subjects'.[9] Leinster and Munster in the south were controlled by Anglo-Norman peers who had settled there in the twelfth century when Henry II attempted to bring the island under England's control. But many of them had gone native: they were connected to the Gaelic chieftains through marriage; they conducted political negotiations in the Irish style at open-air gatherings; and they routinely cemented alliances in the Irish fashion by sending their children to be fostered in each other's families. Particularly disturbing to the English was their inclusion of Gaelic bards and musicians in their household retinues, as the Irish accorded poetry an almost occult power.[10] Constant rivalry between various petty chieftains, who indulged in endless bouts of cattle raiding and pillaging, meant that the country was chronically unstable and violent. Moreover, after the schism with the papacy in 1534, Protestant English monarchs worried that Catholic Ireland would provide political rivals with a base from which to launch an attack on their sovereignty.[11]

Tudor officials diagnosed pastoralism as the source of Ireland's malaise. They argued that rather than following the path of historical progress 'from the woods to the fields and from the fields to settlements and communities of citizens', the Irish had remained a wild and nomadic people.[12] The warm, wet summers produced rich upland grazing and many Irish peasants followed their cattle into higher pastures in the summer. They wore strange, straight trousers and loose coats quite unlike an Englishman's wide breeches and waistcoat but well suited to the activities of wading through bogs and marching over heathland with their cattle. The mantles they wore added to their fearsome appearance, as they were so voluminous that they could serve as a 'cabin for an outlaw in the woods, a bed for a rebel, and a cloak for a thief'.[13]

Since classical times, settled grain-cultivating farmers had dismissed pastoralists as uncivilised. For the Greek historian Herodotus, the use of cookery to transform raw ingredients was the mark of civilised farming populations; barbarian pastoralists drank raw milk and barely cooked their meat.[14] Tudor observers of Ireland, steeped in classical learning, invoked these associations when they described the Irish diet.[15] They were appalled by

The 'wilde Irish man' in this illustration for a map of Ireland is wearing the
long hair and straight trousers English observers thought strange and uncivilised,
while his companion the 'wilde Irish woman' is wrapped in one of the voluminous
mantles favoured by the Irish and that the English considered fit only for a rebel
or a thief. The cartographers will have drawn the figures from a set of instructions
and had probably never seen an Irishman.

their practice of opening their cows' veins to draw off the blood, which they
consumed mixed with butter and salt. They claimed that the Irish devoured
entrails so fresh that they were 'breathing new' and ate barely boiled flesh
with 'whole lumps of filthy butter'.[16] Moryson declared Irish butter so revolt-
ing that no Englishman would touch it 'with his lippes, though he were half
starved'.[17] But the English reserved their greatest disgust for what the Irish
regarded as their finest 'daintie': bonny clabber. John Dunton was treated to
this dish of sour curds the next morning. Confounded by the 'unusualness of
the mess and the sluttishness of the cookery', he went without breakfast and
bade the family adieu.[18]

At the heart of the English intervention in Ireland lay a value judgement about the right way for a people to cultivate their land. The English were in the grip of a movement for agricultural 'improvement' that promoted the practice of mixed livestock and arable farming as man's most 'natural and holie' occupation.[19] Reformers at Henry VIII's court were blind to Ireland's fruitful fields of oats and barley, its stone fortifications, churches and towns.[20] Like Thomas More's Utopians, who drove out of their land any natives who refused to assist in the project to make it yield its natural abundance, the English insisted that Ireland was a barren uncultivated wasteland and that it was incumbent upon them to impose tillage agriculture on its untended landscape.[21] This, the reformers argued, could best be achieved by planting English settlers 'among the weeds of Irish society'.[22] The English cast themselves in the role of 'new Romans': just as Roman settlers had civilised the barbarous ancient Britons, so the English would civilise the Irish.[23]

The settlers would refashion the landscape to resemble the south-eastern English lowlands. Stone manor houses with adjacent orchards, vegetable gardens and fish ponds would dot the landscape, while the tenant farmers would live in orderly nuclear villages surrounded by well-tended enclosed fields. This configuration was considered the fundamental basis for a stable society.[24] If such an example of good husbandry were held up before them, the Irish would surely be persuaded to take up the plough, transforming themselves from unruly cattle-raiding tribesmen into feudal villagers. Their 'messy mish-mashes of gruel', oatcakes, blood puddings and bonny clabber would be replaced with the food of settled farmers: white wheaten bread and well-roasted joints of meat.[25] At the same time, the profitability of this new way of farming would teach them the value of the English principle of private property preserved from division by primogeniture.[26] Thus these reformers conceived agriculture as a prime agent of civilisation.

Tudor rulers, however, showed little enthusiasm for expending the money and effort it would cost to subdue and civilise the Irish. Under Edward VI, English soldiers who had finished their term of service were granted land on the edge of the Pale. They brought English retainers over to farm the land and their estates created a secure buffer zone along the western borders of the area. Under Queen Mary, this strategy was formally extended to the counties of Leix and Offaly, renamed Queen's County and King's County in 1556. But it was not until the reign of Elizabeth I that a concerted effort was made to establish a plantation of English settlers. The prime instigators of this policy were drawn from a circle of men who had been exposed to the idea of Irish plantation at Henry VIII's court and then rose to prominence under Edward VI and his sisters.[27]

The opportunity to put the strategy of settlement into practice came in 1569, when Sir Henry Sidney, the Lord Deputy of Ireland, installed Humphrey Gilbert as military governor in Munster. The Earl of Desmond rebelled in protest at the extension of English power into his domain, and Sidney and Gilbert responded with a scorched-earth campaign of terror. It was said that those Irish who wished to plead with Gilbert in his encampment were forced to walk along a path lined with the severed heads of their kinsmen.[28] The young Walter Raleigh, Gilbert's half-brother, was involved in the suppression of a second wave of rebellion. By the time the Earl of Desmond was executed in 1583, about a third of the population in the provinces of Munster and Leinster had been killed, starved to death or died of the plague. The poet Edmund Spenser, who also took part in the fighting, described how in the devastated countryside survivors crept out of the woods and glens looking like 'Anatomies of death … crying out of their graves', so desperate for food that they 'did eate of the Carrions … and if they found a plott of water-cresses or shamrockes, there they flocked as to a feast'.[29] About 400,000 acres were confiscated from the rebels; both Raleigh and Spenser received estates on what became known as the Munster Plantation.[30]

Meanwhile, northern Ireland appeared to be secure in the hands of Hugh O'Neill, the Earl of Tyrone, one of the few Irish lords who gained Elizabeth's trust. He visited the English court three times and fitted in with ease, adopting English costume and habits. When he returned to his castle at Dungannon, he brought with him expensive English furniture and an English cook. Elizabeth even gave him special permission to import lead to make a fashionable roof. But when in the 1590s it became evident that the queen was determined to thwart his ambition to become supreme in Ulster as 'the O'Neill', he melted down his lead roof to make bullets, donned a suit of armour given to him by Sir Christopher Hatton (one of Elizabeth's favourites) and led a rebellion that spread through much of the rest of Ireland.[31] The unrest was not quelled until the Battle of Kinsale in 1601, after a failed attempt by O'Neill to join forces with Spanish troops; after the queen's death, the Irish leaders fled to the Continent in 1607. The Crown confiscated about one tenth of Ulster's land, and the Ulster Plantation was created on these 500,000 acres.

A mix of wealthy English adventurers and disbanded ex-soldiers who had fought to put down the rebellions were given land on the Plantation. They were known as 'undertakers', because they were granted estates on the understanding that they would undertake to import English tenants to farm the land. Although it was far more difficult to entice English settlers than the masterminds of the plantation schemes envisaged, between 1580 and 1650 at least 100,000 English, Scottish and Dutch emigrants settled in Ireland.[32]

Historians dispute whether Ireland was England's first colony, but for contemporaries, plantations were all part of the same colonial endeavour whether they were established in North America or Ireland. A propaganda pamphlet promoted the Plantation of Ulster as belonging within 'this our new world'.[33] It assured prospective settlers that honest, hard-working English labourers would find just as many opportunities to make their fortunes in Ireland as they would in the Americas. Indeed, for the Lord Deputy, Arthur Chichester, it seemed an 'absurd folly to run all over the world in search of colonies in Virginia or Guiana, whilst Ireland was lying desolate'.[34] The Crown even forced the London livery companies to withdraw their support for the venture to settle Jamestown in Virginia – with disastrous consequences for the settlers in America – so that their funds could be channelled into the setting-up of Londonderry in the Ulster Plantation.[35]

Even before the settlers arrived, Ireland had begun to undergo a process of commercialisation. While the sixteenth-century English economy suffered from inflation, the Irish economy benefited from price stability, and between 1560 and 1630 it began to expand. Irish beef gained a reputation for being sweet and savoury, and a live-cattle trade with England emerged. By the 1630s, about 15,000 animals a year were being imported into England via Chester.[36] In the north, the peasantry participated in the burgeoning of trade by cultivating flax and spinning it into yarn. In the south, peasants hired dairy cattle and sold the butter their wives made from the milk; and they fattened the calves before selling them on for slaughter.[37] At about the same time, the potato became a popular subsistence crop among Munster dairy farmers. They would normally have relied on butter as a staple food, but now they ate potatoes mixed with the sour milk left over from butter-making and instead sold their butter. It was from here that the potato gradually spread over the rest of the country in the eighteenth century.[38] An English commentator observed that Irish men were at first ashamed to be seen at the markets making a cash profit from the industry of their wives, and 'sold their yarn and butter by night, and as privately as possible', but gradually commerce became an accepted way of life.[39] English consumer goods began to flow into Ireland: ribbons and buttons; spectacles and looking glasses; luxury textiles from the Continent; as well as New World goods such as rice, tobacco and sugar.[40] These were mainly consumed by merchants in the port towns, but the flax and dairy farmers also used the proceeds from their yarn and butter to acquire halfpenny combs, coarse hats and woollen stockings, snuff and tobacco brought into the countryside in the packs of pedlars.[41]

Munster's predominantly West Country undertakers were able to attract English settlers from around the Severn Basin to settle on their estates. Catholic and Protestant proprietors outside the Plantation also encouraged these skilled farmers as tenants, and artisans and settlers from the West Country spread throughout the southern counties.[42] They brought with them the English creed of agricultural improvement and applied it with vigour. The miller Richard Harman, for example, raised the annual income of his farm in Tipperary from £7 to £17 by building a corn mill and investing in a herd of English cows.[43] The project of 'improvement' was less well advanced in Ulster. However, the introduction of English bulls and milch cows did improve the region's livestock, and settlers managed to build up valuable herds. The grandson of the Welsh soldier Edward Blayney, who had been rewarded for his service with 2,000 acres in County Monaghan in 1609, in 1641 owned livestock worth an impressive £925.[44] Determined to get their hands on superior animals, the 'wild' Irish would frequently raid the settlers' herds.[45]

The Ulster Plantation began supplying Dublin with butter and cheese, and a thriving trade in Irish butter, wool and hides developed with France.[46] A veteran of the campaign to suppress the Desmond rebellion, Sir Richard Grenville, lord of Bideford manor in north Devon, acquired an estate on the Munster Plantation.[47] Bideford was at the time the centre of English pottery production. The town began sending cargoes of earthenware pots to Ireland, where they were filled with butter and sent back to Devon, from where they were re-exported to France.[48] Clearly the salted butter produced on the Plantation was not the 'rank and strong' stuff that had disgusted John Dunton.

By the 1630s, southern Ireland was increasingly prosperous and Munster was 'probably the wealthiest of any of England's overseas settlements'.[49] Tenant farmers slept in comfortable beds dressed in fine bed linen, ate from pewter ware rather than wooden trenchers and – judging by the sixfold rise in imports of hops – drank well-hopped English-style beer rather than sweeter un-hopped Irish ales. They wore fine hats and linen clothes and were able to admire themselves in looking glasses on their walls.[50] In the early decades of the seventeenth century, Ireland fulfilled the role of a model overseas plantation: it produced commercially desirable raw commodities for export to England and in return acted as a market for English manufactured goods.[51]

But then, in 1641, the country was plunged into more than a decade of warfare when the English conflict between Charles I and Parliament spilled over into Ireland and sparked a rebellion. It soon degenerated into an ethnic conflict between the native Catholic Irish and the new Protestant settlers. Many of the English settlers were driven from their homes by bands of Catholics 'resolved to die in that quarrel' and declaring that 'Noe Englishman or protestant must live among [the Irish].'[52] The Irish Confederation that ruled the rebellious parts of Ireland allied itself with the royalists in England's civil war. This brought Oliver Cromwell to the island in 1649 determined to protect the newly established English Commonwealth from the Catholic threat. Cromwell's campaign of reconquest was merciless. One English soldier described how it was possible to travel twenty or thirty miles through the devastated countryside without seeing a living creature. The skin of the few survivors was blackened 'like an oven because of the terrible famine'.[53] Hunger, the plague and the practice of selling Irish captives to the West Indies as indentured labourers reduced Ireland's population by at least a fifth.[54]

Under Cromwell's land settlement of 1652, 8.5 million acres (about 40 per cent of Ireland's land) were confiscated from Catholic landowners and allocated to a motley group of English adventurers and decommissioned army officers.[55] After 1652, Protestant settlers, who made up only a quarter of the population, now owned an estimated three quarters of the land and controlled two thirds of the trade.[56] By 1700, this power shift in favour of the Protestant English had been firmly established. English officials ran the administration of Ireland, their authority reinforced by a large occupying army of English soldiers, and penal laws restricted the economic and political activity of the Catholics. Catholic landowners had been pushed west into the inhospitable province of Connaught, which Dunton described in 1698 as the stronghold of old Irish barbarism.[57]

During the Commonwealth, the ideology of agricultural improvement was reinvigorated by the redefinition of the pursuit of profit not as sinful covetousness but as a contribution to the nation's wealth, now understood to be the sum of private wealth. Thus the farmer who harnessed the fertility God had bestowed upon the soil in order to increase yields, helped to ensure the prosperity of the Commonwealth as a whole.[58] The parliamentarian Sir Oliver St John applied these ideas to Ireland when he declared, 'Great good will come to this kingdom [Ireland] by transporting cattle and corn from hence into England: for this kingdom will be able to spare great quantities of both, which will bring money into it, and make this barbarous nation feel the sweets thereof, the love of it will sooner effect civility than any other persuasion whatsoever.'[59] The market had become the agent of civilisation.

In the 1660s, Ireland appeared to take St John's advice, and the trade in agricultural exports revived. An annual flow of at least 50,000 cattle and more than 100,000 sheep, as well as several hundredweight of Irish butter, helped to meet England's rising demand for meat and fat as living standards improved among the middling classes.[60] Meanwhile the butter trade with the West Country, which had connected southern Ireland to the French market, now pulled the region into the web of Atlantic trade.

By the 1660s, Newfoundland had become a permanent English settlement of about 2,000 people. Somewhere between 100 and 200 'planters' had established year-round permanent fishing stations varying in size from humble enterprises with only a couple of fishing boats to large operations employing numerous fishermen and household servants.[61] As European settlement encroached on their land, the native Beothuk people who had traditionally lived on seal and fish were forced to rely on alternative food sources. But as Newfoundland's interior supported very little game, scarcity of food resulted in a dramatic decline in the aboriginal population. By 1829, the Beothuk were extinct.[62]

Ironically, even though the Europeans monopolised access to the region's rich marine food sources, they were themselves dependent on food imports. Ireland supplied the settlement with flour, biscuit, salt butter and meat. The supply line came full circle as the fishing settlement that had provided salt cod for the English army in Ireland was now supplied with food from the Irish plantations.

A triangular trade developed conducted by networks of merchants, often with family ties. In 1680, John Smith, a Bideford merchant of southern Irish origin, sent a cargo of 25 dozen earthenware pots with the Bideford vessel the *Delight* to his brother Edward in Ross, Ireland. Later that year, Edward sent back 18 hundredweight of butter packed into the pots. Bideford ships took cargoes of Irish butter to Newfoundland, where it was exchanged for inferior salt cod to be carried on to Virginia, where it was used to feed the African slaves working on the tobacco plantations. John Smith sent his butter directly to Virginia, where another Smith brother, Joseph, was a tobacco planter.[63] By the late seventeenth century, Bideford had become England's main tobacco trading port. Through such interconnections, Ireland became a supplier of provisions to Britain's emerging empire.

The Caribbean sugar islands were to become Ireland's most important market. Sugar was introduced into the West Indies in the mid seventeenth century. It was such a valuable crop that the planters did not want to waste land growing food and the islands became dependent on imported provisions. Irish beef exports doubled between 1641 and 1665 as the trade in barrelled beef developed in tandem with the expansion of sugar cultivation.[64] When, in an effort to protect the higher price of English beef, the English placed a ban on imports of live Irish animals in 1667 and Irish butter in 1681, the New World colonies became Ireland's main market for their exports of salt provisions.[65]

The city of Cork flourished as a result, doubling in size between 1660 and 1685 and doubling again by 1706.[66] In May, the market bustled as great firkins of butter were carried in on horseback from the countryside. The city's connection with the Newfoundland trade gave it access to superior Portuguese salt, and the top-grade 'Rose' butter remained 'sweet and fresh' even in the tropical climate of the Caribbean.[67] In the autumn, Cork's streets would fill with herds of cattle being driven to the slaughterhouse. Old dairy cows and oxen were made into low-grade 'small beef', often with hooves and hide mixed in with the scrawny meat. This was destined for the French West Indies, where it was fed to the African slaves: there was no market for such poor-quality meat in the English West Indies, where the slaves were given the redshanks – spoiled salt cod – from Newfoundland.[68] The necks, fore- and hind-shanks of better-quality animals were packed into two-hundredweight barrels and sold as 'cargo' or 'common mess beef' to provision ships. Prime beef cattle were only driven into the city in November, to be processed into 'planters' beef' and shipped to the West Indies just in time to provide wealthy sugar planters with fresh provisions for their tables at Christmas.[69]

It is unsurprising that when he travelled through Connaught at the end of the seventeenth century, John Dunton thought that this was where old Ireland had survived. The north-west of the island remained poor, dominated by small subsistence-level farms. Although the farmers here participated in the cattle trade by rearing calves, they made little money, as the larger share of the profits went to the farmers in the midland pastoral zone who fattened the cattle and sold them on to the slaughterhouses.[70] In contrast, in southern Ireland the Tudor reformers' vision was realised. Many of the woodlands, bogs and heaths that had been home to the 'barbarous Irish' had been cut down, drained and brought into cultivation. Mixed tillage farms dominated, and tenants lived in villages ranged around a school, a church, and a mill for grinding corn. By 1700, the English plan had succeeded in refashioning Ireland's landscape and it had begun to take on the features familiar to us today.[71] However, it was not English arable farming that had won out, but a commercialised version of Irish pastoralism. In the process, the once wild and unruly country was now firmly integrated into the emerging British Empire.

·3·

In which the Holloway family eat maize bread and salt beef succotash, Sandwich, New England (June 1647)

How the English chased the dream of the yeoman farmer but were forced to compromise

In June 1647, Joseph Holloway returned home worn out after a long morning surveying the highways to eat dinner with his family. He sat down thankfully in one of the two chairs they possessed while his children gathered around the board balanced on trestles that served them as a table. Even though the Holloways were one of the wealthiest of the 61 families who ten years previously had founded the settlement of Sandwich in New England, they did not own a table. The family's other chair was occupied by Joseph's wife Rose, while their eldest children Joseph and Sarah, aged eleven and seven, perched on stools. The two smaller girls, four-year-old Mary and three-year-old Experience, had tree stumps to sit on, and Hopestill the baby was passed around from lap to lap.[1]

Rose had risen early that morning to bake the mixed wheat and corn-meal loaf that she now placed before them. The English preferred unadulterated wheat bread, but even at home wheat flour often had to be eked out with handfuls of barley or rye flour. For New Englanders a wheat loaf was a particular luxury. Joseph grew wheat on about a quarter of his cultivated land, but the crop did not generally do well in this part of America. The harsh winters killed the winter wheat and the spring varieties were afflicted by wheat blast, a form of rust that left the apparently flourishing plant with empty and shrivelled ears. Maize was the only reliable source of grain, and Joseph planted at least five acres with Indian corn.[2]

Fearful that in America's strange climate they would degenerate to the savage state of the Native Americans, the English settlers clung to bread as the food of the civilised. Although cornmeal does not lend itself to bread-making – it lacks the gluten that gives wheat bread its texture – they persisted in using it as they would wheat flour to make loaves. Cornmeal mixed with water and beaten to a batter could be shaped in a wooden dish or slowly ladled, layer after layer, onto a bed of oak or cabbage leaves on the floor of a hot oven to make thick cake-like loaves.[3] Cornmeal bread was most successful when the meal was mixed with rye flour. Of all the European grains, rye did the best in the foreign climate, and loaves of 'ryeaninjun' were the usual staple fare of New Englanders.

Next to the loaf was a large, round hard cheese and a little pot of butter. Joseph's 19 cattle were good milkers, and while most New Englanders made a fairly rudimentary soft cheese from their surplus milk, the well-off Holloways owned two cheese vats and a cheese press that enabled them to produce English-style hard cheeses. Their store also contained salt pork, salt beef and a hogshead of malt.[4]

New England's first settlers may not have wished to replicate their homeland's religious culture, but they certainly aimed to replicate its cookery. Bread, milk, butter, cheese, beef and a good mug of beer were the staples of the seventeenth-century English diet.[5] In all but the cornmeal in the bread, the Holloways' dinner appeared to resemble the food of England's middling farmers. On closer inspection, however, the dish of salt beef yielded telltale signs that the family were sitting down to eat in America rather than England. Rose had been simmering the beef in a pot hung over the fire since early that morning. An English cook would have thrown in a handful of dried peas, turnips or carrots, some parsley or thyme – whatever vegetables and herbs she had to hand in her garden – to make a mess of pottage. But in Joseph's fields, rather than neat rows of carrots and patches of parsley, beans and squash straggled around the maize plants.[6] Lima beans, kernels of maize and American squash took the place of English vegetables in the Holloways' beef stew, transforming it into the Native American one-pot dish known as succotash, the English pronunciation of the Narragansett Indian *sukquttahash*.[7] Despite the fact that they clung on to Old World food habits, once the settlers began substituting English with American foodstuffs, their dishes began to look uncomfortably similar to those of the supposedly savage Native Americans.[8]

Joseph Holloway had sailed to Massachusetts on the *Elizabeth and Ann* in 1635, aged 30. Rose, his wife of seven years, may have joined him later, as she is not on the ship's passenger list.[9] The Holloways were part of the Great Migration of 14,000 English Puritans who left England in the 1630s. The first settlements on the North American continent were Roanoke, established in 1585 using funds provided by Walter Raleigh and his associates; and Sagadahoc in 1606, but they both failed.[10] The one successful early venture was Jamestown, established in the Chesapeake Bay in 1607 and funded by the Virginia Company. The early backers of American plantations hoped to rival Spain's South American possessions by finding rich deposits of gold or silver. When these did not materialise, the investors focused on creating permanent English settlements to act as alternative providers of a range of cash crops such as hemp and flax, silk and indigo, timber, pitch and tar, which England currently sourced from Europe, Africa and Asia.[11]

After several hungry years teetering on the edge of starvation and a long and brutal conflict with the indigenous Powhatan tribe, the settlers in the Chesapeake Bay established the tobacco-producing colony of Virginia.[12] In 1620, a group of Puritan dissenters joined forces with a band of emigrants and set sail from England to join the thousand or so Virginians. Only one of their two ships, the *Mayflower*, made it to America, landing 200 miles northeast of the Chesapeake. Here the 102 surviving members of the expedition founded Plymouth and the separate colony of New England.[13] The venture was given a boost nine years later, when a group of London merchants founded the Massachusetts Bay Company and appointed the Suffolk lawyer John Winthrop to take charge of a new emigration drive. His son Henry made it home from his sugar-planting venture in Barbados just in time to set sail in April 1630 with his father in the fleet carrying 700 emigrants that landed at Cape Ann in June. In the following decade, about a thousand emigrants a year swelled the numbers of this new colony, among them Joseph and Rose Holloway.[14]

Religion is usually portrayed as the main factor motivating New England's colonists to uproot and make the perilous journey across the Atlantic. It certainly galvanised the Puritans, who were the vocal leaders of the settlement. They felt increasingly uncomfortable in Charles I's England, where Catholicism was once again in favour.[15] Roger Clap, a servant in a God-fearing household in Devon, certainly believed that divine providence had 'put it into my heart to incline to live abroad', though he had 'never so much as heard of New England' until a local clergyman spoke of his intention to emigrate.[16] He may have thanked God for giving him the opportunity, but the limited prospects for a poor young man in England must have been what made emigration appealing. The social upheaval of seventeenth-century England rather than a religious calling motivated the majority of those crossing the Atlantic.[17] As smallholdings and common lands were amalgamated into enclosed estates, the smallest and poorest tenant farmers were evicted. As one set of impoverished farmers were pushed off the land, others watched anxiously, fearing that they might be the next to slip into decline. The middling classes in the south-east who depended on the textile trade were already hard hit by the decline in the popularity of England's woollen stuffs, and were now squeezed by rising poor rates, taxes on the propertied to provide poor relief for the needy and destitute of the parish. The depressing economic climate often combined with a spiritual or financial personal crisis to push middling husbandmen into the decision to leave. These wealthier migrants, who could afford to pay their own passages, chose New England rather than Virginia as their destination.[18]

They were attracted to New England as a place where they might realise the dream of becoming respectable and independent yeomen.[19] During the Commonwealth, agricultural reformers promoted the view that a nation's prosperity was best ensured by the dispersal of land into the hands of sturdy yeomen.[20] As enclosure had concentrated land in the hands of the wealthy, this was a difficult ideal to fulfil at home, but in New England emigrants hoped to realise a version of the utopian commonwealth where 'the whole people be landlords', as depicted in the 1656 tract *Oceana* by the republican author James Harrington.[21] New towns proliferated and each immigrant family was allocated its own farm. The 25 founders of the town of Taunton thanked God for bringing them 'to this place, and *settling of us, on lands of our own*, bought with our money ... for a possession for ourselves and for our posterity after us'.[22] When the Holloways and their neighbours established nearby Sandwich, they were motivated by the same drive: to secure their own land as the means of acquiring an independent livelihood.

What the New England settlers stubbornly refused to recognise was that they were stealing other people's land. The first band of settlers did not happen across a pristine wilderness but a landscape that had been managed for centuries by the Native Americans. Indeed, it was the Patuxet people who had made the clearings in the forest where the initial band of settlers planted their first crops. Before these bore fruit, the colonists survived only because they discovered stores of maize buried by the Native Americans before they were wiped out by epidemics of European diseases introduced by the West Countrymen who had tried to found the settlement of Sagadahoc 14 years earlier.[23] There were still plenty of Native Americans in the vicinity of Massachusetts Bay, but John Winthrop applied the same reasoning that the English used to justify their colonisation of Ireland, arguing that because they 'inclose noe Land, neither have they any setled habytation, nor any tame Cattle to improve the Land by', they had not earned the right to own the land.[24] The English settlers in America were, he argued, performing a Christian duty by taming the American wilderness. Winthrop, who had cousins with a farm on the Munster Plantation and had visited Ireland with a view to settling there in 1621, believed that just as plantation was the instrument that would eventually redeem Ireland, so English yeomen were bringing civilisation to America.[25] The Native Americans were cast as versions of the barbarous Irish, who had forfeited their right to the country by their failure to properly order the landscape and realise its potential.[26] The spirit of sharing embodied in the first Thanksgiving meal, when Wampanoag Indians celebrated the harvest with the Plymouth settlers in the autumn of 1621, was soon betrayed as any Indian group that opposed English intrusion onto their land was violently subjugated.

Ideas about land ownership, farming and the right and proper way for a society to acquire its food were central to the ideology of Britain's First Empire. Irish pastoralism was rejected as the practice of barbarians and the English refused to recognise Native American clearings in the forest as farms. But when New England's settlers tried to impose English-style agriculture on American soil, they ran up against a series of obstacles that forced them to compromise their ideals. Organised as it was around small family farms, New England was chronically short of labour. This prevented the first settlers from taking full advantage of the very thing they had come to America for: the abundant land. With only the assistance of their wives and children, they struggled to clear the dense forest and transform it into productive fields. Digging out the tree stumps from newly cleared land to create neatly ploughed fields suitable for European grains was back-breaking and time-consuming. And the endeavour was barely worthwhile, as rust decimated the wheat crops and even the yields of rye and peas were often disappointing. The task was overwhelming, yet the need for food pressing.[27]

In his memoir, Roger Clap recalled that 'many a time, if I could have filled my belly though with mean victuals, it would have been sweet unto me'.[28] Bread and meat were 'very scarce' and the settlers reluctantly relied on seafood such as clams and mussels, although they despised them as food fit only for the poor and desperate as they were exhausting and unpleasant to collect from the mud along the seashore.[29] Having condemned the Native Americans as lazy, the English were forced to adopt their methods of cultivation and crops, which produced as much food as possible in return for the least effort.[30] High-yielding maize could be planted around rotting tree stumps on freshly cleared land, in soil that had been hoed rather than ploughed, and squash and beans could be grown in among the maize plants.[31] Indeed, by 1700, most New England farmers had given up the struggle to grow wheat. Like Joseph Holloway, they were obliged to plant at least half their cultivated land with reliable native crops in straggling fields dotted with tree stumps so that they looked every bit as unkempt as the Native American gardens upon which they poured scorn.[32]

The early settlers worried a great deal about eating strange and unfamiliar foods and initially regarded maize as suitable only as animal fodder. But they had little choice and learned to appreciate it. They made it into loaves like the bread Rose Holloway baked for her family. They also boiled cornmeal in a cloth to make an American version of an English pudding. Mixed with molasses or maple syrup, perhaps some eggs, butter and a few spices, cornmeal was serendipitously well suited to this English technique. And if it was treated as if it were oatmeal, cornflour could be stirred into hot water to make a stiff polenta-like porridge or hasty pudding, eaten with milk or molasses.[33] Clap remembered that in the early days, 'when I could have meal and water and salt boiled together, it was so good, who could wish for better?'[34] From the Native Americans they learned how to beat cooked maize into a powder and then mix it into a thick batter with water and bake it on a flat stone or a hoe over the fire to make flat breads known variously as johnny or journey cake, spoon bread, hoe cake or pone. Eventually, New Englanders identified so strongly with their corn breads, journey cakes, puddings and porridges, and their succotash stews, renamed 'boiled dinners', that their Native American origins were forgotten; they were redefined as plain, unassuming foods eminently suited to the palate of the plain, honest American.[35] By the time they were served at a banquet to celebrate the first Plymouth Forefathers' Day in 1869, they had been thoroughly recast as foods to be proud of rather than slightly shameful compromises born out of necessity.[36]

The early colonists learned how to prepare maize from the Native Americans. The kernels were first dried and then boiled in an alkaline lye made with water and wood ash. This loosened the hulls from the kernels to produce hominy.[37] The hominy could then be ground into cornmeal. Boiling the kernels in lye had the additional advantage of breaking down the niacin within the maize into a digestible form. Those whose diets rely on cornmeal made with maize that has not undergone this process of nixtamalisation risk developing the vitamin deficiency disease of pellagra.

A NICE INDIAN PUDDING

No. 1. Three pints scalded milk, 7 spoons fine Indian meal, stir well together while hot, let stand till cooled; add 7 eggs, half pound raisin, 4 ounces butter, spice and sugar, bake one and an half hour.

No. 2. Three pints scalded milk to one pint meal salted; cool, add 2 eggs, 4 ounces butter, sugar or molasses and spice, it will require two and an half hour baking.

No. 3. Salt a pint meal, wet with one quart of milk, sweeten and put into a strong cloth, brass or bell metal vessel, stone or earthen pot, secure from wet and boil 12 hours.

JOHNNY CAKE OR HOE CAKE

Scald 1 pint of milk and put to 3 pints of Indian meal, and half pint flower – bake before the fire. Or scald with milk, two thirds of the Indian meal, or wet two thirds with boiling water, add salt, molasses and shortening, work up with cold water pretty stiff, and bake as above.[38]

Joseph Holloway had fenced in about 10 acres of his land in order to grow crops and then released his herd of cattle to forage on his remaining 20 acres of unfenced meadow, marsh and woodland.[39] Having failed to bring most of their cultivated fields under the plough, the settlers did not even attempt to properly control their cattle, allowing the animals to lumber around the countryside, trampling and eating any Native American gardens they came across and causing great resentment.[40] Indeed, this free-range form of animal husbandry developed into a mode of conquest.[41] More cattle were imported into the colony than new settlers, and as the herds required more land to sustain them, the settlers moved into neighbouring areas, founding townships and giving rise to new colonies – Maryland, New Hampshire, Rhode Island, New Haven – driving the Native Americans out of their territories and consolidating the European hold on America.[42] By adopting this mode of farming, the settlers hardly lived up to the claim that they were improving the land.

The grandiose plans to 'improve' America may not have been realised, but New England did offer humble men like Roger Clap and Joseph Holloway the opportunity to realise the dream of becoming prosperous and independent yeomen. Roger married four years after arriving in the colony and he and his wife had 14 children. He joined the militia and served as the representative for Dorchester in the colonial assembly. When Joseph Holloway died at the age of 42, he owned a farm of 30 acres, 19 cattle and two horses. He had served as a constable and member of the local militia and in 1647 had been appointed surveyor of the town's highways. He slept in a feather bed, drank his beer from a pewter vessel and ate a nourishing and plentiful diet.[43] While in England rural labourers, paid ever lower wages and deprived of their ability to keep cows by enclosures, were losing their access to meat and dairy products, the American settlers had managed to secure for themselves an almost ideal English diet rich in beef, milk, butter and cheese. Indeed, by the end of the seventeenth century, colonial Americans were probably the best-fed people on the planet. A traveller in Pennsylvania in the 1750s noted that 'even in the humblest or poorest houses, no meals are served without a meat course; and no one eats bread without butter or cheese'.[44] The superiority of American nutrition was revealed by the height of American soldiers during the War of Independence, when they were on average 3.5 inches taller than their British counterparts.[45]

Joseph Holloway's estate was valued at over £200. This was substantially more than the average New Englander was worth. It is unlikely that he achieved his wealth solely by farming. In the West Country he had worked as a millwright, and he probably plied his trade in the new country, where mill-wrights were in demand to build saw and water mills to process lumber and grind corn.[46] Although he lived as a yeoman, Joseph supported himself by his industry. In the same way, New England prided itself on its self-sufficiency but depended on trade for its prosperity. By 1700, the colony's inhabitants felt that they had succeeded in achieving their forefathers' dream of living independently on the land.[47] They grew enough corn, rye and oats to supply their wants for bread-making. The introduction of clover and English meadow grasses meant that the farmers were able to make enough hay to overwinter their cattle. Butter, cheese and beef were plentiful and kitchen gardens supplied a sufficient bounty of vegetables to lay up a store to see them through the winter.[48] But if they were self-sufficient in staple foods, New Englanders were voracious consumers of English manufactured goods, ranging from practical equipment such as farm implements to frivolities like parrot cages.[49] Early American colonial homes were sparsely furnished; even the better off often only possessed a cupboard, a chest and a few cooking implements. At night families 'pigged' together on old blankets on the floor.[50] But as they became more affluent, they bought feather beds, pewter plates, silver spoons and chairs.[51] In the old country a farmer might wear a velvet coat and drink from a pewter goblet, but his reputation rested on the state of his land and livestock and his relationships with his neighbours.[52] In the new world of untidy fields and semi-wild cattle, possessions became important markers of gentility. In order to buy all these goods, New Englanders needed to generate an income.

The colony of family farms had little to sell other than surplus food supplies, mainly barrels of salt beef. These they sold to the increasingly pros-perous West Indian sugar islands. But New England's salt beef was considered 'coarse, black, and much inferior to the Irish'. An Antiguan planter complained to his supplier that the beef he had sent him 'does by no means ansr yr kind intention of regailing our palates; for if it be sound, it be too hard & salt; but generally it stinks'.[53] Still, although for the time being Ireland remained the West Indies' main supplier, salt beef became the second most valuable of all New England's exports. Its prime export, however, was salt fish. In the 1640s, the New England fishery boomed, benefiting from the disruption of the Newfoundland trade when the English Civil War prevented many West Coun-try fishermen from making their annual migration. New England now joined the

Atlantic triangle of trade, sending its best-quality product to southern Europe and the wine islands and over 3,500 barrels of second-rate fish a year to Jamaica to feed the African slaves on the island's newly established sugar plantations.[54]

It was ironic that the commodity that New England relied upon to balance its financial books was fish. The colony's coastal fishing communities were the epitome of everything the settlers had rejected when they emigrated. The fishermen were a motley selection of men who happened to have washed up on New England's shores and decided to settle. Religion was of little interest to them and they did not share the Puritan values of many of the settlers. The farmers regarded the fishing villages as ungodly centres of iniquity and drunkenness, rough and ready outposts that disrupted the harmony of New England's properly ordered agricultural society.[55] But they generated 35 per cent of New England's export income.[56]

The provisions trade spawned a shipbuilding industry. As the farmers cleared their land, they produced plentiful quantities of timber, and by the end of the seventeenth century, Boston had 15 shipyards, making it the Empire's second shipbuilding centre after London. A thriving community of shipwrights, artisans, master mariners and merchants emerged in New England's towns. By 1700, the freight charges for carrying goods on American vessels probably earned New England more than its exports of provisions.[57] Trade with the West Indies dominated, and New England developed in symbiosis with the sugar islands. The two economies were held together by a dense web of trading links, which are exemplified by the business dealings of the Rhode Island merchant Peleg Sandford.

The son of the founder of New England's Portsmouth colony, Sandford travelled to Barbados in the early 1650s to work as an agent for a Rhode Island-based merchant. Having learned the business, in 1666 he returned to Rhode Island, where he set himself up as an independent trader in Newport. His two brothers, William and Elisha, remained in Barbados to act as his agents. Sandford imported English dry goods such as nails, knives, kettles, pistols and hardware and sold them in his store. With the profits he bought locally produced timber, salt meat, dried peas and butter to send to his brothers in Barbados. Elisha and William sold the American provisions and in turn bought sugar to ship to London to pay for the purchase of yet more English dry goods. They also sent sugar, rum and molasses directly from Barbados to New England. By the time Sandford was made governor of

The seal for the Massachusetts Society for Promoting Agriculture showed the New England farmer as the idealised yeoman 'improving' the New World with his plough.

Rhode Island in 1680, more than half the ships arriving and leaving Boston harbour were engaged in trade with the Caribbean, which was becoming the trading hub of the Atlantic Empire.[58]

New England's first settlers sought to establish a society where the middling farmer could enjoy his freedom and independence. Their aim was to secure for themselves a way of life that was becoming increasingly precarious in England.[59] Out of this grew a powerful ideology celebrating the yeoman farmer and idealising the family farm. J. Hector St John Crèvecoeur, the son of a French immigrant and a gentleman farmer in the Hudson valley, expressed this idea in 1770 when he wrote that 'this formerly rude soil has been converted by my father into a pleasant farm and in return, it has established all our rights; on it is founded our rank, our freedom, our power as citizens'.[60] After American independence it became a central tenet of American politics that it was the role of government to protect the citizen's right to live an independent and self-sufficient life on a farmstead.[61] This way of thinking still permeates American republicanism today.

At the heart of this ideology, however, lay a tangle of contradictions. Even though New England owed much of its prosperity to fishermen and cattle breeders, fishing and livestock farming were regarded as secondary and far less noble occupations. Cornbread and boiled dinners were interpreted as the wholesome foods of the family farm, and yet these dishes derived from the farming and food practices of the Native Americans. And while New England's family farms were presented as free of the taint of slave labour, the market for their timber, shingles, salt beef and fish, corn, horses and cattle was the West Indies, where slave labour produced the sugar, molasses and rum that the plantations exchanged for these goods. New England and the West Indies formed a mutually sustaining whole, in which the prosperity of the American yeoman depended on the labour of the West African slave.[62]

·4·

In which Colonel James Drax holds a feast at his sugar plantation on the island of Barbados (1640s)

How the West Indian sugar islands drove the growth of the First British Empire

When Colonel James Drax, the first sugar baron in the English West Indies, slaughtered one of his cattle, he would invite his fellow planters on the island of Barbados to a lavish entertainment. Richard Ligon, the manager at another early sugar plantation, attended one of these occasions and described the splendid feast. The first course was an extravaganza of more than a dozen different beef dishes, from boiled rump and marrow bones to pies of minced tripe and tongue seasoned with sweet herbs, suet, spice and currants. Among them was also an *olio podrido*, a highly spiced Iberian beef stew. The second course included more beef dishes as well as Scottish-style collops of pork; boiled chickens; shoulder of goat dressed with blood and thyme; a loin of veal cooked with oranges, lemons and limes; suckling pig in a brain and claret-wine sauce seasoned with salt, sage and nutmeg; as well as rabbits, pigeons, turkeys, capons, fat hens, and two Muscovy ducks larded and well seasoned with salt and pepper.[1]

The third course consisted of an array of imported delicacies such as Westphalia hams and dried beef tongue; pickled oysters and caviar; anchovies and olives; and 'Virginia Botargo', a fish roe relish, which Ligon thought was the best he had ever tasted. Sweet dishes of custards and creams were dotted among the savoury specialities, including pastry puffs made with imported English flour. Baskets filled with fruit also delighted Ligon, especially the pineapples then virtually unknown in England, which he regarded as so delicious they were 'worth all that went before'.[2] The bewildering array of food was complemented by an equally lavish choice of drinks: mobbie, distilled from sweet potatoes; perino, made from cassava; imported French brandy; Madeira, Rhenish wines and sack; and the 'infinitely strong' Kill-Devil: rum made from the 'skimmings of the Coppers that boil the Sugar'.[3]

TO MAKE PERINO, A DRINK MUCH USED HERE ...

Take a Cake of bad *Cassada* Bread, about a Foot over, and half an Inch thick, burnt black on one side, break it to pieces, and put it to steep in two Gallons of water, let it stand open in a tub twelve hours, then add to it the froth of an Egg and three Gallons more water, and one pound of Sugar, let it work twelve hours, and Bottle it; it will keep good for a week.[4]

Drax lived like a prince in the Jacobean mansion he had built on his plantation. The wealthiest man on Barbados, he entertained according to seventeenth-century aristocratic ideals of hospitality and sociability. But it was no easy feat to emulate the English aristocracy on a country estate thousands of miles from London. The European delicacies he served had weathered an arduous journey to reach his table, first crossing the Atlantic in the hold of a ship and then carried from the port of Bridgetown 'upon Negroes' backs' up and down steep gullies to reach Drax's inland plantation, which was inaccessible by cart. And this had to be done at night so that the heat of the sun did not spoil the comestibles.[5] On an island where beef was rarely eaten, since cattle were too valuable as draught animals, only Drax could afford to set aside animals to raise for meat, and reserve as pasture land that might otherwise have been used to grow sugar. On Barbados this feast centred around dishes of beef was fabulously extravagant.

It was something of an honour for Richard Ligon to be invited, as he occupied a delicate social position, somewhere between friend and socially inferior employee. He worked on a neighbouring sugar plantation as secretary, adviser and occasional overseer. During the English Civil War he had fought alongside the owner, Sir Thomas Modyford, in the royalist Exeter garrison. Although he was allowed to go free when the city finally fell to parliamentary forces, he found himself 'destitute of subsistence' and 'a stranger in my own Country' now that England was a Protestant Commonwealth.[6] At the age of 60, Ligon was rather old for a colonial venture, but he decided to try his luck with Modyford's party of royalist refugees, who initially planned to set up a sugar plantation on the island of Antigua. But with the loss of one of the ships on the voyage out, Modyford's plans changed and he decided to stop in Barbados, where he bought into an established sugar plantation owned by Major William Hilliard, who was keen to leave its running to a partner while he returned home to 'suck in some of the sweet air of England'.[7]

Ligon's arrival in Barbados in 1647 coincided with the moment of the island's transition from a nondescript English settlement into the wealthiest plantation in the British Empire. It far outshone the Munster Plantation, which occupied this position in the 1630s. In the account of his experiences – *A True and Exact History of the Island of Barbados* (1657), written in a debtors' prison on his return to England – Ligon described how the introduction of sugar transformed the island. Land prices skyrocketed. Colonel Modyford paid £7,000 for his half-share in Hilliard's 500-acre sugar plantation, which had cost only £400 five or six years previously, when tobacco and cotton were the island's main crops. Ligon correctly predicted that once all the small plantations of 20 or 30 acres not large enough to embark on the capital-intensive project of growing sugar had been amalgamated into large plantations, this tiny Caribbean island, not much bigger than the Isle of Wight, would become 'one of the richest Spots of earth under the Sun'.[8]

Captain John Powell claimed the uninhabited island of Barbados for the English when sailing home from South America in 1625 on a voyage undertaken on behalf of the Courteen textile trading company. He erected a cross and inscribed the name of the English king on a tree. With William Courteen's financial support he returned two years later, accompanied by his brother, Henry Powell, and 50 hopeful settlers; among them was the 18-year-old James Drax.[9] The new colony was planted just as English attitudes towards empire were changing. By the 1620s, Virginia was sending 200,000 lb of tobacco a year to England, where sales were booming, and one pound of the weed could fetch as much as £1.[10] This was evidence that a colony reliant on an agricultural cash crop could be worthwhile. Henry Powell left the men to construct a makeshift initial settlement and set sail for Dutch Guiana, from where he returned with food, tobacco plants and seeds, as well as three canoe-loads of Arawak Indians. With the help of the Arawaks, on whose agricultural knowledge the settlers depended, the Englishmen hoped to emulate the success of Virginian tobacco planters.[11]

When Richard Ligon arrived on Barbados in the 1640s, every household kept two or three Amerindian slaves to prepare the local staple food, cassava.[12] Before it could be eaten, the toxic prussic acid that permeated the root had to be removed through a labour-intensive process of grating and squeezing. Once the gratings had been dried in the sun, they were ground into flour and made into bread. But the juice did not go to waste. It was boiled until it turned into a benign thick black treacly substance known as casareep, which was an excellent preservative. The meat stew the Amerindians made with it did not putrify as long as the mixture was reboiled every day. According to one traveller, this pepper pot made 'an excellent Breakfast for a Salamander' for 'Three Spoonfuls so Inflam'd my Mouth, that [it was as if he had] devour'd a Peck of Horse-Radish, and Drank after it a Gallon of Brandy and Gunpowder'.[13] The sugar planters clearly acquired a taste for it, as a blackened earthenware pepper pot could be found bubbling on the stove in virtually every plantation kitchen.[14]

During a voyage around the Caribbean islands, William
Paton 'overheard a ship-mate tell his chum how, according to his remembrance ... the Barbadians prepared
their pepper-pot'. Paton instructed his readers: 'in order
to reproduce this surprising invention ... first procure
an earthen jar or Connarhee pot of generous proportions and comfortable rotundity of form'. He went on to
give his shipmate's recipe:

PEPPER-POT

Get a lot of peppers, cayenne, bird's-eye peppers, long,
round, all kinds, green red, yellow, such a jolly lot of
'em. Cut 'em all up. Makes my eyes water to think of it
d'ye know! ... Then you put this mess in a stone pot.
Then, by Jove! Fellow didn't say – I forgot to ask if you
cooked it ... then you put in vinegar and catsup and
spice, all that sort of thing – dash of bitters ... Then
you take any blessed thing left over from dinner or
breakfast, chop, leg of fowl, sausage, bacon (forget
whether he said fish) – anything left of something too
good to throw away ... Tomatoes, pickles, all that lot.
Only fancy! Any time you feel peckish – there you are.
It's always going on is pepper-pot; you never wash the
blooming thing out; keeps for years.

Paton pointed out that the man had forgotten to mention the 'all-important ingredient of a right pepper-pot':
the casareep.[15]

One of the settlers was 19-year-old Henry Winthrop. He optimis-
tically promised his father John in England that, in return for two or three
servants a year plus supplies, he would send back 500–1,000 lb of tobacco.
But Henry's crop was a disappointment. His father complained that it was

'very ill conditioned, foul, full of stalks and evil coloured'. He was only able to sell it for pennies rather than shillings per pound, and he warned Henry that, given that he had to provide for his other children, he would not be able to send him further assistance. By the time John's admonitory letter arrived in Barbados, Henry was already on his way home and ready to try another colonial venture; three years later, he would join his father on his founding voyage to Massachusetts Bay.[16]

Unlike Winthrop, Drax managed to make some profit from his tobacco, and this allowed him to begin buying up more land and servants to work it.[17] Nevertheless, Barbadian tobacco was of poor quality, and when in 1630 the market price of even the superior Virginian product fell to a tenth of its previous value, it became clear that the crop was never going to make the Barbadian planters' fortunes. They experimented with cotton, ginger, indigo and fustic wood (which produced a yellow dye). Drax, Hilliard and another of the first settlers, James Holdip, used their tobacco profits to move into cotton. They acquired plants and know-how from the Dutch, who dominated Caribbean trade in the 1630s. At first cotton did well. New settlers were attracted to the island and its population grew sevenfold. But at the end of the decade, the value of cotton and indigo declined as the market became saturated. The three men cast around looking for a new crop, and sugar caught their attention.[18]

In the 1630s, the north-eastern coast of Brazil was the global hub of sugar production. The world centre of sugar manufacture had gradually moved from northern India to the Levant in the early medieval period, and by the fifteenth century Cyprus and Sicily were Europe's main suppliers. But when the Portuguese discovered the Azores in 1427 and Madeira in 1455, they found that the climate of these Atlantic islands was better suited to growing sugar than the Mediterranean, and when they took Brazil in the 1540s, they expanded production into their new colony.[19] One hundred years later, as Portugal's position as the pre-eminent European maritime power was on the wane, the Dutch West India Company seized control of the Brazilian sugar plantations as well as Portugal's slave-trading forts dotted along the West African coastline. Dutch vessels now criss-crossed the Atlantic Ocean, bringing African slaves to work on the plantations, and returning laden down with huge cargoes of sugar destined for Antwerp's refineries. Drax and his associates would have been aware of this trade, and it was reportedly a Dutch visitor to Barbados who persuaded him and some other planters to try their hands at cultivating this potentially lucrative crop.[20]

Drax visited Brazil in 1640, almost certainly to learn how to cultivate and process sugar cane. Yet when Ligon arrived on Barbados seven years later, sugar planting was still 'in its infancy'.[21] Initially the sugar that Drax, Holdip and Hilliard were producing was wet with molasses and of little worth. However, by the time of Ligon's departure in 1650, they had mastered the art. They had learned that the canes needed to be planted close together so as to hinder the growth of the vigorous vines that would otherwise wind their way up the young plants and kill them.[22] They had worked out that they had to wait 15 rather than 12 months for the cane to ripen, and that in order to prevent bottlenecks at the mill it needed to be planted at intervals so that it matured on a rolling schedule. For once cut, the cane could only be left two days before it soured and spoilt the entire batch of juice.[23]

If the Newfoundland fisheries were pioneering in their industrial scale and organisation, the West Indian sugar plantations were the world's first agro-industrial factories where the human needs of the workforce were subordinated to the demands of production. Rather than adopting the Portuguese system whereby wealthy planters built a sugar mill and were supplied with cane by sharecroppers, Drax emulated the more efficient Dutch factory-plantation units, which controlled every aspect of the process from cultivation to refining.[24] Industrial principles of the division of labour were even applied in the fields, where the workers were separated into specialised planting, weeding and cutting gangs. The careful timing required for the harvesting and grinding of the cane meant that the cutters had to synchronise their efforts with those of the men working on the mill who fed the canes through its immense rollers (turned by five or six oxen) to press out the juice. The system reduced the workers to the role of mechanical parts in a larger machine. Even the mules, carrying the canes from the fields to the rollers, became automatons, plodding backwards and forwards without need of human guides.[25]

The boiling houses where the juice was crystallised into sugar prefigured by more than a hundred years the factory floors of the textile mills. The slaves were organised into shifts so that there was no break in the production process. Ligon described how the work went on from 'Monday morning at one o'clock, till Saturday night ... all hours of the day and night, with fresh supplies of Men, Horses and Cattle'.[26] As with the grinding of the canes, timing was crucial. Once squeezed out of the canes, the juice was channelled into a cistern where it could not remain for more than a day, otherwise it soured. From the cistern it

passed through five enormous heated coppers, constantly surrounded by gangs of men who stirred and skimmed the bubbling juice. A lime temper made of ash and water was added to the last four coppers to aid the crystallisation process. The men working around the final copper had the skilled job of catching the moment when the sugar reached crystallisation point. They would then quickly pour in two spoonfuls of salad oil and hurriedly ladle the juice into the cooling cistern without allowing the copper – still over the furnace – to catch and burn as it was emptied.[27]

The acute time-sensitivity of the process, the need for discipline and careful organisation, the bringing of field and factory together in one place and the fact that the planter owned all the capital assets from land to labour to processing plant – and could therefore take all the profit – made the sugar

A view of an early West Indian sugar mill and boiling house. This picturesque depiction with its focus in the foreground on West Indian foliage and a quaint slave hut would appear to belie the brutality of the first agro-industrial enterprises if it were not for the menacing figure of the white overseer supervising the slaves carrying sugar cane up to the ox-powered mill.

plantation a manifestation of capitalism in its hitherto most rapacious form. The plantations were agro-industrial complexes far in advance of farms and industries in Europe.[28] The sickly miasma that enveloped the sugar works foreshadowed the pall of smoke that would hang over the dark satanic mills of England's Industrial Revolution.

'I never more will drink Sugar in my Tea, for it is nothing but Negroe's blood,' wrote the ship's purser Aaron Thomas in his sea diary at the end of the eighteenth century.[29] When his frigate took part in an expedition to the West Indies, he was shocked to see how sugar was made. But in the early years of sugar production it was as much white men's blood as it was Africans'. Barbadian planters used white indentured servants to do the hard work of clearing the virgin forest and cultivating and processing their first crops.

In the century between 1530 and 1630, about half the rural peasantry in England were pushed off the land by agricultural improvement.[30] Some acquired new skills and found work as artisans, others were able to hire themselves out as labourers on the enclosed estates, but by the 1620s, large numbers of landless labourers roamed the countryside looking for work.[31] The American colonies took advantage of this to secure a labour force for their short-staffed plantations. English merchants would recruit young men and women from the rural poor and transport them across the Atlantic, where they were sold to a planter for a fixed period, normally four to five years. At the end of their term, they were promised a one-off payment of £10 to use to set themselves up in the New World.

Advocates of indenture saw it as a safety valve, ridding the English countryside of a potentially insurrectionary vagrant population and putting them to useful work producing tropical agricultural commodities.[32] Indentured labour was a form of temporary slavery, as servants were bought and sold and were powerless to renegotiate the terms of their contract with masters who frequently abused their position of power.[33] The planters did not feel the sense of paternal responsibility for their workers that, at least theoretically, ameliorated the position of English agricultural labourers. They viewed indentured servants as chattels, and, indeed, referred to these men and women as 'white slaves'.[34] The Cromwellian state made good use of the system: it 'Barbadosed' 12,000 Irish rebels and royalists, transporting them into servitude in the West Indies, whence they were forbidden to return.[35] Seventeenth-century planters did not suffer from the racial delusion (which developed later) that white men were unfit for hard labour in the tropics. Cromwell's political prisoners found themselves 'grinding at the mills, attending the furnaces, digging in this scorching land ... cutting, weeding, and hoeing'.[36]

Despite the arrival of at least 8,000 white servants on Barbados in the 1640s, the demand for workers on the labour-intensive sugar plantations was insatiable. When the first slave-trading ship to visit the island sailed into Bridgetown harbour in 1641 carrying hundreds of enslaved West Africans, they were eagerly bought up by the wealthier planters. More slave ships soon followed.[37] African slaves were more expensive than indentured labourers – a healthy African cost between £25 and £30 compared to £12 for an indentured servant – but the large planters' sugar profits enabled them to make the long-term investment in workers they would own in perpetuity.[38] After a five-month trip to the West Indies in 1645, George Downing, a ship's chaplain, wrote to his uncle, John Winthrop (by then established as governor of Massachusetts), to explain how a planter might get started with indentured servants, but once he had earned enough, he would procure 'Negroes' upon whom the return on investment was excellent: 'The more [Africans] they buie, the better able they are to buye, for in a yeare and halfe they will earne (with gods blessing) as much as they cost.'[39] By 1660, there were around 20,000 enslaved Africans on Barbados.[40] The appalling working conditions, malnutrition and disease led to such a high mortality rate among the slaves that in 1688, English sugar islands needed 20,000 new slaves a year just to maintain their labour force.[41] This constant demand for new workers for the sugar plantations stimulated the growth of the English slave trade.

Over time, slave labour came to dominate, but at first African slaves and indentured servants worked as cogs in the wheels of the sugar machine alongside each other, manuring the fields, digging trenches, trashing and cutting the cane, passing it through the mill and boiling the sugar. It was gruelling and dangerous labour. The cane subjected the workers to numerous painful and easily infected leaf cuts; many lost limbs when they were pulled into the rollers by accident, or were badly scalded by boiling sugar juice. Subject to brutal floggings and cruel punishments for minor indiscretions, they lived 'wearisome and miserable lives'.[42] If they got wet working in the field, they had nothing to change into as they were provided with only one set of clothes. They slept on bare boards, and while their masters gorged on boiled rump steak and marrow bones, the indentured labourers and slaves regarded the skin and entrails of the oxen as a high feast.[43] Their staple food was spoiled Newfoundland salt fish and loblolly, a cornflour gruel they detested.[44] If a slave resorted to stealing food, a common punishment was to string him up on a gibbet with a loaf of bread hung just out of reach for him to contemplate while he starved to death.[45]

Meanwhile, on the back of the slaves' labour, the planters grew rich. Once the sugar juice had passed through the boiling house, it was poured into conical pots and left in a still-house for a month. Liquid molasses slowly drained out of the pots, leaving behind soft, dry brown muscovado sugar. This was packed into bales and carried by mules down to storehouses in Bridgetown to await the arrival of a European ship to take it to the London refineries.[46] Sugar planting required patience – it took 22 months from planting the cane until it was transformed into saleable sugar – but it was worth the wait. Drax calculated that his first crop of good-quality sugar, which sold at £5 per hundredweight on the London market, increased his income per acre fourfold.[47] Those who had the capital to invest in land, labour and equipment followed Drax's lead, and within a couple of decades they had stripped Barbados of its forests and replaced them with a sugar monoculture.[48] Industrial economies of scale applied to sugar planting – contemporaries calculated that a planter needed at least 200 acres of sugar cane to clear a profit after the expensive investment necessary to set up a mill and a boiling house – and so by 1650, land on the island was concentrated in the hands of a tiny elite of fewer than 300 planters.[49] In the last two years of the 1640s, Barbados exported sugar worth over £3 million, catapulting it into the position of England's richest colony and making its planters as wealthy as aristocrats.[50]

Colonial trade – and especially the trade with the West Indian sugar islands – had a profound economic, political and social impact on seventeenth-century England. New World goods required further processing when they arrived at the ports. Tobacco had to be cured and rolled and muscovado sugar refined into white lump sugar. Sugar bakeries, as the refineries were known, sprang up in London and ports around the country. In 1692, there were 19 in the City and another 19 in Southwark, contributing to the great clouds of smoke hanging over London.[51] These promoted subsidiary industries supplying them with coppers and mining the coal to fire the furnaces.[52] But the requirements of the English refineries were nothing compared to the demands arising from Barbados. The deforestation of the island to make way for sugar cane meant that all the coal to fuel the furnaces that heated the coppers had to be imported from England.[53]

Thomas Dalby, who wished to demonstrate the financial and commercial benefits of the West Indian colonies to the British Isles, listed the many other manufactures besides coppers and mills needed by the planters. 'All their Powder, Cannon, Swords, guns, Pikes, and other Weapons ... Axes, Hoes, Saws, Rollers, Shovells, Knives, Nails and other Iron Instruments ... Sadles, Bridles, Coaches ... their Pewter, Brass, Copper and Iron Vessells and

Instruments, their Sail-Cloath, and Cordage ... all which are made in and sent from England.'[54] He claimed that every 'White Man, Woman, and Child, re-siding in the Sugar-Plantations, occasions the Consumption of more of our Native Commodities, and manufactures than ten at home do'.[55] England and Ireland supplied the plantations with 'great quantity of Beef, Pork, Salt, fish, Butter, Cheese, Corn and Flower, as well as Beer'. In the 1680s, the Irish salt beef trade to the West Indies was worth about £45,000 a year, which was equal to 40 per cent of the value of all English exports to the sugar islands.[56] Ligon advised that anyone intending to set up a sugar plantation on Barbados could double his investment by bringing out a cargo of English goods. There was a ready market, he assured would-be investors, for linen shirts and petticoats, Irish rugs for bedding, stockings and Northampton boots and shoes; there was also great demand for black ribbon due to the high rate of mortality on the islands.[57] Dalby pressed his point home when he reminded his readers that all those 'Industrious People Employ'd at home in manufacturing' were increas-ingly reliant on the colonies.[58] There was some truth in his claim. In the 1680s, about 20 per cent of all England's exports of manufactured goods were absorbed by the extra-European market. Barbados alone consumed one third of all the exports London sent to the colonies.[59]

European trade was still the mainstay of the seventeenth-century Eng-lish economy. Europe consumed almost all of England's woollens and stuffs, Yarmouth herrings, lead and tin, and provided most of the flax, iron, timber, pitch and tar needed by the nation's textile, metal and shipbuilding industries.[60] But European trade was stagnant, its value increasing only incrementally each year. From the 1660s onwards, the dynamic sector of the economy was colonial trade, the value of which quadrupled in the last quarter of the century. While England sent the colonies growing quantities of goods and commodities, in return the amount of sugar and molasses, tobacco, coffee, rice, pepper and spices flowing into England increased each year, until by 1700, more than a third of England's imports were tropical groceries.[61] By this time about a third of England's exports were now re-exports of these commodities. In the northern European ports, where the demand for English woollens and fish was low, co-lonial goods helped to balance England's trade deficit.[62]

On the Continent, calicoes and tobacco were the most popular colo-nial goods, but in England the desire for sweetness was overwhelming. The English loved sugar even before they began producing it in their own colonies.

A German traveller in Elizabethan England noticed that the teeth of aristocratic women (including the queen) were rotten, due to the fact that they constantly sucked on comfits, mixed sugar with their wine and even used it to glaze their roast meats.[63] As production got off the ground in Barbados and more sugar than ever before began arriving in the port of London, its price halved and domestic consumption trebled as the circle of people who could afford it widened. By the 1690s, there were 40 confectioners in London, selling jams, bonbons and pastries to the well-heeled.[64] An occasional sugary treat was now within the financial reach of a skilled craftsman, and the economist Gregory King noticed that the availability of sugar had increased the amount of fruit and vegetables eaten by the rural population. Now that it was affordable to make apples and pears, gooseberries and redcurrants palatable, they appeared frequently in pies and preserves on farm dining tables.[65] By the late seventeenth century, sugar was no longer used as a spice but as a principal ingredient in an increasing number of recipes. In the space of a few decades, it had become a kitchen staple.

Unlike the Asian and Middle Eastern trades, dominated by wealthy merchants organised in companies, trade with the Americas was conducted by a medley of men from the middling sort. Shopkeepers, soap boilers, tailors and craftsmen invested in American ventures.[66] These small-scale merchants formed a distinct City-based group, which supported Parliament in the early stages of the civil war, and once the Commonwealth was established in 1649, they gained a level of influence within the government disproportionate to their real social and economic weight. Cromwell embarked on a militant foreign policy promoting English interests against their erstwhile allies the Dutch (resulting in the first Anglo-Dutch War, of 1652–4), and authorised England's first government-led expedition to conquer the colonial territory of a European rival: in December 1654, a fleet sailed for the Caribbean, where the following year it captured the island of Jamaica from the Spanish.[67] In addition, the Cromwellian state sought to shut European competition out of the colonial trade and allow the English government to reap the rewards. The Navigation Act of 1651 stipulated that the produce of English colonies in the Americas could only be transported on English ships. In 1660, a further Act decreed that all colonial goods were to be channelled through England even if their eventual destination was Europe – and they could only be re-exported once the proper customs duties had been paid. Likewise, all slaves, food and manufactures sent to the Atlantic colonies were to be carried on English ships. In return, the 1661 Tariff Act placed prohibitive duties on foreign sugars entering England, thus giving West Indian planters a protected home market.[68]

In sugar the English found a commodity that compensated them for the lack of silver deposits in their colonies. At the end of the seventeenth century, England imported 320,000 hundredweight of West Indian sugar, worth about £630,000. The Crown earned 2s. 8d in customs duties on every hundredweight.[69] But it was not just the intrinsic value of sugar that contributed to England's prosperity. As valuable as the commodity itself was the bustle of commerce and industry that grew out of the sugar trade. The West Indies lay at the heart of the First British Empire, binding all the other colonies together in a web of exchange that stimulated the growth of maritime skills and knowledge, industry and financial services. The seventeenth-century economist Charles Davenant recognised that these were 'more truly [the] riches of a nation than (gold and silver)'.[70] The First British Empire fostered the growth of a new class of planters, merchants, financiers and industrialists whose wealth, based on the proceeds of trade rather than land, eventually gained them sufficient economic, social and political power to challenge the dominance of the landed aristocracy. The Atlantic trading system that developed out of England's American empire underpinned the structural changes and economic development that eventually culminated in Britain's Industrial Revolution.[71]

CHAPTER 5

In which la Belinguere entertains Sieur Michel Jajolet de la Courbe to an African-American meal on the west coast of Africa (June 1686)

How West Africa exchanged men for maize and manioc

Sieur Michel Jajolet de la Courbe had spent the morning buying slaves in Albreda, a trading lodge in the small state of Niumi, on the northern banks of the Gambia River.[1] As a managing director of the Compagnie des Indes, la Courbe commanded the French coastal settlement of Saint-Louis. After a long journey upriver and an uncomfortable night, disturbed by a violent thunderstorm and the unwanted attentions of clouds of mosquitoes, he had risen early that morning to greet the village headman, who arrived at the trading post promptly at eight o'clock. The two men shared the requisite drink – as the chief English factor in Niumi commented, 'without brandy there is no trade' – before the Africans inspected the ivory la Courbe had brought with him as payment.[2] A price per slave was agreed upon and the captives were paraded before the French slave trader. Those he regarded as defective were rejected and then payment was made for those he had chosen. Once the deal was done, la Courbe was taken to the nearby village. Mats were set out for him under a large fig tree, and while the women all came to stare at him, he was entertained by a group of musicians playing wooden wind instruments and beating on drums.[3]

Later he was taken to meet a prominent figure in Senegambia's slave trade. La Belinguere was the glamorous daughter of the former ruler of Niumi. She was tall and beautiful and la Courbe was enchanted.[4] She was wearing 'a small Portuguese-style corset which emphasized her figure' underneath an 'elegant man's shirt' and a beautiful African prestige cloth for a skirt. Her manner was gracious and her conversation – conducted in a mix of Portuguese, French and English – was assured. Clearly, the Frenchman noted in his account of the meeting, she was accustomed to doing business with men of various nations.[5] She lived in a house that was square in the Portuguese style, rather than round, and whose mud walls were coated in white lime. La Belinguere embodied the cultural interchange that took place along the West African coast in the late seventeenth and early eighteenth centuries. With her stylish mixing of customs she was the product of the Atlantic trading world that connected Europe, Africa and the Americas.

The Frenchman and his African hostess sat on mats on the veranda of la Belinguere's house to eat a meal with a similarly intriguing melange of flavours and foodstuffs, many of which were new to la Courbe. In Niumi, where most people could only afford flesh on celebratory occasions, the quantity of meat included in the spread served to demonstrate la Belinguere's elite status.[6] They were served two boiled chickens as well as an elaborate dish of seasoned minced chicken that had been stuffed back into its skin so that it looked as if it were a whole chicken.[7] La Courbe was less impressed by the ingenuity of this deception than by the food he had never before encountered. He judged the small, round, flat millet cakes, known as *batangue*, 'not at all bad'. These were a distinctively Senegambian contribution to the meal, as millet was the local staple crop. A dish of beautifully prepared rice heavily seasoned with chillies was even more surprising. Rice was another African staple but chillies were American and unfamiliar to la Courbe, who explained to his readers that they were 'green or red fruit, shaped like a cucumber and with a taste resembling that of pepper'.[8] West Africa had its own peppery spice in malaguetta pepper – known to medieval Europeans as 'grains of paradise' – but American chilli peppers grew like weeds in the West African climate and were popular with the people of Niumi. To this day, Gambian stews have a reputation for being the fieriest on the continent.[9]

The bananas la Courbe and la Belinguere ate for dessert were by the seventeenth century well established in Africa, even though they had originally come from East Asia. The Frenchman pronounced them 'very sweet, and extremely good' but was more excited by his first encounter with another American interloper: the pineapple. They ate it with wine and sugar to counter its supposedly corrosive effect on the stomach, and la Courbe thought it much

The rice dish described by la Courbe sounds like jollof rice. Now eaten all over West Africa, the spicy, smoky dish probably originated in rice-growing Senegambia. In its modern incarnation the rice is cooked in a tomato-based stew, often with red bell peppers, but as these New World introductions were integrated into African cookery much later than chillies, it is likely that they were not included in la Belinguere's heavily seasoned rice.

JOLLOF RICE

Ingredients

350 g washed and soaked long-grain rice

700 g fresh tomatoes, diced

2 large red peppers, diced

1 habanero chilli, diced (can be replaced with other types of red chilli, but as habanero chillies are very hot, you will need more than one)

2 large onions, 1 diced and 1 sliced

2 tsp smoked paprika

30 g fresh ginger, grated

1 clove of garlic, crushed

4 tbsp groundnut oil

4 tbsp tomato purée

1 green chilli, diced

5 stalks of grains of selim or Guinea pepper (use black pepper and a little nutmeg if unavailable)

15 g fresh thyme and/or other green herbs to taste

salt and pepper to taste

150 ml chicken stock

Wash the rice and soak for at least 15 minutes, then drain. Blend together the tomatoes, red peppers, habanero chilli, diced onion, 1 tsp of smoked paprika, ginger and garlic. Fry the sliced onion in the groundnut oil in a heavy-bottomed saucepan, stirring frequently. Add 1 tsp smoked paprika and fry for another minute. Add the tomato purée and fry for a further 3 minutes. Add the diced green chilli and fry for another minute. Add the blended tomato mix and cook slowly over a gentle heat until it thickens into a paste; this takes about 40–45 minutes. Add the grains of selim, fresh herbs and salt and pepper and stir. Add the soaked and drained rice and stir until all the grains are coated in the sauce. Add the stock. Bring to a simmer, lower the heat and cover with baking paper or foil and the lid of the pan. Cook over a gentle heat for 20–22 minutes until the rice is fluffy. Turn off heat and leave to carry on cooking in its own steam for 7–8 minutes.

better than but 'somewhat like a sugared rennet apple'.[10] La Belinguere politely tried the brandy la Courbe had brought her as a gift.

After leaving la Belinguere, la Courbe journeyed on to Gilfroid (Juffure), where he visited the English trading station. Here the interchange between cultures taking place on African soil was also apparent. The station was built in the Portuguese style and surrounded by a garden where the English cultivated European cabbages and cauliflowers; tropical vegetables like yams; and New World crops such as manioc and potatoes, which la Courbe reported tasted like boiled chestnuts. Here the Frenchman observed the curious pineapple plant growing, with the large fruits balanced on a stem like an artichoke coming out of a crown of prickly thistle-like leaves. While la Belinguere had served la Courbe a sweet and mildly intoxicating African wine made from the fermented sap of a palm tree, the English drank their visitor's health from a large silver bowl of punch, made with brandy, sugar and lime juice and – adding a touch of the East Indies to the medley – spiced with nutmeg.[11]

The French and the English had begun arriving on the West African coast in the mid seventeenth century, their ships loaded with guns, cotton, alcohol, glassware, iron bars and copper bowls, which they traded for slaves. It was the Portuguese who had opened up the African coastline to Europe when they discovered how to negotiate the difficult winds that persistently blow from the north-east, driving ships out of sight of land into the Atlantic Ocean. They succeeded in rounding Cape Bojador in 1434, and a decade later discovered that if on the voyage home they counter-intuitively sailed first in a north-westerly direction, they could pick up trade winds that would blow them back towards the European continent.[12] The Portuguese were seeking access to Africa's gold, but soon tapped into the West African slave trade, bringing the first consignment of slaves to reach Europe by sea back to Lisbon in 1434. Their advances in navigation opened up the Atlantic Ocean to European seafarers and eventually led to the discovery of the Americas, where the Portuguese introduced sugar into Brazil and began to transport Africans across the Atlantic to work on the plantations. In the mid seventeenth century other Europeans – French, Prussians, Danes, Swedes, Dutch and the English – joined the Portuguese on the West African coast, all jostling for a share of the lucrative slave trade.

Markets for African slaves had opened up in the tobacco and rice plantations of North America, but it was rising European demand for West Indian sugar that did most to propel the growth of the British slave trade during the eighteenth century. The great majority of those carried away from the African coast in British ships were taken to the West Indies. Conditions on the islands were so appalling that on reaching them the life expectancy of slaves was only seven years.[13] Therefore the plantations needed a continual flow of new supplies of Africans.

In Senegambia, the French and the English competed with each other, constantly trying to partition the region into exclusive zones of commercial influence. European power, however, was much more limited in Africa than it was in the Americas, where Europeans dominated and destroyed the peoples they encountered. Even in 1800, after 300 years of interaction, the European presence in West Africa was confined to just over 60 forts and factories dotted along a 3,000-mile stretch of coastline. Dilapidated, vulnerable to siege and manned by a rabble of ragtag soldiers, these forts were often indefensible in the case of a concerted attack. European merchants were frequently intimidated and occasionally murdered by the local rulers. Except for a few trading posts established along the course of the rivers, Europeans hardly penetrated into the interior of the continent.[14]

The purpose of la Belinguere and la Courbe's dinner had been to cement trading relations. The Frenchman was aware that he was acting in a treacherous world where the motives of each side were often only dimly understood by the other and in which relationships were unstable and contingent. Despite the fact that he found his dinner companion charming, he recognised that she was a potential enemy who could easily choose to scheme against him. In fact he described her as 'the reef on which many white men had shipwrecked'. When he departed after the meal, having presented her with gifts of coral and amber, he likened himself to Ulysses leaving the home of the enchantress Circe.[15]

Just how dangerous la Belinguere could be if disappointed or annoyed was brought home to the English when they fell out of favour with her a few months later. La Belinguere was invited to a party at the English fort on James Island at the entrance to the Gambia River. During the course of the evening a fight broke out and she was injured by a knife wielded by Captain Cornelius Hodges, a brutal and unsavoury man. (When his African mistress had given birth to a black baby, he was said to have accused her of infidelity, crushed the infant in a mortar and fed it to dogs.) Angered by the incident, the chief of Niumi, Jenung Wuleng Sonko, took the English factor at Juffure hostage and confiscated his trade goods. When the head agent on James Island tried to ne- gotiate with Sonko, he was also taken hostage. Meanwhile, la Belinguere joined forces with the French and began recruiting a network of merchants to break the English monopoly over the slave trade along the upper river. Eventually a neighbouring African ruler intervened and brought about a reconciliation. The English had to pay 200 iron bars to free their unfortunate compatriots. The incident demonstrates the power of the Africans, who were able to use the competition between the Europeans to play one side off against another.[16]

In order to participate in the slave trade, Europeans had to adapt to African trading practices. The most effective way to gain access to slaves was to establish a patron–client relationship with an African chief. The English paid the chief of Niumi 20 gallons of rum a year in order to establish their right to first choice of any slaves that he had to sell. But when the Portuguese had arrived on the West African coast in the fifteenth century, they discovered that the best way to cement this patron–client relationship was for the traders to marry women from the chief's wider family. In this way they became affiliated to him through kinship ties and were treated preferentially. The women who entered into these alliances were known as *nharas* (a corruption of the Portuguese *senhorita*). No mere pawns, they were often active participants in their husbands' affairs, translating and mediating for the men, who were ignorant not only of African languages but also the nuances of African politics and culture.[17]

By the seventeenth century, these unions had given rise to a community of Luso-Africans living along the coast and on the shores of the main trading rivers. They bore Portuguese names, claimed to be Catholic, lived in Portuguese-style houses, wore European clothing and spoke a Portuguese creole.[18] It was this mixed community that acted as the cultural brokers between the British and the French and Senegambia's African rulers. The ledgers from the English fort on James Island list 31 men and several women (known among the English as *signares*) with Portuguese names through whom the English conducted their business. According to la Courbe, it was the Luso-African *signares* who controlled 'almost all the trade of Senegal. They own female slaves who they send far away into the country to buy hides [cotton cloth, grain and other foodstuffs] which they carry for more than 15 leagues on their heads ... they buy them cheaply, and when they have gathered a considerable number they bring them to the fort on boats.'[19] La Belinguere was one such woman. The daughter of a chief, she had been married to several Luso-African traders and become rich and powerful in her own right. It was said that her fortune was worth 40,000 gold livres.[20]

Thus the Africa the Europeans encountered was not a backward continent where they were able to simply impose their will. When they arrived looking for slaves, they were tapping into an established trade. Indeed, slavery was integral to the fabric of African society and slaves were not necessarily treated as mere chattels. Usually captured in a raid, they were put to work

'The Slave Trade'. The text which ran along the bottom of the print read: 'Lo, the poor captive with distraction wild, views his dear partner torn from his embrace. A different Captain buys his wife and Child, What time can from his Soul such ills erase?'

growing crops for the nobility on plantations, mining gold, carrying goods along trading routes, weaving cloth, pounding millet and cooking food. But they also occupied trusted positions within the households of African kings and nobles, acting as administrators, guards and warriors. In the villages, they were often assimilated into the community, caring for children, working in the fields and processing and preparing food alongside the free women of the family.[21] Englishmen stationed on the island of Gorée at the mouth of the Gambia River in the 1770s and 1780s remarked that it was 'impossible to distinguish the [slaves] from free men'.[22]

Those slaves who were surplus to requirements had since the twelfth century been transported across the Sahara Desert to the Muslim world around the Mediterranean basin.[23] Now the insatiable demand for a steady stream of miserable captives to feed the maws of the European slave ships created a burgeoning new market. It was the fate of 12–15 million Africans to be sold into the Atlantic slave trade. With the arrival of the Europeans, West Africa was inexorably drawn into the Atlantic economy.

The Atlantic slave trade placed an immense strain on West Africa's agriculture. The loss of millions of fit and able men and women increased the ratio of dependants to every worker from 65 to 80. The demand for food was particularly intense on the coast. The men and women who were sold to the Europeans were often captured far inland. In Senegal they were purchased 300 miles upriver and brought down to the coast by boat when the water was high in the rainy season. They then had to be held there for several months until the weather and winds were favourable for the transatlantic ships to arrive. Coastal agriculture reoriented to feed the large numbers of captives waiting to embark for America. And once the ships arrived, although they were provisioned with Irish salt beef and butter, cheese and hardtack, they needed to take on substantial quantities of additional food to sustain the slaves on the middle passage across the Atlantic. Even though the importance of the food supply to the workings of the slave trade was rarely acknowledged by the Europeans, the market in foodstuffs that developed in West Africa during the seventeenth and eighteenth centuries underpinned the Atlantic trade.[24]

When famine afflicted the region, it affected the slave trade. In the eighteenth century, West Africa was hit by a prolonged period of dry weather, and periodic droughts sent the cost of food skyrocketing.[25] A French company employee at Saint-Louis complained in 1726 that a hogshead of millet that would normally have cost four livres in iron now cost between 30 and 35 livres in coral. The English governor John Hippisley noted in 1766 that famine had increased the cost of corn on the Gold Coast to 'six times what it is in Ordinary Years'.[26] If the Europeans had sufficient stocks of food themselves, famines could work in their favour. Owners would sell off any slaves they could not feed, and the desperate sold themselves into slavery in order to escape death by starvation. When Senegal was hit by famine between August 1715 and February 1716, the French filled five ships with 1,190 slaves. But when their own stocks of food ran low, the Europeans ran into difficulties. In 1750, the French were forced to turn 500 slaves awaiting shipment to the Americas out of the fort at Saint-Louis as they could not feed them.[27]

Surprisingly, demographic estimates suggest that while the population of West Africa did not grow over the 300 years of the slave trade, it did remain stable.[28] The region managed to achieve the remarkable feat of sustaining its population and the slave trade by holding back women: only about a quarter of the Africans transported to the Americas were female. This was not because there was a greater demand for male slaves in the New World, but because there was reluctance in Africa to sell women. Female slaves were used as concubines and so they allowed the men that were left in Africa to maximise the number of children they fathered. In this way they helped to compensate for the loss of young men. Slave birth rates were low, however, and female slaves were valued less for their fertility and more because African food production depended upon their labour. Traditionally, men cleared the land, but once the trees had been chopped down and troublesome roots had been dug up, it was women who prepared the soil, sowed, weeded, harvested and processed the crops.[29] While Senegambia had been one of the first parts of Africa to supply slaves to the Europeans, in the first half of the eighteenth century the region became more important as a supplier of food.[30]

The only way to increase food production was to bring new land under cultivation and employ more slaves to plant, tend and reap the crops. Indeed, in the first half of the eighteenth century, Senegambia probably imported more slaves than it exported.[31] They were concentrated near the trading ports and set to work in the fields. La Courbe witnessed an African aristocrat standing 'in the middle of his field, with his sword at his side and his spear in his hand' supervising the work of a gang of newly caught naked slaves who wielded their iron hoes as if possessed to the beat of 'the energetic music of six *griots*, who played drums and sang'.[32] No doubt agricultural productivity in the region was also improved by the exchange of slaves for the flat iron bars the blacksmiths fashioned into hoes and machetes.[33]

The millet they grew was sold to the European merchants, and as the Europeans moved along the coast, other areas were integrated into the food supply chain.[34] In what is now south-eastern Nigeria the cultivation of yams intensified. Ships' captains did not like to take yams as a food supply for the middle passage because they were bulky and took up too much room in the hold, besides being prone to turn putrid. But Africans from the Bight of Benin preferred yams above all else, and the slaves' tendency to become ill and refuse to eat when they were given unfamiliar foods placed the Europeans under pressure to take on at least some.[35]

The African–American sea route also opened a channel whereby a host of American plants and foodstuffs entered West African agriculture.[36] It was not just the elite who grew pineapples and experimented with chilli peppers: ordinary African farmers embraced a range of American crops. The two that enabled them to withstand drought and the sustained loss of agricultural workers were maize and manioc (cassava).

The earliest mention of maize in West Africa dates from 1534, when a Portuguese document lists it being loaded onto slave ships as provisions in São Tomé.[37] It seems that the Portuguese islands just off the coast were the launch pad into mainland West Africa for many American crops. The Portuguese planted sugar there in the 1470s and later brought over a range of American foodstuffs to feed the slaves who worked on the plantations. Throughout the sixteenth and seventeenth centuries maize spread along the Gold Coast, where it was referred to as 'Indian sorghum' or 'white man's grain'. Two crops of maize could be grown in the same time span as one crop of sorghum, and because it ripened more quickly it filled the hungry gap when last year's reserves had been eaten and before the yam and sorghum could be harvested.[38] Maize was not more nutritious than yams but it was easier to store. It was therefore a useful food to give to the slaves when they were being transported across the Atlantic.

Maize never replaced millet in the affections of the Senegambian people: it was grown by farmers in the region to sell to European slave ships.[39] However, it eventually displaced both sorghum and millet in Benin, Ghana, Nigeria and Togo, Angola and Cameroon. An Akan proverb in Ghana refers to maize as 'the chief among foods', while in Nigeria, Yoruba folk tales feature mysterious maize figures, and a distinctive 'maize cob roulette' pattern is used to decorate pottery.[40] Today maize is so integrated into African cultures that villagers regard it as an indigenous, 'traditional' crop that has always been part of the African landscape, and are surprised to learn that it was introduced to the continent only relatively recently.[41]

When in 1594 the British privateer Sir Richard Hawkins captured a Portuguese slave ship on its way from Brazil to the Guinea coast, it was carrying a cargo of cassava or manioc as slave provisions.[42] The Portuguese had learned to value this Amerindian root in their Brazilian colony. It was drought-resistant, high-yielding and required little labour to cultivate. Its one great disadvantage was that it was incredibly labour-intensive to process. First the roots had to be soaked in water for up to three days. It was then possible to slip off their skins; the Africans sometimes bypassed this stage, which resulted in a dark and bitter flour. Once the skins had been taken off, the roots were set to soak for another twenty-four hours until they were soft enough for the tough filaments to be removed. Then they were grated and the toxic prussic acid squeezed out of the mass of pulp. Once this process was complete, it could be left to dry in the sun and eventually ground into flour. Manioc meal was easily transportable and, if properly stored, lasted for months.[43]

Manioc was introduced to the Bights of Benin and Biafra and western central Africa by the Portuguese, whose slave-trading activities in the eighteenth century were concentrated on these parts of the coast.[44] Around the port of Ouidah in the Bight of Benin domestic slaves were set to work planting cassava, which they processed into flour to sell to the slaving ships.[45] In western central Africa manioc spread along slave-trading routes.[46] European visitors travelling on the Zaire River in the nineteenth century were struck by the eerie all-female settlements along the riverbanks, with not a man or child in sight. These were slave villages where cassava was grown to supply the trading canoes.[47]

Africans valued manioc for its resistance to drought, the fact that it was impervious to the depredations of locusts, and because it was easy to store, as the mature roots could be left in the ground for up to two years. Besides fitting in well with African ecology, soft maize and manioc flour suited local cookery. Sorghum and millet were made into breads or porridges, stiff pastes of a polenta-like consistency. Maize could be treated in much the same way. Slave cooks at the British fort of Elmina Castle on the Gold Coast would soak dry maize grains in water before grinding them. They would then mix the maize mush with a little water and leave it to ferment. The soft paste could be wrapped in waxy leaves and baked. The resulting *kenkey* soon became the staple food along the Gold Coast, and workmen referred to their wages as 'canky-money'.[48] By the end of the eighteenth century, maize had superseded most indigenous grains throughout large parts of West Africa. In an effort to save millet from extinction, the kings of Dahomey reserved it for royal use, thus hoping to turn millet consumption into a statement of high status.[49]

By deploying female slaves to grow maize and manioc, West African farmers substantially increased the number of available calories in the food supply.[50] This meant that West Africa was able to supply the Atlantic slave trade with men and food while also nourishing enough men, women and children to maintain the population. But the exchange of men for maize had tragic consequences. Manioc was transferred into the Old World with the knowledge of how to process it into an edible food. But the introduction of maize was marred by its arrival in Africa without the technique necessary to optimise its nutritional potential. The proteins and B vitamins present in maize occur in an exceptionally indigestible form. Mesoamericans had learned to break the maize down so as to release these nutrients by boiling the grains in a mixture of water and slaked lime made from burnt seashells. Only if left to soak in this mixture for a day or two before it was ground did maize became a nutritionally satisfactory food. As early as 1600, a Dutch visitor to the Gold Coast noticed that those who relied on maize for their staple food developed 'scabs and itch ... [and] are plagued with great boils', symptoms of pellagra, or niacin deficiency.[51] West African children weaned only on maize porridge would apparently receive plenty to eat but became apathetic and irritable, a condition their mothers named *kwashiorkor*. This is now recognised as a disease caused by protein deficiency. Thus, the slave trade bequeathed to Africa a form of hidden malnutrition that was to plague the continent in the following centuries.

·6·

In which Samuel and Elizabeth Pepys dine on pigeons à l'esteuvé *and* boeuf à la mode *at a French eating house in Covent Garden (12 May 1667)*

How pepper took the British to India, where they discovered calicoes and tea

One afternoon in May 1667, Samuel Pepys and his wife, Elizabeth, were on their way home after failing to pay a social call on Pepys' boss, Sir George Carteret, Treasurer of the Navy. Sir George had already sat down to his meal when the couple arrived at his house and Samuel thought it would not be a good idea to disturb him. He returned with some trepidation to his wife awaiting him in their carriage, aware that his decision would annoy her. That morning they had fought over Elizabeth's desire to wear fashionable 'white locks', which were artificial curls of hair mounted on wire and that Pepys detested. Perhaps he was jealous of the attention she attracted from other men when she wore them. He was still recovering from a bout of jealousy over her relationship with her dancing master. During the argument Elizabeth had been reduced to tears and had voiced her suspicions of Mrs Knipp, one of his mistresses. 'By and by', as he put it, they patched up their quarrel and he gave her 'money to buy lace, and she promised to wear no more white locks while I lived; so all very good friends as ever'.[1] Still wanting to make amends, in the carriage on the way home he hit upon the idea that they could take dinner at a French eating house, or 'ordinary', as they were known, run by his periwig maker, Monsieur Robins. On making enquiries, they were directed to an 'ugly street' in Covent

Garden where they found Monsieur Robins standing in the doorway of his establishment. Within moments the Pepyses had been ushered in and were seated at a table set for dinner. Pepys was mightily taken with the 'pleasant and ready attendance'.[2]

The first course was a potage: chicken simmered in a bouillon of herbs, salt and pepper, served on a slice of bread, the whole smothered with the cooking liquid and garnished with capers and mushrooms.[3] This liquid starter was typical of the French cookery all the rage at the time among

POTAGE OF CHICKEN GARNISHED WITH ASPARAGUS

After the chickens have been properly trussed up, blanch them well and put them into a pot with lard on top. Fill your pot with your best bouillon and season the chickens with salt and a very little pepper.

Do not let them cook too much. Dry your [slices of] bread, simmer them and garnish them with your chickens, with asparagus that has been broken and a few fricasseed mushrooms, cockscombs or tidbits from your chickens, a few pistachios and mutton stock. Garnish the rim of your platter with lemon. Then serve.

SQUAB IN RAGOUT

Pluck them dry, clean them out and sauté them in a pan in plain or clarified lard. Put them into a pot with good bouillon and cook them with a bouquet of herbs. When they are cooked, garnish them with their livers and veal sweetbreads, with everything seasoned with salt and spice. Then serve.[4]

London's fashionable elite. In the last half of the seventeenth century, French high society invented a new way of eating. Rather than all the dishes being placed on the table at once, the food was served in courses, each accompanied by a different, complementary wine.[5] This was a novel experience for the Pepyses, whose idea of a 'specially good dinner' was a leg of veal, a knuckle of bacon, roast capons and sausages ranged on the table alongside a few sweet dishes such as fritters and fruit.[6] The new French cookery, as defined in its manifesto, *The French Cook* – published in 1653 by La Varenne, the kitchen clerk of a Burgundian nobleman – replaced medieval abundance with refined moderation.[7]

Less was turned into more by the care and attention lavished on each dish. A cook of the new school might spend hours reducing meat to produce a delicate jus in which to poach a chicken. The newly invented raised stove gave off a gentler and more regular heat than a fire and allowed for the concoction of emulsified egg yolk and cream sauces.[8] The cook's ultimate aim was to stimulate the appetite by bringing out the flavour of the meat with one or two choice ingredients.[9] The *pigeons à l'esteuvé* the Pepyses were served after their potage was just such a ragout. The pigeons had been well seasoned with salt and pepper and sautéed in lard before being placed in a pot with a little stock and a few herbs and vegetables and then (with the lid tightly closed) set to braise on hot coals inside a metal oven or *estuve*. Garnished with slices of liver and veal sweetbreads, they would have been exquisite.[10]

The third course was *boeuf à la mode*. Beef brisket casseroled in a mixture of wine and bouillon flavoured with onions, orange peel and bay leaf, it would have been familiar to the couple as it was part of Elizabeth's domestic repertoire.[11] Elizabeth was, in fact, of French origin, but the food they ate at home was decidedly English. The merry dinner they had with eight friends on 4 April 1663, for example, was a typically English celebration of abundance. To Samuel's 'great content', they served 'a Fricasse of rabbets and chickens – a leg of mutton boiled – three carps in a dish – a great dish of a side of lamb – a dish of roasted pigeons – a dish of four lobsters – three tarts – a lamprey pie, a most rare pie – a dish of anchovies – good wine of several sorts'.[12] It was the elite of Restoration London, Pepys' employers, who ate French food at home. They employed French cooks, and on several occasions Pepys mentioned in his diary being served 'a fine neat French dinner' or 'a most noble French dinner' at the houses of various lords of his acquaintance.[13]

A decidedly Francophile atmosphere pervaded the re-established royal court. Charles II, his French mother, and the royalist gentlemen who had fled into exile with him had spent many years in Paris. On his return to England, the king employed a French cook to make 'Potages for Our Dyet' and the rich and the fashionable were keen to emulate the court.[14] French eating houses became part of the landscape of Restoration London. Throughout the latter half of his diary Pepys would regularly mention visiting French 'ordinaries' in Covent Garden, where he enjoyed the many-coursed dinners and the wide varieties of wine.[15]

In November 1665, Pepys was taken down into the hold of a 'Dutch India Shipp' that had been captured by the Earl of Sandwich. Here he crunched peppercorns underfoot and waded up to his knees through rooms full of nut-megs and cloves. He felt as though he were walking through piles of gold and marvelled at the way in which 'the greatest wealth ... a man can see in the world' was scattered about in confusion.[16] In London in 1668 a pound of pepper cost 16s. 8d, nutmegs were worth 13s. and cloves 8s. a pound. At the time a labourer would have earned about 5s. a week and a pound of beef cost around 3d.[17] But within a decade the price of pepper had more than halved due to a struggle between the English and the Dutch East India companies. Both were determined not to let the other dominate the spice trade and consequently imported such large quantities of pepper into Europe that pepper mountains formed in the warehouses of London and Antwerp and the value of this once rare and precious commodity plummeted.[18]

In 1498, the Portuguese had discovered the sea route to India. When three years later seven Portuguese carracks returned to Lisbon from India's west coast laden down with 100 tons of pepper, cinnamon and ginger, this was the first consignment of spices to reach Europe without passing through Arab hands.[19] However, although they monopolised the sea route to the Indies throughout the sixteenth century, the Portuguese never imported enough spices for Lisbon to rival Venice as Europe's spice entrepôt. Venice was only ousted from this position at the turn of the century, when between 1595 and 1601 the Dutch sent fourteen fleets to the East Indies. Their return with cargoes of spicy loot galvanised English merchants into action. In 1601, the English East India

Company was formed, and two years later the merchant James Lancaster triumphantly unloaded a million pounds of pepper onto London's docks – a quantity amounting to one quarter of the whole of Europe's annual consumption. In the same year, the Dutch East India Company brought back another three million pounds.[20] The contributions of both the Portuguese and the Levant merchants were now surplus to Europe's requirements.

In England, pepper had always been the most popular of all the spices. If a poor man could afford to sprinkle something piquant over his potage, it was pepper that he chose. Many of the drowned sailors on the *Mary Rose* were carrying a stash of corns in their personal baggage or in their pockets; no doubt a grinding of pepper helped to make a mess of 'poor John' palatable.[21] But now that their place of origin had been located and spices no longer came from beyond the known world, they had lost some of their magical aura. Their affordability meant that all classes of society could spice their ale or savour a meat pie fragrant with ginger and saffron, and so larding one's food with cinnamon and cloves lost its ability to signal wealth and status.

As spices fell out of favour, the complex, multi-layered tastes that had distinguished medieval and Renaissance cuisine all but disappeared from French and English cookery. The fashionable French cooking that the Pepyses sampled in Monsieur Robins' Covent Garden 'ordinary' rejected spice mixtures on the grounds that they disguised rather than enhanced flavour. This style of cookery signalled its consumers' elevated social position by using expensive perishable foods and placing fussy emphasis on the use of only the thinnest of asparagus stalks or rare varieties of fruits or vegetables.[22] Meanwhile, as spices disappeared from English food, it became increasingly plain, dominated by roast and boiled meats, pastries and pies. These plain meat dishes were, however, always accompanied by pungent condiments: mustard, horseradish sauce, pickles or fruit jellies.[23] Black pepper, the spice that had been treated with most caution by medieval cooks, also survived the expulsion of spices from savoury food. When Pepys dined with the Duke of Norfolk at Whitehall in February 1669, the duke served him the 'best universal sauce in the world', pronouncing with satisfaction that it could be eaten with 'flesh, or fowl or fish'.[24] It consisted of parsley and dry toast beaten together in a mortar with vinegar, salt and pepper.

Medieval cooks who associated black with melancholy preferred to use a combination of ginger and saffron known as 'yellow pepper'. In the medieval cosmic view of the universe, golden, saffron-coloured food was considered to be nourishing because it was thought to be imbued with the vitality of the sun.[25] But in the seventeenth century, black pepper rose to prominence as the everyday all-purpose spice. This may have been helped by the fact that it found favour with the new scientific dietary theory. Doctors such as Thomas Willis, a founding member of the Royal Society of London, re-envisaged digestion as a chemical process of fermentation rather than one of cooking aided by hot spices.[26] Fashionable foods such as anchovies and oysters, mushrooms, asparagus, artichokes and fruit were all thought to ferment readily. It made sense in terms of the new science of digestion to season one's food with pepper because in 1606 the pioneering French chemist Joseph Duchesne had concluded that its fiery taste was attributable to aronic salts, which were now identified as key in the process of fermentation.[27] Virtually every recipe in the *nouvelle cuisine* cookbooks was seasoned with salt *and* pepper.[28] It may have lost its glamorous aura as a rare and costly spice but black pepper's recategorisation as salt's partner meant that its position as a kitchen staple was secure.

Hippocratic dietetics regarded sugar as a perfectly balanced food, neither too dry nor too moist, too warm nor too cold, and therefore a sprinkling was thought to render any dish suitable for anyone from the choleric to the sanguine, the melancholic to the phlegmatic, the old to the very young.[29] As late as 1730, the botanist Richard Bradley complained that it was still common practice in many parts of England for 'good provisions' such as bacon and eggs to be 'murder'd in the dressing' by strewing sugar over them.[30] French cookery, however, eschewed sugar, as it dulled the appetite and this ran counter to its aim to stimulate the taste buds. The devotees of the new fashion began to serve sweet dishes in a separate, final course. Sugar at the end of a meal was thought to close the stomach and induce a feeling of satiation. Though spices were pushed out of savoury dishes, they retained a place in the sweet course and were redefined as suitable flavourings for desserts and cakes.[31] This established a sweet-versus-savoury divide in cookery that has survived to the present day.

As spices were incorporated into England's commercial empire they lost their high-status position in the culinary world and became mundane store cupboard staples. The English domestic market was not large enough to absorb the great quantities of pepper the East India Company imported and so it was re-exported to the Baltic and eastern Europe, where the middle classes still ate dishes so thick with saffron, pepper, cinnamon and nutmeg that Frenchmen dismissed them as inedible.[32] In this way pepper stimulated the growth of the re-export sector, in the seventeenth century the fastest-growing sector of the English economy.

The proceeds from the sale of pepper on the Continent were used to buy Spanish silver reales. These were diverted into the East Indian trade, which was perennially short of cash.[33] But East Indian trading patterns were far more complicated than a straightforward exchange of silver for spices. The Europeans who sailed to the Indies muscled their way into the liveliest commercial zone in the early-modern world. Diverse communities of Gujarati, Fujian, Arabian, Persian, Jewish and Armenian merchants lived in the ports dotted around the Indian Ocean and traded in a bewildering array of goods.[34] Complex chains of exchange involved swapping Malabar pepper for cowrie shells in the Maldives and using these to buy rice in Burma to take to Malabar, where the harvest was small.

English merchants soon learned that in order to succeed in this Asian trading world they needed to adapt to the existing patterns of exchange. Pepper grew in south-west India but cloves and nutmeg came from tiny islands in the Indonesian archipelago, where Indian textiles were more sought after than silver. The East India Company duly established trading posts, known as factories, at Surat and Masulipatnam on the west and east coasts of India. Employing Indian merchants as intermediaries, the factors used bullion to advance loans to the weavers who were contracted to supply a certain quantity of goods. They then stockpiled the calicoes, chintzes, ginghams, fine muslins and silks until the East Indiamen arrived bringing more bullion. The ships took the textiles on to Java, Sumatra and the Moluccas, where they were exchanged for spices. In order to sail home before the monsoon they had to set out by the end of December, and would arrive back in London in the summer with cargoes of spices to be auctioned to merchants engaged in the re-export trade with the Continent.

In the East, England's empire was very much a trading empire, whereas in the Atlantic it was based on English settlements. By 1660, around 2,000 English, Scots and Irish were living in Newfoundland, while a population of about 60,000 Englishmen was settled on the North American mainland and another 80,000 were distributed across six Caribbean islands.[35] The East India Company, by contrast, operated out of a chain of factories each inhabited by a handful of employees. Fort St George on India's Coromandel coast attracted communities of skilled weavers to settle in the area and by the 1640s was surrounded by the thriving commercial community of Madras, home to Portuguese, Muslim and Armenian merchants, who brought with them trading connections that stretched across the Indian Ocean.[36] In 1661, as part of her dowry, Charles II's Portuguese bride, Catherine of Braganza, gave England Bombay, which was to become the Company's most important port on the west coast, while the scruffy huddle of bungalows around Fort William eventually grew into Calcutta.[37] These were to become British India's three most important towns, though in the seventeenth century the factors were focused on conducting the Company's business rather than on the acquisition of territory.

These Company employees also traded in their own right, often in partnership with Indian merchants, and participated in the local or 'country' networks that circulated camphor and ivory, hides and dyestuffs, elephants and parakeets around the Indian Ocean. They met in the coffee houses and taverns in the ports to exchange news about where Bengal silks were selling at a good price and what Surat factors would pay for betel nut. It was through the networks and connections forged by entrepreneurial Company officers that the East India Company was integrated into the commercial world of the Indian Ocean.[38]

Spices had brought the Company to India, but it quickly became more interested in the subcontinent's textiles. These were popular in Europe, where they were at first used to decorate domestic interiors. Pepys bought his wife 'a painted East India calico for to line her new study'.[39] Gradually people began to use Indian textiles to make clothing; Elizabeth Pepys owned an 'Indian blue gown which is very pretty'.[40] The wealthy were enchanted by the exquisite hand-painted chintzes, while the poorer valued the calicoes because their vibrant dyes did not fade in the wash, besides being much easier to clean than woollens.[41] By the 1660s, textile piece goods were the East India Company's most important commodity, accounting for nearly three quarters of the value of their trade. Pepper now only accounted for 7 per cent of East Indian imports and had been relegated to the status of a ballast cargo, poured into the holds to help stabilise the ships. Calicoes also interlinked the Indian Ocean trading circuit with that of the Atlantic as the Royal East African Company began buying up Indian cottons in London and using them to purchase slaves in West Africa. By 1700, the ultimate destination of most East Indiamen was India and its textile markets rather than the Spice Islands.[42]

The arrival of Indian calicoes did not immediately stimulate a 'calico craze' among Europeans as has often been argued. In fact, the adoption of cottons for clothing was a gradual process, and East India Company directors clearly felt that in order to assure sales of their new commodity they needed to engage in large-scale promotion. In the 1670s, they ordered 200,000 ready-made calico shifts from their factory in Madras in order to introduce people to the idea that calico could be used to make underclothes.[43] But by the last quarter of the century, if people had a little ready money, they might spend it on a printed cotton shawl that mimicked the design of embroidered silk but was far more affordable.[44] By this time new consumables were arriving in England from the colonies in unprecedented quantities, and they might also have treated themselves to a pipe of tobacco, a dram of rum, or perhaps a twist of sugar and a few spices to liven up a suet pudding. Gentlemen like Pepys could sample the new colonial drinks in the London coffee houses, and from his diaries it is clear that both chocolate and coffee were by this time integrated into the daily lives of the middling classes. When he was breakfasting with friends, Pepys often mentioned drinking coffee or chocolate for his 'morning draught'.[45]

Tea was the last of the new colonial groceries to arrive on the English market. Garaway's London coffee house began selling tea in 1658, and on 25 September 1660, Pepys mentioned sending 'for a cup of tee (a China drink) of which I never drank before'.[46] Tea was as yet a rare and expensive item. It reached London not directly through the English East India Company but via the Netherlands under the auspices of Dutch East India Company merchants, who acquired it from Chinese traders in Batavia. Pepys only mentions tea-drinking on a couple of other occasions, and on both of these it was drunk for medicinal purposes rather than for pleasure. In June 1667, he arrived home to find 'my wife making of Tea, a drink which Mr Pelling the apothecary tells her is good for her cold and defluxions'.[47] Tea might not have been a popular drink with the Pepyses, but it soon became fashionable among gentlewomen, who revelled in the beauty of the paraphernalia that surrounded its consumption: the lockable polished wooden tea caddies; the delightfully patterned china teapots; delicate porcelain cups and saucers; sugar bowls, silver strainers and silver spoons. In the last decades of the seventeenth century, two or three East India Company ships a year began visiting Canton in order to pick up supplies of tea, but the Chinese resisted Company attempts to set up a factory.

A gentlewoman enjoying her breakfast tea drunk from a porcelain cup and wearing a printed shawl that imitated an Indian chintz.

The English drank their tea heavily sweetened with sugar. Sugar bowls, tongs and small silver spoons for stirring the sugar into the beverage were essential items in the tea-making equipment that fashionable ladies kept in their closets.[48] As sugar and spices ceased to play a role in savoury cooking, they became central to the ritual of afternoon tea. When a gentlewoman of social standing invited friends to take tea with her, she would place a bowl of sugar lumps on the table and serve sweet ginger biscuits or sugary cakes.[49] It is unclear when the practice of sweetening tea became commonplace in England. It certainly was not an Asian habit. But the popularity of sugar may be a key to understanding why the English embraced tea. Just as with spices, no sooner had sugar become widely available than it fell out of favour with both cooks and the medical profession. Far from regarding it as a perfect food, late-seventeenth-century physicians saw it as a dangerous substance that heated the blood, and its unbridled consumption was blamed for an epidemic of tooth decay, corpulence and gout. Health manuals of the time suggested that one way of countering its harmful sweetness was to imbibe it in bitter herbal or fruit infusions. There was no explicit mention of tea in these tracts; however, sweetened tea would have complied with this advice.[50] Tea-drinking may have been construed as a restrained and therefore legitimate way of consuming sugar. Over the next century, their use increased in tandem. Between 1663 and 1773, the amount of sugar consumed per head of the population increased twentyfold, while that of tea increased fifteenfold.[51] As tea's popularity grew, it was eventually to overtake textiles as the East India Company's most valuable trading commodity.

When Britain was created by the Act of Union in 1707, it was in possession of a flourishing maritime trading empire. To contemporaries, empire meant more than just a scattered collection of Irish and American territories, West African and East Indian trading posts; rather, it was the web of trade that held them all together.[52]

England's empire of trade reinvigorated its economy.[53] In the seventeenth century, labourers worked harder in order to be able to buy the new colonial commodities, and in a virtuous circle, the more sugar they ate, the more money West Indian planters had to spend on English provisions and manufactures.[54] By the end of the century, the American colonies were absorbing 10 per cent of English exports as the planters adopted an ever more costly 'peacock wardrobe' and filled their houses with mahogany sideboards, oak escritoires, japanned tea tables, damask bedsteads, silver tankards, spoons and fruit stands.[55] Virtually every payment in the Atlantic trading world could eventually be traced back to sugar. Even the purchases of English goods by the mainland American colonies were at bottom funded by sales of salt fish and timber to the sugar islands.[56]

Meanwhile, another 30 per cent of England's exports were in fact re-exports of colonial commodities: calicoes, pepper, tobacco, sugar and rice.

The bullion obtained for these goods on the Continent financed yet more colonial voyages. Surpluses in one area of commerce compensated for deficits in another. Rather than narrowly weighing up the costs and benefits of one branch of trade at a time, English economic thinkers began to view the nation's trade as a whole.[57]

PART
2

CHAPTER

In which the Latham family eat beef and potato stew, pudding and treacle: Scarisbrick, Lancashire (22 January 1748)

How the impoverishment of the English rural labourer gave rise to the industrial ration

At noon on Monday 22 January 1748, Nany Latham heard the sound of the family's newly shod mare trotting into the yard as her husband, Richard, returned from the blacksmith. There was a great deal of squawking as he released the two new hens he had bought to replace the ones that had stopped laying. The children, Sara, Rachael and Ann, put aside their spinning to help their mother set the food on the table. Sara doled helpings of beef and potato stew onto pewter platters and Rachael unwrapped the cloth from around the pudding, which had been simmering in a cauldron of water. Ann put a crock of treacle on the table so that everyone could pour a generous measure over their pudding while Nany set out mugs of strong, sweet ale.[1] Dicy, the Lathams' only son, came in from cutting turf for fuel on a neighbour's farm and their two other daughters, Alice and Martha, rushed breathlessly into the room a few minutes later, having run all the way home from school. While they ate, the parents exchanged a few words about the hens, which had cost Richard 1s. 3d, but for most of the mealtime the family were silent, concentrating on the pleasure of consuming the food.[2]

This was a solidly English dinner of the kind that New Englanders like the Holloways aspired to eat. Richard recorded in a little leather-bound notebook the family's expenditure between 1724, when he married Ann (Nany) Barton, and 1767, when he died. From these careful records we can see that the family of a carter with a smallholding was able to lead the kind of comfortable rural life that the harried middling emigrants of the seventeenth century felt they could not achieve in England, and which they had attempted to create in the New World.

On his smallholding in south Lancashire, Richard practised the mixed farming that agrarian reformers advocated. He grew wheat and barley, and Nany made most of the family's bread, eking the wheat out with additions of barley flour. That morning Nany had not baked, however, because she and her daughters were too busy trying to finish spinning into yarn that week's cotton consignment. They wanted to have it finished so it would be ready for Thomas Holecroft, the representative of a Manchester textile manufacturer, who was due to pick the yarn up the next day, when he would also deliver more supplies of cotton. Making pudding was much quicker and easier than baking bread, and earlier that morning Nany had mixed a dough out of flour, beef suet, milk and some eggs. She had flavoured it with a spoonful of ginger powder and a handful of raisins and formed it into a ball, which she wrapped in a cloth and set to simmer in a cauldron of water hung over the turf fire. In the seventeenth century the British began wrapping dough in cloth and then boiling it to make puddings eaten with treacle and by the eighteenth century it had became the favourite fare of the rural population: the sweet–savoury divide that character-ised elite cookery had not yet penetrated the countryside.[3]

The Lathams owned three cows, which made them virtually self-sufficient in milk, butter and cheese; and as there is scant mention in Richard's accounts of purchasing pork products, it seems likely that they slaughtered their own pigs to make salt pork and bacon. But beef they had to buy, and on a trip to the nearby town of Liverpool a few days earlier, Richard had bought 12 lb, some of which had now found its way into the hearty beef and potato stew that Nany served her family.[4] The stew was typical of the meat, grain and vegetable pottages that ever since the Middle Ages rural cottagers had let simmer slowly over the fire while they went about their household tasks.[5] Nany would have grown the vegetables and herbs in her kitchen garden; Richard frequently recorded payments for seed potatoes. The family may even have grown potatoes as a cash crop to sell on the Liverpool market.[6] Although the English lower classes are thought to have regarded potatoes with suspicion when they were introduced from the New World, labourers in northern areas, where they relied on peat as a cooking fuel, seem to have willingly integrated them into their diet. Slow-burning turf fires were well suited to cooking potatoes, which could be set to simmer slowly over smouldering peat or buried in the ashes.[7]

Labourers' wives like Nany Latham would not have consulted recipes. Hannah Glasse's *Art of Cookery Made Plain and Easy* was aimed at a middle-class audience, but although Nany would probably have used fewer eggs in her pudding, and stewed her beef in water or ale rather than in red wine, these recipes give a sense of what her cooking might have been like.

TO MAKE A FINE PLAIN PUDDING

Take a Quart of Milk, put into it six Laurel-leaves, boil it, then take out your Leaves, and stir in as much Flour as will make it a Hasty-pudding pretty thick; take it off and then stir in half a Pound of Butter, then a quarter of a Pound of Sugar, a small Nutmeg grated, and twelve Yolks and six Whites of Eggs well beaten; mix it well together, butter a Dish, and put in your Stuff: A little more than half an Hour will bake it.

ANOTHER WAY TO STEW A RUMP OF BEEF

You must cut the Meat off the Bone, lay it in your Stew-pan, cover it with Water, put in a Spoonful of Whole Pepper, two Onions, a Bundle of Sweet Herbs, some Salt, and a Pint of Red Wine; cover it close, set it over a Stove or slow Fire for four Hours, shaking it sometimes, and turning it four or five Times; make Gravy as for Soop, put in three Quarts, keep it stirring till Dinner is ready: Take ten or twelve Turnips, cut them into Slices the broad Way, then cut them into four, flour them, and fry them Brown in Beef Dripping. Be sure to let your Dripping boil before you put them in, then drain them well from the Fat, lay the Beef

into your Soup dish, toast a little Bread very nice and
brown, cut in three Corner Dice, lay them into the
Dish, and the Turnips likewise, strain the Gravy, and
send it to Table.[8]

The first half of the eighteenth century was a prosperous period for British agriculture. The rise in the value of land – and the consequent rise in rental income – made landlords embark on agricultural innovations that greatly increased productivity. Smallholders like Richard Latham also tried to improve their plots. Richard's account book records frequent purchases of marl to use as manure, and he also grew the new fodder crops – clover and turnips – to feed his livestock.[9] Farming was productive while population growth had slowed, so food was both more plentiful and relatively affordable. But the real key to the prosperity of the eighteenth-century countryside was the increase in women's earning capacity.[10] Nany and her daughters were able to substantially boost their household's ability to spend by joining an army of putting-out workers spinning yarn for the textile manufacturers who had begun setting up around Manchester. In 1739, when the two oldest girls had reached the age when they were able to spin, Thomas Holecroft had sold the Lathams two new cotton spinning wheels at 2s. each. That year the family had also invested in cotton cards, steel spindles and whorls, which altogether cost them about 10s. – a sizeable proportion of the £12 they spent in the entire year.[11] We do not know how much Nany and her daughters earned, but a history of the village of Wilmslow, south of Manchester, claimed that in the 1740s, a diligent woman spinning yarn on a Jersey wheel in her cottage could make up to 4s. a week, while seven- or eight-year-old children could earn 3d or 4d a day.[12]

The Latham women's earnings allowed the family to participate in the consumer revolution that swept through Britain in the eighteenth century.[13] The cottage in which Richard and Nany began their married life in 1724 was much more comfortable than a seventeenth-century labourer's would have been. They spent 82s. on a horse and cart, a feather bed and bolster, a spinning wheel and bobbins, various pots, cups and earthenware 'mugs' for cooking and butter-making, a large stew pot, chafing dishes, knives, ladles, a sieve and six wooden trenchers, some platters and twelve pewter plates. Over the next 16 years, Nany gave birth to eight children (one died in early infancy), and the family had little spare cash to spend on items to add to their domestic comfort. Indeed, most of the goods they bought when they married seem to have lasted the family a lifetime.[14]

Once the older girls began contributing to the household income, however, the Lathams' cottage was gradually made more elegant, with the addition of window curtains, four upholstered and two rush chairs, a clock and a looking glass. Richard bought himself and the children books and newspapers on a regular basis, and his account book shows that the family were drawn into the consumption of textiles that had infected all levels of society.[15] This had been sparked by the East India Company's introduction of Indian textiles, but by the mid eighteenth century, the popularity of these had stimulated the home textile industry – in which the Latham women themselves participated – into the production of fine cottons and stuffs.[16] The family purchased hats, gloves, caps, trimmings, handkerchiefs, lace, lengths of blue flowered damask, plainer woollen cloths and linen, as well as ready-made plain and check gowns. When the eldest daughter, Betty, went into service in 1747, she was given a new gown and a red cloak and shoes.[17]

The Lathams enjoyed their new-found prosperity just as colonial goods began entering the country in unprecedentedly large quantities. This brought their price down sufficiently for people from all walks of life – blacksmiths and miners, midwives and dancing masters – to be able to afford them.[18] The Lathams began to buy small treats, such as three pennies' worth of raisins, a few cloves and a little gingerbread. The combination of efficient industrial production methods and the systematic exploitation of slave labour meant that the West Indian plantations produced millions of hogsheads of sugar a year. The further the price of sugar fell, the more people could afford to buy and so the greater the amounts that were imported. In the first half of the eighteenth century, the per capita consumption of sugar doubled from 4 lb to 8 lb and more than doubled again to 20 lb by the end of the century.[19] Throughout the 43 years that Richard Latham recorded his family's expenses, sugar and treacle were the most frequently purchased foodstuffs. In the 1740s, when their family was at its largest, the Lathams consumed an average of 50 lb of sugar and 20 lb of treacle a year.[20] Sugar and treacle had become staples of the English labourer's diet.

If the consumption of empire goods changed ordinary people's diet, it also transformed their shopping habits.[21] The Lathams probably purchased

This illustration for an eighteenth-century pastoral comedy gives an impression of how the Lathams' kitchen might have looked, with a few china plates displayed on a shelf and one of the girls binding up her hair with a newly purchased ribbon.

their sugar and treacle in one of the many small local shops that began to appear in England's villages and towns during the eighteenth century. Before the advent of the village shop, people bought trinkets and small luxuries from pedlars or at fairs; if they needed to buy staple foodstuffs, they visited the local town on a market day. The influx of colonial groceries radically altered the way poor people shopped. It soon became a habit among labourers to pop into their local shop on a daily basis, sometimes twice or thrice a day. In the 1780s, William Wood, who ran the Ring O' Bells Inn in Didsbury, catered to the needs of the humbler village folk in a room on the side of the inn.[22] On the morning of 3 January 1787 Matha (*sic*) Chase is recorded in the shop ledger as having bought 1 lb of treacle for 3½d. She came in again later in the day to pick up three pennies' worth of currants and a clove.[23] No doubt they were destined to flavour that evening's pudding, which Matha and her family would have eaten with a generous helping of treacle.

Colonial groceries were the backbone of these small shops' trade, and sugar and treacle in particular were among the most frequent items on the shopping list of the villagers who frequented Wood's store.[24] William Cash was typical of Wood's customers: in just one week in February 1786 he bought 6 lb of treacle and 1 lb of sugar.[25] Sugar and tea accounted for three quarters of Mrs Taylor's trade in the tiny shop she ran in Niddry near Edinburgh.[26] Larger enterprises like the shop Mrs Elizabeth Kennett ran out of her front parlour in Folkestone in the 1730s sold a small range of useful household items such as soap and powder blue, tape and binding, mops, candles and brushes as well as foreign and colonial groceries – raisins and currants, spices, snuff, rice, lump sugar and tea.[27]

In some parts of the country these commodities were still seen as luxurious fripperies. The ironmonger known as 'Roberts' who sold agricultural supplies, textiles and medicines in the remote village of Penmorfa in North Wales added colonial groceries and haberdashery to his stock in the 1790s. While their husbands came in to buy alum, indigo, logwood, linen and thread, the wives would buy pennyworths of sugar, screws of tea, handkerchiefs and lace. Many of these purchases evidently had to be smuggled past the men, as Roberts frequently noted down 'nor to tell' next to the record of the sales.[28] But even if they were still frowned upon in Britain's remoter regions, colonial goods – bought in small quantities on a daily basis – had become integral to the lives of eighteenth-century rural labourers.

It is remarkable that while they embraced sugar and treacle, the Lathams do not appear to have fallen under the spell of tea. Tea-drinking did, however, become a widespread habit in the eighteenth century, especially in the south of England.[29] In 1713, the East India Company finally managed to persuade the Chinese authorities to allow them to establish a trading post at Canton.[30] Now that they had easier access to the Chinese market, the number of Company ships calling in at the new trading post rose steadily from three or four to around twenty a year, and the quantity of tea arriving at Britain's docks rose from 142,000 lb in 1711 to 890,000 lb in 1741, reaching 15 million lb a year by 1791.[31] Once the infusion was widely available and affordable, the practice of taking afternoon tea spread throughout the whole population and was even adopted by the most humble. When Arthur Young travelled through England in the 1760s, he found that the inmates of alms houses at Nacton in Suffolk had petitioned to replace the pease porridge served on Fridays and Saturdays with bread and butter, which was 'their favourite dinner, because they have tea to it'.[32] When he expressed surprise that they were allowed this indulgence, he was told that 'they were permitted to spend 2d in the shilling of what they earned, as they please; and they laid it all out in tea and sugar to drink with their bread and butter dinners'.[33]

The consumption of colonial goods integrated the Empire into ordinary people's everyday lives. The images on the trade cards shops used to advertise their wares would have left people in no doubt as to where these goods came from or how they were produced.[34] Tobacco, known as the 'Indian weed', was advertised with images of American Indians in feathered headdresses smoking pipes, while black African slaves were shown toiling in the fields and processing sheds of the Virginian plantations. Pictures of crates of tea marked with mock Chinese writing being loaded onto an East Indiaman by pigtailed Chinese peasants depicted the tea trade. Sometimes the cards showed the East India Company's headquarters in Leadenhall Street in London. It would have been easy for people to recognise the connection between the foodstuffs they enjoyed and Britain's commercial empire.[35]

In the eighteenth century, the English, Scots and Welsh were united into a single state and began to define themselves as British. This new identity derived from a sense of a shared Protestantism, which was highlighted by their opposition to Catholic France. With the British triumph over the French in Canada and India during the Seven Years War (1756–63), public pride in Britain's navy and imperial strength grew.[36] Victories at sea were now marked by the ringing of church bells, and there was a populist dimension to the celebration of empire – merchants, artisans, people in the provinces all took pride in Britain's overseas triumphs.[37] National morale was affected by imperial success (or failure). And Britain's military might was financed by its empire. In the 1760s, the duty the government made on sugar imports was roughly equivalent to the cost of

This trade card for Hodson's Tea dealers brings together standard images of empire to sell its stocks of sugar and tea. The ship in the background symbolises imperial trade while the pagoda and plants evoke the exotic origins of tea and sugar. The African slave and the sugar cones bring to mind the West Indies while the Chinaman holds up a sprig of tea. Above the scene floats a teapot of British manufacture ready to transform these imperial goods into a quintessentially English cup of tea.

maintaining all the ships in the British navy.[38] More directly, the government raised loans from the East India Company to finance its wars.[39] The consumption of colonial goods became linked to pride in Britain's imperial greatness, and both became an integral part of what it meant to be British.[40]

Ironically, the origins of the colonial product of which British people consumed the most were the least visible in advertising. Pictures of slaves cutting cane, refining the juice in boiling houses or loading muscovado sugar onto ships rarely appeared on trade cards. Sugar appears to have been considered such a standard commodity that traders did not feel the need to assure their customers of its authentically West Indian origins. It was sold according to the level of its refinement – brown muscovado or white lump sugar – not according to its place of origin. One did not need to be a connoisseur to judge the quality of sugar, unlike the teas it was used to sweeten, which came in a variety of types and grades.[41] In her shop near Edinburgh, Mrs Taylor sold a range of middle-quality Congou teas, which the labouring classes preferred as they were stronger than the cheaper teas. And for every pound of tea she sold, she sold seven pounds of sugar.[42]

Tea sweetened with sugar eventually displaced beer as the primary drink of the poor. Tea itself does not seem an obvious alternative to beer until the sweetness of the eighteenth-century brew is taken into account: the amount of malt it contained would have produced a heady, sweet beer that may have predisposed people to develop a liking for strong, sugary tea.[43] In 1767, the social reformer Jonas Hanway was outraged by the indulgence of beggars, road menders and haymakers, who he observed had developed a passion for tea, a luxury he considered they could ill afford.[44] What Hanway and other middle-class commentators who condemned the habit failed to understand was that rather than a sign of profligate spending, tea-drinking was in fact a symptom of the worrying impoverishment of the labouring classes.

Enclosure had left many rural labourers without access to even a small patch of common land on which to graze a cow or some sheep. It also denied them access to woodlands, where they had gleaned firewood and caught the odd rabbit for the pot. In addition, employment for live-in agricultural servants declined as farmers began to hire in labour only as and when they needed it. The rural labouring population thus gradually turned into a wage-earning proletariat as they lost their means of economic independence and, most importantly, the means to produce their own food. This was less troubling when the cost of food was reasonable.[45] But the rural population's dependence on wages became a grave problem when the population explosion from the middle of the century began to put pressure on food supplies. Poor harvests in the 1760s and 1770s pushed wheat prices up by 40 per cent.[46] The Revolutionary and Napoleonic wars of 1792–1815 caused further inflation and food prices went spiralling upwards. Those rural families who did not own a cow lost their access to milk as its price rose from 4d a gallon in 1770 to 10d in 1800. At the same time, deforestation also led to a rise in fuel prices in southern England, where people were dependent on wood for cooking and heating and the cheaper coal that was being mined in the north was not available. Brewing beer therefore became an expensive process: the wort had to be boiled, and this was preferably done over a fire made with high-grade fuel, as impurities affected the flavour.[47] Many labourers who could no longer afford to brew their own beer turned to sweetened tea as a less expensive alternative.

Those who criticised the labourers' tea-drinking habit were correct in their assertion that it was detrimental to their nutrition and health. Brewing beer was an alternative way of turning grain into edible food. Beer was, in effect, liquid bread. It was nutritious, containing protein and vitamin B, as well as providing energy (about 350 calories per pint).[48] Tea, on the other hand, contained neither vitamins nor protein, and even when it was heavily sweetened, it provided far less energy. Even if a man heaped his cup with four teaspoonfuls of sugar, it would only have contained about 64 calories. Labourers would have been under the illusion, however, that tea gave them more energy because the sugar would have been immediately accessible to the body, whereas the sugars in beer are released far more slowly.[49] Tea had the added advantage that it was hot, which must have been welcome to labourers working outside in the inclement English climate, and to the increasing number of families who could no longer afford to cook on a daily basis. For if the rise in fuel prices led to a decline in brewing, it also had a calamitous impact on the ability of many people to prepare a warm meal.

Those who could not afford fuel to cook or heat their homes were now forced to buy in bread. Bakeries began to appear in England's villages in the middle of the eighteenth century. There were striking regional differences. In the southern county of Berkshire by 1815 there was one baker to every 295 inhabitants; in comparison, there was only one for every 2,200 people in the northern county of Cumberland.[50] Surveys conducted in the 1790s found that although the north too had been hard hit by price rises, porridge, potatoes and barley broths still constituted an important part of the diet of labourers there. Cheaper peat and coal in the north meant that people could still afford to cook warm meals.[51] Southern labouring families, on the other hand, were barely able to scrape a living together. Not only warm, home-cooked broths and stews but milk and butter had virtually disappeared from their diet. They subsisted on an industrial ration of shop-bought bread and the occasional bit of cheese or scrap of bacon. What irritated Sir Frederick Eden, who conducted one of the surveys, was that these poor families spent at least 10 per cent of their annual income on tea and sugar.[52] A family of seven in Northamptonshire, for example, spent £2 7s. 6d a year on tea and sugar out of an annual income of £26 8s.[53] While Eden's instinct was to judge the poor as shamefully wasteful, a fellow surveyor, David Davies, understood that they were now entirely reliant on hot sweet tea to give them some small measure of comfort: 'Spring water, just coloured with the leaves of the lowest-priced tea and sweetened with the brownest sugar is the luxury for which you reprove them. To this they have recourse from mere necessity, and were they now to be deprived of this they would immediately be reduced to bread and water. Tea-drinking is not the cause, but the consequence of the distresses of the poor.'[54]

Initially, the lower classes bought sugar and treacle in order to fulfil a novel desire for sweetness, but before long they metamorphosed from luxuries into necessities. When milk became unaffordable, porridge made with water tasted much better if it was covered in treacle.[55] Treacle spread on a slice of bread was a good substitute for butter, which was now too expensive. It was cheaper to boil a kettle to make a cup of tea than simmer the wort to brew beer at home. And a cup of sweet tea with a slice of bread and treacle at least created the illusion that this was a warm meal. Last but not least, tea also had the advantage that it acted as an effective suppressor of appetite.[56] Sugar and treacle replaced the fresh meat, milk, butter, cheese and vegetables that had disappeared from labourers' diets. The problem was that the calories they contained were empty of any additional nutritional value: sugar contains neither vitamins, minerals nor protein. Looking back in the 1890s on the change in the labourer's diet, an old man complained to Arthur Fox, a commissioner for the Royal Commission on Labour, that the reliance on 'foreign stuff' had had a deleterious effect on the poor. 'Tea is no forage for a man,' he complained. 'Bannocks made of barley and peas made a man as hard as a brick. Men would take a lump of bannock out for the day, and drink water, but now they eat white bread and drink tea, and ain't half so hard.'[57]

By the end of the eighteenth century, the meat and vegetable pottages, the porridges and puddings had all but disappeared from the tables of rural labourers in the south. The prosperity they had enjoyed in the first half of the century had allowed them to take part in the consumer revolution and integrate colonial foodstuffs into their diets. These foods changed the way the British ate and shopped. But when population growth and food shortages sent the price of fuel and foodstuffs spiralling, the colonial groceries that had once supplemented their diet became essential to their sustenance. This marked an important shift in the contribution of the Empire to Britain's economy and society. And the Empire's underlying importance was reinforced when the rural labouring classes took these eating habits with them as they moved into the urban slums that grew up around the textile mills.

·8·

In which a slave family eat maize mush and possum on Middleburg plantation, South Carolina (1730s)

How the American colony of South Carolina was built on African rice

In a scene that could have been transposed from Africa, a family gathered in the moonlight around the open hearth in front of their cabin on the Middleburg plantation. Tasty food at the end of the day was their principal source of comfort after working in the rice fields since first light.[1] The father was a good hunter and had found an opossum in one of his traps the previous evening; the animal was now roasting on a stick stuck in the ground next to the fire.[2] Squatting on their haunches, the family each tore a piece of maize 'porridge' off the mass in the big iron pot, rolled it into a ball and dipped it into a small clay jar of sauce. This evening the family's relish was made of sorrel and watercress, which the children had collected from the edges of the rice fields. It was delicately flavoured with sesame, which grew in the small garden they were allowed to cultivate next to their cabin. Sesame, brought over from Africa, was a favourite seasoning among those enslaved on Carolina's rice plantations.[3]

After they had eaten, the father went off to plant peas in their garden patch. A Carolina slave proverb that made a virtue out of a necessity said that only the pods of peas planted at full moon would fill.[4] Throughout the American South, the hours of darkness were a busy time for the slaves, as this was when they carried out their own chores after the slog of working all day for their masters. South Carolina slave life was lived almost entirely in the open. The family only retired to their cabin to sleep on a pile of palm fronds,

97

The sheaves are beaten with flails.

These sketches of work on a South Carolina rice plantation were drawn after the civil war and the emancipation of the slaves but the work of rice production had changed little since rice was first introduced in the eighteenth century.[4]

wrapped up in blankets. While the father worked in the garden, the rest of the family huddled closer to the fire. The mother was sewing a patchwork quilt out of rags to provide a warm covering at night. The children were fashioning seagrass baskets that the family would sell in exchange for a little sugar or some bottles of porter. One of them told a Buh Rabbit story to keep everyone awake. Buh Rabbit was up to his usual tricks trying to deceive a more powerful animal. That evening he managed to trick Buh Bear out of a large fish.[5]

African slaves outnumbered their white masters by four to one in South Carolina.[6] For at least half the year, the planters and their families fled from the unhealthy malarial stench of the stagnant water in the rice paddies, leaving a few white overseers to supervise the slaves on the plantations. The Africans therefore lived in relative isolation and these conditions fostered the development of a distinctive slave culture heavily influenced by memories of their homeland. They developed their own language, Gullah, a mix of African languages and English; lived in African-style windowless cob-wall huts with

Her little log cottage was as clean
as possible.

palmetto-leaf thatched roofs; decorated their few possessions with traditional African patterns and symbols; and in their gardens planted a wide variety of African vegetables – okra, cowpeas, groundnuts, West African red pepper, and sesame – alongside American squashes and pumpkins and European turnips, collards and cabbage.[7]

In the 1980s, a team of archaeologists located the remains of the cabins where Middleburg plantation's slave workforce had lived in the eighteenth century. Beneath layers of wind-blown sand, they discovered the charcoal that had built up from years of open fires in the yards in front of the cabins, and a series of refuse pits from which they unearthed pieces of glass, buttons, broken clay tobacco pipes decorated with African designs, small animal bones and hundreds of fire-charred shards from earthenware jars and bowls.[8] Many of these bore abrasion marks made when the contents of the pot was stirred; some were scorched on the outside where they had been balanced on stones over a fire; others contained charred food. These were the remains of many decades of slave meals.[9] For years it had been assumed that the slaves had bought their cooking pots from Native American potters. But the team excavating Middleburg noticed that the archaeological trace of Carolina slave meals was almost identical to that found by their colleagues working in West Africa.[10] Indeed, the cooking pots the eighteenth-century Carolina slaves had used were indistinguishable from the flat-bottomed grit- or sand-tempered vessels that were still being made and used in twentieth-century Ghana.[11] The slaves had brought not only their eating habits with them from Africa but also their potting skills.[12]

Earthenware jars were the best vessels in which to prepare the pulpy vegetable relishes Africans made to accompany the staple starchy porridge. Moisture evaporated through the clay walls, allowing the mixture to cook slowly at a low temperature.[13] The slaves also taught their white masters how to make these African stews. Among the recipes collected in the 1840s from the women of Charleston and published in *The Carolina Housewife* were a range of gumba, okra, peanut and sesame soups. And a good Carolina house-wife knew that these dishes were best prepared in African cookware. A group of ladies interviewed by a journalist for *The Magnolia: or Southern Monthly* declared that 'Okra soup was always inferior if cooked in any but an earthen-ware pot.'[14] Cooking techniques and recipes were not all that Carolina whites learned from their African slaves. The plantation economies of the Americas rested on the slaves' hard labour, growing the tobacco, sugar and rice that made the planters' fortunes. But the Carolinas were particularly indebted to their black workforce, for it was the Africans who taught the Carolina planters how to grow the colony's cash crop, rice.

OKRA SOUP

Cut up, in small pieces, a quarter of a peck of okra; skin half a peck of tomatoes, and put them, with a shin or leg of beef, into ten quarts of cold water. Boil it gently for seven hours, skimming it well. Season with cayenne or black pepper and salt.

A ham-bone, boiled with the other ingredients is thought an improvement by some persons.[15]

This recipe was included in *The Carolina Housewife*, but the African origins of the dish can be seen in the recipe below. This is a more elaborate version of the soup that was presented to Ghanaian schoolgirls in the 1960s as belonging to the West African culinary heritage.

ENOMI WONU (OKRA SOUP)

1 lb of meat

1 lb of smoked or fresh fish

some smoked shrimps or prawns,
crabs and/or mushrooms

3 tomatoes

3 gardeneggs [Guinea squash]

pepper and salt to taste

6 okroes

4–5 spring onions

5 pints water

Method

1. Wash and cut the meat into pieces. Put into a sauce-pan with chopped onions and salt. Place on the fire for about 5 minutes, stirring occasionally.

2. Add water, and cook for about 10 minutes.

3. Wash okroes, gardeneggs, tomatoes, pepper and add to the soup. Cook until the vegetables are tender. Remove the vegetables from the soup.

4. Wash crabs, mushrooms, shrimps or prawns, and fish and add to the soup.

5. Grind tomatoes, pepper and gardeneggs. Return these to the pot.

6. Mash the okroes and return to the pot.

7. Cook the soup gently for 30 minutes.

8. Serve with fufu or bankju.[16]

The story of the development of Middleburg plantation encapsulates the story of the colony of South Carolina. The slaves eating their meal in the 1730s were the property of Benjamin Simons. We know only that he owned slaves; there is no record of their names or how they came to live in the Carolinas. In contrast, the lives of the Simonses are well documented. Benjamin was the son of a Huguenot (the first Benjamin Simons) who had escaped France to come to the Americas in the 1680s via the Dutch port after which the plantation was named. In 1692, he was granted 100 acres of land on the eastern bank of the Cooper River, about 25 miles north of Charleston, and he moved there with his wife, Esther, and their infant son.[17] Benjamin arrived in the colony when it was only a couple of decades old. In 1663, a band of adventurers and bankrupt pirates, sponsored by eight English noblemen known as the Lords Proprietors, had established the first settlement in the area of Charleston. One of the Proprietors and many of the first settlers came from Barbados, and these men brought slaves with them whom they set to work clearing the land of trees and scrub and planting food crops.[18]

Benjamin would eventually have bought himself some slaves to help with the back-breaking work of clearing the land, but it is likely that initially he and his wife felled the trees and burned the brushwood themselves. Another Huguenot immigrant, Judith Manigault, who arrived in the colony around the same time, described how for the first six months after they had laid claim to their land she had 'worked the ground like a slave'.[19] The Simons family Bible records the couple's next three children as having been born 'at Maptica', which was in all likelihood the Native American name for their patch of land. Six years later, however, Benjamin wrote that their first daughter had been born at '6 o'clock in the evening in the house at Middleburg Plantation'. Benjamin Simons had succeeded in transforming the wilderness into a house and farm with a respectable European name. The house was simple: two storeys, each with two rooms on either side of a central chimney and with wide porches to the front and back to afford shade. Later on he added another room to each floor to accommodate his growing family of fourteen children.[20]

The first priority was to plant food crops to feed his family. The early Carolina settlers were unperturbed by New England-style notions of improving the land and expediently planted maize and beans Native American style in among the burnt tree stumps.[21] Maize-flour hominy, milk and baked sweet potatoes were the staple foods on their tables, supplemented by game and wild fruits, which could be foraged in the woods.[22] The early settler John Lawson relished the opportunities the colony afforded him to hunt, remarking with satisfaction that even the 'poor Labourer, that is Master of his Gun … hath as good a Claim to have continu'd Coarses of Delicacies crouded upon his Table, as he [that] is Master of a greater Purse'.[23] Early colonial woods abounded in deer, but much of the game would have been unfamiliar to European settlers. Lawson considered beaver tail 'choice Food', and Mark Catesby, a naturalist who visited South Carolina in the 1720s, noted that the colonists considered 'a young bear fed with Autumn's plenty … an exquisite dish'.[24] Another visitor, the Reverend Charles Woodmason, was disturbed by these 'irregular and unchaste' consumption habits.[25] To him, wild foods gleaned from the American wilderness carried a whiff of danger and impropriety, unlike tame, domesticated crops and animals.[26] But most settlers in the Carolinas cheerfully adapted to their new surroundings without a care for whether their fields were properly ploughed or whether their food replicated that of the English yeoman.

These colonists were not chasing the dream of becoming self-sufficient mixed farmers. The Barbadians who founded the colony had planned to expand sugar production onto the North American mainland. They were disappointed to find that sugar would not grow in the sandy coastal swamplands of Carolina.[27] All the early colony could muster to export were deer skins, timber and naval stores. As Benjamin Simons felled the trees on his land, he sold the good-quality timber and transformed the lower-quality pine into pitch by burning the resin in clay-lined pits.[28] With the proceeds he was able to stock up on supplies of sugar and British manufactures from the stores just beginning to spring up in Charleston.

The fortunes of Benjamin's plantation mirrored those of South Carolina. He spent most of his profit on acquiring more slaves. When he died in 1717, he had expanded his plantation from its initial 100 acres to 1,545.[29] By then the slaves living at Middleburg would have outnumbered his large family, just as in South Carolina as a whole the African slaves outnumbered the white population.[30] From about 1700, ships began to make their way directly from West Africa to Charleston, where slaves from the Gambia, renowned for their cattle-herding skills, were in particular demand.[31] The Lords Proprietors had supplied Carolina with cattle and hogs from Virginia, and these animals thrived by foraging in the savannahs and woodlands. The colony was soon dotted with cow pens and hog crawls into which the slaves herded the animals at night to protect them from wild predators. Thousands of barrels of salt beef and pork became the colony's main export. But the colonists had not come to Carolina to become graziers. Looking for a cash crop, they experimented with ginger, silk, vines, olive and citrus trees.[32]

The first planter to be credited with trying to grow rice was Nathaniel Johnson, who had been governor of the Leeward Islands. Forced out of his position by the Glorious Revolution, he arrived in South Carolina in 1689 with 100 African slaves. On his Silk Hope plantation (15 miles further north along the Cooper River from Middleburg), he began by growing silk but soon gave up on planting mulberry bushes in favour of upland rice. He had no previous experience with rice cultivation. White planters later claimed that a passing East Indiaman first introduced rice into Carolina. But the rice species that the settlers first cultivated was red rice – *Orzya glaberrima*, domesticated in the Niger River region around AD 300.[33] Thus the allegorical story the African slaves told of one of their ancestors bringing seed rice with her on the middle passage, hidden in the curls of her hair, seems to have more than a grain of truth in it.

The meal that la Courbe and la Belinguere shared at around this time on Africa's west coast was a demonstration that the exchange of foodstuffs between Africa and the Americas was well established. The Portuguese were active agents in this botanical exchange, and there is a record of a Portuguese slave vessel calling at Charleston in the 1690s carrying supplies of rice.[34] We also know from the records of European forts on the West African coast that African rice was a favoured provision for slave ships, and if some of it was carried on the ships unmilled, then it could have served as seed rice. Rice probably arrived in the Carolinas on many different occasions and was eagerly seized upon by the slaves as a favoured food that they could grow on their private plots of land.[35]

No matter the means by which rice was introduced into Carolina, it would have been the African slaves who knew how to cultivate it. In Senegambia, cattle herding went hand in hand with upland rice cultivation. Rainwater was conserved in reservoirs at the top of upland fields and channelled via a series of dams onto the crops when it was needed. Once the rice had been harvested, pastoralists herded their cattle onto the fields to graze on the rice stubble and manure the ground in preparation for the next sowing. The upland rice-and-cattle farming that emerged in early South Carolina followed precisely this West African style of farming. By the end of the seventeenth century, rice cultivation had spread to a number of plantations, and in 1700, Edward Randolph, Collector of Customs for the Southern Department of

Gibbie and the oxen.

North America, reported that more than 300 tons had been shipped to England and more than 30 to the Caribbean, while the Lords Commissioners of Trade and Plantations crowed that the colony 'hath made more rice … then we have Ships to Transport'.[36] When in the same year John Lawson called at a plantation as part of a hunting party seeking provisions, the old African slave looking after the property sold them rice rather than maize.[37] The Carolina settlers had acquired a taste for rice.

Apart from a few old India hands, the British rarely ate rice, but in South Carolina it became 'a constant article of food'. In 1758, the wife of a planter sent a large barrel to her sons, who were at school in England, explaining to the headmaster that 'the children love it boiled dry to eat with their meat instead of bread'.[38] The colonists often treated it as they would wheat and baked an array of breads, cakes, biscuits and muffins using rice flour.[39] But their slaves taught them to appreciate African-style dishes such as 'Hoppin' John', which consists of rice and beans boiled together and is still widely eaten for luck on New Year's Day throughout the American South. Good slave cooks fetched high prices, and one Virginia colonist mentioned in a letter to her sister that her cook was so accomplished that 'a great many wealthy gentlemen' had offered to buy him 'at any price'.[40] Nowadays, when Southerners use slabs of cornbread to mop up the 'pot likkor' at the bottom of a pan of leafy greens slow-cooked with fatback, they are relishing the culinary legacy of the African slaves.[41]

When the meal that began this chapter took place in the 1730s, rice had become Middleburg's main crop. Although the family sitting round the campfire would surely have preferred it, rice was now too valuable to be given to slaves; their standard ration was cornmeal. By the 1730s, the rice paddies they would have been working during the day were no longer in the uplands.

A Dutch geographer, Olfert Dapper, described in the 1640s how West African farmers would 'sow the first rice on low ground, the second a little higher and the third ... on the high ground, each a month after the previous one, in order not to have all the rice ripe at the same time'.[42] This spread not only labour requirements but also the risk of crop failure. One of the first men to experiment with growing rice in the lowlands was John Stewart, the manager of Governor James Colleton's plantation on the western branch of the Cooper River.[43] Rice grown in swamps required a lot less weeding, and the alluvial soil produced a better yield.[44] By the 1710s, the success of Stewart's experiment was apparent, and other planters began to follow suit.

In 1717, Benjamin Simons *père* died and his sons Peter and Simon took over the management of the plantation. They immediately followed John Stewart's example and set the slaves to work transforming the swamp lands into rice paddies.[45] It was a hard slog. First the gum and cypress trees needed to be felled and their roots grubbed out of the earth. A five-foot-deep ditch then had to be dug all the way around the field before it was, in turn, crossed by smaller ditches every quarter of an acre.[46] The slaves dug these ditches and built up embankments, equipped only with shovels and baskets, standing up to their knees in the soft Carolina mud, often up to their waists in water, amid clouds of malaria-carrying mosquitoes.[47] A verse from a slave song conveyed rather mildly how unpleasant it was to work in the stinking stagnant water of the rice fields:

> Come listen, all you darkies, come listen to my song,
> It am about ole Massa, who use me bery wrong:
> In de cole, frosty mornin', it ain't so bery nice,
> Wid de water to de middle to hoe among de rice.[48]

South Carolina had found its cash crop. By the 1720s, rice was the colony's leading export and the pioneering John Stewart proudly proclaimed that in Jamaica, Carolina rice was 'better esteem'd ... than that from Europe'.[49] Between 1750 and 1770, the number of slaves in the colony doubled from 39,000 to 75,000.[50] The Carolina landscape was 'transformed into a pattern of causeways with rice plants appearing above the flooded fields', which was how Sieur de la Courbe described the landscape along the Geba River in Guinea-Bissau when he travelled there in 1685.[51] It was as if a piece of the West African countryside had been transported to North America.

A rice field " flowed."

In 1772, the third Benjamin Simons inherited Middleburg, by then a modest rice plantation with 59 slaves.[52] At this time, rice cultivation in Carolina was undergoing its third revolutionary change. Innovative planters upgraded their flood-prone systems of irrigation to a more sophisticated tidal flooding-and-drainage arrangement whereby the movement of the tides up and down the rivers was harnessed to irrigate the fields by means of a series of dykes. André Alvares de Almada, a Luso-African trader based in Santiago, Cape Verde, described in the 1590s how all along the African coast from the Gambia River south to Guinea Conakry, the Africans had built huge embankments for miles to keep back overspill from marine tides and constructed a complex network of canals and dykes that enabled them to flood and drain their rice fields.[53] During his seventeen years of ownership, the third Benjamin introduced this tidal system to Middleburg's rice fields.[54]

Sloshing about in the mud, the slaves built more than 55 miles of banks along a 12-mile stretch of the Cooper River. To do this they shovelled and worked into shape more than 6.4 million cubic feet of earth, in the process installing a complicated network of 'trunk gates' into the banks that controlled the flow of water (so called because they were made out of hollow tree trunks).[55] Tidal rice cultivation increased the amount of land each slave could work, from three to

"The girls shuffled the rice about with their feet until it was clayed."

Before it was sown the rice seed was coated in liquid clay.

five acres.[56] The 89 slaves living at Middleburg would have been able to cultivate 445 acres. No wonder rice was the third most valuable export from all the North American colonies at the time of the revolution, after tobacco and flour.[57]

By the nineteenth century, the sophisticated rice cultivation that Europeans had observed on the West African coast in the sixteenth and seventeenth centuries had all but died out. Labour-intensive rice cultivation fell victim to the loss of manpower to the slave trade. Ignorant of West Africa's rice-cultivating history, the Carolina planters arrogantly assumed that the ancestors of the Africans who laboured on their rice fields could not possibly have been the progenitors of the sophisticated cultivation system that had made them so rich. But it is difficult to see who else would have been in a position to teach the early Carolina planters how to cultivate rice. Italian rice-growers were not among the Europeans who emigrated to Carolina, and the East India Company ships' captains, who did eventually bring Asian rice varieties into the colony, were in no position to show the planters how to farm it.[58]

Once rice was established, Carolina planters did study papers and reports about Asiatic rice cultivation, and some employed Dutch engineers knowledgeable about the construction of dykes and drainage systems.[59] However, the planters' involvement in the day-to-day practicalities of rice cultivation was limited. Both the white proprietor and the white overseer 'defer[red] to the … more experienced judgement' of the African slave drivers, who were the 'de facto managers of the plantations … managing the work of the other slaves, allotting their tasks for the day, and deciding when and for how long to flood or drain the rice fields'.[60] The slave drivers were allowed to use their initiative to an extent that would have been unthinkable on the West Indian sugar plantations. Despite their enslaved status, this undoubtedly gave them a sense of ownership over the fields they worked. Indeed, J. Motte Alston, the master of a rice plantation at Woodbourne, claimed that his 'head man', Cudjo, 'looked upon my property as belonging to him'.[61]

The plantations produced more rice than they were able to process. Throughout the colonial period, labour-intensive West African techniques were used. The sheaves of rice were threshed manually with a flail; winnowing was done using hand-made seagrass baskets, and the rice was polished using hand-held pestle-and-mortars with pestles that weighed between seven and ten pounds. It was slow and gruelling work. Men were assigned 66 lb of rice to pound each day, women 44 lb. Even an accomplished slave would have had to pound rice for at least five hours each day to process their allotted quantity. Tired or less skilled workers ran the risk of damaging the rice and rendering a proportion of the crop unmarketable.[62]

It was not until after the American Revolution that Jonathan Lucas, the English son of a mill owner, was shipwrecked off South Carolina and stayed to invent the first steam-powered rice mill. Milling revolutionised rice processing and allowed production to increase, enriching the planters even further. The fourth owner of Middleburg plantation was Lucas's son, who had married one of Benjamin Simon III's daughters. Under his management, the fortunes of the plantation no longer simply mirrored those of rice production in South Carolina: it became a site of innovation when he built South Carolina's first public toll rice mill.[63]

The Carolina planters, like the West Indian sugar planters, were proto-industrialists, running their plantations as capital-intensive agricultural factories according to the principle of maximising profit.[64] Most of the rice they

Pounding rice.

produced was exported. About 18 per cent went to the West Indies to feed the sugar planters and their slaves. In 1714, the planters managed to negotiate with Parliament to allow the 18 per cent that went to southern Europe to be shipped there directly. The bulk of the crop, however, went to London in order to satisfy the rules of the Navigation Acts, which stipulated that colonial goods had to be transported to Britain, where entry duties were charged. The rice was then re-exported to the Netherlands and the German states, where it tided the peasants over the winter months when supplies of dried peas and barley ran short.[65] A number of Jamaican planters had moved into coffee growing, and this also found favour on the Continent. Along with West Indian coffee and Chinese tea, Carolina rice contributed to a boom in Britain's re-export sector in the late eighteenth century.[66]

The first planters failed in their attempt to transplant sugar cane to the North American continent. Instead, the slave trade supplied them with the means to expropriate an entire agricultural system from the west coast of Africa. While the West African mangrove rice fields fell into disrepair, erstwhile African rice farmers rebuilt them on North America's eastern seaboard. Rice made the Carolina planters fabulously wealthy, and as white Carolina society saw itself as an extension of English polite society, it spent its money on imports from

Fanning and pounding rice for household use.

Britain. No sooner had tea become a fashionable drink in 1690s London than tea-drinking was taken up by the Carolina gentry; in the Chesapeake, tea-drinking did not become fashionable until the 1730s.[67] There was a craze for mahogany furniture in 1730s London, and by the 1740s, mahogany tables and chairs had begun to find their way into the fine town houses of Charleston.[68] On the eve of the revolution, rice had made Carolina planters by far the wealthiest of all the American colonists. A comparison of probate records shows that South Carolinians left estates worth on average four times as much as those left by Virginians and ten times more valuable than the fortunes left by the inhabitants of Massachusetts.[69]

·9·

In which Lady Anne Barnard enjoys fine cabin dinners on a voyage to the Cape of Good Hope (February to May 1797)

How the Empire stimulated the growth of the provisions industry

Every day at two o'clock, the passengers on board the *Sir Edward Hughes* assembled in the ship's cuddy to dine. According to Lady Anne Barnard, for the most part they 'got on like lambs'. There was gentle and brave General Hartley, and the amiable Mrs Saul, an Irishwoman whom the gentlemen enjoyed teasing; the modest and well-bred Dr Paterson, and Mr Green – a collector of customs – and his wife; Colonel Lloyd, an honest Welshman, and Mr Keith, an aide-de-camp; and Mrs Patterson, who was travelling with 'a crumb of a sister'. The only disagreeable members of the party were Captain Campbell, and his wife, who 'might have been handsome if not so ill-tempered'.[1] As the principal lady, Anne sat next to the ship's captain. She was accompanying her husband, Andrew Barnard, who had just been appointed Colonial Secretary to the Cape of Good Hope. Lord Macartney, the new governor, was sailing alongside in another ship.[2] The French revolutionary army had overrun the Netherlands in 1795, and the British were determined that the Dutch colony on the southern tip of Africa should not fall into French hands, as it was a key staging post on the sea route to India. That the Barnards were members of the new colonial administration was the cause of Mrs Campbell's displeasure. As a Cape Dutch-woman, she was evidently unhappy about the British occupation of her home and continually made rude remarks about the 'parcel of people' the British were sending to the colony. Lady Anne and her companions were obliged 'to drop common conversation with them beyond the necessities of society'.[3]

Lady Anne did not, however, allow the Campbells to spoil her enjoy-
ment of the voyage. Captain James Urmuston, whom she found a most civil and
pleasant dinner companion, kept a generous table. In her letter about the voyage
to Henry Dundas, Secretary for the Colonies and her husband's patron (as well
as her erstwhile suitor), she included a typical menu:

Pease soup
Roast Leg of Mutton

Hogs' puddings	Two fowls	Pork Pye
Stewed Cabbage	Two hams	Potatoes
Mutton Pyes	Two ducks	Mutton chops

Corned Round of Beef
Removed by an enormous Plumb Pudding
Porter, Spruce Beer, Port Wine, Sherry, Gin, Rum etc.[4]

The captain's table was clearly well supplied with fresh meat from the farmyard
on deck. Dozens of oxen, pigs, sheep, chickens and ducks were routinely carried
on sea voyages to provide the officers (and occasionally the men) with fresh
meat. The sailors were allowed to bring their own goats on board and these
would roam freely about the ship, indulging their unpopular habit of nibbling
from any bread bags the sailors had neglected to hang out of their reach.[5] Yet
the hams, potatoes and (presumably pickled) cabbage on the menu, as well as
the dried fruit to make the 'plumb pudding' and the fine selection of wines and
spirits, would have been drawn from the captain's special stores.

By the end of the eighteenth century, London had become a hub for a thriving European trade in provisions. Aristocratic families residing on their country
estates sent their stewards down to the metropolis to fetch stocks of chocolate,
coffee and tea. Italian warehouses in the capital specialised in Parmesan cheeses,
Florence oil, vermicelli and prunes. Oil men had begun adding condiments such
as olives, anchovies and pickles to their stores of animal and vegetable oils used
for making lubricants, lamps, varnishes and soaps.[6] Before putting to sea, ships'
captains routinely stocked up with herb- and elder-flavoured vinegars, cayenne
pepper and spices, Naples biscuits and currant jelly.[7] These were considered part
of the furniture of a good table, and no doubt Lady Anne and her companions
were able to dip their meat in ketchups and pickles from Urmuston's store. Ordinary sailors eating their stodgy duffs (boiled puddings) and 'scouse' of broken

A life on the Ocean Wave!

Lady Ann Barnard described how the heavy load of great guns the *Sir Edward Hughes* was carrying out to Bengal made the ship rock violently in heavy seas. This must have made it difficult to avoid a similar mishap at dinner time in the ship's cuddy.

biscuit mixed with bits of salt beef and 'slush' (the greasy mess the cook skimmed off vats of boiling meat) looked on the captain's table with envy.[8]

The British occupation of the Dutch Cape colony was only the latest twist in a century and a half of conflict. For most of the time between 1650 and 1815, the British were at war with either the French, the Spanish or the Dutch. As each side sought to reduce its opponents' commercial power within Europe, the fighting frequently spilled over into attacks on the others' colonial commerce and overseas territories.[9] Britain's determination to defend her empire was evident on board the *Sir Edward Hughes*: the heavy load it was carrying of 227 great guns bound for Bengal made it rock violently in strong seas.[10] With every conflict, the Royal Navy grew. Between 1650 and 1740 it doubled from around 20,000 to 40,000 men, and at the height of the 1793–1815 war with France, it mustered over 147,000 men sailing in more than 800 ships.[11] In 1808, the British fleet in the Baltic alone required 960,000 lb of bread, 36,000 gallons of rum, 60,000 pieces of pork and 33,000 pieces of beef.[12] At the turn of the century, between 10,000 and 20,000 extra cattle were slaughtered each year at London's Smithfield market to supply the ships of the line with fresh beef. Pig farms proliferated around London, using the waste barley and malt from breweries to fatten the hogs.[13]

In the same way that the increase in the Tudor navy had stimulated the development of the Newfoundland fishery, so the expansion of the navy in the eighteenth century now stimulated the growth of the provisions industry. Local suppliers found it difficult to meet the unpredictable surges in demand, and so the victualling department set up slaughterhouses, breweries and bakehouses at the naval dockyards.[14] Here intense demand promoted innovation and encouraged the rationalisation of food preparation. Just as the curing of cod on Newfoundland's shores was organised into a set of repetitive tasks, so was the baking of ship's biscuit in the naval bakeries. Every oven was assigned a team of bakers. A 'kneader' made the dough, while the 'breakman' was turned into a human machine, shuffling on his bottom up and down the pivoted beam that kneaded the great mass, which was too heavy to manipulate by hand. The 'moulder' then shaped pieces of the dough into biscuits and passed them on to a 'stamper', whose task was to mark them with holes on each side. A 'thrower' chucked the biscuits onto the peel, which a baker then placed in the oven.[15] This division of labour speeded up the process to the point where each team was able to produce an impressive 1,500 lb of biscuits in an hour.[16] With all 12 ovens working at full stretch, the naval bakery at Deptford could produce enough biscuit for more than 12,000 men every year.[17] Nevertheless, wartime demand was sometimes so great that extra gangs had to be employed to bake biscuits through the night. On occasion, they were no sooner out of the ovens than they were packed into bags and hurried onto the warships waiting to put to sea.

The navy eventually turned to Ireland to make up its shortfall. At first, the seventeenth-century Cattle Acts, banning the import of Irish goods into England, prevented the Admiralty from taking advantage of the fact that Irish salt beef and butter were cheap. But when naval stores ran dry, the victuallers were given permission to buy meat and butter in Ireland. A series of Acts reopened trade after 1758, and from then on, Ireland became a major naval supplier. Its exports of salted beef, pork and butter doubled, and 'Irish horse' became sailors' slang for salt beef.[18] Anglo-Irish landlords were now in the ascendancy, and they carried on the English obsession with improving the land, building lime kilns on their estates to produce fertiliser and engaging in a flurry of hedging and ditching. The rich Munster pastureland around the busy ports was consolidated into neat fields dotted with beef and dairy cattle.[19] At the same time, their Irish tenants – subsisting on the diet of potatoes that was to make them so vulnerable to famine in the nineteenth century – grew flax for the linen trade. And on the sour milk left over from butter-making they raised pigs for Newfoundland, where salt pork was the most popular meat.[20] Home to an array of butchers, salters, packers, coopers, carters and porters, Cork gained such a reputation for efficient and effective packaging that herring from Gothenburg in Sweden was sent there to be repackaged before being exported to the West Indies, where it was fed to African slaves.[21]

In an effort to improve the sailors' health, oatmeal, sugar, pickled cabbage, lemon juice, cocoa, dried fruit, suet and rum were added to their ration.[22] In 1754, the pioneering ship's surgeon James Lind suggested that portable soup might alleviate scurvy. It was made by simmering meat in water for hours until it was reduced to a jelly. In her popular cookery book of 1747, Hannah Glasse claimed in the section devoted to cookery for the 'Captains of ships' that a square of portable soup added to pease soup would improve it no end.[23] By 1793, Ratcliffe's Soup House in London was producing 897 tons a year, which it sold to both the army and the navy. Ship's chandlers added it to their list of groceries for the merchant marine, and adverts for 'portable soup of the best Sorts' began appearing in London newspapers.[24]

Innovation in food processing was not confined to marine suppliers. In 1775, in the kitchen at the back of his shop on the Strand, John Burgess began pounding the Dutch herrings and anchovies he normally sold straight from the barrel and packing the resulting anchovy paste into small earthenware jars. His fish sauce made his shop so well known that in his poem *Beppo*, Byron suggested that travellers should make a trip there before venturing abroad:

> And therefore humbly I would recommend
> 'The curious in fish-sauce', before they cross

The sea, to bid their cook, or wife, or friend,
Walk or ride to the Strand, and buy in gross
(Or if set out beforehand, these many send
By any means least liable to loss).
Ketchup, Soy, Chili-vinegar, and Harvey,
Or by the Lord! a Lent will well nigh starve ye.[25]

The Harvey's sauce that Byron referred to was produced by Elizabeth Lazenby, an impoverished shopkeeper who had been given a fish-sauce recipe in the 1790s by her innkeeper brother, Peter Harvey, with the idea that she might use it to generate a modest living. Within a decade it was so popular that she set up a small factory in Southwark, where a heady scent of spices mixed with sharp notes of vinegar hung in the air over a small group of food workshops and vinegar breweries.[26] From the 1750s, advances in food processing and preserving methods using sugar and vinegar made it possible to conquer the limits that time and distance placed on the transportation of foodstuffs. Durham mustard, Gorgona anchovies and Yorkshire hams were now available to the prosperous, whether they were away from London on a country estate, travelling in Europe, or colonists in distant lands.

In the eighteenth century, Britain's export trade to the colonies was the fastest-growing sector of the economy. North America absorbed about a third of its output of woollens, while West Africa exchanged slaves for English cottons and chintzes and the West Indies took abundant quantities of Scottish and Irish linen to clothe the slaves who toiled on the sugar plantations. Fledgling societies in the colonies imported British manufactures ranging from farming equipment and sugar-refining pots to watches and clocks; pewter and brass basins, pots and tankards were popular among the West African slave traders.[27] The figures for exports of provisions were subsumed under miscellaneous goods and so tend to be overlooked. However, they also played an important part in this colonial trade. Americans were as eager for English cheeses, pickles and hams as they were for buttons, clocks and nails.[28] North American newspapers began to advertise the arrival of parcels of pickled mushrooms and London-made jellies, sauces and pickles.[29] In among Connecticut onions, Philadelphian wheat flour and Carolina rice, grocers such as Gregory Purcell in Portsmouth, New Hampshire, stocked a range of imported foods: Irish 'May Butter' and salt pork, Dorchester ale, Florence oil, bohea and hyson teas and West Indian rum and citrus fruits.[30] By mid century, the American colonies were importing £1.3 million worth of British goods each year.[31]

India too was a growing market, absorbing just under 10 per cent of Britain's exports, among them 'preserved salmon, lobsters, oysters, herrings, and other exotic fish, hams, reindeer-tongues, liqueurs, dried fruits, and a long list of foreign dainties'.[32] When a ship called into Calcutta, wholesale purchasers 'anxious to sell the[ir wares] in their freshest and purest state, usually put forth a series of advertisements, in which the art of puffing is carried to its fullest extent'.[33] Officers on East India Company ships were encouraged to take with them to eastern ports a variety of domestic commodities. On a 755-ton ship they were allotted about 90 tons of cargo space as an 'indulgence', which they could fill with any goods as long as they did not come under the Company's monopoly; restricted goods were Company staples such as nankeen cloth, raw silk, tea and China ware. This system ensured that the 'Europe shops' in the Asian ports were well stocked with hats, haberdashery, perfumery and provisions.[34] Most of the time the officers could be fairly certain of making a profit of 100 per cent on their investment. In the 1770s, the memoirist and rake William Hickey reported that cheese and ham that would have sold in London for 1s. a pound were selling in Calcutta for 12s. 6d.[35] Occasionally things did not go quite to plan. In May 1769, the East India Company officers on board the fleet bound for Madras suffered the misfortune that not only did all the ships arrive within ten days of each other, but they had all brought glassware with them as there had been such demand for it the previous year. They were forced to sell their goods at a 60 per cent loss.[36]

Colonial demand was one of the engines driving the growth of the provisions industry in Britain. Although for most of the eighteenth century food processing was predominantly small-scale, with most pickles, hams, pastes and comfitures manufactured in back kitchens, the provisions industry gave rise to busy workshops and small-scale factories making the packaging for the foodstuffs. Artisans produced barrels, firkins, casks and kits for salt meat, butter and pickled tripe. Others wove baskets for salt, canvas to make bales for pepper and wrappings for cheeses, and hessian to make sacks for flour and biscuits. Earthenware pots and jars were needed for split peas and oils and vinegars, and glass 'squares' for mustard and spices.[37] English customs preferred wines and spirits to be imported in barrels and casks to prevent the smuggling of easily hidden bottles. The wine then had to be bottled in England before being sold at home or shipped out to foreign climes. The result was the rapid growth of a bottle-making industry.[38] Thus the provisions industry was at the heart of eighteenth-century British industriousness.

The empire trade in provisions gave rise to new products. Indian pale ale was developed to cater to the market of thirsty colonists. Traditionally, in October the English landed classes brewed a well-hopped and therefore very bitter pale ale known as 'stock' beer. It was designed to take a few months to mature and so could be kept over the winter. For this reason it was thought the most suitable beer to ship to the colonies, as it would best survive the long journey. A small Bow brewery, just up the Thames from the East India docks at Blackwall, was popular with Company captains, as its owner, George Hodgson, extended them 18 months' credit. In fact, the four- to five-month-long journey to India was discovered to have a beneficial impact on Hodgson's 'stock' beer.[39] The rocking motion of the ship combined with the gradual application of heat as it sailed first to the Atlantic wine islands and then on to Rio de Janeiro, from where the trade winds blew it back east across the southern Atlantic to Cape Town and on to India, resulted in a beer with a depth of flavour that could be achieved in England only after years in the cellar.

In the 1780s, George Hodgson's son, Mark, perfected the brew by using pale malt and plenty of hops, both with strong preservative qualities. A final touch was to add dry hops to the barrel of finished beer; this helped stabilise the beverage so that it could withstand the pitching motion of the ship.[40] The idea of drinking cold beer was alien to the British, but Company officials in India took the novel step of cooling the pale ale in saltpetre, which made it all the more refreshing.[41] Hodgson's became an icon of British life in India. The chronicler of London street life Henry Mayhew recalled that when he made his first journey to India in 1825 as a 'midshipman in the Leadenhall-street Navy ... no other malt liquor was drunk at tiffin or at dinner, in Calcutta, but this same Hodgson's Pale Ale – for at that time there was none other to compete with it'.[42] It became so much a part of Company culture that failing to omit the 'g' in the pronunciation of the beer's name had the effect of instantly marking out the newcomer to India.[43]

Competition for the colonial market led food businesses to hone their products, sharpen their marketing tactics and introduce new distribution techniques. In the 1820s, Hodgson's were joined in India by Bass and Samuel Allsopp & Sons, whose pale ales were popular because the hard water in Burton upon

Trent was particularly suited to brewing a sharp, dry and thirst-quenching beer. Even though they failed to oust Hodgson's from its iconic position in the public mind as *the* Indian pale ale, these companies eventually gained the larger market share. Bass and Allsopp also applied the lessons they had learned in India with good effect to the home market. Hodgson's had cut out the ships' officers who acted as middlemen in the Indian provisions trade and sold their beer directly to agency houses in the port towns. In the same way, the Burton brewers now circumvented the public house, which in Britain acted as the middleman between a brewery and its customers, and looked to the shopkeepers. They bottled their pale ale on site and distributed it by canal and rail to shops round the country. If in Britain Hodgson's targeted their advertising at returned old-India hands, Bass and Allsopp identified as their potential customers the rising lower-middle class of shopkeepers and clerks, eager to find a beer that would set them apart from the porter-drinking labouring classes. They revolutionised the English brewing trade and transformed Burton into England's first brewing town.[44] When Mayhew visited in 1865, he picturesquely claimed that the 'brewers' tall chimney-shafts … now bristle almost as thickly as the minarets of some Turkish city'.[45] He noted that while the Hodgson brewery had long since closed down, the Burton brewers had become 'merchant princes', with Bass & Co. paying 'as much as £500 a-day in excise dues to the Government'.[46]

The ability to spot an opportunity and then adapt and improve a product to suit the market was displayed equally by Madeiran wine makers. Wine producers and export merchants in Madeira participated in a dialogue with colonial shopkeepers and customers around the world that eventually transformed a nondescript *vin de table* into a luxurious fortified wine drunk throughout the Empire. Madeira's strategic position on the sailing routes between Britain, the Americas and the Indies meant that ships would call in there and pick up some of the local wine. As with pale ale, it was discovered that the liquor was greatly improved by the heat and agitation of a prolonged voyage. In Britain, distributors found they could sell a bottle of Madeira that had been subjected to a long journey around the West Indies for £10 or £12 more than wine shipped directly to Britain. If it was fortified with brandy, it was found to taste even better. The wine makers were responsive to the feedback they received from their various markets. Eventually they constructed special steam-powered machinery to simulate the heat and agitation of long-distance maritime travel. They made the pipes to transport the wine in various lengths according to the differing East India Company and American colonial customs requirements. Thus Madeira became a different drink in every market. Dark, sweet wines were made for the West Indian sugar barons; heavily fortified pale, dry white Madeira for the South Carolina rice planters. Every taste was catered for and no colonial meal was complete without a bottle of Madeira on the table.[47]

This process of exchange and adaptability marked the imperial commercial world. While organising the transport or sale of cargoes of provisions, letter-writers swapped news about world events as well as domestic occurrences. Trust was built up across immense distances. Family ties, marital alliances and contracts created security, as did the shared sense of what constituted financial and moral probity that arose out the process of communication and negotiation. The trade in provisions made up an important strand in this 'dense, integrated, inter-imperial' commercial world.[48]

The exchange of provisions was two-way. While barrels of Bristol tripe, jars of preserves and Harvey's sauce, bottles of vinegar and pipes of Madeira made their way to the colonies, colonials had assorted exotic goods sent home for their own use or as gifts for relatives and friends. In 1679, Henry Drax wrote a detailed document for his overseer on how, in his absence, to run the sugar plantation he had inherited from his father James (whose beef extravaganza Richard Ligon described in Chapter Four). In an appendix, he instructed his overseer:

> I would have every year 200 weight of green ginger well preserved with the best sugar sent home in ... good Cask. Let all the citron peels you can get be put into good brandy and sent to me in England, also two barrels of the best and largest Yams, 2 Barrels of the Largest and best Eddoes and 2 barrels of the largest and driest potatoes ... all the orange blossoms that you can get be stilled in alembic and the water sent me. Send four times every year a ten gallon runlet of Jamaica pepper well pickled in good vinegar and about 50 pounds of Okra stilled and well dried and a chest of china oranges, a chest of sweet lemons and some shaddocks yearly.[49]

Drax clearly intended to replicate in England the mongrel cuisine of the West Indies, heavily influenced by the cookery of the African slaves. The slaves had introduced yams to the sugar islands from Africa, while eddoes were of Asian origin and had probably been brought to the Caribbean by the Portuguese from China or Japan. The slaves used salt fish, capsicums and eddoes, which were 'not unlike a rough irregular potato', to make 'an excellent pot of soup' enjoyed by black and white alike.[50] No doubt Drax intended to have a similar dish made with his 'largest and best eddoes'.

In 1765, Simon Taylor, one of the most important landowners in Jamaica, took over the running of the Golden Grove plantation for its absentee proprietor, Chaloner Arcedekne, who lived in Suffolk. Taylor regularly sent Arcedekne turtles and pipes of Madeira in the care of various ships' captains.[51] Traditionally when a host wanted to impress his dinner guests he served venison. Venison celebrated the established social order: power and status was derived from land, which gave the aristocracy exclusive access to deer. In the second half of the eighteenth century, commercial men began to celebrate their links to the world of trade with turtle dinners.[52]

These were hearty affairs, as some of the animals weighed as much as 500 lb, and consisted of five different dishes. One was made from the fins; another from the calipash, the green gelatinous substance that adhered to the shell; the third from the yellow gelatinous belly known as the calipee; while the rest of the meat was made into a fricassee and a soup. Despite the meat's slightly musky smell, epicures raved that it had the consistency of butter and that the calipash and calipee tasted like bone marrow.[53] It was only when she visited the West Indies in the 1770s that Janet Schaw came to appreciate turtle. In her account of her journey she wrote, 'here is the green fat, not the slobbery thing my stomach used to stand at, but firm and more delicate than it is possible to describe. Could an Alderman of true taste conceive the difference between it here and in the city, he would make the Voyage on purpose, and I fancy he would make a voyage into the other world before he left the table.'[54]

Schaw was referring to the fact that turtle was routinely served at the Lord Mayor of London's banquet for the aldermen of London's city council. Indeed, turtle dinners became so popular with scientific, gambling and male dining clubs that some feared the meat might displace roast beef as the symbol of whole-hearted Englishness.[55] It is an indication of how embedded the

Empire was within British culture that a feast based on an exotic foreign creature could be seen as symbolic of Englishness.[56]

The growing pride in the Empire within Britain can be traced through contemporary cookbooks. From the mid eighteenth century, recipes for 'oatmeal pudding after the New England manner', 'Carolina Rice pudding' and 'China Chilo' began to appear often in sections devoted to 'oriental' and 'colonial' recipes.[57] Luxury cookbooks began including recipes for turtle. Turtle meat was best eaten fresh, and so the poor creatures were transported live in barrels of water. In *The Lady's Complete Guide; or Cookery in all its Branches*, Mary Cole gave the grisly instruction to remove the animal from the barrel of water and chop off its head and then bleed the carcass before butchering it into the separate cuts. She gave a recipe for dressing the meat 'the West India Way' with Madeira, cloves, nutmeg, mace and cayenne pepper. For those who could not run to the expense of the real thing, she included a mock-turtle soup recipe using a calf's head as a substitute.[58] Thus an exotic dish was incorporated into the British culinary repertoire transformed into an elaborate offal soup.

TO DRESS A MOCK TURTLE

Take the largest calf's head you can get, with the skin on, put it in scalding water till you find the hair will come off, clean it well, and wash it in warm water, and boil it three quarters of an hour. Then take it out of the water, and slit it down the face, cut off all the meat along with the skin as clean from the bone as you can, and be careful you do not break the ears off. Lay it on a flat dish, and stuff the ears with forcemeat, and tie them round with cloths. Take the eyes out, and pick all the rest of the meat clean from the bone, put it in a tossing-pan, with the nicest and fattest part of another calf's head, without the skin on, boiled as long as the above, and three quarts of veal gravy. Lay the skin in the pan on the meat, with the flesh side up, cover the pan close, and let it stew over a moderate fire one hour; then put in three sweetbreads, fried a little brown, one ounce of morels, the same of truffles, five artichoke bottoms boiled, one anchovy boned and chopped small, a tea-spoonful of chyan pepper, a little salt, half a lemon, three pints of Madeira wine, two-spoonsful of mushroom catchup, one of lemon-pickle and half a pint of mushrooms. Let them stew slowly half an hour longer, and thicken it with flour and butter. Have ready the yolks of four eggs boiled hard, and the brains of both heads boiled; cut the brains, the size of nutmegs, and make a rich force-meat, and spread it on the caul of a leg of veal, roll it up, and boil it in a cloth one hour. When boiled, cut it into the dish, and lay the head over it with the skin side up, and put the largest piece of forcemeat between the ears, and make the top of the ears to meet round it (this is called the crown of the turtle), lay the other slices of the forcemeat opposite to each other at the narrow end, and lay a few of the truffles, morels, brains, mushrooms, eggs, and artichoke bottoms upon the face, and round it; strain the gravy boiling hot upon it. Be as quick in dishing it up as possible, for it soon grows cold.[59]

HASHED MUTTON A L'INDIENNE

Cut some slices for a cold roast leg or shoulder of mutton, free them from skin, etc., and reserve on a plate; chop a large onion finely, and fry it in clarified butter with a teaspoonful of minced parsley. When of a light brown hue, add a large dessertspoonful of 'Empress' curry paste, half a pint of either stock or gravy, and a dessertspoonful of 'Empress' Lucknow chutney; make very hot, then thicken with a little flour and butter kneaded together, add the sliced mutton, make hot again, and serve with a border of well-boiled rice or mashed potato. Curry powder may be used instead of the paste, if desired, but the paste gives the best results.[60]

This was typical of the way the British integrated foreign foods into the cuisine and is illustrated in their treatment of the exotic dish they really made their own – curry. Early cooks remained faithful to Indian practices when cooking curries and added specific freshly ground spices at different stages in the cooking process. J. Skeat even appeared to be attempting to re-create a particular garnish when he suggested drying long pieces of cucumber over a slow fire before strewing them over a finished curry.[61] But over time British cooks began to take short cuts using pre-prepared spice mixtures and eventually the variety and multiplicity of Indian cookery was lost. British curries tended to be made according to a standardised method which involved first frying the onions in butter, then adding a spice mix, followed by the meat which was simmered in stock to produce a spicy casserole. British cooks also had an unfortunate tendency to regard curry as a way of using up leftovers. Charlotte Mason informed the readers of her cookbook that a pre-prepared spice mix could transform cold meats and introduce 'a very acceptable variety at table in place of *toujours* hash'.[62] As he contemplated one such 'hash flavoured with turmeric and cayenne' an Indian visitor to England lamented, 'where are our chutneys, and our sweet pickles – the far-famed compositions of Lucknow!'[63]

As with turtle, the British transformed curry into an economical and convenient dish that according to one cookery writer was 'now so completely naturalized, that few dinners are thought complete unless one is on the table'.[64] They had appropriated Indian food and made it their own. British cookery was at its most adventurous, interesting and innovative when it incorporated colonial dishes. In the notebooks that Wilhelmina and Stephana Malcolm used to collect recipes, the exotic ones like 'mulgatawy soup' and Indian pickle sent to the girls in Dumfriesshire by their brothers from various locations in the Empire stand out among the more pedestrian instructions for making Brown Windsor soup.[65]

The lively contribution the Empire made to British cookery mirrored the wider contribution it made to the British economy. By the end of the eighteenth century, it seemed perfectly normal to transport potentially perishable food and drink over immense distances.[66] Flexible and ingenious manufacturers who listened carefully to their customers and adapted their goods to their tastes had produced a wide range of ready-made foods and sophisticated drinks that meant the moneyed traveller and colonist could replace hardtack with crackers, salt meat with hams, and beer with refined pale ales and fortified wine.

The branding of food products had begun with the association of foods with particular places – ham with Yorkshire, tripe with Bristol and oil with Florence – to give them an air of authenticity and quality.[67] It had been discovered that intensive marketing and advertising reaped rewards, and producers and distributors had taken to the practice with enthusiasm.[68] In all these ways the colonial trade in provisions laid the groundwork for the rise of the industrialised food industry.

The roots of Britain's Industrial Revolution can be traced back to the rapid technological change the textile industry underwent over the eighteenth century, beginning with the spinning jenny and culminating in the introduction of the mechanised loom. But the growing provisions industry also made a significant contribution to the industriousness that was the precursor to the Industrial Revolution. In fact, it was probably a food-processing factory rather than a textile mill that inspired William Blake's phrase 'dark satanic mills' in his poem 'Jerusalem'. On the south-eastern bank of the Thames near Blackfriars Bridge, close to where Blake lived, stood the Albion flour mill. Built in 1786, this was the first steam-powered flour mill in Britain, equipped with machinery designed by Matthew Boulton and James Watt, two of the architects of the Industrial Revolution. The small independent millers that the mill put out of business denounced it as 'satanic'.[69]

10

In which Sons of Liberty drink rum punch at the Golden Ball Tavern, Merchants Row, Boston (a cold evening in January 1769)

How rum brought the American colonies together and split Britain's First Empire apart

'May the Sons of Liberty Shine with Lustre!'[1] called out Nathaniel Barber as he raised his glass. His companions raised theirs and drank with him. John Marston ladled out more rum punch. 'All true patriots throughout the world!' he rejoined, and the company raised their glasses again.[2] It was considered ungentlemanly to propose a toast the rest of the company would not want to uphold.[3] For the fifteen men gathered round the table in a Boston tavern on a cold January night in 1769, the toasts they proposed affirmed their political affiliation.[4] They saw themselves as Sons of Liberty, men who were prepared to resist the British Crown's arrogant imposition of taxation on their colony.[5] A group of New York radicals had been the first to call themselves the Sons of Liberty when in 1765 a cash-strapped British metropole attempted to raise revenue from its American colonies by introducing the Stamp Act, which imposed a tax on printed paper. The New Yorkers called on others to form themselves into similar oppositional groups, and before long there were hundreds of men throughout the Thirteen Colonies calling themselves Sons of Liberty.[6]

The fifteen men had gathered that January evening in John Marston's tavern, a convenient meeting place as it was situated in a small street just off the town's busiest thoroughfare. It was en route between Benjamin Cobb's distillery and his home at 22 Long Wharf, and merchant William Mackay frequently passed by when business took him to the wharf. The friends often called into the tavern to talk and exchange news, read the newspapers or the latest political pamphlet and occasionally dip into a book from Marston's extensive library. On the shelves were volumes of *North Briton*, the journal published by the Whig John Wilkes, and all eight volumes of Addison and Steele's *Spectator*, the avowed aim of which had been to promote discussion in England's coffee houses. Indeed, the friends sipped coffee on occasion, but like most of Marston's customers, they preferred something stronger. More often than not they drank rum punch.

That evening the punch that was flowing freely into their glasses was ladled from a fine silver bowl of which the assembled company were inordinately proud. Barber had brought it to the tavern from the offices of his insurance company, where it was kept safe.[7] The names of the fifteen men were engraved around the outer rim of the bowl, but as a further inscription made clear, the vessel had been made to celebrate 'the glorious NINETY-TWO'.[8] These were the 92 members of the Massachusetts Assembly who had voted not to rescind a letter written a few months earlier questioning the right of the British Crown to tax the American colonies when they did not have representation in Parliament and were therefore unable to protest the measures.[9]

The men gathered round the punch bowl were typical Sons of Liberty. At least five of them had been captains in the militia. The Irishman Captain Daniel Malcolm imported wines, and Ichabod Jones traded in provisions. In contemporary documents John White and William Mackay were both referred to as gentlemen and may have been merchants.[10] These men's livelihoods depended less on imperial connections to Britain than on intercolonial networks of trade. This meant that they were more invested in maintaining the strength of the American economy than propping up the sagging fortunes of the metropole. Another of the friends, Caleb Hopkins, was a Freemason and a cousin of one of Boston's most influential Sons of Liberty, Benjamin Edes, the publisher of the *Boston Gazette*. Two of his other cousins were Daniel Parker, a silversmith, and John Welsh, an ironmonger.[11] They too would have had little economic reason to support the imperial system, which assigned the colonies the role of consuming British manufactures rather than making their own wares. It was men such as these, gathered around bowls of rum punch in taverns throughout the thirteen North American colonies, who fomented the dissent that was to end in the Declaration of American Independence in 1776.

In the instructions Henry Drax left for the overseer of his Barbados sugar plantation before he went on a trip to England in 1679, he warned him to make sure 'that at any time [the Stiller] have occasion to be absent or a Sleep that he Certainly keep the Still house door Locked and the Key in his pocket'.[12] Drax did not want the rum to be stolen by the slaves, who he knew would siphon off the liquor to sell to tavern keepers in Bridgetown if they were given the slightest opportunity. While his father had served rum at his dining table, Henry Drax would have seen it as a drink more suitable for fortifying slaves against the perpetual Barbadian damp. In his instructions he stipulated that the overseer should be sure to give the slaves a dram every morning in wet weather and 'at other times as you shall see convenient'.[13] Although Drax himself preferred fine wines and Madeira, he noted with some satisfaction that the still house 'brings in very Considerable profit with little charge'.[14] Indeed, while the planters originally distilled rum as a sideline to sugar-making, by 1700 they were producing 600,000 gallons a year and it accounted for 19 per cent of the value of Barbadian exports.[15]

The common fuddling liquor of the more ordinary sort
is Rum Punch, to the composition of which goes Rum,
Water, Lime-Juice, Sugar and a little Nutmeg scrap'd
on top of it. This as 'tis very strong, so 'tis sower, and
being made usually of the Sugar-Pot bottoms, is very
unhealthy and because 'tis cheap, Servants, and other
of the poorer sort are very easily fuddled with it, when
they come home from their Masters Plantations: this …
puts them into a fast Sleep, whereby they fall off their
Horses going home.[16]

British merchants were the first to transform rum from a local Caribbean drink into a global trading commodity. Both the French and the Spanish saw it as an unwelcome competitor with home-produced liquors and outlawed either its production or its entry into their home ports. But the British discovered that it was popular with African slave traders and that it made an excellent cargo for Irish provisions ships returning from the New World. The Navigation Acts stipulated that even sugar bound for Ireland had to first pass through British customs. But in the 1730s, restrictions on rum were lifted and ships that would otherwise have sailed home empty now brought hundreds of thousands of gallons of the liquor to Ireland's southern ports. The bountiful flow of cheap rum established liquor consumption among Ireland's peasantry, especially in the hinterland of the southern ports, where whiskey had less of a hold on popular drinking habits. By the 1760s, the Irish drank twice as much rum as the English. It was not until the 1780s that whiskey rose to ascendancy and pushed rum into second place as the Irishman's favourite tipple.[17]

In the Americas, the continental colonies were the region's most enthusiastic consumers, and in the 1670s, they began to distil their own. Captain John Turner of Salem was among the pioneers in the American manufacture of the liquor. The sons of a Suffolk shoemaker who had come to New England as part of Winthrop's Great Migration, John and his brother Habakkuk established themselves in the intercolonial shipping trade. They took New England fish, lumber, shingles and ships' stores to the West Indies and exchanged them for sugar, rum and molasses. A relative owned a sugar plantation in Barbados, and perhaps it was through this connection that John Turner acquired the knowledge of how to distil his own liquor. Although the rum Turner made seems to have been rather rough stuff, its manufacture propelled him to a position of wealth and respectability. Throughout the 1670s, he served as a Salem selectman, and he built a fine house across the street from his warehouses.[18] If he had lived a hundred years later, he would surely have joined the Sons of Liberty.

On the eve of the War of Independence, there were 140 rum distilleries in colonial America, concentrated around Massachusetts, the hub for the West Indies trade. American slave traders found it a useful commodity, as they had few other goods to barter for slaves in West Africa.[19] A triangular trade now emerged in American rum, West African slaves and West Indian molasses. But less than 10 per cent of the rum brewed in America found its way onto the global market: lacking its depth of flavour, it could not compete with the West Indian product.[20] Its real economic importance lay in stimulating trade between the thirteen continental American colonies.

Until the 1720s, the different colonies did not trade much with each other. But once Massachusetts began producing rum, it found eager buyers in Newfoundland, Nova Scotia, Quebec, Prince Edward Island, New York, Maryland, Virginia, the Carolinas and Georgia. New England rum became the tipple of choice among America's fishermen and lumberjacks, washerwomen, farmers and workmen. Just as the sugar planters used rum to inoculate their slaves against the damp, American labourers administered themselves fortifying doses of the liquor.[21] Derived from sugar, it was one of the most calorific of all spirits and was a cheap and agreeable way to give themselves an injection of energy. Indeed, the American working man's use of rum bore some resemblance to the English labourer's reliance on heavily sugared tea.[22] This may account for the discrepancy between the English, whose annual consumption of distilled spirits amounted to only 0.6 gallons per member of the population, and the heavy-drinking Americans, who consumed enough rum for everyone in the Thirteen Colonies to have drunk four gallons a year.[23]

In the same way that in Britain the elite worried about the democratisation of tea-drinking, the New England Puritan elite were perturbed by the fact that the cheap, home-produced rum allowed workmen access to a regular drop of comfort. When the poorer section of society had been confined to other home-brewed alcoholic products, their drinking habits had not impacted on America's balance of trade. But the molasses needed to manufacture rum had to be bought with hard currency or traded for goods. How much would America be forced to pay, worried commentators in the newspapers, in order to satisfy the masses' growing desire for imported luxuries? For some, the workman's thirst for rum recalled the fall of Rome, when the populace had lost their virtuous simplicity and fallen prey to sin and extravagance. Vocal Puritan leaders warned that New England's carefully harnessed reserves would be squandered in the pursuit of imported fripperies and drunkenness. The authorities were, however, reluctant to place too much of a curb on the rum trade as it brought in welcome tax revenue.[24] Ironically, a colony founded on a commitment to suppress intemperance had become the centre of New World rum production.

In fact, the commercialisation of American drinking habits fostered beneficial internal trading links. Traditionally the countryside had supplied the towns with beer and cider; now barrels of rum and brandy made the return journey and other foodstuffs followed in their wake.[25] The Southern colonies

Note the row of small barrels labelled rum behind the bar of this country tavern in America.

began importing northern-grown Indian corn and wheat as well as rum, and sent back supplies of rice, limes, turtles and yams. New England began to rely on the Middle Colonies for its bread flour and grains. Moreover, Americans developed nuanced tastes for regional specialities: New York State produced the best beef, North Carolina the best pork and Philadelphia the best beer. As the Thirteen Colonies evolved into a network of co-operating units, it is no wonder that eighteenth-century Americans were the best-fed and tallest people on the globe.[26]

Taverns were at the heart of their local communities. Visiting Philadelphia in 1744, William Black observed that it was possible to 'learn more of the

constitution of the place, their trade and manner of living, in one hour' spent in a local tavern than 'I could [in] … a week's sauntering up and down the City'.[27] The Boston minister Benjamin Wadsworth complained that it was common practice for every bargain or payment to be solemnised by a visit to a tavern to 'swallow strong drink'.[28] The militia mustered at the tavern and concluded a morning of drills with a drink. Local court hearings were often held in a separate room in a tavern, and while waiting to be called into the court chamber, many a witness violated the 1645 law stipulating that only a single half-pint of wine should be served to any one customer at a time.[29] On court days, everyone in the area would congregate to pick up the latest news and gossip.

John Adams, the snooty Harvard graduate who was to become America's second president, bemoaned the fact that in order to win an election it was necessary to 'mix with the crowd in a tavern'.[30] Indeed, he noted with resentment that tavern keepers were exceptionally well placed to gain political office because they spent the whole day drinking drams with their potential electorate.[31] The practice of distributing free liquor to voters was facilitated by the fact that taverns were frequently polling stations. Most of their regular patrons were entitled to vote, as the opportunity America afforded to own property had greatly extended the franchise.[32]

Taverns were places where men picked up news. The German physician John David Schoepf complained that strangers were plied with constant questions, and Daniel Fisher described how he was quizzed by the landlord of a country tavern as soon as he discovered that Fisher had come 'from the metropolis (and the assembly now sitting)'. The man positively 'gaped after news', but once 'I had answered all his interrogations, and he had picked what intelligence out of me he was able … he vanished'.[33] Taverns were also the site where men formed opinions about what they had heard. They stocked newspapers and the latest political pamphlets, and it was here that groups of like-minded men formed societies and clubs that met to debate, pontificate and gossip over a bowl of rum punch – as the Sons of Liberty would in 1769. A 'Mrs Amy Prudent' pointed out to the *American Weekly Mercury* that when the Meridional Club – of which her husband was a member – 'got together over a flowing bowl of fresh limes', they were more fluent than ever their wives were 'over a dish of tea'.[34] A French visitor to Annapolis enjoyed the 'large and agreeable company at my tavern. Where we had nothing but feasting and Drinking, after the King's health, the Virginia Assembly and then Damnation to the Stamp Act, and a great Deal to that purpose in wine, we scarce used to go to bed sober.'[35]

In 1692, the self-governing colony of Massachusetts had been made a Crown colony. A royally appointed governor and a layer of Crown-appointed officials were placed in authority over the elected American assemblymen. Resentment over royal interference with the colony's independence grew as alien governors distributed patronage to their own men, appointing members of the judiciary, vetoing legislation, and on occasion dismissing the Assembly. In the eighteenth

century, taverns became forums in which discontent with this system of government was expressed. Here rum and sociability fostered the growing awareness
that the colonists belonged to an American community with its own interests
and political grievances.[36]

British Whig politics found a receptive audience in Massachusetts
among men like the fifteen Sons of Liberty who had gathered in John
Marston's tavern. The Whigs asserted the public's right to criticise and
censure government actions and called for checks on the abuse of power.
They cast themselves as defenders of the constitution in opposition to the
king's ministers, who indulged in bribery and distributed pensions and offices
as favours. In 1763, in issue number 45 of his journal *North Briton*, John Wilkes
had gone so far as to attack King George III himself as a threat to Magna
Carta and 500 years of representative government.[37] Whig rhetoric resonated
in a colony that had been founded as 'a self-conscious alternative to English
corruption', especially now that it was felt that the corrupt politics of the old
country was being forced upon it.[38] While royal officers were seen as corrupt
and self-seeking, the elected members of the Massachusetts Assembly were
cast in the role of 'guardians of the public interest'.[39] Engraved on the Sons of
Liberty's silver punch bowl were representations of Magna Carta and the Bill
of Rights flanked by flags and topped by a liberty cap with the central inscription
'No. 45 Wilks and liberty'.[40]

In 1733, the British had introduced the Molasses Act, which imposed a tax
of 6d a gallon on imports of molasses produced outside the British Empire. This
was to prevent the American distillers from sourcing their molasses from the French
sugar islands, which lacked their own rum industry and sold off their molasses at
4d a gallon, undercutting Barbados molasses, which cost between 9d and 10d. The
Act was introduced as a result of pressure from West Indian planters, who were
organised into a formidable lobby group. They claimed that trade in molasses with
a foreign power was against the national interest. In fact, what they objected to
was that supplies of French molasses made New Englanders independent of the
British planters and therefore able to charge more for their goods on the sugar
islands. Indignation was felt throughout the thirteen mainland colonies at this
blatant act of favouring one colony's interests over another. However, it provoked
little reaction other than indignation, as the measure was ineffective. New England
distillers evaded British patrols and smuggled in French molasses. Often they paid
the customs officials to simply look the other way.[41]

But in 1764, the British provoked the wrath of the Americans by re-forming the terms of the Act. Throughout the Seven Years War (1756–63), a good many New England merchants had carried on a semi-clandestine trade with the French, which did the Americans' reputation in London no good. Although the French were expelled from mainland America during the war, increasing hostility from the Native Americans meant that a large force of British soldiers was stationed in the colonies and a squadron of 26 ships and more than 3,000 men was kept offshore. With a massive war debt to pay off, Prime Minister George Grenville was determined that the disloyal Americans should shoulder some of the cost for paying for this expensive military force.[42] The 1764 Sugar Act reduced the duty on non-British molasses to 3d a gallon, while at the same time it was announced that the collection of the tax would now be enforced. This transformed what had been an ineffective attempt at prohibition into a revenue-collecting exercise.[43] Matters were made worse when in 1767 Charles Townshend as Chancellor of the Exchequer sought to raise government revenues through the Tariff Act, which imposed taxes on the import of paper, paint, glass and tea. Included in this legislation was a reiteration of the British customs officers' right to use writs of assistance (akin to an British general warrant) to search for goods that they suspected had been smuggled in without paying the necessary duties.[44]

For the men whose names were engraved on the silver punch bowl, the dispute over taxation was more than theoretical. Engraved below 'No. 45 Wilks and liberty' was a representation of a torn page labelled 'General Warrants'.[45] The tearing-up of such documents was not merely symbolic. At least one of the group, Captain Daniel Malcolm, had several violent run-ins with British customs officers. On 24 September, the Deputy Collector of Customs, William Sheafe, arrived at his house with a writ of assistance authorising him to search Malcolm's house. He had received an anonymous tip that Malcolm was storing pipes of wine in his cellar on which he had not paid duties. He was almost certainly right. Malcolm routinely smuggled wine in from schooners that anchored out of sight of the customs officers. But the hot-headed Irishman, armed with a pistol in each hand and a sword at his side, refused Sheafe entry, threatening to 'blow his brains out' if he tried to force his way in. Sheafe returned later that day with a search warrant signed by a judge, only to retreat again when met by a crowd of 200 men and boys surrounding the house. They told him that they would not allow him to search the cellars until he named his informant. The stand-off was brought to an end by the Attorney and Solicitor General, who, to the customs officer's annoyance, refused to uphold the writ of assistance, arguing that it was invalid in the American colonies. The charges were dropped.[46]

Captain Malcolm died, aged 44, in October 1769. His memorial plaque in the Old North Church states that he was 'buried 10 feet deep, safe from British bullets'. But when British soldiers occupied Boston during the War of Independence, they used his gravestone for target practice. The stone with its defiant inscription stating that he was 'a true Son of Liberty. An enemy to oppression and one of the foremost in opposing the revenue acts on America' is still pockmarked with bullet holes.[47]

The British government succeeded in provoking a constitutional crisis with the very same colonies that had been vital to securing Britain's success in the Seven Years War. Just as Britain emerged as the globe's foremost imperial power, its desperate attempts to overcome the financial crisis the war had precipitated led to the dissolution of its empire. The injustice of unrepresentative taxation galvanised the Thirteen Colonies into political co-operation and protest against the motherland.[48] Looking back on events, John Adams remarked that 'molasses was an essential ingredient in American Independence'.[49]

The colonists began a boycott of British imports. Some commentators castigated their fellow Americans, pointing out that by becoming dependent on imported luxuries, they had made themselves easy targets for the British, who sought to extract revenue by taxing their vices. But the majority were outraged that Parliament appeared to be trying to deny colonists the accoutrements necessary to gentility. The protection of their right to consume united merchants, planters, farmers and artisans. The Townshend Acts were eventually repealed, apart from the duty on tea, which was retained to demonstrate to the colonists that Parliament had a right to levy taxes. This is why tea rather than molasses became the commodity that brought to a head the Americans' refusal to tolerate taxation without representation. In December 1773, three Bostonians disguised as Amerindians boarded British vessels waiting to unload their cargo of tea and threw it in the harbour.

The British attempted to demonstrate the Crown's authority by closing Boston harbour, but instead provoked a conflict that developed into a revolution. The other mainland colonies stood with Massachusetts in opposition to the government's high-handed treatment. John Adams overheard farmers in Shrewsbury, who were fearful that the government would soon impose a cattle tax, concluding, 'We had better rebel now ... If we put it off ... they will get a strong party among us and plague us a deal more than they can now.'[50] When British troops marched on Lexington and Concord in April 1775 in order to confiscate the military stores the American militia had stockpiled there, Paul Revere, the maker of the Sons of Liberty's silver punch bowl, set off on his legendary ride to warn the colonists. The exchange of fire at Concord that fateful day triggered the American War of Independence.

The Atlantic trading world of the First British Empire encouraged the symbiotic growth of the various colonies, which were bound together by a web of commerce. It was a system that benefited the Americans, allowing them to profit from a roaring trade in salt fish, provisions and naval goods in the West Indies, where they bought molasses that they distilled into rum and exchanged for slaves, all the while benefiting from the protection of the British navy. During the Seven Years War, however, they discovered that being a colony in this metropole-centred empire had its costs. Britain saw its colonies as subsidiaries or extensions of its landed estate: Barbados was where it happened to grow its sugar, Carolina its rice. It favoured one colony over another according to its own interests and felt entitled to extract revenue from the colonies when and how it saw fit.

America's thirteen mainland colonies were distinctively different from British settlements in the rest of the Empire. In the West Indies, the downtrodden slaves were in no position to stage an effective rebellion, while the sugar planters, with an effective lobby in Westminster, felt that their voices were heard. Besides, like the East India Company merchants and officials who lived in British outposts in the East Indies, most saw Britain as their home and intended to return one day. Many of the inhabitants of the North American colonies, on the other hand, were by now third- or fourth-generation Americans with their own distinctive identity and the means to express it. The free land that had attracted settlers meant that a far larger proportion of the population than in Britain owned property and were enfranchised. The need to protect their settlements against hostile Native Americans meant that most freemen were members of armed and well-trained militias. Thus, American colonists had a well-developed sense of entitlement and the power to protest effectively when they were provoked. When the British decided to draw a line and demonstrate their authority to what they considered to be a bunch of colonial upstarts, they were given something of a shock.

At the beginning of the eighteenth century, Britain was still an integral part of the European economy, with the Continent absorbing 85 per cent of its exports and sending it 68 per cent of its imports.[51] Yet by 1800, the country had turned its back on Europe to look outwards to its empire; the Americas, Africa and Asia now absorbed 70 per cent of its exports.[52] In return for a flood of British manufactures, the Empire sent Britain cargoes of pepper, calicoes, rice, sugar and tea, which encouraged industriousness among its population, stimulated industry and provided foodstuffs to sustain its working people. The loss of the thirteen mainland American colonies was a blow to Britain's pride, but its economy was able to withstand their loss because trading links were re-established after 1783. Indeed, economic ties between the two countries can be said to have strengthened, and for the first eighty years of its existence, the United States remained an important member of Britain's informal commercial empire.[53]

Britain may have lost territory in the Americas, but its war with France had spilled over onto the Indian subcontinent, and here it gained substantial victories that secured its position in the East. India took over America's dominant role in the Second British Empire, which emerged in the nineteenth century.

PART
3

11

In which Kamala prepares a meal for her family, near Patna, Bihar (February 1811)

How the East India Company turned opium into tea

Freshly bathed, Kamala set about preparing her family's evening meal. First she smoothed fresh cow dung in a circle to define a purified cooking space and sprinkled it with a few drops of water. Then she took some of the chillies she had plucked from the plants that grew near the family's hut and cast them on the grinding stone with a few drops of safflower oil, made from the seeds of the thistle-like plants that formed a picturesque hedge surrounding their plot of land. She crushed the chillies to a fine paste and added them, with salt, to flour made from finely ground parched maize. When she stepped outside the area of the hearth to fetch water, she was careful to wash her hands and feet again before returning to her cooking.[1] She poured a little of the water into the cornflour and kneaded it vigorously to make an unboiled pudding known as *chhattu*.[2]

Meanwhile, Kamala's daughter prepared a chutney by grinding together a few black peppercorns, some salt and a little ginger with a handful of Bengali currants, small red-black berries foraged from *Carissa carandas* bushes that grew wild in the fields around the village.[3] When the food was ready, the women called the men to come and eat. They broke off from their work of strewing the fertilising ashes from the fireplace around the poppies. They too washed their hands and feet, then cast a small amount of food into the fire. Together with her daughter, Kamala served her husband first, and then their two sons, the elder followed by the younger. The women would eat later, once the men had had their fill.[4] They were all hungry, having eaten only a handful of parched maize at midday. The meal that they savoured at the end of their long working day bore an uncanny resemblance to the cornmeal mush and sorrel stew eaten by African slaves on a Carolina rice plantation. The starchy component of their meal was another version of the porridge that was the staple food of slaves in the Americas. The sauce they dipped it in was distinctively Indian, but they ate it in a similar fashion to the Africans, using their right hands to tear off a piece of *chhattu*, which they rolled into a neat ball and dipped into the chutney.

BENGALI CURRANT CHUTNEY

Cut the currants in half and deseed. Grind them with a teaspoon of salt, some red chillies, a teaspoon of cumin seeds and a handful of fresh coriander leaves. Add water if the mixture is too thick. When ground, add the freshly squeezed juice of one lemon and mix well.

Gooseberries or cranberries can be substituted for the Bengali currants.

Kamala and her family lived near Patna in the province of Bihar. In 1811, when she and her family sat down to their meal, the province had been under East India Company rule for nearly forty years. During the eighteenth century, the Company had become embroiled in territorial disputes with Indian rulers, and in 1765 their army had defeated the combined forces of the Mughal emperor and the Nawab of Bengal at the Battle of Buxar. As a result of their victory, they were able to force the emperor to grant the Company itself – rather than an Indian noble – the governorship of the province. This had transformed a trading enterprise into an autonomous ruling power in control of one of the largest private armies in the world.[5]

The British idea of themselves as the new Romans bringing civilisation to barbarians gained fresh vigour with their acquisition of Indian territory. Company merchants were converted into administrators, dispensing justice and supervising the collection of the tax revenue of one of India's wealthiest regions.

The British politician Edmund Burke believed that private ownership of land was the foundation of a stable society, and he argued that it was incumbent on the British to introduce this first principle of civilisation to India. Consequently, in 1793 the Company imposed what became known as the Permanent Settlement on Bengal. Under its terms, ownership of the land was transferred to the tax-collecting nobility, or zamindaris, who were thus transformed into a version of Britain's landed aristocracy. But rather than creating a body of English-style improving landlords, the Company brought into being a rapacious rentier class whose aim was to extract as much revenue from their tenants as possible.[6]

To the satisfaction of the East India Company, the peasantry raised the money to pay their taxes by growing cash crops such as indigo and cotton. The military and administrative costs of ruling Indian territory absorbed an alarmingly large proportion of the Bengal revenue, and these export crops helped to keep the Company afloat financially.[7] The cash crop of most value to the Company was opium.

Kamala and her family belonged to a small sub-caste of market gardeners who specialised in the cultivation of opium poppies. Although Bihar was famed for its high-quality rice, it was only eaten by the wealthy: the cultivators of the land themselves lived on coarse grains. Traditionally, poppy farmers grew finger millet because the timetable for planting and harvesting it harmonised with raising the winter crop of poppies: they planted it in the spring and it could be harvested in August and September, leaving time to prepare the fields for the sowing of poppy seeds. Sometimes the millet was boiled in imitation of rice, but more often than not the peasants roasted it, ground it into a flour and used it to make *chhattu*.[8]

The *chhattu* that Kamala prepared for her family was unusual, however, because it was made with maize rather than millet flour. In the early nineteenth century, maize had begun to infiltrate the Indian subcontinent and was particularly taken up by poppy-growers: like farmers in West Africa, they found it could be grown in the same short summer season but its yields were much higher. Francis Buchanan, an Englishman who in the early nineteenth century spent seven years surveying the provinces of Bengal and Bihar, observed that around Patna, in the areas closest to the Ganges, millet was being replaced by maize.[9] He was pleased to note that in these areas 'the people have entirely lost the prejudice of considering [maize] unwholesome' and used it to prepare both roti (flat breads) and *chhattu*.[10]

The importance of maize in the food world of the British Empire is easily overlooked because it never made any inroads into the British diet. American maize was, however, a key staple foodstuff underpinning an array of imperial commercial activities. As we have seen, the Atlantic slave trade relied on maize and manioc to supply the slave traders and their ships with food, and they formed the basis of the slaves' diet as they laboured on the American sugar, tobacco and rice plantations. When late-nineteenth-century surveyors followed in Buchanan's footsteps, they found that maize had completely replaced millet as the summer crop of Bihar's poppy cultivators.[11] Thus it played an important role in sustaining the opium trade, one of the Empire's most lucrative commercial endeavours.

As a result of the preference among the labouring classes for liberally sweetened tea, the value of East India Company imports of the herb increased one hundred-fold between 1700 and 1774 and tea now overtook textiles as the Company's most valuable trading commodity.[12] The loss of the American colonies in 1783 made the British government all the more determined to raise revenue from its remaining colonies.[13] In 1784, in an attempt to boost the China trade, while at the same time pulling the rug from under the feet of tea smugglers, Parliament slashed the tax on tea imports, bringing the price of the lowest-quality bohea dust down from 12s. to 2s. a pound. Tea imports more than doubled within a year, and by the 1830s had doubled again to 30 million lb per annum. Tea was by now a truly mass consumer item and the Exchequer reaped the rewards: tea duties in the 1830s amounted to over £3 million and accounted for one tenth of the government's income.[14]

The Company welcomed the increase in demand for imports from China, but this also intensified the problem that the Chinese showed little interest in buying the goods the Company had to offer in exchange for tea. They bought some English woollens and Indian cotton, and an array of exotic goods such as sandalwood, bêche-de-mer, bird's nests, sharks' fins and coral moss. These the East India Company acquired in South East Asia in exchange for Indian textiles. But the supply of sandalwood and marine animals was not sufficiently large to pay for 15 shiploads of tea per year, and the Company found itself covering about half the cost with hard currency from its Bengal revenues.[15] This was unsatisfactory as it was considered very poor economics to allow Bengali silver to drain into China. And so the Company had begun casting about in search of a commodity that would unlock the Chinese market.

East India Company merchants were aware that there was a steady demand for Bengal opium among the Chinese living in Indonesian and Malay ports.[16] Since European traders had introduced tobacco to China in the late sixteenth century, smoking and drinking tea had become such complementary activities for the Chinese that they found it hard to imagine engaging in one without the other and referred to the practice as *yancha* (smoke and tea). Early in the eighteenth century, tea-house owners had introduced a new, expensive blend of tobacco cut with opium, and by the end of the century the wealthy had dispensed with the tobacco altogether. In China, smoking pure opium became a mark of elite social status. Just as British gentlewomen used Chinese tea paraphernalia to display their wealth and sophistication, Chinese gentlemen demonstrated their affluence and good taste with the elaborate equipment associated with opium inhalation – inlaid wooden boxes, intricate lamps, decorated spoons and pipes.[17] Opium devotees showed a marked preference for the mild Patna opium from eastern India over the more fiery and potentially irritating Malwa opium grown in the west. The East India Company realised that the Indian district over which they now ruled produced a commodity for which there was a potentially vast Chinese market. In 1773, they took over the production and sale of opium in Bengal.

Each September, peasants were issued licences to cultivate poppies. The Company granted them to the skilled market gardeners from the Kachhi and Koiri sub-castes who lived around Patna and Benares and who eventually made up a hereditary pool of poppy producers.[18] At least 1.3 million peasants opted to grow poppies each year. There were some advantages to holding a poppy-growing licence. The Company advanced loans to farmers to cover the costs of rent, seed and fertiliser; on occasion, it also loaned money for agricultural improvements such as digging wells.[19] These interest-free cash advances were appealing to the peasants because they were made at the time of year when they needed ready cash to pay their rent and allowed them to avoid the usurious rates of interest offered on loans by the village moneylender.[20] Altogether the credit extended to opium cultivators injected 5–6 million rupees a year into local economies.[21]

Poppies were a temperamental crop and the harvesting of the opium was labour-intensive: small incisions had to be made in the thousands of seed heads every two or three days over a period of three to four weeks. It was back-breaking work to scrape the latex oozing from the incisions into a shallow brass bowl. The work involved the farmer's entire family, and in this way the East India Company co-opted a large body of hidden and unpaid labour.[22] Cultivators received a fixed sum of five rupees per seer (about 5 oz) of raw opium. In theory, the fixed price cushioned them from fluctuations in the wider market. However, when the poppies failed to yield sufficient latex to cover the costs, it was the farmer and his family who were forced to carry the loss. And when the cultivator enjoyed a bumper crop, his profit was limited. If the market price of opium rose, the Company creamed off the profits.[23] By increasing the numbers of peasants who relied on cash incomes, opium production contributed to the growth of a large section in Bengali society who were vulnerable to famine when food prices spiralled in times of scarcity. However, given that only a tiny proportion of cultivated land was planted with poppies, opium production in itself was not to blame for the food scarcity that was to afflict the subcontinent with ever-increasing regularity.[24]

In the spring, the Company's Assistant Sub-Deputy would tour the villages, supervising the various headmen as they weighed and graded the cakes of crude opium. It was packed into large earthenware jars, loaded onto carts and transported under armed guard to one of two Company processing factories at Bankipur and Ghazipur. Here it was refined, shaped into balls, covered with a protective wrapper of steamed poppy petals and packed into 140 lb chests.[25] These were then transported to Calcutta, where they were sold at auction to private shipping companies. This was where the Company's official involvement with the opium trade ended.

The Company delegated the illegal section of the trade to private merchants. In theory, imports of opium into China were banned. However, lying at anchor just off the southern Chinese coast were a number of heavily armed broken-down East Indiamen. The merchants used these as floating opium warehouses. The ships from Calcutta would unload their chests of opium onto the receiving ships, and at night Chinese smugglers would row out to them in their longboats with many oars, known as 'scrambling dragons'. Drawing alongside, they would place a bag of silver in one side of a scale and the merchants would balance it with opium. 'The price', the captain of an American opium brig explained, 'being weight for weight.'[26] The longboats then made their way up the Pearl River past Canton, running the gauntlet of the numerous checkpoints and patrols that were supposed to make it impossible for European goods to enter China without the permission of the Chinese authorities. But the customs officers and soldiers manning the patrols were in the pay of the smugglers and turned a blind eye to their comings and goings.[27]

The stacking room in the East India Company's opium factory at Patna where the raw opium was refined, shaped into balls and wrapped in steamed poppy petals and then packed into chests ready to be taken to auction in Calcutta.

Before receiving a Company licence to trade with China, the private merchants signed bonds obliging them to pay the proceeds of their trade into the Company's Canton treasury. In return for their bags of silver, the merchants were issued with credit bills of exchange. These could be cashed in with the Company in Bengal or with the Company's Court of Directors in London.[28] The exchange rates between the Spanish dollar – in which the Canton receipts were registered – and the pound sterling – which the bearer of the bill was paid in London – were usually generous. In this way, profits from goods bought in India and sold in China were transferred back to Britain. A similar mechanism was put in place for the Indian cotton loaded at Bombay and sold at Canton.[29] Meanwhile, the Company's agents used the silver the Canton treasury acquired in this manner to pay the Chinese for chests of tea. These were sold in London at quarterly auctions and the proceeds were used to pay those bills of exchange the merchants chose to cash in London.

In India, the circle of trade was maintained by the large funds the opium auctions raised. The Company paid the poppy cultivators the bare minimum, while they auctioned the chests of opium in Calcutta for sums far exceeding the production costs. In 1881, a chest of opium that had cost the Company 370 rupees to produce was auctioned for 1,362 rupees.[30] The profits allowed the Company to pay with ease the credit bills of the private opium merchants who cashed their bills of exchange in Calcutta. The auctions also provided the funds for the next round of advance loans to the peasants, who then planted a new crop of poppies and began the cycle again.[31]

In the 1790s, about 4,000 chests of opium were sold by auction in Calcutta; by the 1830s, the number had risen to about 15,000. By then, the silver the private traders received from the Chinese smugglers and then in turn paid into the Canton treasury financed nearly 80 per cent of the Company's China trade.[32] The exchange of opium for Chinese silver, some of which was then paid back to the Chinese for tea, silk and porcelain, solved the Company's problem of the balance of trade with China. At the same time it created a lucrative source of income for the Bengal government. From the late eighteenth century until the end of British rule in India in 1947, opium revenues were the third most important source of income for the Indian government after land revenue and the salt tax.[33] In the 1880s, about two million peasants working less than 2 per cent of the cultivated land in the Gangetic valley generated 93.5 million rupees for the Company.[34]

Only a small proportion of the opium revenue was reinvested in the Bengali economy. The Company opium agencies employed a range of local administrators and collectors, whose salaries amounted to a quarter of a million rupees.[35] The poppy cultivators themselves supplemented their incomes by selling various by-products of opium production. The women gathered the petals from the flowers, steamed them and sold the soft thin discs to the Company opium-processing factories, where they were used to wrap around the balls of refined opium. The surplus seeds were sold as a spice or pressed to obtain cooking oil. The residue was formed into cakes – 'remarkably sweet and nutritious [and] wholesome food often resorted to by the poor, and greedily eaten by cattle'.[36] Indeed, no part of the poppy was wasted. At the turn of the year, when the seedlings were thinned, the peasants used the leaves of the discarded plants as greens in their dhal, and the stalks could be added to the messy thatch on their huts. If they had any surplus summer maize, this was turned into an additional cash crop and sold to the wealthy in the nearby towns, who liked to eat roast corn on the cob. Most lucrative of all, even though it was illegal, the peasants would retain some of their raw opium to sell to itinerant salesmen.[37]

Although the system of opium production was exploitative, the small community of market gardeners around Benares and Patna appear to have been able to use poppy cultivation to lift themselves out of poverty.[38] When H. H. Risley conducted an ethnographic survey a century after Francis Buchanan, he observed 'a high rate of saving' among poppy cultivators and noted that some had even been able to purchase their own land and lift themselves into the class of revenue-paying proprietors.[39] Nevertheless, rather than being reinvested in India, by far the greater proportion of the money generated by their labour was remitted back to Britain. By means of the China trade, opium production allowed the Company and its agents to siphon off India's wealth.[40]

The opium trade tends to attract almost as much moral opprobrium as the Atlantic slave trade. The Chinese state is presented as having been 'powerless against the pernicious forces of an imperialist drug cartel'.[41] The evil of opium is supposed to have drained silver out of the economy while turning the Chinese into 'a nation of hopeless addicts, smoking themselves to death while their country descended into chaos'.[42] However, a number of European and Chinese scholars have argued that by repeatedly retelling the story of the opium trade in these terms, we have fallen victim to an 'opium myth'. They argue that opium's reputation as a demon drug is hyperbole, and that China's early-nineteenth-century financial crisis had as much to do with internal economic difficulties as it did with silver payments for opium.

In the 1820s, the East India Company accepted that they were unable to prevent the production and sale of opium in the independent princely states in western India. Instead, they opted to incorporate this Malwa opium into their revenue-generating system by charging pass fees on opium exported via Bombay. Malwa opium was half the price of the higher-quality Bengal product, which meant that the drug was now within the financial reach of the labouring poor, thus expanding the Chinese market. By 1835, European and Indian traders were supplying China with enough opium to provide two million people with a daily smoke.[43] For Chinese labourers, a pipe of opium was the equivalent of the British workman's cup of sweetened tea. Travelling up the Yangtze River in the 1890s, Isabella Bird observed that after a hard day's scrambling over rocks and negotiating narrow paths in order to haul her boat upstream through the rapids, the boatmen would huddle in blankets and share a pipe of opium.[44]

Opium was at times abused and it was addictive but its inhalation was probably one of the least physically damaging ways of taking any of the recreational drugs available at the time. The worst health side-effect was constipation, and the vast majority of opium smokers – like most compulsive inhalers of tobacco and tipplers of gin or rum – were able to function as useful members of their society despite their foible. The idea that China was incapacitated by a hopelessly drug-addicted population was absurd propaganda. A British consul based in Hainan was surprised to find that 'although nearly everyone uses [opium] … one never meets the opium-skeleton so vividly depicted in philanthropic works, rather the reverse – a hardy peasantry, healthy and energetic'.[45]

Opium was as commonly used in Britain as it was in China, with the difference that the British consumed it. Dissolved into alcohol to make laudanum, it was a common remedy for everything from stomach ache to infant colic.

TO MAKE THE BEST LIQUID LAUDANUM

Take a Quart of Sack, and half a Pint of Spirit of Wine, and four Ounces of Opium, two Ounces of Saffron; slice the Opium and pull the Saffron, and put it in a Bottle with the Sack, and Spirit of Wine, and one Ounce of Salt of Tartar, and of Cinamoa, Cloves, and Mace of each a Drachm, cork and tie down the Bottle, and set it in the Sun or by the Fire twenty Days, pour it off the Dregs, and 'tis fine to use; ten, fifteen, twenty, or twenty five Drops.[46]

Why then did the Chinese government demonise the opium habit and take precipitate measures against foreign merchants in order to suppress the trade? Ch'ing officials blamed the opium trade for the silver famine the Chinese economy was experiencing.[47] By 1835, the Chinese desire for opium outweighed the British thirst for tea and the Chinese worried that every year purchases of opium were draining $18 million worth of silver out of their economy. Company and Indian merchant ships returning to London, Calcutta and Bombay did stash silver bullion in their holds as well as crates of tea, but the Chinese seem to have been unaware that about three quarters of the silver paid for opium was channelled straight back to them in payment for tea and silk.[48] The causes of China's silver famine were, in fact, far more complex.

In 1827, the depletion of Spain's American silver mines triggered a worldwide depression and the quantity of silver entering the global market declined. The flow of silver into the Chinese economy from the other foreign merchants trading in Canton was therefore diminished.[49] At the same time, declining production in the Yunnan copper mines led to the debasement of the copper and bronze coins that were China's real currency. The inflation affecting copper hit ordinary peasants hard: although they paid their taxes in copper, the amount they had to pay was calculated in silver. They were faced with ever-increasing tax bills while the government's income (because it was paid in copper) remained static. As people needed more and more cash, the price of silver skyrocketed, and rather than spend it, private individuals and the government began to hoard the metal. In the circumstances of this inflationary crisis, silver's value as a currency was marginalised. It therefore made economic sense to export silver in exchange for consumer goods, even opium.[50] But it was much easier for officials to blame China's economic crisis on the imbalance of trade inflicted upon them by unscrupulous foreign merchants than it was to address the problem by improving the copper coinage and creating a stable silver currency.[51] The issue of silver, opium and the balance of trade was a smokescreen.

The Ch'ing government oscillated between xenophobic resentment and opportunism in its attitude towards foreign trade.[52] The emperor wanted to preserve social stability by keeping the foreigners at arm's length. Their intrusion into the country was therefore limited to designated trading entrepôts. However, it was in the interests of the government, and the emperor himself, to keep the Canton trade open and buoyant. The Hoppo, the superintendent of the maritime customs at Canton, paid a large share of the trading revenue into the emperor's private purse.[53] By the 1830s, a good proportion of this would have come indirectly from the trade in opium; thus it was not really to the advantage of either side to bring it to a halt. Nevertheless, it was becoming something of an embarrassment. The emperor and his government were humiliated by rumours that both the military and the Chinese merchants were openly conniving in the illegal trade.[54]

An 'inner opium war' broke out between rival factions within the Chinese governing classes. The response of the xenophobic section among Chinese officials was to call for a trade embargo. The emperor and his government, however, knew that this was neither in the government's financial interest, nor was it enforceable. In May 1836, Juan Yuan, the leader of a group of bureaucrats in alliance with a Canton-based merchants' academy, the Hsueh-hai't'ang, suggested to the emperor that the problem would best be tackled by both legalising the import of Indian opium and encouraging domestic production. This would hopefully pull the carpet out from under the smugglers' feet and allow the government to regulate both the trade and the drug's consumption. But while Yuan's measures were being deliberated, and enthusiastically endorsed by the leader of the Canton merchants, a group of dissatisfied literati calling themselves the Spring Purification movement persuaded the emperor to drop his legalisation plans and embark on a crusade against opium addiction.[55]

The Spring Purification party were intent on implementing a moral programme to rejuvenate the scholarly official class, who were some of the most notorious opium users in society.[56] Motivated by a desire for a more powerful position within the government, their leader, Juang Chueh-tzu, provided the emperor with proof that the Canton merchants were implicated in illegal currency dealings and the opium trade.[57] In response, the emperor scrapped Yuan's legalisation plans and appointed the Spring Purification party's ally, Lin Tse-hsu, as governor general of Canton. It was Lin who forced a diplomatic impasse in June 1839 by seizing and destroying the opium in the European factories within Canton and closing the channel to shipping, in effect imprisoning the foreign traders in the city.[58]

By the mid nineteenth century, British imperialists had embraced the ideology of free trade and were embarked upon a tireless crusade to break down protectionism in foreign countries in order to open up new markets for their own export industries. Having discovered in India how expensive territorial acquisitions could be, they sought to create an 'informal empire' of economic hegemony. In Latin America, they were in dispute over what they considered to be unfair tariffs with the new nations that had arisen from the wreck of the Spanish Empire. Earlier that year, the Foreign Secretary, Lord Palmerston, had sent gun boats to the Bay of Naples to force the Neapolitans to reduce their trading tariffs.[59] The India–China opium trade was too lucrative to relinquish. The sale of opium accounted for 20 per cent of Indian revenues, the duties on tea imports earned the British Exchequer one tenth of their total revenue and the sale of Chinese goods on the international market funded Britain's purchases of raw cotton from America to feed its textile mills.[60] When William Jardine, until recently the foremost of Canton's opium merchants, arrived in London two months after the Chinese seizure of the Europeans' opium (having retired from Canton that January), he immediately began pressing Lord Palmerston to wage war on China in retaliation. It had long been his aim to use force to open up trade with China, and he now saw his opportunity to persuade the British government to help.

In November 1839, a British fleet arrived off the coast of Canton – including the *Nemesis*, the first iron paddle steamer to round the Cape of Good Hope – equipped with shells and Congreve rockets against which China's defences were hopelessly inadequate.[61] The Chinese lacked both the military structure and the bureaucratic organisation to resist the imposition of the imperial global trading system, and the war ended ignominiously for them in August 1842 when they signed the Treaty of Nanking, still referred to in China as 'the first of the unequal treaties'. The British succeeded in their crusade to access new markets for their growing export industries and forced the Chinese to open five 'treaty ports' to their ships. The British government was uninterested in gaining anything other than a secure trading regime with the Chinese. It was even reluctant to take on the unpromising rocky island of Hong Kong, which the merchants wanted as a safe haven.[62]

Canton returned to business as usual, with Chinese officials once more taking a cut as part of the smugglers' protection racket. Opium smoking continued to grow in popularity and the government carried on blaming its fiscal problems on the imbalance caused by the flow of silver to pay for opium imports. The drug became the focus of a mass movement of young gentry and students, for whom opium smokers came to symbolise China's inability to resist Europe's intrusion into its economy. They campaigned tirelessly against its use as demeaning and unpatriotic.[63] In colonial America, tea had similarly become a symbol of the arrogant imposition of British power.[64] There, however, tea drinking was at worst presented as disloyal, whereas in China opium smoking was regarded as a degenerate practice. Opium was, therefore, an ideal scapegoat for both Chinese nationalists and critics of colonialism's exploitative economics.[65]

For this reason, the shocked accounts of foreign missionaries and travellers who described the havoc wrought on Chinese society by opium should be treated with some caution. The Chinese opium dens supposedly occupied by skeletal addicts were in fact doss houses where labourers could eat, sleep and relax by 'chasing the dragon' in the bowl of an opium pipe.[66] When the American journalist F. H. Nichols travelled through the famine-stricken province of Shensi in 1900, the peasants he described – their faces 'drawn and leathery, their eyes dull and glazed' – were victims of starvation rather than opium addiction, and those he observed smoking were probably using the drug's appetite-suppressing qualities to stave off hunger pangs.[67] The end result of the campaign of moral outrage was the first international Opium Commission, which met in Shanghai in 1909. The Commission agreed to make illegal all trade in narcotic substances and to apply this principle globally. These commitments are the source of our contemporary legal framework outlawing opium and its derivatives.[68]

Elements of the opium myth are undoubtedly true. That the East India Company exploited poppy cultivators is undeniable; that it immiserated them is more questionable. That the opium trade was a mechanism whereby the East India Company was able to drain substantial amounts of money out of India is undoubtedly correct, but the causes of China's silver famine were far more complex than a simple trade imbalance. That the British were ruthless in their determination to impose their trading system on China in order to secure supplies of the stimulant that was by now essential to their working classes is without a doubt the case, but that in doing so they inflicted a heinous drug on the Chinese people is hyperbole.

12

In which Sarah Harding and her family grow fat eating plenty of good food in Waipawa, Hawke's Bay, New Zealand (29 July 1874)

How hunger drove the explosion of European emigration in the nineteenth century

Sarah Harding's mother arrived at John and Mary Pinfold's run-down cottage on a July morning in 1874 just as the family had finished their paltry breakfast of tea-kettle broth: 'bread in the breakfast pot with hot water poured on it'.[1] The previous November, Sarah, her husband Ted and their five children had packed up their few belongings and left their home village of Taynton in Oxfordshire to seek a better life on the other side of the world. Now that they were established in their new home in Waipawa, on New Zealand's North Island, Sarah had written to her mother with news of how they were getting on. She instructed her to show the letter to her friends and specially asked after John Pinfold. 'Tell him,' she wrote, that here 'there is no sitting under the hedge knawing [*sic*] a piece of bread and an onion, and talking over the bad times ... I can't remember the time when I felt so strong and well; I suppose it is having plenty to eat of good substantial food, for we do have plenty of good food – beef, mutton and pork. I must tell you the children are getting quite fat, and so is Ted.'[2]

It is not difficult to imagine the effect of such words on the Pinfolds. John had been laid off by his employer, and the family were struggling. Sarah's letter must have conjured images of their own family gathered round a table piled high with roast and boiled meats, their children growing fat in a far-off land. 'You know we did not have enough in the old country, we could not have

A cottage and farm buildings of the kind the Pinfolds would have inhabited.

it and pay for it,' Sarah had written, describing the Pinfolds' present situation. 'There is no fear of that here.' Ted Harding and his elder son Frank had found construction work on a rail line, and if the weather stayed fine, Ted hoped to earn £13 that month. 'Don't you think that is better than working at home for two pounds sixteen shillings?' Sarah asked.[3]

The Hardings and the Pinfolds belonged to the group of rural labourers that, throughout the eighteenth and nineteenth centuries, paid the price of increasing agricultural efficiency. Enclosure had only just reached their part of Oxfordshire. During the first half of the nineteenth century, the extensive tracts of waste ground in the local forest of Wychwood had still provided the villagers of Taynton with a place to graze horses, sheep and cattle. But in 1856, the local landowners, the Churchill family, cleared the forest, subdivided the land into seven new farms and rented them out to tenant farmers. For the first few years the farmers had plenty of work to offer the villagers, grubbing out tree roots and breast-ploughing the land so that it could be brought under cultivation.[4] But by the early 1870s, they were no longer needed; as a result, the local wage had dropped to 8–11s. a week and unemployment was a persistent problem.[5]

Already on 13s. a week a labourer could not cover the cost of his rent, food, clothes and shoes, and maybe a few pennies for his children's school fees. Food had to be bought on credit and the family were restricted to a diet of 'potatoes, dry bread, greens, and herbs, kettle broth, and tea which was coloured water … a bit of bacon for the man now and then, but fresh meat … like Christmas, [only] once a year'.[6] The outspoken hedger and Methodist preacher Joseph Arch pointed out that this did not make for a strong and healthy family but rather for 'poor blood and poor bones and poor flesh'.[7] The Reverend Sidney Godolphin Osborne thought it a wonder the rural poor were able to live at all on their paltry diet.[8] William Cobbett, who travelled the country to investigate the condition of rural England, felt ashamed of his fat horse and full belly when confronted with poor faces of 'nothing but skin and bone'.[9] A contemporary scribbled in the margin of his copy of Cobbett's *Cottage Economy*, 'Homes have ceased in England and that is why we emigrate.'[10]

In the winter of 1870–1, labourers in the village of 'Hungry Harbury' in Warwickshire asked Joseph Arch to speak to a gathering about forming a labourers' union. Winter was the worst time of year for the rural poor, when there was little work and many had to fall back on parish relief funds to feed their families, or ended in the workhouse. Looking down from his upturned pig-killing stool on their 'faces gaunt with hunger and pinched with want', Arch felt as though he were addressing 'the children of Israel waiting for someone to lead them out of the land of Egypt'.[11] As a result of the meeting, the labourers formed the Warwickshire Agricultural Labourers' Union, with the aim of securing for the rural workers an increase in their wages, 'adequate food, decent homes … a secure stake in the land, and the right to be treated with full respect as free men'.[12] These were hardly outrageous demands, given that on the back of their labour most farmers had yearly incomes of hundreds, and the landlords thousands, of pounds. Ted Harding was a founding member of the Taynton branch of the new union and John Pinfold became its secretary. The man who led them and thousands of hungry labourers 'out of Egypt', however, was not Joseph Arch but C. R. Carter, an emigration agent who had been commissioned to recruit more than 2,000 able-bodied men to work as navvies on the construction of railways in New Zealand.[13]

In July 1872, Carter was invited by the union to Shipton under Wychwood to give a speech about the opportunities open to a hard-working man in New Zealand. Many came direct from the harvest fields to listen to him while others in the audience were out of work; the local farmer had just dismissed six of his twenty-five labourers for joining the union. Embittered by their treatment, they would have been ripe for recruitment and Carter selected ten men and their families straight away. Among them was George Smith, a 31-year-old farm labourer with a wife and three children who was also an active unionist.[14]

The Smith family sailed on the *Chile* in September 1872 for the new bush settlements in Hawke's Bay, on New Zealand's North Island. Less than a year later, George Smith wrote to his friends back home and John Pinfold published the letter in the *Labourers' Union Chronicle* in September 1873. Food and the chances New Zealand offered for those who were willing to work featured strongly in the letter. Smith described 'the first rate dinner ... [of] fresh beef, young potatoes and carrots' they had on the day they arrived. He wrote that he was just about to buy a cow and his wife had her fowls. The family lived in a two-roomed cottage with a garden and he owned a horse, which was unthinkable in England, where horseback was the gentry's means of transport. Work was plentiful, so that 'I have no anxiety now about how I am to get food and clothing for myself and children.' Whereas in England his family had considered a pig's cheek or a bit of bacon a 'fine thing', in New Zealand he bought half and sometimes a whole sheep at a time, 80 or 90 lb of beef as well as whole legs of mutton for just 6d. 'We used to be told that the beef and mutton of this country were not so good as at home; come and try them', he urged his friends. 'I assure you you will find out your mistake.'[15]

A year later, Carter visited the Wychwood area again, this time recruiting directly for the New Zealand government, which was offering assisted passages to would-be emigrants. On 4 November 1873, he spoke at Milton under Wychwood, only a few miles from Taynton. Between 500 and 600 people from all over the area listened to him speaking for nearly two hours. It was at this meeting that Ted and Sarah Harding resolved to follow the Smiths and signed up to sail on the *Inverene* on 22 November. When they arrived at Hawke's Bay, they stayed with George and Maria Smith for the first few weeks while their own cottage was constructed. In the letter she wrote home to her mother in July 1874, Sarah reported that George was doing well and was now the proud owner of two horses, two cows, two calves and between sixty and seventy fowls.[16] Emigration had allowed them to move back in time to the rural world destroyed by enclosure in England. Sarah Harding was adamant that the move to New Zealand 'was the best thing we [have] ever done for ourselves and children'.[17]

Only a minority of those who streamed out of Europe in the nineteenth century were seeking religious or political freedom. Some, like the Irish, were fleeing famine. Potato blight affected a large part of Europe in the 1840s, but in Ireland, over-reliance on the potato for food meant that both the plant and the poor were decimated. Between 1846 and 1850, a million Irish died of starvation and another million joined the economic migrants drawn to the New World by the promise of a good life.[18] But even for those who were not fleeing starvation, what the abstract notion of a 'good life' meant in concrete terms was that they would have enough to eat. Poles described emigration as a quest for food: '*za chlebem*' (to emigrate) literally meant 'to bread'.[19] Britons and Germans too spoke of emigrating in order to 'put food on the table'.[20] British game laws prevented labourers even from knocking a rabbit on the head. But in the New World, 'a man is at liberty to do as he pleases', wrote Thomas Goodwin in triumph from Illinois. 'I can go with my gun, and shoot what I like, and no one says where are you going? No game laws here!'[21] This access to abundant wild animals, John Worsfold assured his parents from Hamilton in Canada, meant that in the New World 'there is little danger of starving'.[22]

Emigrants' letters abound with lists of prices for foodstuffs, and read aloud to friends and family, passed around communities and published in newspapers, they spread the word that working men in the colonies could afford the best joints of meat and ate as much suet in a fortnight as they would normally have eaten in six months. Boasts that after a working day of only eight rather than twelve hours labourers could afford to 'go to the shop, and get a bag of sugar, and half-chest of tea, and pay for it ready money' would have aroused envy among those left behind at home, who scrimped along buying pennyworths of tea and sugar on credit.[23] Sarah Harding's letter must have helped to make up the minds of the Pinfolds, who were struggling on the lock-out pay John had been allocated by the district union. On 20 November, John and Mary too sailed for Hawke's Bay, with their five children, who they no doubt hoped would soon be as fat as the small Hardings.[24]

The Hardings, the Smiths and the Pinfolds were part of a nineteenth-century explosion in European migration. Millions moved within the Continent itself, streaming into the cities looking for work. But often the cities were stepping stones to the wider world. For every nine people who migrated within Europe, one person left the Continent. Between 1815 and 1930, this amounted to an outward migration of around 50 million people.[25] The majority of these emigrants went to the United States. The rest gave rise to prosperous settler societies in Canada, Australia, New Zealand and South Africa, with a smaller number settling in East Africa and the newly independent South American republics.

In Britain, the outward flow of emigrants was given a kick-start by a government keen to foster a strong British presence and loyalty to the Crown in its empire after the loss of the American colonies. It drew on the pool of the dissatisfied and dispossessed who were suffering from what one artisan evocatively called the 'Great Damp in trade' when the Napoleonic Wars were followed by an economic recession.[26] The ranks of the rural unemployed were swelled by 200,000 demobilised soldiers and sailors, all competing for fewer jobs.[27] The government recruited 4,000 Britons to emigrate to the Cape of Good Hope, and 2,000 Scottish farmers and labourers were dispatched to what was left of Britain's North American empire in Upper Canada.[28]

The Cape of Good Hope scheme attracted a great deal of interest from young men who felt they had 'no prospect of securing a start in life in the Cape of Despair, in this our Native land'.[29] In October 1819, Jeremiah Goldswain, a 17-year-old pit-sawyer from Great Marlow in Buckinghamshire, was caught up in the scheme when he joined a crowd gathered around William Wait, a wine merchant who had come down from London to drum up takers for what was essentially an indentured labour scheme. Jeremiah was enthused by the offer of a free passage and provisions, half an acre of land and a supply of wheat seed in return for six years' labour on Wait's land grant. His family were dismayed. He was his mother's only child and she must have feared what would happen to her in old age without her son to care for her. She protested that he was a 'very undutiful son' and that he would be killed by wild beasts. But he replied that it was 'better for me to leave my native home and go where I could do better than stopping there [sic] as I had got but little work to do and had no prospect of getting any more'.[30] Rather than hanging around the village waiting for trade to pick up, he resolved to emigrate, and against his mother's vehemently expressed wishes he left home on Boxing Day, never to return.

Peace had created a dismal economic climate in the English countryside, but it did make the seas safer. Now that Britain had crushed not only the French, but also the Dutch and Spanish navies, piracy was virtually eliminated from the world's oceans. This brought down insurance costs and, correspondingly, the cost of transporting freight. The volume of world trade increased substantially.[31] Timber, wool, hides and whale products flowed into Britain, but many of the ships sailing out to collect these goods were virtually empty. The shipping interest brought pressure to bear on the government to lift restrictions on the number of paying passengers that merchant ships were allowed to accommodate. Consequently, the number of passenger berths to foreign destinations multiplied.[32] Isaac Stephenson, an Irishman of Scottish ancestry and the fifth of a flax-farming family's seventeen children, joined the steady stream of Irish and Scottish settlers who made their way across the Atlantic Ocean. Having gone to Londonderry to look for work, he was attracted by the prospect of the New World and bought himself a passage on a timber ship sailing for New Brunswick. Straight off the ship, he found work looking after the lumbering operations of loyalist grandees along the Oromocto River. Thirty years later, he was established as an independent logging contractor supplying masts to the Royal Navy.[33]

By the 1830s, 55,000 migrants had left the British Isles, with the majority coming from the depressed agricultural counties in the south and southeast.[34] Between 1850 and 1854, another two million Irish swelled their ranks. The government used the famine to effect a programme of eviction and land clearance. From 1847, the only way for the starving to receive relief was if they entered the workhouse, and if they did so, they were forced to relinquish their land to the government, who tore down their cabins and consolidated their plots into larger holdings. One witness described how he appeared 'to be tracking the course of an invading army' as he travelled through County Clare in the wake of the 'levellers'.[35] By 1858, about one tenth of Irish land had been placed under new ownership. As the dispossessed fled to the United States, the government achieved its aim of ridding the Irish countryside of the surplus population of potato-eating cottiers.

In the 1840s, Britain's industrial workers began to make up the majority of the 250,000 a year who decided to emigrate.[36] The introduction of steamships in the 1860s brought down the cost of passage so that emigration was now affordable for increasing numbers of people further down the social scale.[37] While in the cities real wages were higher than in the countryside and the opportunities to find work were expanding, living standards could hardly be described as idyllic. Urban emigrants sought a better life than the one they led in the slums, with their damp, overcrowded terraces, shared toilets and overflowing drains. Although he struggled to make a living on his farm in Wisconsin, Edwin Bottomley was glad to have escaped the harsh drudgery of English industrial life. 'Thank God', he wrote, 'I have not to rouse my children at the sound of a bell from their beds and Drag them through the pelting storm of a Dark winters morning to earn a small pittance at a factory. O thank god such is not the case with us.'[38]

For the potters who left Staffordshire with the Potters' Emigration Society, the colonies promised the chance of escaping the minute division of labour that characterised modern manufacture.[39] If the emigrating agricultural labourers wished to recapture the lost rural world before enclosure, the craftsmen sought to go back in time to the proto-industrial world when the skilled artisan was master of all the stages of production. In the Staffordshire potteries, master potters had been replaced with slip-makers, throwers, flat pressers, kiln loaders, painters and glazers – each repetitively performing only one task in a production line. This increased efficiency and reduced labour costs, as unskilled and semi-skilled workers could be paid less.[40] In mid-century America, by contrast, it was still possible to achieve the old ideal of setting oneself up as an independent craftsman, as Samuel Walker did in Utica, where he had his own pot works.[41] English hand-loom weavers likewise took refuge from industrialisation in New England and Philadelphia.[42] However, as America also industrialised after the civil war, and the American pottery and textile industries became increasingly mechanised, English emigrants were no longer able to recapture the old ways. From then on they were attracted by the fact that wages were higher in the United States rather than by the dream of working independence.[43]

In the New World, British emigrants were able to realise the modest aims that the National Agricultural Labourers' Union had for its members: adequate homes, food, respect, and a stake in the land. Emigrant homes were often basic: a photograph of the Hardings' homestead shows a sturdy single-storey clapboard house with a veranda and a chimney.[44] If not luxurious, it was certainly better than the much-patched cob-and-thatch cottage they had left behind in England. James Randall, who also came out to work on the New Zealand railways, acknowledged that 'there is not the comfort here as regards feather beds'. But he thought this was beside the point when it was possible to go out and catch a pig in the bush any time he wanted pork, and wages were such that 'a working man here can spend more in comforts than he can earn in England'.[45]

Conditions were often rough in the early years. Laurence Kennaway, who helped to set up one of the first sheep runs near Canterbury on New

'Ulrich's bakery'. Pioneer settlers went to great lengths to make proper leavened bread. This man baked bread for the gum diggers on the Ahipara gum fields north of Auckland, New Zealand. Pioneer farmers struggling to break in their land would spend the winters here digging for kauri gum. They sold it to raise cash to support their families and pay for farm improvements.

Zealand's South Island in the 1850s, recalled the 'granulous and nobby' puddings and bread the shepherds were forced to subsist on, as the only equipment they possessed for grinding wheat into flour was a coffee mill. He felt that the 'decrease in quality was [not] quite made up for by the increase of novelty'.[46] Still, it was a far cry from the 'growy bread' many labourers were reduced to eating back home in the 1840s, made out of the residue left after the bran had been separated from the wheat flour. These 'crammings' produced a heavy, doughy loaf that could be pulled in 'long strings out of your mouth'.[47] Once established, however, settlers were quickly able to improve on the paltry meals they were used to at home. Using mixtures of warm water, bran, salt, hops, sugar, and potato peelings to replace yeast, they were able to make leavened bread. Inventive settlers in Ohio added yeast, milk and a generous helping of butter to dumplings made with flour, lard, water and salt, known as doughboys, and dropped them into hot fat rather than boiling water. Dusted with sugar, they were transformed into doughnuts.[48] For a Swedish immigrant who was served doughnuts and coffee when she arrived at America's emigrant processing depot on Ellis Island, this delicious fatty, sugary concoction affirmed to her that she had at last reached the land of plenty.[49]

On the farms in the wooded zone of Texas, a slice of buttered bread or some cheese and crackers – a whole supper for a tired English textile worker – was considered a mere 'snack'.[50] Meat was the food most emigrants had longed for in Britain. Joseph Arch stated that it was 'the ambition and glory of every loving father … to sit at his own table … with a good joint of meat', and when he travelled to Canada to assess the prospects for emigrating Britons, he saw 'plenty of great lumps of beef in working-men's houses'.[51] In the New World, where widespread pastoral farming produced plentiful supplies of beef and mutton, it was considered the norm to eat meat for breakfast, dinner and supper. Edward Dale recalled that everyone in the Texas of his boyhood in the 1880s 'demanded three square meals' a day, all including meat.[52] On New Zealand's sheep stations, mutton chops, mutton curry or mutton and mushrooms, made with tender steaks off a leg, were the standard breakfast fare. For dinner, a joint

MUTTON DEVILLED

Season 8 or 9 slices of cold roast mutton with salt, pepper, and cayenne, sprinkle with lemon-juice, and put aside for ½ an hour. When ready, dip them into oiled butter, coat lightly with browned breadcrumbs, and bake in a moderately hot oven for a few minutes. Arrange in a close circle on a hot dish, fill the centre with watercress seasoned with salt, pepper, and lemon-juice, and serve.

of mutton and vegetables was the norm, and supper again featured mutton 'cooked in some form of entrée'.[53] George Hancox, a farm labourer from Tysoe in Warwickshire, thought it 'enough to make a man dance' to come home after a hard day's work building New Zealand's railways to find 'two legs of mutton in the boiler for our supper'.[54]

As Sarah Harding wrote, there was no sitting down under a hedge in the cold to eat their dinner for farm labourers in New Zealand. 'The "boss" is with us working, and sits down and smokes his pipe and chats like yourself. There is no bowing and scraping here', wrote John Traves, a 38-year-old farm labourer, to his sister in Lincolnshire.[55] The genteel immigrant Lady Barker noted that some people objected to the 'independence of manner' exhibited by the New Zealand settlers, but found that she liked 'to see the upright gait, the well-fed, healthy look, the decent clothes (even if no one touches his hat to you), instead of the half-starved, depressed appearance, and too often cringing servility of the mass of our English population'.[56] Freedom from the fear of the workhouse was liberating, as was the fact that it was not necessary to be forever pulling one's cap to a social superior. 'In this country are no Lords, nor Dukes, nor Counts, nor Marquises, nor Earls, nor Royal Family to support nor no King', rejoiced Joseph Hollingworth in a letter from America to his aunt and uncle in Huddersfield.[57]

It was the dream of many emigrants to earn enough money in their new country to buy their own farm. The ideal of the hardy colonial yeoman farmer pioneered by the New Englanders in the seventeenth century was still alive among Britain's nineteenth-century migrants. New Zealand's emigration literature was full of tales of the emigrant hero who subdued the wilderness and earned himself a bucolic idyll through hard work and perseverance.[58] Talking to pioneer farmers in the prairie province of Alberta, the missionary Burgon Bickersteth found the same spirit at work among Canadian settlers. The home-steaders he spoke to were 'always talking of what the country *will* be – what a fine farm his homestead will one day become'. He believed that many of the emigrants would have been less enthusiastic if they had been able to buy 'a ready-made farm … It is the actual conquering and taming of the land which has a peculiar attraction … The seeing of acre after acre gradually reclaimed from the bush and brought under cultivation constitutes the real fascination of pioneer farming.'[59]

The emigrants from the Wychwood area of Oxfordshire achieved in New Zealand the last of the Agricultural Labourers' Union's aims that it found so difficult to realise for its members at home: secure access to the land. Hawke's Bay in 1870 was an isolated settlement only recently purchased from its indigenous Maori owners. The railway the navvies were contracted to build was intended to link it to the west-coast port of Foxton. George Smith, the first of the Wychwood labourers to emigrate, found work constructing the Great South Road running parallel to the railway.[60] As we have seen, on his daily wage of 6s. he was able to rent a house with a garden, keep a horse and a cow, eat well, and clothe his children. Ted Harding, who followed him out the next year, found work constructing the railway. Sarah's letter home mentioned that he was hoping to get some land 'before the summer is over'.[61] The settlement's administration was keen to convert the navvies into settled colonists and was selling plots of bush land on easy terms of credit. When John Pinfold arrived, he found employment on a new government project, clearing bush land for the planned settlement of Woodville.[62] All three men joined the Woodville Small Farm Association in April 1876 and each was allotted a 150-acre plot of land. The following year, a *Hawke's Bay Herald* reporter visited the settlement, which now had a hotel, two stores, a butcher and a carpenter, as well as a boot- and shoemaker. The farmers had already burnt off most of the bush and felled the trees and were beginning to fence off the land. Cattle wandered among the tree stumps, and here and there a settler had managed to sow a field of wheat or oats. They were beginning to erect comfortable houses in place of their temporary huts. The next year they had clubbed together to build a school for the sixty school-age children, and four years later they had built a church.[63]

Not all emigration stories had quite such happy endings, and not all the emigrants ended up in such idyllic rural settings. Many of them found work in the burgeoning towns and cities of the New World. Jeremiah Goldswain became a farmer in the Albany district of South Africa. Frequent stock raids and conflict with the Xhosa over the land meant that the farm was never particularly successful but he also built up a lucrative ox-carting business transporting supplies.[64] Like the farm labourers of Wychwood he left unemployment, hunger and humiliation behind. In the settler colonies the emigrants were able to eat meat three times a day, including beef steaks for breakfast; own their own homes and land; ride and hunt; plant an orchard; and doff their cap to no one. Throughout the nineteenth century, European emigrants extended the world's arable fields and productive pastures by somewhere between 1.5 and 2 billion acres.[65] This was to have a profound impact on agricultural production, and laid the foundations for the new global food regime that emerged in the last quarter of the nineteenth century.

13

In which Frank Swannell eats bean stew, bannock and prune pie in British Columbia (15 November 1901)

How the industrial ration fed those who pushed out the boundaries of empire and processed foods became magical symbols of home

As darkness fell in British Columbia on 15 November 1901, Frank Swannell and his companions tramped back to their camp in the fir woods of Texada Island, where they were surveying mining claims for the Cap Sheaf Copper & Gold Company. They were the advance guard of a short-lived copper boom in the Straits of Georgia. It had been a miserable, drizzling wet day with 'a leaden sky overhead [and] a bog underneath'.[1] Frank had to take sights standing ankle-deep in water and he received a shower from every bush he brushed against. By 3.30 in the afternoon it was too dark to read his instruments without the light of matches, and the team gave up for the day. They fought their way back to their camp through the tangled, soaking hemlock scrub, stumbling over rocks and logs and wading through pools of water on the way, arriving 'at dark – boots and leggings like soggy blotting paper'.[2] Having last eaten some bread and butter with a cup of tea at 11.30 in the morning, the men were hungry. In the meantime the camp cook had been busy. Supper was 'Beans mixed with Australian rabbit. Bread and prunes pie. (All side orders extra and unobtainable.)'[3] Even though it had been a tough day, the men's spirits lifted once they had eaten, and they had 'a fine time' singing 'every song they could remember from "My Bonnie" to "Clementine"'.[4]

Frank Swannell cooking venison for his crew at a survey camp in British Columbia.

The supplies Frank and his crew relied on were the same cheap, durable foods that had enabled the sixteenth-century exploration of the oceans: salt meat, hardtack and flour, beans and pulses, and a little grease or butter. This was similar to the industrial ration that fed Britain's labourers, and the men and women who continued to push outwards the boundaries of empire in the nineteenth century packed the same foods into their ships and canoes, packhorse saddlebags, wheelbarrows and wagons.[5] Over time, dried fruit, salt, sugar, tea, coffee and rum were added to the ration, and canned meat and biscuits packed in airtight tins became available. With these supplies Europeans made themselves warm and sustaining meals as they explored, exploited and settled the globe. Over the course of the nineteenth century, explorers, whalers, loggers, cowboys, shepherds and pioneer settlers harvested the world's marine resources and moved into what they told themselves was virgin territory, encroaching on forests and moving out over grasslands and prairies, continually incorporating peripheral areas into the core regions of white settlement.[6]

Even on the frontiers of settlement, Europeans went to great lengths to make proper leavened bread. In 1839, Kitturah Belknap and her husband were travelling west from Ohio onto the prairie lands of Iowa. As soon as they made camp, she would prepare 'salt rising' by mixing water, cornmeal, sliced potatoes and salt in a bowl. This she would leave on the warm ground to ferment overnight. Early the next morning she added the 'rising' to a flour-and-water dough to leaven it. She then baked the bread in a Dutch oven before they broke camp. That way they always had a supply of good bread for their journey.[7] In her account of the trek her family made from the Cape to the Hope Mountain mission (in what is now Zimbabwe) in 1874, Jessie Lovemore recalled how her mother had a similar camp routine. Each night she would prepare a leaven sponge and then bake the bread the next morning in her Dutch oven, a 'heavy cast-iron or wrought-iron flat pot, with a lid, on which one could heap coals. The procedure was to make a good fire and when there were enough hot embers, to put the pot containing bread or cake or meat on them and cover the lid with more.'[8]

Camp cooks who lacked a yeast substitute made soda breads. Frank Swannell's 'jewel' of a cook was a dab hand at making bannock, or scone bread. In August 1901, Frank wrote to his fiancée 'against the time when aforesaid mademoiselle will have to make cake for some fellow or other' to give her the cook's 'latest evolved recipe: Cake à la Survey: Musty flour – a sufficiency. Baking powder: a fistful. Raisins galore. Marmalade – as much as will stick to a clasp knife blade: syrup (with sandflies therein) – considerable. "Tin cow" – half tin cupful. Water: ad libitum. Mix. Place before a reflector [oven] with lots of fir bark on fire. Test for doneness with a hemlock sliver.' But if supplies were running short, at a pinch Frank's cook could make 'very iron clad affairs' out of just flour and snow water.[9]

Another camp standby was doughboys, or flour and lard dumplings. These were cooked by dropping them into the broth that formed around salt meat as it was cooking. 'Doughboys' were a favourite among the gangs of men who pushed into the world's forests and oceans, hunting for furs, logging timber, mining for minerals and precious metals, and harpooning whales in a frenzy of extraction that despoiled great tracts of land and drove the wildlife to the edge of extinction.[10] In Newfoundland, doughboys were known as 'lassie buns' as they were made with generous amounts of molasses and 'fat pork'. These substantial balls of carbohydrate gave lumberjacks and fishermen the energy they needed to fell timber and fish for cod.[11]

Reduced to its bare bones, however, the ration was severely vitamin-deficient. It needed to be supplemented with fresh meat and, if possible, local fruit and vegetables. Meals of salt beef stew poured over damper, and

173

cups of sweet tea, enabled Robert O'Hara Burke and William John Wills to cross the Australian continent from south to north in 1860. But they failed to take enough supplies for the return journey, and reduced to surviving on a few sticks of rotten meat and a handful of flour a day, they became too apathetic and weak to hunt the abundant wildlife. By the time they stumbled back into the territory of the Yandruwandha people, they were suffering from such dreadful vitamin B deficiency that their legs were virtually paralysed. Both men died.[12]

Naval officers understood that scurvy was a dietary disease caused by the shortcomings of the ration. Many thought that the salinity of sailors' food was the cause of their ill health, and for this reason the Admiralty dropped salt fish from the naval ration in 1733 and replaced it with oatmeal and sugar.[13] It was well known that fresh food alleviated scorbutic symptoms, and whenever the ships were in port, fresh meat and vegetables were issued; when they were at sea, lime juice and vinegar were doled out to the sailors. However, although scurvy was not a major cause of death in the eighteenth-century navy, it continued to be a problem and severely restricted naval efficiency, as it limited the amount of time ships could stay at sea.[14] The need to find a way of providing fresh food for sailors was pressing, for as the London physician Andrew Wynter described, 'England, with regard to her dependencies ... is like a city situated in the midst of a desert; vast foodless tracts have to be traversed by her ships, the camels of the ocean; and if [their] provisions are not entirely to be depended on, the position of the mariners might be likened to the people of a caravan whose water-bags are liable at any moment, without previous warning to burst, and to discharge the means of preserving life into the thirsting sands.'[15] The search for a solution to the problem stimulated the development of new food industries.

In 1804, the French government awarded Nicholas Appert a 12,000-franc prize for his innovative bottling method. This involved heating hermetically sealed glass jars of food to very high temperatures. His technique could be used to preserve virtually anything, from beef bouillon to green beans. The French newspapers praised Appert for having found a way to 'fix the seasons'. The British inventor Peter Durand learned of this process and patented the idea using tin cans instead of glass bottles. He then sold the patent to Bryan Donkin, a partner in an ironworks who had an eye for new ideas. In 1813, Gamble,

The Newfoundland cod fishery.

The hot and dangerous work of boiling sugar.

A scene from a London coffee house where gentlemen like Samuel Pepys were able to sample the new colonial drinks.

In the West Indies slaves were allowed to sell the vegetables they grew in their gardens at Sunday markets.

In the eighteenth century tea time became an established afternoon ritual in the homes of the wealthy.

A village scene in nineteenth-century India.

A Chinese sailor relaxing with a pipe of opium.

The interior of a nineteenth-century labourer's cottage of the kind so many left when they emigrated. Note the brown teapot on the table.

Meat was so plentiful and cheap in New Zealand that it was 'enough to make a man dance'.

Maori women preparing food in a traditional earth oven.

A group of Indian indentured labourers in British Guiana.

Indian indentured labourers on arrival in British Guiana.

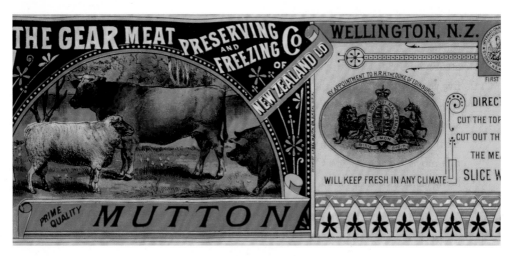

The Gear Meat Company won prizes for their tinned meats at the Sydney and Melbourne International Exhibitions in 1879 and 1880.

Donkin and Hall opened Britain's first food-canning factory in Blue Anchor Road, Bermondsey. Their canned meat received praise from illustrious celebrities: Joseph Banks tested it on behalf of the Royal Society, Lord Wellesley (later the Duke of Wellington) recommended it to the navy, and even King George III and Queen Charlotte claimed to have enjoyed their meal of canned beef.[16]

The commander of the navy's West India station immediately put in a request to the Admiralty to be sent a sample of Gamble, Donkin and Hall's 'patented preserved meats' for the hospital stores. He had heard that their canned 'bouilli' kept fresh even in the hottest climates. In 1815, he reported that it was far superior to the portable soup that had been introduced as a remedy for scorbutic sailors in the mid eighteenth century.[17] In 1819, an expedition to search for the Northwest Passage was one of the first to add tins from Gamble & Co. to the usual stores of flour and salt meat. On their return, the expedition surgeon attributed the good health of the men to the preserved meats and soups.[18] Only five years after setting up the factory, Gamble, Donkin and Hall were supplying the Admiralty with more than £5,000 worth of canned roast, corned, seasoned and boiled beef, mutton and veal, as well as beef bouillon and vegetable soup.[19] As the navy was their main customer, in 1821 John Gamble (now sole proprietor) moved the factory to Cork, the centre for naval beef supplies. Rather than being salted down in barrels to make 'Irish horse', Irish cattle were now packed into tin cans and renamed 'clews and lashing' (hammock cords), as the overcooked beef tended to form into an unappetising 'conglomeration of strings'.[20] In 1831, the Admiralty made it compulsory for all ships of the line to carry tinned meat as medical provisions for sick and ailing sailors, and in 1847, it was added to the ration scale for the ordinary sailor.[21] On alternate beef days they were allotted three quarters of a pound of canned meat along with a quarter of a pound of canned potatoes or rice. Each naval mess was issued with a special lever knife so that they could open the tins.[22] In the sailors' parlance, 'boeuf bouilli' became 'bully beef', a term still used by the army in the twentieth century.[23]

Many people were convinced that canned meats were the means of saving sailors from their 'salt junk' diet.[24] However, faith in the new-fangled preservation method was shaken by the Goldner scandal, when in 1852 inspectors at the Royal Clarence Victualling Yard in Portsmouth discovered that hundreds of tins in the navy store contained putrid meat. As they made their grim discovery they were overcome by nausea, and afterwards the stench could only be removed by coating the storeroom floor with chloride of lime.[25]

Eventually the navy had to throw away cans to the value of more than £6,000. Stephen Goldner, the navy's supplier since 1845, had set up a factory in Moldova, where both meat and labour were cheap, but he made the mistake of trying to cut costs further by using larger tins holding 9 and 14 lb of meat. This overstretched the infant canning technology as they were too big to be heated to a sufficient temperature all the way through. The navy cancelled its contract with him and instead set up its own canning factory.[26] The hostile, anti-Semitic press coverage of the government enquiry drove Goldner's London agent, Samuel Sextus Ritchie, into exile in Australia. He arrived in Melbourne in 1857 and set himself up as a wine and spirit merchant, but by the 1870s he had opened a canning operation, which quickly became the largest in Australia. By the turn of the century, Melbourne's exports of canned meat were virtually all rabbit; this was almost certainly the source of the 'Australian rabbit' that Frank Swannell and his men had in their bean stew in British Columbia in 1901.[27]

The furore did nothing to promote the cause of canned meat among the general public, who now associated canned goods with food poisoning. Joseph Banks's testimonial was also of limited value, as his description of Gamble's canned goods as 'embalmed Provisions' conjured up images of mummified rather than fresh and nutritious food.[28] In a similar vein, because the meat was cut up into small pieces in order to be inserted into the cans through a small stud hole, sailors gave it the grim moniker 'Fanny Adams', after an 8-year-old girl who was dismembered by her murderer.[29] Advertising emphasised that cans could be opened years later to reveal good meat, but for many this seemed to suggest that the 'freshness' of the product was illusory. According to Anthony Trollope, the working man preferred half a pound of fresh meat to even a whole pound of coarse-grained, fatty tinned mutton.[30] Besides, canned goods were expensive: Gamble charged the navy between 1s. 8d and 3s. a pound for his products.[31] Canned meat made little economic sense except for those such as sailors and explorers who needed to take stores with them on long journeys. By the last quarter of the nineteenth century, cans had become standard issue on any expedition.

If the domestic response to canned goods was lacklustre, in the colonies their reception was enthusiastic. Tins of pâté de foie gras and truffles joined the jars of pickles and bottles of Indian pale ale on the shelves of grocery stores in India and America.[32] In the 1830s, Emma Roberts observed that the 'delicacies of an entertainment consist of hermetically-sealed salmon … raspberry jam and dried fruits; these articles coming from Europe and being sometimes very difficult to procure in a fresh and palmy state, are prized accordingly'.[33] Tinned foods were a boon to those living in isolation. There was no supply of fresh eggs at Fort Abraham Lincoln on the Missouri River in the 1870s. Lieutenant Colonel Custer was stationed there with his cavalry unit in order to provide protection from the Sioux for the survey crews and railroad workers who were advancing the Northern Pacific Railroad across the plains of North Dakota. Mrs Custer was able to compensate for the lack by procuring 'crystallized eggs' in airtight cans.[34]

By the 1850s, John Gamble's canning firm had turned from naval supplies towards the colonial market. When he displayed his wares at the Great Exhibition in 1851, the pyramid of his company's tins contained preserved ham 'for use in India, China etc. … soup and boili, for emigrants and troops at sea. Pheasants, partridges etc., preserved … whole … so as to keep in any climate, and for an unlimited length of time.'[35] Soon afterwards, Gamble's firm was bought by Crosse & Blackwell. In the 1830s, Edmund Crosse and Thomas Blackwell reoriented their oilman's business away from the provision of seal and whale fat towards luxury provisions. In 1840, they sent their first consignment of pickles, fruits, mustard, vinegar and capers to India and began to look towards the empire market. Now, in the mid nineteenth century, the manufacture of provisions began to turn into an industry; by the 1860s, Crosse & Blackwell had three purpose-built factories and two warehouses on the Thames.[36]

When Henry Mayhew visited one of these factories in 1865, he was struck by the scale of production. In the gas-lit bottling room, hundreds of women, their arms stained as yellow as the legs of game cocks with the pickle juice, stood along a gallery packing the 'primrose-coloured cauliflower-sprouts … white onions, like so many glass marbles [and] … huge olive-green caterpillar-like gherkins' into square glass jars.[37] He was astonished by the mountains of sugar (a ton a day) and rivers of vinegar (2,500 gallons a week) they used, and the fact that they churned out 350 hogsheads of anchovy sauce a year. He could not imagine 'where on earth all the fish comes from that has to be eaten with this amount of sauce'.[38] The fish was in the colonies, Crosse & Blackwell's major market. In 1871, Edmund Hull, author of a handbook to India, acknowledged that 'the Englishman abroad owes a debt of gratitude to the enterprise of such firms as Crosse & Blackwell ... whose pickles, preserved fruits, meats, soups, tin hams, tongues, bacon, and indeed oilman's stores are probably unsurpassed, and for soundness generally to be depended upon'.[39]

In biscuit factories mechanisation was in full swing. Contemporaries had just become accustomed to the idea that shirts and trousers could be stitched by sewing machines; now they were confronted by the astonishing fact that biscuits could be manufactured in such a way that 'from the time when the flour and other ingredients are put into the mixers to the time when the biscuits are packed into tins ... they are scarcely touched by the hands of the work people'.[40] Pioneering bakers Thomas Huntley, William Palmer and J. D. Carr had moved biscuit manufacture out of their baker's shops and into purpose-built factories where steam-powered machines rolled out the dough and cut the biscuits and 'travelling ovens' baked them while they passed through on a conveyor belt on their way to the packing area. 'Biscuits by machinery!' exclaimed Mayhew. 'It strikes on the ear almost as funnily, at first, as chickens produced by steam.'[41]

The biscuit factories manufactured thousands of tons of biscuits a year.[42] Indeed, they produced such large quantities that Mayhew remarked that 'it seemed as though biscuits constituted the staple article of the food of the entire human race, rather than being the mere toothsome snacks of a small portion of mankind'.[43] They were making enough biscuits to supply a mass market, but not at mass-market prices. At 6d for a quarter of a pound, even the most ordinary ginger nuts cost as much as a labourer might earn in a day.[44] Their market was the rest of the world. France, Belgium and the Netherlands absorbed 70 per cent of Britain's biscuit exports in 1870, but the remaining 30 per cent were sent all over the globe.[45] Packed into airtight tin boxes, manufactured biscuits remained fresh for months or even years, no matter what the external climatic conditions. This made them excellent provisions for explorers, military men and colonial officials. In the 1880s, a geological survey team in Southern Rhodesia wrote to Carr's to inform them that a tin of their biscuits kept in the toolbox of a car for two years had recently been opened. To their delight, the biscuits were still crisp and delicious.[46]

Biscuit tins, unlike cans and bottles, were not thrown away, as they could be used for a variety of purposes even when empty of their original contents. In the 1860s, an English traveller noticed that a nomadic Mongolian chieftainess used a large biscuit tin as a travelling garden in which to grow garlic to flavour her mutton stews.[47] In 1879, British troops fought the Zulus at the Battle of Rorke's Drift from behind barricades constructed out of Carr's of Carlisle biscuit tins.[48] When the British defeated Mahdist forces near Khartoum in 1898, they retrieved from the battlefield a scabbard held together with strips of metal cut from a Huntley & Palmer's biscuit tin. In the twentieth century, a Christian congregation in Uganda used 2 lb biscuit tins as containers for their Bibles to protect them from the ravages of white ants.[49] And in the 1940s, there was a craze in Nubia, on the River Nile, for decorating mud houses with relief work of flowers and art deco designs inspired by the 'Bouquet Assorted' and 'Wisteria' Huntley & Palmer Christmas biscuit tins.[50]

After the Indian Rebellion in 1857, the East India Company was relieved of its territorial possessions and in 1858 India was made a Crown colony. The old-style Company merchant who behaved like an Indian grandee, wore comfortable white pyjamas, smoked a hookah, often had an Indian mistress and socialised easily with the Indian elite had long since been replaced by the burra sahib: the personification of polite middle-class British society. The notion took hold in the 1820s and 1830s that Company officials should act as agents of Western civilisation. Their task was to bring India into the modern age by eradicating disturbing Indian practices such as *suttee* (widow burning) and promoting the rule of law and justice. In his neat black suit the burra sahib demonstrated that he was prepared to endure any amount of discomfort in order to keep up standards.[51] Now that the officers of the Indian civil service were representatives of the British Crown, they were more than ever expected to enact the physical and moral superiority of the British race and maintain national prestige at all times.

Prestige was a concept that in the nineteenth century came to govern the behaviour of British officials throughout the Empire. It found expression in the adoption of an authoritative manner and an air of invincibility. In the colonies, British men and women were permanently on display to the 'natives'. In all areas of life, no matter how trivial or domestic, they were expected to uphold proper standards of dress, cleanliness and deportment.[52] In particular, the colonial dining room was seen as a stage where the official put on a perform-ance of civilisation. Handbooks such as *The Englishwoman in India* (1864) offering advice to 'ladies proceeding to ... the East Indies' recommended shipping out crates of table linen and Wedgwood china, silver cruets, cutlery and crystal glasses so that their dining tables would mirror those of the 'best

Colonial officials in India putting on a performance of Britishness at their dining table.

regulated establishments' at 'home'.[53] When in February 1900 Isabella Russel found herself entertaining the Roman Catholic Bishop of Senegambia while he was on a visit to Bathurst in British Gambia, she relied heavily on the town's collective stock of tableware to create the desired effect. In a letter home to her sister, she described the table covered with pink silk and laid with pretty dishes and silver spoons, borrowed sherry glasses and her good Wedgwood grey, white and gold dinner service.[54]

The ideal menu was of 'dishes approved by the taste of polite society at home'.[55] But this could be difficult to achieve. Market gardens growing European vegetables did spring up around European cantonments in India, but more often than not colonial memsahibs were forced to resort to tinned foods in order to create a semblance of a European meal. At dinner parties in India, often 'the fish would be tinned, the bacon, the pâté de foie gras, asparagus and cheese'.[56] Isabella Russel enclosed the menu for the bishop's dinner in her letter to her sister. 'It may interest you to know what West Africa can produce', she wrote with pride, even though 'we have tinned things and no ice or such luxuries'. The basis of the meal was the local fare of groundnuts made into a soup, boiled mutton ('too poor to roast here') and roast pigeon, transformed into the more elegant-sounding 'Potage d'arrachides', 'Gigot de Mouton' and 'Pigeon rotis'. Tinned peas, marrons glacé and bottled almonds and raisins added a touch of finesse.[57]

IN THE STORE-ROOM

Although I am strongly against the use of tinned things
to the extent that many allow, there are nevertheless
many articles which you *must* have in the store-room:
pickles, sauces, jams, bacon, cheese, macaroni, vermicelli, vinegars, flavouring essences, the invaluable
truffle, tart fruits, biscuits, isinglass, arrowroot, oatmeal, pearl barley, cornflour, olives, capers, dried herbs
and so on. Grated Parmesan cheese (sold in bottles by
Crosse & Blackwell) should never be forgotten, the salad
oil should be the best procurable, and no store-room
should be without tarragon vinegar, anchovy vinegar,
French vinegar, and white wine vinegar. Amongst sauces
I consider 'Harvey' the best for general use; Sutton's
'Empress of India' is a strong sauce with a real flavour
of mushrooms; Moir's sauces and 'Reading Sauce' are
very trustworthy ... but I denounce 'Worcester sauce'
and 'Tapp's sauce' as agents too powerful to be trusted
to the hands of the native cook. Sutton's essence of anchovies is said to possess the charm of not clotting, or
forming a stoppage in the neck of the bottle. I have deep
respect for both walnut and mushroom ketchup, soy,
and tomato conserve. Then, as special trifles, we must
not forget caviar, *olives farcies*, and anchovies in oil.[58]

Wherever they were, the men and women who made the Empire tried to create moments of Britishness in their unfamiliar surroundings. European provisions took on magical qualities in these distant settings. In 1914, Laura Boyle and her husband were entertained by the outgoing district officer in their Gold Coast posting deep in the West African bush. 'Anyone looking from the dark African night into the lighted rest-house dining-room across the wide verandah' would have witnessed the enactment of an 'almost European dinner party', she wrote. 'The men in white mess jackets with bright yellow cummerbunds and I in a cool white dress … records of Wagner and Beethoven's Moonlight Sonata playing as an accompaniment.'[59] Tinned food played an essential part in this re-creation of 'home'. As the Boyles set off on the ten-day journey to Wenchi from the railhead at Kumasi, the carriers hoisted onto their heads box after box containing tins of tomato and turtle soup; asparagus and mushrooms; sardines, bacon and kidneys; cherries, pears, plums and strawberries.[60]

Not every colonial officer could afford to rely on tins to re-create Britain in their patch of empire. When in 1943 Margery Hall moved into her new home in the remote town of Phutipura, near Jacobabad in British India's Sind Desert, she was horrified by what she found. The compound was overrun by rats, and on inspecting the kitchen, she discovered that it was 'black all over … obviously scrubbing was not in the cook's schedule'.[61] Isolated and unbearably hot, she thought Phutipura 'a vile and horrible place'.[62] She could not believe that her husband, a member of the Indian Political Service, had been posted there with a young family. At night she was tortured by the heat and a terrible stench seeping into their bedroom. It was coming from the servants' latrine, which she discovered was overflowing and crawling with maggots.

The Halls could not afford to eat tinned food on a daily basis. For most of the year the only vegetables available in the local bazaar were potatoes, pumpkins and 'some green attenuated things like desiccated cucumbers', probably bitter gourds.[63] Their cook made these into simple curries and the family ate them with rice and chapattis, as yeast to make leavened bread was unobtainable. Then, in the cold weather, they were told that a number of senior officials would be passing through on their district tour: Margery and her husband, Henry, would be expected to entertain them. The requirements of prestige sent her to her store cupboard. On the evening in question, the small party sat down to a simulacrum of a British meal. The centrepiece was cold roast pigeon. Little did Margery's guests know that the bird had, only that morning, been cooing contentedly on the walls that surrounded their compound. Henry had shot it and then Margery had plucked and roasted it in the freshly scrubbed, but still primitive, kitchen. It was accompanied by 'tinned vegetables topped by home-made salad-dressing'. Dessert was 'tinned fruit topped by meringue and served with cream from my own pasteurized milk'. Margery had prepared everything herself before the guests arrived and then joined the party 'as hostess, pretend-ing I had a cook'. In order to complete the charade, she even dug out her hus-band's dinner jacket and put on a 'rather nice sort of rayon dress ... Rather chic at home; now clinging in a great soaking wet patch to my back and waist. Not at all chic in the tropics.'[64]

It was, as Margery herself pointed out, 'all very silly, really', but the con-ventions of the Empire meant that it was always of paramount importance to keep up appearances. Margery would have been mortified if her guests had dis-covered the reason why she was without a cook. Only a few weeks before, he had bolted when she discovered the brothel he had been running in a spare hut in the compound. She had 'flung open the door' and her eyes had fallen on 'familiar objects. My spare bed, my mattress, my lamps ... All, no doubt, crawling with syphilis and goodness knows what other filthy germs from the filthy bazaar.'[65] It was one of the few times in her life that Margery completely lost her temper.

This insistence on maintaining British standards was not just about an apparently relentless demonstration of racial superiority. The colonial imitation of British meals was an attempt to cling to the familiar in unfamiliar and often threatening surroundings. In Phutipura, Margery felt besieged by filth and disease. Years later, she was able to see the incident with her brothel-keeping cook as amusing, but at the time, she was angry because she was fright-ened. 'Everything revolved around the safety of the family,' she explained, and 'everything that threatened that safety was very important'.[66] Cheshire cheese, Huntley & Palmer biscuits and tins of Crosse & Blackwell mushroom soup helped to construct safe British oases in the wilds of the Empire. A peculiar by-product of this was that, regardless of their actual place of origin, preserved, processed, tinned and industrial foods were transmogrified in the British col-onies into emblems of 'home'. Scandinavian reindeer tongues, sardines caught off the coast of Brittany, soup made from West Indian turtles, marmalade made with Spanish oranges – all acted as potent triggers for nostalgic memories and thus carried with them an aura of Britishness.[67] So important was the association of these products with 'home' that William Underwood, who opened a bottling and canning factory in America, sold his pickles, ketchups, bottled tomatoes, tinned lobster and tinned milk in India, Batavia, Hong Kong, Gibraltar, Manila, the West Indies and South America under a label on which was clearly printed, 'Made in England'.[68]

A typical Anglo-Indian dinner-party dish, heavily reliant on the tinned goods and bottled sauces the good house-keeper in India was instructed to keep in her storeroom.

DARNES DE SEER À LA PÉRIGUEUX

Stew a couple of handsome slices of seer fish in a good broth made from bones and trimmings, assisted by an onion, a carrot, a bunch of parsley, a dessert-spoonful of preserved thyme and marjoram, a minced anchovy, a dozen pepper corns, a table-spoonful of mushroom ketchup, a table-spoonful of Harvey sauce, a table-spoonful of vinegar, a table-spoonful of chablis or sauterne. Let the fish slices cook slowly in this broth, and when done, drain and place them in a very hot dish, carefully covered up. Strain the broth in which they were cooked, thicken it, add a little well browned gravy, and throw into it a couple of table-spoonfuls of chopped truffles (previously tossed in a frying-pan in an ounce of butter, and a table-spoonful of Madeira) and let the sauce simmer for ten minutes to extract the flavour of the truffles. When ready, pour it over the slices and serve.[69]

The contribution of the food sector to Britain's industrial growth is easily over-looked. The sorting, peeling, chopping, brining and cooking was still largely done by calloused hands, and therefore the emergence of food-processing factories does not naturally fit into the dominant narrative of mechanisation.[70] However, food processing made a significant contribution to the foundation of Britain's industrial might.[71] In the same way that the Newfoundland fisheries and London sugar refineries stimulated the growth of supplementary industries in the seventeenth century, the canning, pickle and biscuit factories of the nineteenth century were supported by a host of flour mills, vinegar breweries and market gardens.[72] The Maling pottery in Newcastle, producing the stoneware jars used by the preserves and pickles industry, became the biggest pottery in the world. T. T. Vicars, run by William Palmer's cousins with whom he invented the coal-fired travelling oven in 1856, went on to become one of the country's foremost engineering firms.[73]

Moreover, the growth and success of the British food-processing industry relied on the worldwide market of Britain's commercial empire.[74] Given that they manufactured foods that barely featured in the diets of most of the population, it was impressive that Huntley & Palmer's production represented one thousandth of Britain's total industrial production; by 1905, they were the country's thirty-eighth largest company by value.[75] In the 1870s, Britain's top three food exports were refined sugar, fish, and pickles and table sauces. Every year, Crosse & Blackwell sent to India, Australia and China more than 30,000 one-pound tins of Oxford sausages, 34,000 half-pint cans of oysters, more than 3,000 dried ox tongues, 17,000 cans of Cheddar and Berkeley cheese, and over a thousand plum puddings.[76] The company's slogan, 'The name that is known to the ends of the earth', said it all.

14

In which the Reverend Daniel Tyerman and Mr George Bennet attend a tea party in Raiatea, the Society Islands (4 December 1822)

How the spread of European provisions colonised taste

On 4 December 1822, the Reverend Daniel Tyerman and Mr George Bennet were delighted to take part in a 'public festival' held at the City of David settlement on the island of Raiatea, one of the Society Islands, north-west of Tahiti. The two men had come to the South Pacific on behalf of the London Missionary Society as part of a world tour of the society's various mission stations. The festival, held on a large stone pier stretching out into the sea, made a picturesque spectacle. The 'rough coral pavement' had been strewn with a carpet of grass and awnings of bark had been rigged up in order to provide shade. The two visitors counted 'two hundred and forty-one sofas, and about half as many tables', 'loaded with the rich provision which Nature throws from her lap at the feet of her children in these remote nurseries'.[1]

The missionaries remarked that the food was 'principally vegetable', although a few families brought along 'baked hogs and fish'.[2] But they were less interested in what the party was eating than in their table manners and general conduct. The two men were impressed by the islanders' tablecloths fashioned out of native bark cloth, and the fact that cheerful family groups were seated on chairs and stools they had made themselves. They dismissed the dinner services as 'motley', but praised the hats and bonnets everyone wore, made out of plaited bark and, in the case of the women, decorated with colourful bark ribbons.[3] Many of the islanders, they noted with satisfaction, were 'decently' dressed, and some even 'gracefully clad', although a few wore a 'mongrel mixture of European and native habilments'; an aged chief had put his white shirt on *over* his black coat, 'taking care that … the laps fall below the linen behind'.[4] Various chiefs gave after-dinner speeches comparing the islanders' 'former glutton, nakedness, riot, brutality, filthy customs, and obscene talk' to their 'present manner of feasting … dress … purer enjoyments … more courteous behaviour, the cleanliness of their persons, and the delicacy of their language'.[5] Tyerman and Bennet were convinced that the islanders had been transformed by their missionaries into respectable Christians.

In 1822, the concept of respectability was still relatively new. The word had only just begun to be used to imply good character and that a person was 'worthy of respect … by reason of moral excellence', rather than simply describing someone's position in the social hierarchy.[6] Within the new definition, to be respectable was to be conversant with genteel behaviour. The London Missionary Society's representatives were pleased to note that the Raiateans had embraced a range of behaviours that allowed them to claim entrance into the global community of respectable, God-fearing Christians.[7] Their missionary had taught them well. Their manners were pleasant, they were clean and decently clad; they gathered together in family groups, the nineteenth century's ideal social instrument for instilling moral behaviour; and they had adopted one of the central rituals of respectable British family life: tea-drinking.

Once the feast had been eaten, speeches had been made, and everyone had sheltered from a rain shower, the assembly reconvened to take tea, or, as the islanders called it, *pape mahauahana*, meaning 'warm water'. Their 'equipage for tea-drinking was quite as heterogeneous as the dinner-services … some had kettles, and others had tea-pots; these could manage very well together, if, in addition, one could raise a cup, a second a saucer, and a third a porringer. A few – a few only – had got tea, many had no sugar; but everyone had something – whether an ingredient or a utensil – employed in preparing or partaking this favourite refreshment.'[8] The visiting missionaries were amused to notice that 'one party heated water in a frying-pan'. The majority of the company collected their drink from 'a large vat, or sugar-boiler, which was brought down to the shore, and filled with water slightly sweetened, but without any infusion of the Chinese plant'. The variety of drinking vessels included 'pots, plates, delft-ware, porringers, cans, glasses, and even bottles', but most used 'their own native and elegantly-sculptured cups' made from coconut shells.[9] Tyerman and Bennet were so impressed

'The Reception of the Reverend J. Williams at Tanna the Day Before He Was Massacred' (and eaten). In 1841 the islanders of Tanna put a sudden end to Williams' mission to introduce South Sea islanders to tea, time-keeping and Christianity.

by the sober yet joyous nature of the occasion that they were convinced that even the missionary society's enemies would have been won over.[10]

According to the resident missionary, John Williams, a more effective tool for conversion than a succession of prayer meetings was to instil in the islanders a number of civilised habits. He installed a large clock on the island and expected them to organise their lives according to its chimes.[11] He gave them lessons in furniture- and dress-making, and he was a particularly firm believer in the civilising power of tea-drinking. Soon after he came to live on Raiatea, he made a trip to Sydney, returning not only with cows, calves, sheep, two chapel bells, decent clothes for the women, shoes and stockings, but also a selection of kettles, cups and tea itself. 'When they have Tea,' he explained, 'they will want Sugar, Tea Cups – they will want a Table ... then they will want seats to set on. Thus, we hope that European customs in a very short time will be wholly introduced in the leeward stations.'[12]

In Britain, the ritual of afternoon tea allowed middle-class women to participate in a respectable form of consumption. The purchase of a china tea service was not the profligate spending of the aristocracy but the measured acquisition of goods to make the home a comfortable sanctuary. When Josiah Wedgwood began to manufacture porcelain tea sets in his Staffordshire factory in the 1760s, the middle-class housewife's respectable habits contributed to Britain's economic growth.[13] Williams was attempting to set a similar process in motion in the South Pacific. He brought a young man back from Sydney with him to instruct the islanders in the arts of growing tobacco and boiling sugar. Just as a craving for sweetness and smoke had encouraged industriousness among the British labouring classes, Williams hoped that a liking for these small luxuries would encourage the islanders to work hard enough to earn the money to buy them. The desire to consume would inextricably link them to the outside world, reinforcing their newly learned habits and providing constant motivation to continue to behave respectably. The missionary hoped that, eventually, belief would follow and that the habits of respectability would become the outward manifestation of the islanders' inward transformation.[14] He used tea as a bait to draw them into the capitalist economy. Throughout the Empire, colonial administrations used rations in the same way: to draw native peoples into their sphere of control.

In Australia, settlers began moving inland from their coastal settlements in the 1830s and 1840s, bringing with them flocks of sheep and herds of cattle. Prospecting for new sheep runs north of Melbourne along the Murray River in the 1840s, Edward Curr gazed out over 'open, grassy, forest land' extending as far as he could see. 'The grass underfoot, as yet undefiled by flock or herd … as green and fresh as Eden, and the landscape generally bathed in a sort of hazy sunlight.'[15] His vision of the country as untouched and empty was an illusion, of course. The area was home to the Wurundjeri, Boonwurrung and Walthaurong people, who had managed the grassland – and the animals that grazed on it – for centuries. In a series of violent spats and skirmishes, the Aborigines were dispossessed of their land. As the settlers created new sheep runs and cattle ranches, they wiped out traditional food sources, shut the Aborigines out of their hunting and foraging ranges, and cut them off from water holes.[16]

On the other side of the continent, the Yalonga people, who managed the land around the Swan River settlement that would eventually become Perth, tried to continue using their land according to their time-honoured seasonal pattern, despite the arrival of European sheep farmers on the high alluvial terraces. The grasslands were dotted with yam patches marked by thickets of dogwood. The Yalonga had been careful to preserve them from the fires they used to burn off the undergrowth, as yams were their chief food during the rainy season, when the earth softened sufficiently for them to dig out the long, thin, tasty roots. In 1833, George Fletcher Moore allowed them onto his up-river farm to harvest yams despite his disquiet that digging them out of the ground left it pitted with deep holes dangerous to his sheep. When the group arrived the following year, they discovered that the animals had eaten the yam vines to the ground. Instead, they began harvesting red gum blossoms to make into a festive drink. In May, the group were still on what Moore thought of as his land, now digging the root of a swamp flag to make a starchy flour that they baked into damper. Moore summoned the army, whose mere arrival drove the Aborigines away. They were now regarded as trespassers on their own land.[17] When a Yalonga woman went onto William Leeder's farm in 1836 to harvest reed rhizomes, the settler declared her 'a notorious thief'.[18]

Recognising that agricultural settlement had encroached on native hunting grounds to the extent that it was no longer feasible for the continent's Aboriginal inhabitants to live by hunting and gathering, the Australian administration felt obliged to hand out food rations.[19] On outback farms the itinerant white workforce were paid 'Ten, ten, two & a Quarter: 10 lb flour, 10 lb meat, 2 lb sugar, ¼ lb tea'. Out of these supplies, the men made the signature frontier meal of meat fry and damper, swallowed down with copious amounts of sweet tea.[20] The Aboriginal feeding stations the government set up in frontier districts doled out similar rations − 1 lb bread, ⅓ oz tea, and 1½ oz sugar − in return for 'good behaviour'. Even though the ration did not include meat, when the Aborigines were found to have speared livestock, the rations were withheld. Tobacco was given out as a reward for compliance.[21]

Cattle and sheep stations were perennially short of cheap labour. In an effort to persuade Aborigines to come and work as shepherds and cattle herders, the ranchers began doling out rations to their dependants.[22] In this way, the Aborigines were transformed into resident station workforces. In Queensland, the natives watched the cattle ranchers and learned how to train their dogs to round up the livestock and corral them in pens built out of scrub. Using these techniques, they were able to run off large numbers of the settlers' cattle.[23] To persuade them to desist, the ranchers included beef in the rations they gave out.

In the end, it was easier to have a stationary population of natives living in a camp on the ranch than to deal with bands of Aborigines roaming about the property. Therefore any newcomer who wandered in was given a small parcel of food rations to entice them to stay.[24]

As we have seen with the Wychwood farm labourers who settled in Hawke's Bay, New Zealand, land hunger – the desire to secure a stake in the land that could then be passed on to the children – was a major driving force propelling the nineteenth-century surge of European emigration. As Europeans began to move out onto the Canadian prairies in the 1870s, the native peoples watching gangs of men dragging chains, sighting straight lines between landmarks, and hammering posts into the ground must have felt the same sense of dread as the Catholics in Cromwell's Ireland, where William Petty's Down Survey presaged the arrival of English and Scottish settlers. Petty's scaled maps, accurately showing the acreage, rental value and ownership of every scrap of land, set the standard for the many colonial surveys that were to follow.[25] Demoralised by European diseases, alcoholism and malnutrition, the Canadian First Nations did not have the strength to defend their territories, unlike their compatriots to the south, who met American encroachment with violence.[26] On the prairies west of Winnipeg, they did, however, show their contempt for the annexation of their land by 'defecat[ing] on the top of every available stake'.[27] The First Nations were corralled into reserves. Here, like the Australian Aborigines, they became dependent on handouts of meat, flour, sugar and tea. The government manipulated the rations shamelessly, withdrawing them when the people refused to co-operate and increasing them to encourage compliance.[28]

The same ration was doled out throughout the Empire to natives who worked as porters, servants and labourers. The universal distribution of the ration accustomed native peoples to British foodstuffs. Like the working classes in Britain, they fell under the spell of tea and sugar: those addictive groceries that staved off hunger and provided empty calories. In 1896, the issuer of rations at Mount Serle, about 600 kilometres north of Adelaide, made a desperate appeal for supplies of sugar and tea to be sent post-haste. Although he had plenty of flour, this did not appease the Aborigines. It was no use, he explained, 'telling them I have no tea & sugar, they expect their usual ration every Week'.[29]

Not all indigenous peoples were reduced to abject subjugation by their encounter with white settlers. The New Zealand Maoris acquired white men's boats for themselves and used them to go muttonbirding, gathering tasty fledgling shearwater from their nests on sea cliffs. They took to stock-raising and integrated the white potato into their diet, which helped to make them such ferocious warriors that the British had trouble defeating them. But even the Maoris were seduced by the white man's foods, which needed far less time to prepare, and began to reserve their traditional foods for special occasions.[30]

The deluge of white settlers eventually obliterated the indigenous ways of life. By 1900, a brewery stood on the site of the Yalonga clan's favourite camp-site, and city blocks covered the ground where they had hunted for wallabies, lizards and crayfish and gathered yams and zamia nuts.[31] The beans, squash and maize of the North Americans; the cured buffalo of the Plains Indians; the fern root, taro and kumara preparations of the Maori; the reed rhizome dampers and grilled frog of the Australian Aborigines – all were vanquished by the bland and unsophisticated frontier meal.[32] During the nineteenth century, a comprehensive colonisation of taste took place. Salt-beef stew and damper or salt pork and doughboys were the first truly global meals.[33] Made with foodstuffs sourced from all over the world, the British diet tied an ever-increasing proportion of the world's population into the trading system of the British Empire.

On the tables of the colonial elites, canned salmon, tinned mushrooms, bottled peas, Carr's Captain's Thins, and Crosse & Blackwell's pickles, sauces, jellies and jams were the tools of prestige that, as we saw in the previous chapter, enabled colonial officials to put on a theatrical performance of their British identity at their dining tables. The importance colonial officials placed on preserving their national eating habits meant that the dismal, pseudo-British colonial cuisine was accorded more respect than it warranted. Margery Hall was given a taste of her own medicine in Phutipura when a local Indian dignitary invited the Halls to dine. As we have seen, rather than serving some visiting civil service officials the family's usual semi-Indian-style dinner of chapattis and pumpkin curry, Margery had concocted an English dinner out of roast pigeon, tinned vegetables and fruit. Likewise, her Indian acquaintance wished 'to show off his skill and sophistication' by demonstrating that he was capable of emulating British eating habits. Margery arrived hoping for a 'nice curry' only to be confronted with a 'terrible soup, terrible roast meat – looked like fried entrails which I think it was – followed by very, very old cheese, and biscuits with little walkies [weevils] and their eggs clinging to the sides'.[34] A number of other locals were invited to the dinner and 'were presented with knives and forks for the first time ... the food was shot all round the plates, the tables, themselves, their beards, and us. The cowards abandoned the chase and ceased to eat; the brave abandoned the knives and forks and used their fingers.'[35]

Margery's account sought to entertain rather than disparage, but a lofty tone of distanced amusement was the standard British response towards any Indian who adopted British manners and habits. The London Missionary Society's representatives displayed this attitude when they described the Pacific Islanders' motley tea services and their eccentric use of European garb. For Tyerman and Bennet the islanders were children whose savagery could be glimpsed through the holes in their armour of respectability. That they should strive to emulate European ways was laudable, but the prospect of actually giving these 'natives' full admission to the club of respectable Christian gentlemen made the two men palpably uneasy. In India, Western-educated Indians fully conversant with British manners and customs posed a particular challenge. By mastering the outward symbols of British superiority, they claimed to also possess the inner qualities of an Englishman, and this strengthened their claim to political and social equality. As the Indian elite took on one British habit after another, officials engaged in an unedifying struggle to put them in their place, objecting, for example, when Indians in their presence did not remove their European lace-up shoes as they would have done if they had been wearing sandals, and poking fun at those who swapped their turbans for brimless caps so as to be able to doff them.[36]

Even though the British routinely dismissed the idea that the 'natives' might be able to produce a proper English meal, colonial elites persisted in their efforts. In British Honduras, the indigenous middle classes denigrated local 'bush' foods and favoured the consumption of imported European produce. As a result, they eschewed game and freshly caught shellfish in favour of tinned Australian rabbit and cans of American lobster. The ultimate absurdity was their purchase of 'English' boxes of imported tapioca (cassava granules) to make 'shape', a bland and archetypical colonial dessert, when cassava grew in the colony in abundance.[37] Indeed, throughout the nineteenth century, food imports made up 60 per cent by value of all the goods imported into British Honduras.[38]

Some upper-class Indian households employed an 'English' and an 'Indian' cook. When he was studying in Hyderabad in the 1930s, Prakash Tandon was invited to dine with a friend. He was disappointed when in succession watery soup, chops, fried fish, roast mutton and steamed pudding appeared on the table. However, he had mistaken for the meal itself what in fact was simply a demonstration that the family were au fait with British customs. As the servants were removing the dishes, his host turned to him and explained that this part of the meal was just a 'touch of modern formality'. Prakash regretted that he had politely swallowed down the insipid fare, as now the servants brought in 'an un-believable succession of ... pullaos, biryanis, naans and famaishes, rogan joshes and qormas ... quails and patrtridges'. Having picked at the British dishes, the family fell upon these with gusto.[39] Indian state banquets today mirror the practice of this Hyderabadi family. Although the majority of the dishes are a medley drawn from India's different regions in an effort to showcase Indian culture to the visiting dignitary, the first course is always a European-style soup.[40]

In Africa, the influence of Western eating habits was at its greatest in the cities. Bread and rice were much easier to prepare than indigenous grains, and urban Africans became increasingly reliant on industrially processed wheat flour, white rice, mealie (maize) meal and sugar, all imported by colonial wholesalers.[41] In the twentieth century, West Africa began importing rice from Indochina and wheat from the United States.[42] Tinned sardines, condensed milk and white sugar penetrated deep into the African countryside. In Northern Rhodesia in 1939, the anthropologist Audrey Richards observed four young Bemba men who lived in a village close to a white settlement eating 'white' foodstuffs 'apparently entirely for their kudos value'. After their customary meal of porridge and relish, they sat down at a table in full view of the rest of the community and shared a tin of sardines.[43] Colonial contact inexorably drew peripheral areas into its sphere of influence, undermining indigenous eating cultures and integrating them into the commercial food world of the Empire. Richards commented: 'it is an unfortunate fact that the diet of many primitive peoples has deteriorated in contact with white civilization rather than the reverse'.[44]

PART

4

In which diamond miners cook up an iguana curry at a rum shop in Guyana during the rainy season (1993)

How non-Europeans migrated to work on plantations producing tropical foods for the British

One Sunday morning, 'Bushman', 'Spider', 'Tall Boy' and 'Crab Dog', all Afro-Guyanese diamond miners, gathered at a rum shop in the Guyanese coastal village of Mahaica, about thirty kilometres east of the capital, George-town. They were joined by Terry Roopnaraine, an anthropologist gathering information for his study of gold and diamond mining in the Pakaraima Moun-tains in the interior. A man in a hurry might quickly knock back his 'quarter' of rum, just as Italians on the way to work gulp down an espresso standing at the counter of their local café. But with a 'large' (whole bottle), a bowl of ice and some glasses on the table, these men had clearly gathered for a lime: a companionable session of drinking accompanied by gaffing or aimless conver-sation. The rainy season had driven them out of the interior, where they dug for diamonds, and Spider, who was flush with the proceeds from a big strike, was treating the others from his earnings. As they sat and drank, the men regaled each other with stories of missed strikes, stumbling over seams of gold, and difficult periods when they were out of luck and had run out of credit. As the level in the rum bottle steadily fell and another bottle was called for, the talk inevitably drifted round to sex. Crab Dog waxed lyrical about the willingness of the Brazilian girls in the mining settlement of Monkey Mountain to engage in acts that Guyanese girls always refused to perform.

Eventually Bushman announced that he had killed an iguana the day before. 'So, let's cook him,' the men declared. The exceptionally short Tall Boy, who worked as a cook out in the mining camps, was assigned the task of preparing the food. The owner of the rum shop was a friend and allowed him to use the kitchen in the back of the shack. He set some cheap coconut oil to sizzle in a pot over the fire and threw in some onions. While they softened, he slit the belly of the iguana, cleaned out its guts and roughly chopped up the carcass. After adding a generous helping of curry powder, he threw the meat into the pot and poured in a good glug of high wine. Bush-meat cooks assert that this strong cane spirit is an essential ingredient, as it counters the rank, musty odour of the flesh of wild animals. While the curry was simmering, Tall Boy set a pot of rice to cook and the men drank yet more rum. When the food was ready, they eagerly wolfed it down and then sauntered off to doze away the afternoon.[1]

How did a group of diamond miners descended from African slaves come to be making a bush-meat version of an Indian curry on a Sunday morning in 1993? The answer lay 15 kilometres down the road from Mahaica, in the village of Annandale, where, on that same Sunday morning, Savitri Persaud was preparing a breakfast of roti and dhal for her family. She had set the lentils to simmer an hour earlier and was frying up garlic, chillies and cumin seeds to add flavour to the soupy mix. Most of the family's cooking was done in the bottom house, the shady concrete space in between the stilts that most coastal houses in Guyana stand on to raise them above the water during the seasonal floods.

Unlike weekday breakfasts, when Hari Pal had to hurry off to his work at the state-owned Guysuco sugar-cane plantation, the Persauds were able to eat a leisurely Sunday breakfast. As the family drifted in, Savitri took a disc of dough, and set it to heat on the tawa. The Indo-Guyanese oil their rotis generously, and as they take them off the heat, the women clap them between their hands. The result is a rich, flaky, paratha-like bread.[2] Savitri's hands were bright red from the heat by the time she had finished making the rotis. She handed each of her family a bowl of dhal, and a roti as it came off the griddle pan. Sitting on benches, they dipped pieces of the warm, soft, oily bread into the spicy lentils, savouring the food as they enjoyed a light morning breeze and chatted happily about the Bollywood movie they had watched the night before at the village cinema hall.[3]

Indian food had come to Guyana with the Persauds' ancestors. Between 1838 and 1916, about 240,000 Indians were shipped to the colony to provide a disciplined workforce for the sugar plantations when the abolition of slavery enabled the Africans to turn their backs on sugar work. And it was they who taught the ex-slaves how to make curry.

The old mercantilist system of imperial trade began to crumble when the doctrine of free trade undermined its rationale. The Navigation Acts had been introduced in order to guarantee that England would be able to secure a sizeable slice of the world's finite wealth. But in the second half of the eighteenth century, liberal economists like Adam Smith argued that commerce itself increased the sum of the world's riches and a nation could best secure a share of that wealth by participating in its creation. After the American Declaration of Independence, the Navigation Acts had to be amended. They excluded other countries' shipping from the commercial world of the British Empire but British North America (Canada) and the West Indies were dependent on supplies brought in by American ships now sailing under the flag of the United States. The Acts were further dismantled when in order to counter the growing influence of United States shipping in British ports, concessions were extended to other European powers. Liberal economists also objected to state-supported monopolistic trading companies.[4] With Britain's lower classes increasingly dependent on imports of sugar and tea, it made no sense to create pressure for higher wages by protecting the East India Company's monopoly over these commodities and thus artificially maintaining their high price. Parliament revoked the Company's monopoly over the tea trade with China in 1833, and in 1846, the Sugar Duties Act opened the British market to foreign sugars.[5]

The influence of liberal economics on British commerce coincided with the triumph of the humanitarian campaign to abolish slavery. The Act was passed in 1834 and came into effect in the Caribbean in 1838. This had a far-reaching impact on the way trade was conducted within the Empire. The sugar planters were now faced with the challenge of producing sugar cheaply enough to compete with the slave-produced sugars of Brazil and Cuba. At the same time, the East India Company had to find a way of dealing with foreign competition in a branch of their trade worth over £70 million.[6] Indian indentured labourers played an important part in solving the problems of both the sugar planters and the East India Company, and it was thanks to them that plentiful supplies of cheap sugar and tea continued to flow into Britain.

Britain gained a raft of new sugar-producing colonies as a result of the Napoleonic Wars: the French islands of Mauritius in the Indian Ocean; St Lucia and Trinidad in the West Indies; and the Dutch colonies of Essequibo, Berbice and Demerara on the North Atlantic coast of South America, which were amalgamated into British Guiana in 1831. But the abolition of slavery in the Caribbean seven years later precipitated a breakdown in the economies of Britain's sugar-producing colonies. Many slaves continued to work only long enough to accumulate some savings and then pooled together with others to buy declining coffee, cotton and sugar plantations, where they were able to found independent villages away from intrusive planter supervision.[7] More than half chose not to continue to work in the cane fields and sugar refineries. Those who stayed insisted on a shorter working week. The planters complained that the quality of their work declined, but their ability to punish negligence was curtailed as the freed Africans could now simply walk away from the job. British colonial sugar production fell drastically and the planters went in search of an alternative workforce: one they could control.[8]

A parliamentary committee had already been appointed in 1810 to address the question of colonial labour. A Royal Naval officer recommended the Chinese, whom he had noticed were 'indefatigable' workers on Dutch sugar, cotton and coffee plantations in South East Asia. The committee investigated the possibility of tapping into the Chinese 'credit-ticket' system of 'free' migrant labour, whereby about 10,000 Chinese a year pawned themselves to junk captains, paying for their passage once they reached their destination and found work on a plantation.[9] Two hundred able-bodied Chinese were procured to work on Trinidad, and once the system of indenture was systematically organised in the 1840s, supplies of Chinese 'coolies' were regularly sent to the West Indies.[10] But it was in India that British sugar planters eventually found a workforce that would keep their costs low enough to be able to compete on the world market.

The economic balance of power had tipped against India by the nineteenth century. Its textile-producing areas had enjoyed a period of prosperity when East India Company ships took huge consignments of Indian textiles back to eager consumers in Europe. But Britain now had its own industrial cotton mills, and protective tariffs were introduced in the 1820s that closed the British market to Indian manufactures. Instead, cheap Manchester cottons flooded into India and millions of handicraft producers went out of business.[11] Governor General William Bentinck described the misery this caused when in 1835 he remarked that 'the bones of cotton weavers are bleaching on the plains of India'.[12] Mauritian sugar planters were the first to commission Calcutta firms to find them workers from India's reservoir of impoverished craftsmen and labourers. They targeted men like Paravadee, a landless labourer from the Neilgherry Hills. As he was walking along the road to the town of Hazaribag in Bihar, where he intended to look for work, a recruitment agent fell into step with him. The promise of 'five Rupees a month, besides daily Batta ... of rice, doll [and] curry stuff' was enough to overcome his fear of losing caste by crossing the *kala pani* (black water). He signed up to a term of five years' indentured labour on a Mauritian sugar plantation.[13]

Over the course of the nineteenth century, hundreds of thousands of Indian indentured labourers – an exceptionally high proportion of them ex-weavers – were taken to work on British, French and Dutch sugar plantations all over the Caribbean, as well as in Natal, Australia, Malaysia, Fiji and Hawaii.[14] To the freed slaves they were akin to strike-breakers, as they undermined the Africans' new-found bargaining power with the plantocracy, who were supplied with an alternative 'quiet, docile and industrious' labour force.[15] The planters were satisfied with the new arrangement. One Mauritius-based firm calculated that if all the costs of passage, food, board and lodging were included, each labourer cost the planter a mere five shillings a week.[16] The British West Indian plantations recovered, and on Mauritius, production rose above the levels reached during the days of slavery.[17]

The indentured labourer Totaram Sanadyha later likened to slaves the 500 Indians with whom he boarded the ship bound for Fiji in 1893. The sea voyage was traumatic. Each labourer was allotted a tiny space of 1½ by 6 feet, the conditions were insanitary, the water brackish and the food horrible. When he was issued with hardtack, which he heard the sailors refer to as 'dog biscuits' (a common mariner's nickname), Sanadyha – perhaps wilfully – misunderstood. 'Oh God!' he wrote. 'Are we Indians like dogs?'[18] The disregard for caste sensibilities was painful, especially for those ordered to clean the ship's heads, and the crew were drunken and physically abusive. The few women on these ships were especially vulnerable, and in Mauritius, the Protector of Immigrants received numerous complaints of rape during the voyage. Around 10 per cent of indentured labourers died on the ships bringing them out to the plantations – about half the rate of mortality suffered on the disease-ridden slave ships.[19]

Most of the indentured labourers did not fully understand what they had signed up for, but a clear contract did exist between planters and labourers – they were not regarded as chattels. The planter did not own their children nor did he have the right to break up families; these were important differences to slavery. The overseers (often ex-slaves) were accustomed to driving a slave workforce and treated the labourers with brutality, beating them with rattans if they were slow or inattentive. However, the harsh regime became more in-stitutionalised under indenture. Paravadee described how the planters would accuse labourers of breach of contract for the 'least negligence or trifling fault' and take them to court, where the justices would pass sentence of a few days' stone-breaking.[20] Indentured labour was not the same as slavery, but rather the application of capitalist rationale to wage labour at its most brutal.[21]

When their contract came to an end, the majority of indentured labour-ers chose to commute their passage home into a land grant.[22] By the end of the nineteenth century, the Africans on Mauritius were outnumbered by Indians; there were more Indians living in Natal than Europeans; and in Trinidad and British Guiana, they made up a third of the population.[23] Unlike British mi-grants, who brought to their new homes the unimaginative food culture based on the industrial ration of flour, sugar and tea, the Indians carried with them the ability to use spices to create flavourful meals even with the most basic rations. The plantation managers soon realised that their new workforce would not re-main docile if they were forced to eat the cornmeal normally doled out to the slaves, and so it was replaced with rice and lentils.[24] But the range of foodstuffs accessible to them was restricted, and this meant that the culinary variety to be found across Indian communities and regions disappeared in Indo-Guyanese cooking.

Only split peas and chickpeas were available, so it was possible to make just two types of dhal. In India, different oils are used to give a range of fla-vours to dishes, but in British Guiana everything was cooked in coconut oil, the cheapest oil available and fortunately well suited to Indian cookery.[25] Mustard oil was sometimes imported, but as it was precious, the workers reserved it for making pickles.[26] The greatest limitation was the distribution of a pre-mixed masala of spices, or curry powder. Much of the variety in Indian cooking comes from the use of a wide range of freshly ground spices, added to dishes in varying combinations and at different stages in the cooking process. Over time, British cooks had begun to take short cuts with laborious Indian recipes and they started using pre-prepared spice mixtures that would have horrified most Indian cooks. Indeed, in the 1820s, one cookery book writer admonished her readers that 'to use currie-powder mixed in the same proportions for every sort of viand and of taste may do very well for those who entertain a mysterious veneration for the oriental characters inscribed on the packages, but will not suit a gourmand of any knowledge or experience'.[27] Nevertheless, Victorian Britons took to adding a spoonful of curry powder to what was in effect a recipe for an English stew and 'curried' everything, from beef to periwinkles, sheep's trotters and brain. Thus, this typically British invention repackaged fresh aromatic ingredients and turned them into a handy, industrially manufactured flavouring. In British Guiana, indentured labourers were more discerning in their use of the pre-mixed masala and developed a range of distinctive flavour combinations such as mutton with aubergine and shrimp with pumpkin, but curry powder reduced the possibilities for inventiveness and forced them to prepare dishes that were more generic than those they would have made in their homeland.[28]

NELLIE HUSANARA ABDOOL'S PUMPKIN AND SHRIMP CURRY

100 g shrimp

1 lime

1 small onion, diced

5 cloves of garlic, crushed

2 red chilli peppers (or to taste), diced

3 tbsp oil

1 large tomato, diced

600 g pumpkin, diced

½ tsp curry powder

½ tsp brown sugar

sprig of fresh thyme

salt and black pepper to taste

pinch of cayenne powder

Soak shrimp in cold water and juice of one lime for at
least 25 minutes to rid them of any rank smell or taste.
Rinse twice in cold water. Set aside.

Sauté the onion, garlic and chilli in oil until soft, then
add the tomato and cook until it has softened to make
a sauce. Add the pumpkin and cook for 10–12 minutes
on a medium heat. Add curry powder, brown sugar,
thyme, salt and pepper. Stir and cook for another
15 minutes. Add 250 ml of water and cook for 20–25
minutes until the pumpkin is soft. The pumpkin should
begin to dissolve and hardly any water should be left
in the pan. Mash the pumpkin with a spoon to break up
any whole pieces.

Meanwhile, add a little oil to a frying pan and cook
the shrimp, salt and pepper and cayenne powder on a
medium heat. Cook until all the water has evaporated
and the shrimp are dry and crisp. Add the shrimp to the
pumpkin mixture. Eat with a paratha roti.[29]

Once the Afro-Guyanese learned the currying technique from their
Indian neighbours, they too applied it with British-style enthusiasm to a range of
meats. After they were freed, the Africans had developed a different relationship
with their new homeland, venturing away from the coastal sugar plantations into
the interior to tap rubber and prospect for gold and diamonds.[30] Here they inter-
acted with the Amerindians, who taught them how to hunt and cook the forest
animals. And this was how one Sunday morning in 1993, descendants of Africans

who had been brought there to cultivate sugar came to be making an Indian-style curry out of a wild animal caught in the rainforests of South America.

If Indian indentured labourers ensured the survival of Britain's colonial sugar plantations, they were also key to the creation of an imperial tea industry. In the early 1800s, the British did not have the first idea how to grow, pluck or manufacture tea. The Chinese preferred to keep this knowledge to themselves and discouraged any European exploration of the tea-growing area of Fujian.[31] However, as it became clear that the government was likely to end the East India Company's monopoly on the China trade, the Company began to cast around for alternative sources of its most valuable trading commodity. In the early 1820s, an officer passing through Assam on his way to the wars in Burma had noticed that tea plants, thought previously to be indigenous to China, grew wild in the Assamese hills. At the same time, the British administration began to focus on the potential of vast tracts of Indian tribal land supposedly lying idle. When the Company lost its monopoly in 1833, provision was also made in its revised charter for Europeans to own land in India, and Governor General Bentinck set up a Tea Committee to investigate the possibility of European planters using Assamese 'wasteland' to grow tea.[32]

The British had little faith that the indigenous Assamese plant would make good tea and in 1835 dispatched the opium trader George Gordon on a mission to China to acquire by whatever methods it took – including deceit and subterfuge – seeds, plants and, if possible, some Chinese artisanal tea manufacturers.[33] Gordon sent back 80,000 plants and two tea makers from Fujian's Wuyi Mountains, where they produced the semi-fermented dark teas popular with the British.[34] Nevertheless, it took three decades to perfect the plant stock, establish viable plantations and find a suitable labour force in India. The Chinese shoemakers and carpenters the Assam Tea Company re-cruited in Calcutta and Singapore had 'never seen a tea plant in their lifetime' and had no idea how to cultivate it, while those tea makers they did manage to find were indignant when they discovered that they were expected to grub out tree roots and clear the forest to make new plantations.[35] The conditions on the plantations were so poor and, at half the rate normally paid to a free labourer, the wages so low that the local Assamese were unenthusiastic about

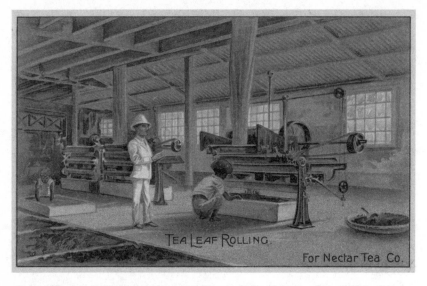

The planter in his topee supervising the industrial manufacture of tea.

working there too, even when the British banned the private cultivation of the local cash crop – opium – hoping that this would push them into waged work.[36] In the end, the Assamese tea planters drew on the same pool of the impoverished and dispossessed who provided labour for the colonial sugar plantations.

In China, tea was grown by peasants on smallholdings and manufactured by travelling artisans.[37] On British colonial territory, tea-making was transformed into an industrial undertaking. The process of growing and plucking the fresh green leaves was performed by gangs of indentured labourers working under the supervision of an overseer; this made the tea gardens reminiscent of the slave plantations in the Caribbean. In the 1860s, one planter wrote of driving the 'coolies' up and down the line, 'shov[ing] them on exactly as nigger drivers in America'.[38] The processing of green leaves into brown tea was mechanised, and inside the factory each worker was assigned a simple repetitive task. The pay was pitiful, the housing squalid, disease rife and medical provision virtually non-existent. Under newly enacted labour laws, the indentured labourers could be prosecuted for refusing to work; if they fled, they were pursued and usually captured, given the difficult terrain that surrounded the plantations.[39] Recalcitrant labourers were routinely flogged, and there were reports of planters beating their workers to death.[40] Even among other Europeans, tea planters soon gained a dreadful reputation.

However, by the 1870s, Assam was producing a passable product. When coffee blight hit planters in southern India and Ceylon, they too switched to growing tea, and 1.5 million indentured labourers from the famine-struck areas of Tamil Nadu were recruited to work in Ceylon's plantations.[41] By the 1880s, India was producing large quantities of tea. British consumers, though, had to be persuaded to switch to the strong black fermented Indian product. In the 1870s, the promoters of Indian tea were able to capitalise on the advertising campaign that John Horniman had been running since the 1830s demonising Chinese practices. Horniman's advertisements, which had begun to appear soon after the East India Company lost its monopoly, claimed that British consumers were no longer protected from the dastardly adulteration practices of the Chinese, who supposedly mixed tea dust, dirt and sand in with their tea leaves, coated them in a gummy rice flour to make the dyes stick, and then coloured them with either Prussian blue to make the leaves look darker or, if they were green, with arsenate of copper.[42] Horniman assured his customers that his Chinese tea – the first to be sold in pre-sealed packages – was free from such impurities. The Indian tea makers built on these prejudices to present their product as a complete contrast to the dubious stuff produced by the opium-eating Chinese. Indian tea was robust and flavourful, and grown, processed and packaged in a clean, orderly, British-controlled environment. By 1900, China had lost the British market to Indian and Ceylonese tea.[43]

During the nineteenth century, almost as many non-Europeans migrated around the globe as the 50 million Europeans who left the Continent.[44] Hunger, war and the disruptive intrusion of European trade into traditional societies pushed hundreds of thousands from their homes and onto the global labour market. China was a major source of migrants. The majority came from four coastal counties in Guangdong and Fujian where explosive population growth resulted in a vicious ethnic conflict between the valley farmers and the peasants cultivating the less fertile hilly terrain. Millions fled to the nearby port towns of Guangzhou, Macao and Hong Kong and from there migrated across the globe.[45]

Many Chinese joined the gold rush to California in the 1840s – the Chinese ideogram for California translates as 'Gold Mountain' – but they quickly realised that gold was unlikely to make them their fortunes and turned to other employment. Chinese migrants helped to lay the bedrock of the infrastructure on America's West Coast, working as navvies on railway construction crews, cutting timber and labouring in sawmills. They worked as domestic and camp cooks; made shoes and cigars; supplied the towns with fruit and vegetables grown in their truck gardens; and ran virtually every laundry on the West Coast.[46] The 1858 gold rush to the Fraser Valley drew Chinese into British Columbia, where they ended up providing the workforce for the salmon canneries that began opening on the rivers in the 1860s and 1870s, transforming the erstwhile foodstuff of the disappearing First Nations into an industrial commodity.[47] On a steamer voyage up the West Coast in 1888, Rudyard Kipling contrasted the immense silence and solitude of a cannery's pine-forested setting with the bloodstained, scale-spangled, oily, noisy atmosphere within, where offal-smeared Chinamen, looking like 'yellow devils', stuffed salmon into cans with 'crooked fingers'.[48]

The Chinese were as unwilling to give up their habitual foods as the Indian migrants to the sugar plantations. The steamship companies that plied the emigrant route between Hong Kong and San Francisco carried jars and packets of lychees, water chestnuts, dried mushrooms and powdered shrimp, preserved ginger and duck livers to supply the Chinese grocery stores to be found wherever there were Chinese communities.[49] East Asian migrants often ended up living on an adapted industrial ration. A Japanese railroad labourer described how he and his fellow workers ate a strange fusion diet of fried bacon, potatoes and onions added to salt water to make a soup, and *bottera* (flour-and-water pancakes) with bacon and soy sauce, all washed down with coffee.[50]

If the Chinese migrated in the hope of making their fortunes, so too did the 60,000 young Melanesians who signed up with passage masters to work on Queensland's sugar plantations. For three years they endured insanitary conditions, malnutrition, disease and violent abuse – their death rate of one in four was the worst among any group of colonial indentured labourers – in order to earn their prize: a 'bokis'. This was a lockable box packed full of Western goods – weapons, fishing implements, steel tools, household wares, medicines, textiles, clothing, tobacco, jewellery, umbrellas, tin whistles and other musical instruments. With the key to the lock hanging ostentatiously from their belts, the young men would return to their villages and deploy their goods in the gift economy to claim a wife and an honourable position in the village hierarchy. Such was the impossibility of living down the shame of returning home without a 'bokis' that the authorities would even give a box to those men they rejected as unfit at the colonial ports.[51]

In West Africa, thousands of young men from eastern Senegal and Mali would migrate to the peanut-growing region of Gambia in a similar quest for Western goods. They would pay a local chief to rent a suitable field and spend two or three seasons cultivating peanuts before returning home with their earnings converted into consumer goods.[52] With the abolition of slavery, West Africa had begun supplying the Europeans with agricultural commodities rather than men. In the same way that local rulers had put slaves to work cultivating maize and cassava to sell to the slaving ships, they now employed them collecting palm oil kernels and cultivating peanuts. In the 1830s, groundnut production took off in the dry savannas of Senegambia, where the French and the British continued to struggle over control of the area's trade. In 1845, the acting governor of Senegal gleefully reported from Albreda (the fort where la Courbe met with la Belinguere in Chapter Five) that French traders were managing to smuggle great quantities of peanuts out from under the noses of the British without paying customs duties.[53] Eventually the British conceded to the French and switched to buying Nigerian palm oil to meet their needs for vegetable oil to make candles and soap. In the 1880s, cocoa was introduced on the Gold Coast and around the Bight of Benin. Following the lines of the newly constructed railways, immigrant smallholders began to move into the sparsely populated interior to set up cocoa farms.[54]

By the end of the nineteenth century, the British Empire had recovered from the setbacks caused by the restructuring of colonial trade and created a new system for supplying its colonies with a compliant labour force. The specialisation that the Industrial Revolution had introduced into manufacturing was applied to the world's agricultural land, as particular regions concentrated on the cultivation of specific crops. John Stuart Mill argued that the trade between Britain and her colonies could 'hardly ... be considered an external trade, but more resemble[d] the traffic between town and country'. Tropical colonies, he went on, were 'to be looked upon ... as outlying agricultural or manufacturing estates belonging to a larger community'.[55] Having eradicated the peasantry at home, Britain had acquired an enormous peasantry abroad. It was the coercion and exploitation of colonial subjects that provided the country with raw materials for its industries and sugar and tea for its industrial workers.

16

In which the Bartons entertain the Wilsons to tea in the London Road slum district of Manchester (May 1839)

How the wheat for the working-class loaf came to be grown in America and the settler colonies

At Whitsuntide in May 1839, the mill workers of Manchester enjoyed a rare holiday from the toil and noise of the factories, savouring the fresh air while walking in the countryside. Afterwards, the Bartons invited their friends the Wilsons back to their home for tea. The two families wended their way through the maze of narrow streets into the London Road slum district and crowded into the Bartons' little house in a back courtyard. As John Barton stoked the fire, the light revealed a room furnished with a dresser, a cupboard displaying their few bits of china, and a deal table and chairs. Blue-and-white check curtains at the windows and a couple of straggling geranium plants on the windowsill added a cheerful touch, as did the green japanned tea tray propped up on the table next to a crimson tea caddy. A brightly coloured piece of oil cloth covered the floor between the coal hole and the fireplace.

George and Jane Wilson sat in the chairs on either side of the fire, distracting their young twins with bread and milk. They politely pretended not to notice the clinking of small change as Mrs Barton gave her daughter Mary some money and instructed her to run to the shop round the corner to fetch five eggs, some Cumberland ham, a pennyworth of milk and a fresh loaf of bread. Her father John added that she should stop at the Grapes public house for 'six-pennyworth of rum to warm the tea'.[1] On her way to the shop, Mary was instructed to call on Alice, George Wilson's sister, who lived in a cellar round the corner, and invite her to come and join them. But she was not to forget to tell her to bring her own teacup, as the family only had five. By the time Alice had hobbled to the Bartons' home, Mary had returned with her purchases and was busy frying the ham and eggs while her mother presided over the making of tea at the table. The two families ate in silence, for the poor believed in savouring their food rather than engaging in distracting chit-chat.[2]

The Bartons and the Wilsons were the invention of Elizabeth Gaskell, who begins her novel *Mary Barton*, published in 1848, with these scenes. Gaskell wrote the book in an attempt to elicit middle-class sympathy for the plight of the working classes. She introduces us to the characters at a prosperous moment, but the rest of the novel is set during the trade depression of the early 1840s, when the northern mill workers were reduced to hunger and want. In the early nineteenth century, Britain's industrial towns tripled in size within a few decades, swelling into cities as hundreds of thousands migrated from the countryside in search of work.[3] While some, like the Harding and Pinfold families (whom we met in Chapter Twelve), exchanged their damp, run-down cottages for colonial cabins, the majority moved into the urban slums. Here the air reeked of coal smoke, and the houses, thrown up by unscrupulous speculative builders, were crowded together around inner courts where wet washing flapped damply above pools of filthy water contaminated with undrained sewage.[4] Nevertheless, the new arrivals hoped to improve their lives, for while a rural labourer might scrape along on a weekly wage of as little as 8s., a skilled storeman in Manchester could earn as much as £2 17s. and his family could eat meat and potatoes every day.[5]

Although urban wages were potentially higher, industrial workers led insecure lives. As the philanthropist Florence Bell observed, even the thriftiest working man with a decent job walked along the 'margin of disaster' at all times.[6] The slightest sickness or disability, a downturn in work or some other ill fortune could plunge a relatively prosperous family into immediate poverty. And as nineteenth-century industry lurched through a series of depressions, tens of thousands of workers were intermittently thrown out of their jobs.[7] The 1840s recession described in *Mary Barton* was one of the worst. More than half the workers were laid off in mill towns across northern England, and the unemployed were reduced to penury.[8] Elizabeth Gaskell visited the families of the poor during that time and was haunted by the words of a man who grasped her arm tightly and asked, 'Ay ma'am, but have ye ever seen a child clemmed [starved] to death?'[9] Middle-class critics condemned the workers as improvident for failing to accumulate savings that could tide them over these difficult periods. But even the best industrial wages were never sufficient to allow workers to do more than live from hand to mouth: 'consum[ing] today what they earned yesterday'.[10] Charles Dickens condemned the manufacturers, who treated their workers like objects rather than people, 'to be worked so much, and paid so much, and there ended; something to be infallibly settled by laws of supply and demand'.[11]

Like the rural labourers in the late eighteenth century, the industrial poor were reduced to eating shop-bought bread, sugar and tea. Those who could not afford to light a fire for the twenty minutes or more it took to boil potatoes had to eat a slice of wheat bread smeared with treacle. In Sheffield, where coal was relatively expensive, there were twice as many bakers as in Leeds, where coal was cheaper.[12] The poorer the family, the more they spent on bread. Bread absorbed more than 30 per cent of the wages of a Manchester mechanic's assistant, while the better-off storeman spent less than 20 per cent of his weekly wage on bread.[13]

The more bread the industrial workers ate, the more sweetened tea they drank. Friedrich Engels, who had turned his back on the 'port wine and champagne' lifestyle of his own mill-owning class in order to explore Manchester's slums, noted that tea was 'quite indispensable' to the poor and was forgone only when the 'bitterest poverty reigns'.[14] This was not, as judgemental commentators claimed, because tea satisfied a debauched working-class craving for nervous stimulation, but because, as one more empathetic physician understood, it had a 'reviving influence when the body was fatigued'.[15] This was no wonder considering the amount of sugar a working-class cup of tea contained. A family of iron workers whose diet was investigated by Florence Bell dissolved 4 lb of sugar – enough to fill ten teacups – in their weekly ½ lb of tea.[16] Dr Edward Smith, investigating the diets of mill workers caught up in the 'cotton famine' of 1861, found that even when they cut back on the amount of foodstuffs they bought, including bread, the amount of sugar they purchased remained the same. The only difference was that rather than buying it in the form of lumps to put in their tea, they purchased it as treacle to spread on their bread. This made economic sense, as a pennyworth of treacle will have given them around four times more energy than a pennyworth of margarine.[17] Cotton workers in the 1860s ate as much as double the amount of sugar as other workers: sugar really did fuel the Industrial Revolution.[18]

A working-class family finding comfort in a warm cup of tea.

Children brought up on this impoverished diet were malnourished, and in the insanitary conditions of the industrial conurbations they fell victim to pneumonia and tuberculosis, diarrhoea and rheumatic fever. Those that survived childhood were severely stunted, as their bodies had diverted what nutrients could be gleaned from their food into recovery rather than growth.[19] Working-class adolescent boys from the industrial cities were on average a staggering 10 inches shorter than those from privileged backgrounds.[20] The grinding poverty and squalor reduced life expectancy in Manchester to just 26, a full 10 years less than the national average.[21] Elizabeth Gaskell was at her best in her novel when she allowed John Barton to express the injustice of the system: 'If I am out of work for weeks in the bad times, and winter comes, with black frost, and keen east wind ... does the rich man share his plenty with me, as he ought to do, if his religion wasn't a humbug? ... don't think to come over me with th' old tale, that the rich know nothing of the trials of the poor; I say, if they don't know, they ought to know. We're their slaves as long as we can work; we pile up their fortunes with the sweat of our brows.'[22] It was clear that something needed to be done about the plight of the workers. Dissatisfaction was fuelling demands for political change. In her novel, Gaskell has John Barton travel to London with the Chartists, who in 1842 handed in a petition of 3.5 million signatures to Parliament calling for manhood suffrage. Friedrich Engels was convinced that if the middle classes continued to ignore the poverty and distress of the workers, they would surely rise up in revolution as they had done in France in 1789.[23]

The Anti-Corn Law League argued that the solution would be to repeal the Corn Laws. These had been introduced in 1815 and were designed to favour British farmers by effectively preventing imports of cheaper Russian and American wheat from entering the British market.[24] The founders of the League, Richard Cobden and John Bright, insisted that if cheap wheat imports were allowed, this would force down British wheat prices and consequently bring down the price of bread, freeing the working man from the tyranny of hunger. Many industrialists supported the League for the cynical reason that if the price of bread were to fall, it would allow them to keep wages low. Of course, the aristocracy, who derived their income from the land, were opposed, as decreasing wheat prices were likely to push down farm rents. However, although the aristocracy dominated Sir Robert Peel's Tory government, the prime minister himself was in favour of opening up the British domestic market to free trade. Apart from anything else, it was difficult for the government to justify effectively barring cheap American grain imports when due to the failure of the potato crop in Ireland, the Irish were 'reduced to the last extremity for want of food'.[25] Peel was convinced that imports of cheap 'Indian cornmeal' (maize) from America would minimise the need for expensive relief efforts.[26] By a series of complicated political manoeuvres, he managed to defeat the two thirds of his own party members who opposed him.[27] In 1846, the Corn Laws were repealed and the British wheat market was opened up to foreign competition.

The triumph of the doctrine of free trade created the conditions for the emergence of a new imperial food regime. Until now, the colonies had supplied the mother country with useful raw materials and tropical agricultural goods such as sugar that could not be cultivated in Britain's temperate climate. But those European migrants who had chosen colonial farms over urban slums had extended Britain's agricultural estate into parts of the world suited to the cultivation of temperate crops. On these distant fields it was possible to grow more than enough to provide Britain's ever-increasing workforce with enough cheap food to distract them from all thought of revolution. In effect, Britain had exported not just its farming population but almost its entire agricultural sector to the United States and the new settler colonies. From the mid nineteenth century, the country looked to its trading empire to supply it with staple foodstuffs.

During the parliamentary debate on the repeal of the Corn Laws, the Tory landed interest warned that the foundations of British democracy would be undermined if British farmers lost their protection from foreign competition. And immediately after the repeal there was a flurry of panic among small farmers. A disproportionately large number of those emigrating to the United States in 1850 were tenants from counties such as Surrey and Lancashire where it was a struggle to grow wheat on undercapitalised farms with heavy clay soils. Rather than lose their livelihoods to the Americans, with their limitless access to 'untaxed and fertile soil', they went to join them.[28]

America's family farms may have been anachronistic in their idealisation of the sturdy yeoman farmer, but they were progressive in their farming technique. The pioneers who ventured onto the prairies of northern Illinois, Wisconsin, Iowa and eastern Minnesota used mechanical reapers, which substantially increased the amount a farmer working on his own could harvest.[29] When, in the 1870s, they moved onto the great plains of Kansas, Nebraska and the Dakotas, they added the wire binder to their battery of machines, which doubled their productivity.[30] But the mechanical innovation that assured American wheat's competitiveness was the invention in 1848 of the steam-powered grain elevator. Elevators transformed wheat from a product that individual farmers transported in sacks, and that took days to load and unload on the backs of stevedores, into a quality-controlled bulk commodity. By means of a series of mechanised buckets, grain was scooped out of boats on the Illinois and Michigan canals and taken up to the top of the elevator to be weighed and graded. Using the force of gravity, the wheat was then channelled into appropriate storage bins from where it could be poured down a chute into a rail car or ship's hold. In 1857, when all twelve of Chicago's elevators were in operation, they could process half a million bushels of grain in ten hours at the cost of only half a cent a bushel.[31] Low freight charges on the sailing ships that transported the wheat across the Atlantic meant that it cost less to ship grain from New York to Liverpool than it did to transport Irish wheat on the canals to Dublin and from there across the Irish Sea.[32]

From the mid 1860s, at times more than half the American wheat arriving in Britain was grown not in the Midwest but in California. The fact that wheat from the arid Sacramento and San Joaquin valleys could be transported in sailing ships 14,000 nautical miles down the west coast of South America, around Cape Horn and across the Atlantic and still compete with wheat grown in East Anglia was a triumph of organisation and efficiency.[33] Using the most up-to-date farming methods, Californian farms produced far more wheat than the population of San Francisco and the gold-mining towns dotted around the state could possibly eat. When they went in search of a market, the Californians discovered that British and Irish millers were prepared to pay top prices for their hard, dry, unusually white wheat. But transporting it to the eastern seaboard on the new transcontinental rail lines was too expensive, and steam ships were out of the question, as the cost of the coal necessary to fuel the long and arduous route round Cape Horn was prohibitive.[34] Isaac Friedlander, a German-Jewish immigrant who had moved to California from South Carolina during the 1849 gold rush, found the solution. He used the newly established transatlantic and transcontinental telegraph systems to co-ordinate the arrival of a flotilla of clipper ships in San Francisco harbour just as the wheat harvest was flooding onto the market. Clippers had been invented for the China trade in the 1840s after the East India Company had lost its monopoly. Narrow and yacht-like, they were designed to race cargoes of the new season's tea back to Britain, where the first ships to arrive were able to capitalise on the highest prices. As the California wheat trade flourished, New England shipbuilders responded by producing bigger, stronger ships, thus reducing the four-to-five-month journey between San Francisco and Liverpool to 100 days.[35]

In 1882, when the Pacific wheat trade peaked, 550 ships sailed under the Golden Gate on their way to Liverpool, where Californian wheat dominated the market. On the Liverpool exchange, wheat was sold by the cental (100 lb) rather than the more usual bushel, as the Californian wheat was shipped in 100 lb sacks. Meanwhile, the trade meant that Britain dominated the American state. The clipper ships were almost all British-owned, and insured by British brokers; two of San Francisco's leading banks were British; and it was British capital that funded the building of railways in the late 1860s that linked the wheat-growing valleys to the port. For the decades during which wheat was California's leading export crop, the state was effectively a British colony.[36]

The San Francisco–Liverpool wheat run was, however, the last hurrah of the sailing ships. In 1863, the compound engine, developed in the textile mills, was applied to marine steam engines. This was quickly followed by the invention of triple and quadruple expansion engines. Within the decade, marine-engine fuel consumption was halved.[37] Steamships could now make much longer sea journeys, and larger steamships created economies of scale that caused freight prices to plummet throughout the last quarter of the century. In 1902, the freight rate for a quarter of wheat from New York to Liverpool was a mere 11½d, down from 5s. 2d in 1872.[38] It was the drop in freight prices that brought about the collapse of British wheat farming. By embarking on a concerted campaign of drainage, manuring and investment in machinery, British farmers had managed to maintain a respectable share of the market: in 1870, they still supplied half the wheat in a loaf.[39] But as freight prices dropped and American exports increased from 5 million hectolitres of wheat in the 1840s to 100 million hectolitres in the 1870s, British wheat farming went into steep decline.[40]

The landed interest had been correct when they argued that the repeal of the Corn Laws would adversely affect them. Once the fall in transport costs allowed foodstuffs to flow into Britain from around the world, the landlords' rental incomes fell dramatically.[41] In 1897, Herbrand, the 11th Duke of Bedford, published *A Great Agricultural Estate*, a polemic in which he alleged that the repeal of the Corn Laws had brought about the ruin of the landed aristocracy. He detailed how his estates of Thorney and Woburn were now running at a deficit due to falls in rents between 45 and 22 per cent. As George Russell, a radical Liberal and distant relative of the Duke of Bedford, pointed out, the aristocrat failed to mention that his estate in the West Country was financially buoyant and his urban landholding between the Strand and Euston Road brought in a substantial rental income. Indeed, when Bedford wrote his tale of landed woe, he was a very wealthy man, with an annual income of £319,369.[42] While aristocrats did begin to sell their estates, it would take more than a decline in land value to undermine the patrician elite. The shrewd among them diversified their portfolios and invested in urban land, American railways, government bonds, mortgage companies and breweries, joining the gentlemanly capitalists of the City.[43]

By the 1880s, there was growing disenchantment on both sides with the mutual dependence of the British and American wheat markets.[44] The Americans sought to escape Liverpool's dominance by opening up new markets, while the British, having favoured dependence on America over Russia, now preferred the idea of relying on the Empire. In the 1880s and 1890s, measures were taken to stimulate wheat exports from India, Australia, Canada and Argentina. British investment in schemes to construct railways in these countries was frequently promoted on the grounds that this would allow them to replace the United States as Britain's wheat supplier.[45] In the 1880s, an enthusiastic group of private investors even suggested introducing into India an American-style wheat grading system, and grain elevators along the railways, in order to facilitate the export of wheat from the colony.[46]

When India became a Crown colony in 1858, internal commerce was facilitated by the unification of most of the subcontinent under one administration, using a single currency. Farmers were able to move their surplus rice and wheat crops to market more easily as bullock carts began replacing pack animals, roads were metalled and steamboats were introduced on the Ganges. Between 1850 and 1870, the British built an extensive rail network linking the twenty major cities. All this inexorably drew the Indian peasant into the market.[47] There was a scramble to bring agriculturally marginal land into production, and farmers were encouraged to replace hardy subsistence crops such as millet with wheat.[48] By the 1870s, district officers noted that the peasantry had given up storing surplus foodstuffs and instead sold their entire harvest. But this left them vulnerable at times of food scarcity and dependent on charity or government relief in the event of famine.[49] And with the regular failure of the south-west monsoon, famines were a frequent occurrence.

As many as 16 million Indians died in famines between 1875 and 1914.[50] The colonial government did very little to alleviate the misery, insisting that this was nature's way of keeping a check on the burgeoning Indian population.[51] But famines were not a natural consequence of poor harvests. They were the result of the unchecked functioning of the free market, which allowed merchants to continue to sell their wheat to the highest international bidders while inflation priced the poor out of their ability to buy food. Some administrators argued that famines were good for India's agricultural sector, as they forced unproductive and indebted smallholders off the land.[52] In fact, every famine had the effect of pauperising an ever greater proportion of the Indian population. And yet in 1900, one fifth of Britain's wheat imports came from India.[53]

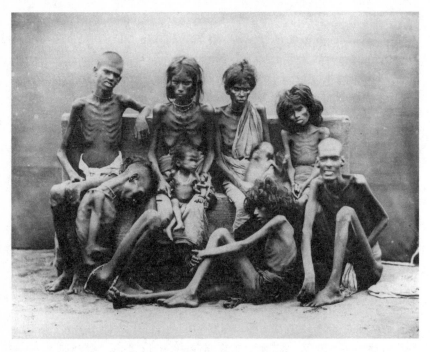

Victims of the Madras Famine, 1877.

While Britain's preference for empire wheat had a destabilising effect on Indian agriculture, it was a boon for Australian farmers looking for a way out of the economic slump of the 1890s. Farmers ploughed up their sheep runs and planted them with wheat varieties bred to suit the Antipodean climate. From exports of only a couple of hundred thousand tons in the early 1890s, Australia was exporting about two million tons by 1919, three quarters of it to Britain.[54] At the same time, in Latin America, millions of southern European migrants spread out over the Argentinian pampas as the last of the Amerindians were driven off their lands. Although they practised a poor sort of extensive agriculture, with low yields, grain exports from their farms supported the national economy, earning most of Argentina's foreign exchange.[55] The country was drawn into Britain's informal empire as its infrastructure of railways and ports was funded by British banks, investors and companies, and the Argentinian wheat trade became bound up with coal exports from South Wales.[56] Welsh coal was used by navies and steamship companies throughout the world as it was slow-burning and did not reach damagingly high temperatures, making it the optimum fuel for marine engines. Grain ships sailing out to Argentina, which would have been more or less empty otherwise, took out cargoes of Welsh coal, which helped reduce the return freight rates for wheat.[57] There had been expectations of Canada feeding Britain as early as the 1870s, when Canadian prime minister John A. Macdonald passed the Homestead Act and British investors sank millions of pounds into financing the building of the Canadian Pacific transcontinental railway. But it was not until freight rates were reduced in 1896 that it became economically viable for settlers to grow wheat for sale to Britain. Over a million farmers now drove the Métis and Plains Indians into reservations as they brought 9.2 million hectares under cultivation. By 1910, Canada had become the world's leading wheat exporter.[58]

By the end of the nineteenth century, Britain absorbed between 30 and 40 per cent of the world's wheat exports. Agriculture's relative importance to the country's economy declined dramatically, from contributing a third of the national income at the beginning of the nineteenth century to about 7 per cent at the end.[59]

The repeal of the Corn Laws and the influx of American wheat imports brought down the price of bread. In 1880, a 4 lb loaf cost as little as 6d, half what it had cost in 1840.[60] The money this saved working-class families meant they were able to add a bit of bacon to their bread and butter at breakfast, some sausages or a piece of liver to their midday meal of potatoes.[61] British dairy farmers took advantage of the nation's new rail network to supply the towns with fresh milk, and working-class people were now able to enjoy the occasional glass.[62] Two thirds of Britain's wheat acreage disappeared as a result of cheap imports, and in Cambridgeshire, farmers switched to market gardening; fields of corn were replaced by orchards and rows of soft fruit.[63] The further extension of the free market with the abolition of duties on sugar in 1874 was followed by a flood of unprecedentedly cheap German beet sugar in the 1880s, and this made it economically viable to convert the less-than-perfect strawberries, raspberries, damsons and plums into affordable jams.[64] 'Strawberry flavour' at twopence halfpenny a pound became such a ubiquitous spread that whereas a middle-class child in the nursery looked forward to the treat of bread and jam for tea, 'when given the opportunity at a party or a picnic, [the working-class child] will devote his attention to the luxury of bread-and-butter'.[65] By the end of the century, sugar accounted for as much as 15 per cent of a worker's daily intake of energy.[66]

The repeal of the Corn Laws and the supply of foreign wheat enabled Britain to feed its mushrooming industrial population; it may even have diverted them from social revolution, although it could be argued that the workers were simply drugged into compliance by lavish quantities of sugar. By 1880, their living standards had improved. Those earning the highest wages were able to spare a little for boots, clothing, bedding and cooking utensils.[67] In most of Britain's larger cities, life expectancy was now only a few years below the national average – although in Manchester it remained stubbornly at 37, ten years lower than the average.[68] Yet overcrowding and insanitary conditions, irregular employment and poverty still afflicted about a quarter of the working population. Although the poorest no longer starved, their diet could hardly be described as healthy. Free trade did not bring about a marked improvement in the working-class diet until the Empire began sending Britain cargoes of meat as well as wheat.

In which Prakash Tandon enjoys a Sunday roast with his landlady's family in a Manchester council house (1931)

How foreign food imports improved the working-class diet and made Britain dependent on its Empire

Prakash Tandon's landlady looked at her husband with satisfaction as he carved the roast leg of best New Zealand lamb. It was Prakash's host family's first Sunday in their new home. When he moved in with them, they lived in 'a street of an unbroken row of houses with backyards and front steps' in the centre of Manchester.[1] His landlady's bell-shaped hair would shake as she tossed her head defiantly and declared her determination to get away from this street as it symbolised her hateful slippage into the lower rungs of the working classes. 'It may not have been posh where I came from', she would pronounce, but 'at least we had a little lawn and a couple of trees at the back'.[2] The money their 'Indian gentleman' paid for board and lodging had enabled the family to move up in the world. They were 'in raptures' over their new council house with 'its own gate and a wire fence' on a named housing estate with 'a shopping parade with a Co-op [and] a public house with a car park' – all signs of class. The house had a small back garden where the husband grew vegetables, which was so much better than having an allotment 'like a working man'. Instead of the privy in the yard, they now had a 'proper bathroom with a tub and a separate water closet ... two bedrooms and a small one for the children, a front room ... a dining room and a kitchen ... a tiny hall and a cupboard under the stairs'.[3] The children went to a better school, where they wore a uniform. Prakash watched with interest as his landlady invested her new-found wealth in a half-moon rug, an easy chair and a dining suite in good wood. Whereas in the Punjab, where he came from, women would spend any extra money on gold ornaments and fine clothes, Prakash's landlady channelled her energies into her home, which she scrubbed and polished with an enthusiasm that astonished him.[4]

Brought up on thick chapattis, chalk-white butter, curd and sharp mustard greens, Prakash had at first struggled with English food. On the voyage to Britain in 1929, he and his fellow Indian passengers had been revolted by the vast quantities of 'ham and bacon, roast pork and beef, steaks and ribs' that the British cheerfully gobbled. Having caught sight of a plate of sausages, they concluded that they ate every conceivable part of the unfortunate animal, from its head to its feet, including its stomach and 'its most private part'. (Fortunately they did not encounter sweetbreads or lamb fries.)[5] In Manchester, where Prakash studied chartered accountancy, the Indian students searched in vain for an Indian restaurant and cherished their landladies if they could conjure up a recognisable curry. After a while, Prakash broke out of his Indian circle and, despite the fact that his compatriots labelled him a traitor, 'dropped all inhibitions, developed a liking for beer, fish and chips, hot-pot and parkin, smutty stories, soft aitches and broad a's and generally got as close to the heart of Lancashire as one could'.[6]

Prakash joined in the life of his host family with enthusiasm and was as pleased as they were that the leg of roast lamb was a sign of their better fortune. That by the 1930s the Sunday roast was becoming an institution among the Manchester working class was an indication of just how much the lives of workers had improved since the hungry 1840s. The key to the rise in living standards was the import of cheap foreign food. The lamb that Prakash and his host family savoured that Sunday would have been fattened on New Zealand pastureland on the other side of the world, slaughtered in an abattoir at the port and transported to Britain in the freezer hold of a ship. From the butcher's, the joint would have continued its journey to the Sunday dinner table in the bicycle basket of the butcher's boy, as Prakash's landlady could now afford the middle-class luxury of having her shopping delivered. Just as Prakash's family were dependent on their Indian gentleman's rent to fund their new-found rise in the world, the British working classes in the inter-war years were dependent on the Empire to feed them.

The influx of foreign wheat from the 1870s had ensured the workers their daily loaf of white wheaten bread. But as the population grew steadily and wages rose, the working classes' desire to eat more meat put pressure on the supply. After the repeal of the Corn Laws, new imports of high-calorie oil-seed cakes had boosted meat and dairy farming. Farmers were producing prime Angus beef, Welsh lamb and full-fat creamy milk for eager middle-class consumers. But meat farming soon hit a ceiling. There was no new pastureland for farmers to extend their operations onto, and rather than stimulating supply, the increasing demand had pushed up meat prices.[7] The cost of bread had been lowered by extending Britain's farmland onto the American prairies; now the cost of meat could also be brought down if Britain were able to extend its pastures over the grasslands of the New World.

The meat trade was still reliant on old-fashioned methods of meat preservation. Whenever American meat packers had a surplus of pork, they would rub salt on it and pack it loosely between layers of dry salt in the hold of a transatlantic ship. By the time it reached its destination, the meat had cured into bacon.[8] Dr Edward Smith recommended American bacon to the poor in his *Practical Dietary* (1864) as it was less than half the price of English bacon, but British customers disliked its fattiness.[9] Sensitive to the needs of their market, the Americans brought meat packers from Cork and Liverpool to Cincinnati and Chicago to show them how to cut and cure pork to satisfy British tastes, and American bacon eventually became popular.[10] Another source of extra meat supplies was the Argentinian dried beef peddled by the South American Beef Company, but Dr Smith drew the line at recommending this to the poor. The stuff was so dry and fibrous, he complained, that even slow boiling for 12 hours could not make it palatable and certainly did not render it, as the promotional literature claimed, 'perfectly tender'.[11] Given that in many parts of Britain the poor only had sufficient fuel to cook warm food once a week, he thought it a ridiculous proposition to try to persuade them to buy the awful stuff, which at 4d a pound was no cheaper than cuts of fresh meat. The idea that it might be fed to workhouse inmates he pronounced 'a cruelty'.[12] Dr Smith did, however, reiterate that if a way could be found to bring Argentinian beef to Britain in a moist state, it would indeed 'be a great boon to the masses of the people'.[13]

The physician Andrew Wynter identified canning as the technology to defeat distance and allow 'every man [to] have a slice of good [colonial] beef sandwiched between his free-trade bread'.[14] The British public disagreed, however. Emigrants had taken canning know-how to Australia and begun turning the thousands of waste sheep carcasses that the wool industry produced into canned mutton. Tins of Australian mutton may have won a prize medal at the Great Exhibition in 1851, but after the debacle with the Admiralty over Goldner's spoiled Moldovan tins, the British remained unimpressed.[15] In the 1860s and 1870s, Daniel Tallerman, the Australian industry's agent in London, conducted a vigorous campaign of mass demonstrations of how to cook with canned meat, and set up dining rooms around the country where working men and women could buy 3d dinners of pies and stews, puddings and dumplings, all made with Australian canned meat.[16] Despite the workers' apparent enthusiasm for the cheap dinners – more than a thousand people a day ate in 'Tallerman's Hall' in London – tins of Australian mutton did not fly off the shelves.[17] Tinned meat was only bought by workhouses, gaols and hospitals, whose inmates had no influence over the decision – although in a Cardiff lock hospital, one dinner too many made of the 'nauseous' stuff caused the patients to protest by pelting a nurse with spoons, bread and other missiles and disporting themselves in the garden like lunatics; the troublemakers received 21 days in gaol.[18]

It was only with the invention of tinned corned beef that canned meat gained any traction in the British market. In 1876, Samuel Vestey, a provisions broker from Liverpool, sent his son William out to America to look for new lines for his business. In the Chicago slaughterhouses Samuel realised that the trimmings from the better cuts were going to waste. He borrowed money from his father and set up a canning factory, where he applied a recently invented American technique: packing the meat tightly into the can and cooking it quickly, which produced a more appetising product.[19] His tapered rectangular cans, which allowed the meat to slide out, became the distinctive hallmark of corned beef.[20] The canners streamlined the production of tin cans with machinery and mastered the art of boiling them in a solution containing calcium chloride. This reduced the length of the process from five hours to thirty minutes.[21] But canned meats never secured a dominant positon in the kitchen cupboards of the urban working classes, and tins only ever accounted for less than 6 per cent of British meat consumption. It was clear that canning would not solve Britain's meat crisis.[22]

The United States shipped thousands of live animals to Britain every year, but the expense of installing special decks increased the cost of shipping, the animals suffered from the stress of the voyage and lost weight and a large percentage of them died. It was an emigrant farmer from Croydon who first succeeded in finding a way of shipping meat rather than cattle across the Atlantic.[23] Timothy C. Eastman owned a ranch in Ohio and a slaughterhouse in New York City, where in 1875 he prepared 36,000 lb of beef to be sent to London in an experimental refrigerator known as a 'Bates' tank. Steam-driven fans drew air through a box of ice and then blew it onto the carcasses hanging from hooks so that the cold draught could circulate freely around them. Eastman's beef was a hit. Fed on the blue-stem grass of the prairies, it was juicy, full of flavour and appetisingly streaked with solid lines of fat.[24] New York's 'Cattle King' was soon joined by other enterprising American businessmen, who discovered that they could transport mutton virtually for free by hanging sheep carcasses in the spaces between the sides of beef.

In response to the threat of American competition, English and Scottish cattle farmers opened their own ranches in the United States. By 1882, British-owned ranching companies had invested more than $30 million in transforming the Great Plains, once thick with herds of buffalo, into 'cow country'.[25] British consumers were not particularly keen on the lean meat from the predominant Texas Longhorn cattle, so stockier British beasts were imported to improve the stock. The cattle were bred on the ranges and then sent to specialised feeder farms in Iowa and Illinois, where they were fattened on maize to produce the fat-marbled beef popular with the British.[26] From Chicago's stockyards they were railroaded to slaughterhouses on the East Coast.

Gustavus Swift, a partner in a Boston wholesale meat business, thought that it would also make more sense on this journey to transport the cattle as meat. However, having invested in stockyards and livestock wagons, the American rail companies were unwilling to reinvest in refrigerated railroad cars. In 1880, Swift turned to the Canadian Grand Trunk rail line, as its northern route was too cold for live cattle. He built refrigerated facilities at the railheads in Chicago and Boston, as well as a fleet of refrigerated rail cars. Chicago now became a centre for huge slaughterhouses cum meat-packing factories, handling thousands of animals each day.[27] The more traffic on the rail lines, the more cost-effective this mode of transport became, and by the end of the 1880s, freight rates had fallen by 90 per cent.[28]

In 1881, America shipped 106 million lb of dressed beef to Britain.[29] One in four joints of meat on British dinner tables now came from abroad; in the 1860s, it would have been one in twelve.[30] Industrial-scale American meat processing had solved the problem of Britain's meat supply. But hearty joints of roast beef were integral to British national identity, as they were seen as the source of the Englishman's vitality. The nation's increasing dependence on the United States to supply its beef was therefore something of a blow to national pride. A *Punch* cartoon for Christmas Day 1907, entitled 'Alien Cheer', has a despondent John Bull eyeing his plate dubiously, for the roast beef has been 'killed and chilled in Chicago'.[31]

The Antipodes were keen to follow America's example and gain access to Britain's meat market. But while chilled meat could withstand the short journey across the Atlantic, a more radical preservation method than a Bates tank was needed for a voyage of 13,000 miles, passing through the tropics. Initial experiments with freezing meat were unsuccessful. In 1873, £2,500 raised by subscription from Australian pastoralists was wasted when the shipment of frozen meat became so rank on its way to Britain that it had to be thrown overboard.[32] The Australians watched French attempts to transport frozen meat from Argentina with great interest. In 1878, the Queenslander Thomas McIlwraith sent his brother to France to investigate when it was reported that a cargo of frozen beef had successfully been shipped to Le Havre from Buenos Aires. Based on his brother's investigations of the ammonia compression refrigerators the French had used, McIlwraith put in an order with the Glaswegian firm of Bell and Coleman for air compression and expansion refrigerators to be fitted on his own ship. The SS *Strathleven* collected her cargo from Australia in December 1879 and arrived in London two months later with all 40 tons of beef and mutton in excellent condition. Butchers in Smithfield market claimed it was impossible to tell the difference between the Australian and fresh British meat.[33]

The New Zealand newspapers were filled with reports of the British reception of Australian mutton, and from 1882, New Zealand began exporting frozen sheep carcasses.[34] At first, British consumers had been reluctant to eat the flesh of animals that had been killed as long as nine months ago. The liquid that oozed out of frozen meat as it defrosted led people to think it lost its nutritional value during the thawing process.[35] And there were fears that, like canned food, frozen food might be the source of food poisoning. But the price soon overcame any prejudices. Australian beef undercut American beef by a halfpenny per pound, and New Zealand lamb was at least tuppence cheaper than British lamb. And once they had tasted it, the British relished the meat of the carefully interbred New Zealand Corriedale sheep, preferring it to the rangy mutton derived from Australia's hardy Spanish merinos, bred to withstand the hot, dry climate.[36] 'Prime Canterbury' soon became associated with good-quality meat.[37] British farmers expressed fears that they would be driven out of business. The American prairies had already been brought to their doorstep; now they had to contend with the new proximity of the Australasian grasslands.[38]

DIRECTIONS FOR COOKING NEW ZEALAND AND OTHER FROZEN MUTTON ISSUED BY THE NEW ZEALAND LOAN AND MERCAN-TILE AGENCY CO., 1880s

Frozen meat, like English, improves by hanging. The hindquarters will keep a week in cool weather, the fore-quarters may be cooked sooner. As there is a tendency for the juice to run from the mutton while thawing, it should be hung in such a way to check this. The hind-quarter, haunch, and leg, should be hung by the flaps, the knuckles hanging down, the loins and saddles also by the flaps, giving them a horizontal position. This meat should not be soaked in water for the purpose of thawing (as some suppose), but hung in the larder or other dry, draughty place, and wiped occasionally with a dry cloth in damp weather. Flour should not be used, as it is apt to turn sour. When put down for cooking, the chump part of the leg or loin should be exposed to the fire, or hottest part of the oven, for a few minutes, to toast the part cut and so seal it up, thus keeping the gravy in the joint.[39]

Argentina was a latecomer to the British meat market. It built its first *frigorífico* (meat freezing plant) in 1882, but Argentinian beef and mutton were too low in quality to compete with American corn-fed beef cattle and New Zealand's Corriedale sheep. It was only during the Boer War of 1899–1902 that the Argentinian meat industry was given a boost as British-owned firms spent millions constructing new *frigoríficos* in response to the rise in demand for beef to feed the troops. This made the Argentinian cattle ranchers aware of the potential of the meat trade, and they started to improve their stock, bringing in pedigree bulls from Britain to interbreed with their own animals; they also began to fatten them in specialised finishing farms. By 1910, Argentina was producing quality beef. By now, refrigeration technology had advanced and the cargo ships were equipped with sterilisers and dehumidifiers, which kept chilled beef free of mould.[40] This made it possible to ship chilled as well as frozen meat from South America to Europe. These developments also attracted American investment to Argentina. The American domestic market was beginning to absorb almost all the meat produced in the United States, and the huge meat-packing companies needed an alternative source for their exports to Britain. A vicious price war ensued as British, Argentinian and American meat companies fought for dominance of the industry. The beneficiaries were British consumers, as beef prices fell to all-time lows.[41] Argentina's beef exports doubled, then tripled, until beef came second to wheat as the country's most valuable export. In the first three decades of the twentieth century, Argentina was transformed from a small South American backwater into the ninth richest country in the world.[42]

The technological revolution that made it possible to bring 'fresh' meat to Britain from around the world was indeed the 'great boon to the masses of the people' Dr Edward Smith had predicted.[43] By the 1890s, Britain absorbed 60 per cent of the meat that was traded globally. A fleet of steel steamships equipped with Glaswegian Bell-Coleman patented refrigerators unloaded at Britain's docks huge quantities of lamb from the Antipodes, chilled beef from Argentina and ham and bacon from America.[44] While the middle and upper classes continued to buy the more expensive home-produced meat, imports allowed the working classes to eat a roast once a week.[45] In 1913, an Oxfordshire labourer with a wife and four young children living on a miserable wage of 8s. a week – a wage that in the 1840s would have condemned his family to a diet of bread, tea and treacle – was able to buy 5 lb of frozen brisket for 2s. and 28 lb of bread for 3s. 2½d, as well as Quaker oats, condensed milk and margarine.[46]

In the last quarter of the nineteenth century, besides corned beef and frozen meat, the diet of the working classes began to include three Dutch imports: margarine, condensed milk and cocoa. In the 1880s and 1890s, the temperance movement gave cocoa consumption a boost by opening 'cocoa rooms' or 'coffee palaces' where workers could read the newspapers or play board games while sipping a non-alcoholic cup of tea, coffee or cocoa. The social reformer Charles Booth described how these establishments encouraged custom by allowing those men 'who drink the cocoa … to eat the dinner or breakfast they have brought from home, or bringing the bread and butter … they can add [a] sausage or whatever completes the meal'.[47] For the best part of the nineteenth century cocoa powder was heavily adulterated with lentils, tapioca or arrowroot in order to counter its fattiness, and the bowls of cocoa the early cafés served were more like chocolate soup or gruel than a drink.[48] But as they evolved into more commercial enterprises, the cocoa rooms began to serve a better-quality beverage made with drinking chocolate powder. In the 1860s, cocoa producers had greatly improved the product by adopting the Van Houten cocoa press. By extracting the cocoa butter from the mass of pressed beans, it allowed for the manufacture of a light and digestible powder.[49] 'Pure drinking chocolate' was transformed into a superior drink and gained the edge on coffee, which remained a heavily adulterated product until well into the twentieth century.[50]

A plethora of advertisements now proclaimed that cocoa was a nourishing and wholesome addition to the diet. Most of the cocoa the British drank in the late nineteenth century was made by the Dutch company Van Houten, although Cadbury's began making drinking chocolate in 1866 and Rowntree's followed suit a decade later.[51] But possibly the most successful brand in establishing the drink in the working-class dietary repertoire has long since been forgotten. In his 1898 budget statement, the Chancellor of the Exchequer attributed the fact that 'people are turning their attention to cocoa … to the remarkable success of a certain well-advertised article which, in gratitude to the manufacturer, I am half tempted to name'.[52] He was referring to Dr Tibbles' Vi-Cocoa. Between 1895 and 1910, this blend of cocoa, hops, malt and kola nut was so popular that the Chancellor thought the brand was responsible over the last year for a 25 per cent increase in government duties on imports of manufactured cocoa. Vi-Cocoa was half the price of Cadbury's drinking chocolate, and while Cadbury's aimed to capture the attention of the middle-class housewife looking for a nourishing drink for her family, Vi-Cocoa was promoted as a powerful alternative to tea for the working man. Advertisements claimed that it was by chewing kola nut all day that West Africans were able to endure arduous labour and that Vi-Cocoa would likewise improve the stamina of the British worker. In a typical testimonial, a Mr T. Cox of Trowbridge, who worked a 14-hour day as a roller man in a flour mill, asserted that it was 'a first-class cocoa to work by' and that (no doubt due to the caffeine content of the kola nuts) he felt 'no fatigue with one and a half pint of Vi-cocoa per day in place of 2 pints of tea'.[53]

Margarine had been invented in 1869 as a butter substitute for the French navy, and tinned condensed milk was created in the late 1860s for the troops during the American Civil War. Both were manufactured by the Dutch in large quantities using the leftover skimmed milk that was a by-product of the butter-making industry. Cheaper than both butter and strawberry jam, margarine became the working-class spread of choice, while by 1914 Britain imported more tinned condensed milk than the combined total of canned beef and fish imports. In the days before refrigeration, tinned milk appeared to be a convenient alternative to fresh. But both margarine and condensed milk were lacking in vitamins A and D, as well as fat, and tinned milk was dangerously detrimental to the health of the numerous working-class infants to whom it was fed.[54] However, working-class nutrition changed for the better when New Zealand dairy farmers realised that they could take advantage of the advent of refrigerated ships to capture the world market for butter and cheese. In 1883, a New Zealand dairy inspector wrote enthusiastically, 'We have only to make the prime article in butter and cheese, then no power on earth can stay the flow of gold in this direction.'[55] The farmers organised themselves into co-operatives and brought in a Danish butter expert to help them crack open the British market. On his advice they built up herds of Jersey cows, producing rich milk high in butterfat. Rather than making the butter on the farm, they sent the milk to factories to be processed into a uniform, high-quality product.

By 1914 there were over a thousand River Plate Meat Company butchers shops in Britain, selling chilled Argentinean beef to the working classes.

The influx of imported foods into Britain gave rise to a new form of retailing. The main stumbling block to the sale of imported meat was the lack of cold storage at Britain's ports and in the butchers' shops. Unwilling to aid and abet foreign competitors, butchers were reluctant to install the new technology. Initially, the meat had to be sold direct from the shipboard refrigerators, and inland markets therefore remained out of the importers' reach.[56] Not so easily defeated, American meat-packing companies set up their own chains of shops. This enabled them to carefully stagger the arrival of meat-bearing ships in British ports, as chilled meat had only a limited shelf life of about 10 days once it arrived after a 40-day voyage.[57] Not far behind the Americans were the New Zealanders, who set up James Nelson & Sons, and they were followed by the Argentinian River Plate Meat Company, which by 1914 had established the largest chain, with over a thousand branches.[58] In 1929, the New Zealand Co-operative Dairy Company followed the meat-packers' example and opened the Empire Dairies chain of stores as the sole sales outlet for New Zealand Anchor butter.[59]

As the butcher's chains moved into the working-class districts of the large industrial towns, they were joined by a new breed of specialised grocery store. Lipton's, the Home & Colonial stores, the Maypole Dairy Company and the Co-operative stocked a limited range of working-class staples, most of them imports. They set themselves apart from small corner shops as they did not offer credit: all goods had to be paid for on the spot in cash. Moreover, rather than selling a pennyworth of tea here, a screw of sugar there, they sold their goods in pre-weighed and sealed packages.[60] The chain stores of the colonial meat companies had been set up to distribute a particular product; the new grocery stores reversed this process, establishing their own factories and buying colonial plantations to supply their stores with the goods they wanted to sell. The Home & Colonial Stores set up a company to buy groundnuts in the Gambia and processed them into vegetable oil at the firm's refinery at Erith in Kent.[61] Thomas Lipton went from setting up an egg-packing station in Ireland and a jam factory in London to purchasing a tea estate in Ceylon in 1890.[62] He proudly proclaimed that his teas went directly 'from the tea garden to the tea pot' and pictures of the Tamil tea pickers featured prominently on the packaging.[63]

Combining the roles of producer, buyer, packager, distributor and retailer within one firm allowed these companies to take advantage of economies of scale that they then translated into reasonable prices for their customers.[64] At the same time, the chain stores anticipated demand and transformed high-class goods into items of mass consumption.[65] This now brought biscuits within the reach of ordinary people. In 1873, the Co-operative Wholesale Society opened a biscuit-making factory in Crumpsall, Manchester, while Lipton's, the Home & Colonial Stores and the Maypole Dairy were catered for by the mushrooming number of small, independent manufacturers. A survey conducted in 1936–7 by the William Crawford London advertising agency found that workers had added biscuits to their evening meal of a cup of tea and a slice of bread and butter.[66]

As the working classes' disposable income increased and more firms pre-packaged their goods, the selection of items for sale in the chain stores widened. In 1885, Tate & Lyle began to pour their golden syrup into tins. Pre-packaged pudding rice, custard powder, shredded suet and pickles, once the preserve of the middle classes, now found their way onto the shelves aimed at working-class consumers. The only colonial import that remained out of reach for the working classes was fruit. Refrigerated shipping allowed Tasmania and the Cape to take advantage of the southern hemisphere's reversed seasons to supply Britain with apples and pears during the winter, but these ended up largely in middle-class fruit bowls.[67] Even Hawaiian tinned pineapple was too expensive for working-class budgets until an enterprising Chinese Malay set up a pineapple canning factory in Singapore.[68] As a result, in the 1920s, thousands of cases of affordable tinned pineapple were imported from British Malaya. The British prejudice against Chinese foods meant that the tins were not stamped by the Malayan factories but were sold by various British companies under their own brand name.[69] In addition, tins of apples and pears, cherries, grapefruit, loganberries, peaches, apricots and fruit salad began pouring in from Canada, Australia and the United States. Sunday high tea at six o'clock was another of the rituals associated with prosperity in Prakash Tandon's host family. It consisted of tinned Canadian salmon with bread and butter, and 'instead of the cheap fresh fruit in season', canned Australian pears with tinned Carnation milk.[70]

Thanks to food imports, the working-class diet had substantially improved. However, in the 1930s, the British government became concerned that too many of these foods were imported from outside the Empire.[71] Most of the cocoa consumed in Britain was grown in Portuguese West Africa, and more than half of chilled beef imports came from Argentina. Amid the atmosphere of protectionism during the inter-war years, the government worried about its dependency on unpredictable foreign partners outside its sphere of official influence. The Empire Marketing Board was duly founded in 1926 and ran a vigorous campaign of press and poster advertising in which the white settler colonies were cast as Britain's siblings and the colonies as her children. The public were urged to 'keep your money in the Empire', 'drink Empire grown tea', 'buy Jaffa Oranges' and 'smoke Empire tobacco'.[72] Trade agreements favouring Empire suppliers over foreign competitors reinforced the campaign. Consequently, by 1939, the Empire supplied more than half of Britain's agricultural imports.[73] Britain depended on overseas sources for more than 50 per cent of its meat, about 70 per cent of its sugar and cheese, and 90 per cent of its fats and cereals.[74] This was the culmination of Britain's quest for food that had begun with West Country fishermen going in search of cod in the sixteenth century. By the 1930s, Britain had transformed itself into the world's manufacturing centre and its working classes were fed by its empire.[75]

In which the recipe for irio changes (Kenya, 1900–2016)

How the Empire impacted on subsistence farming in East Africa and introduced colonial malnutrition

IRIO

Ingredients

2 kg floury potatoes – King Edward for preference

300 g fresh or frozen green peas

3 fresh corncobs (if unavailable, you could use a tin of creamed corn, but it really is much nicer with fresh maize)

50 g butter

A handful of fresh spinach leaves

Salt and freshly ground black pepper to taste

Wash and peel the potatoes and cut into chunks. Arrange them at the bottom of a large saucepan. With a sharp knife, cut the sweet kernels off the corncobs, making sure not to cut too deep into the inedible and fibrous core, and add to the potatoes. Fill the pan to cover the vegetables, and add a pinch of salt, before bringing to the boil. Turn the heat down slightly and boil for twelve minutes, or until the potatoes are just cooked through. Add the peas and cook for a further two minutes then drain and switch off the heat. While the vegetables are draining, place the butter and spinach in the bottom of the pan and allow the residual heat to begin melting the butter. Add the cooked vegetables, and thoroughly mash together with a potato masher. Add salt and black pepper to taste. Kenyans swear by mchuzi seasoning made by Royco, which gives a particularly spicy and tasty finish to irio – you may find Mchuzi in African or Caribbean grocery stores.[1]

Note: You can refrigerate any leftovers and form them into patties and pan-fry them the next day.

Contemporary recipes for the Kikuyu porridge or paste known as irio, Kenya's national dish, suggest that it should be made with potatoes, peas and maize.[2] But in June 1988, a nostalgic correspondent in the letters section of the Nairobi newspaper the *Daily Nation* recalled how in his youth the irio that gave him the lovely feeling of a tight stomach after a good meal was made with plantains and njahi (lablab beans). And indeed, over the course of the twentieth century, the recipe for irio has changed. By the 1960s, njahi had been replaced by *Phaseolus* (e.g. kidney and lima) beans. These were introduced to Africa from South America by the Portuguese in the seventeenth century. The Kikuyu subsequently grew them to sell to the trading caravans that used to pass through their lands, but it was not until the twentieth century, under the influence of colonial agricultural officers, that they started to eat these beans themselves.[3] By the early 1970s, they had become such a key ingredient that on 12 June 1971, the *Daily Nation* reported that local kiosk restaurants were likely to take irio off their menus because of a shortage of beans. There seemed to be a consensus that the dish simply was not irio unless at least half of the paste consisted of mashed *Phaseolus* beans.[4] The paper bemoaned the fact that Kenyans were witnessing the disappearance of a traditional food. But in fact, the 1960s incarnation was already a reinterpretation of the original dish. The ever-changing irio recipe reflected the changes in the Kikuyu diet as a result of the pressures colonialism placed on indigenous agriculture.

Published in 1931, *Studies in Nutrition* summarised the results of the first survey of human nutrition in a colonial context. Between 1927 and 1929, the medical student John Foster examined 27,000 Kenyans on the reservations. His colleague Dr John Henderson chemically evaluated the diet of hospital and prison inmates in Nairobi. He was joined by Dr Francis Kelly, who conducted a series of experiments that involved adding iodine, cod liver oil, milk, bone meal and chalk to the hapless inmates' meals.[5] The importance of vitamins and minerals in the human diet had only just been discovered, and scientists and doctors were beginning to apply this knowledge in a number of dietary investigations around the world. The study was ground-breaking because this was the first time a colonial government had assessed not whether their subjects had access to enough food in order to survive, but whether the food they ate was sufficiently nutritious to safeguard their health. It accorded the Kenyans an unprecedented measure of respect by assessing the quality of their diet using the same League of Nations' minimum standards that were applied by researchers to the diets of the urban working classes in the 'civilised' world.[6] The results were written up by J. L. Gilks, the Director of Medical Services in Kenya, and John Boyd Orr. Orr had just published the findings of a British survey showing that about a tenth of British citizens were suffering from hidden malnutrition, in that while they appeared to have enough to eat, their diets did not provide them with enough iron, calcium or vitamins.[7] The Kenyan study revealed equally depressing levels of hidden malnutrition among the Kikuyu.

The scientists concluded that the Kikuyu were malnourished because they were vegetarians. In contrast, they thought the Maasai were particularly well nourished as they consumed large quantities of meat and milk. British nutritionists regarded meat, milk and eggs as the panacea for all dietary ills. It had been demonstrated that if Britain's poor were given access to these foods, it was possible to significantly improve maternal and infant mortality rates while virtually eradicating deficiency diseases. However, the scientists' interpretation of the Kenyan data rested on a fundamental misconception that assigned one particular diet to each tribe and failed to perceive differentiation within the African communities. It was only the Maasai warriors whose diet was rich in animal protein. The non-warrior Maasai were, in fact, largely vegetarian: they ate maize, millet, plantains and beans, supplemented by a few berries and a little honey. This diet was similar to that of the Kikuyu women. A careful reading of Foster's data shows that despite the fact that they avoided milk (as they thought it interfered with their reproductive capacity), Kikuyu women ate surprisingly healthily. They injected beneficial quantities of calcium and manganese into their food by adding greens and the specially prepared ash of swamp plants to their irio, taking the place of spinach in the recipe at the beginning of the chapter.[8] Foreign beans were beginning to make inroads into the Kikuyu reserves, but protein-rich njahi beans were an almost sacred part of the women's diet, associated with health and fertility. Irio made of njahi and plantain was eaten at all the important female rituals such as clitoridectomy, marriage negotiations, weddings and after childbirth.[9]

It was the Kikuyu men who were malnourished. Kikuyu life had been severely disrupted by the arrival of white settlers in the early twentieth century. Few of the haughty Maasai deigned to work for the whites, but the Kikuyu were treated as a labour pool. While their wives and children stayed behind on the reserves, the men went to work on the railways – Nairobi was founded in 1899 as a rail camp – or as labourers on farms. They were given daily rations of 2 lb of *posho*, a cheap maize meal. In much of south and eastern Africa in the 1920s millet was still the staple grain, and the men found cornmeal porridge insubstantial and unsatisfying in comparison.[10] One old Bemba man from Northern Rhodesia told the anthropologist Audrey Richards that when he moved to work in the southern industrial area, he at first ate his way through 'one bag of flour and then a second. Then at last I said, "Well, there it is! There is no food to be found among the Europeans. Their foods are 'light'."'[11] Not only did maize porridge fail to produce the satisfying feeling of a tight, full stomach, it was severely deficient in protein and vitamin B. The 'Kikuyu diet' that the study condemned was, in fact, a version of the industrial ration that was doled out to indigenous workers around the Empire – African slaves, indentured labourers, Aboriginal farm hands, Canadian First Nations. The researchers do not seem to have realised that Kikuyu men were more prone to malaria, respiratory diseases, intestinal disorders and tropical ulcers not because of an inadequate 'traditional' diet but due to the poverty of the rations the cheapskate British fed to their workers.[12]

Studies in Nutrition recommended that the health of the Kikuyu would be improved by the introduction of better animal husbandry. It blithely suggested that every family should have access to cows.[13] The authors' intentions were good, but their recommendations demonstrated their ignorance of African circumstances. The Kikuyu on the reserves had been forced to relinquish their cattle. This was why the 1920s researchers had found no evidence of them eating the sour milk, blood puddings and broiled meat that as recently as 1910 European observers had noted were an integral part of their diet. That the Kikuyu should drink milk was therefore not a practical solution. It would have been more sensible to suggest that the men should add greens and ash to their maize porridge.[14] The aim of the study was to improve the nutritional situation of the East Africans, but in the end it probably did more damage than good, as it confirmed the long-held but misguided colonial belief that the best way to help the natives was to 'improve' indigenous agricultural practices.[15]

When J. L. Gilks retired from the Kenyan Medical Service in 1935, he was replaced by A. R. Paterson. While in office, Paterson wrote an excruciating monument to imperial condescension in the form of a guidebook for Africans entitled *The Book of Civilization*. 'Folk are poorly fed in Africa because most Africans are not good farmers, and particularly are they not good farmers because they do not know how to keep the soil fertile', he postulated. He went on in a vein reminiscent of those seventeenth-century agricultural reformers who insisted that the Irish would never be civilised until they took to the plough: 'When cattle in Africa are used for their proper purposes – to provide milk for the children and meat for [them]selves, and manure for [their] fields, and to draw carts and ploughs – then, but not sooner will people thrive.'[16]

In the inter-war years the colonial authorities in East Africa strove to transform subsistence peasants into commercial farmers. They claimed that economic prosperity would naturally lead to an improvement in nutrition. But the policies the administrations imposed were designed primarily to benefit Britain rather than the African population. The economic strain of the First World War, followed by the Depression, intensified the British determination to reconfigure the African colonies so that they fulfilled the role that had been assigned to colonies since the beginning of the Empire as producers of use-

The African countryside as it is today ...

ful agricultural commodities and importers of British manufactured goods.[17] The Kenyan agricultural department experimented with bean varieties, giving out lima, rose coco, Canadian Wonder and Boston bean seeds in search of a suitable candidate for the colony's infant canning industry.[18] But the most concerted campaign was directed towards extending and intensifying maize farming. The aim was to persuade East Africans to relinquish the traditional staples of sorghum and millet in preference for maize. The surplus crop could then be released onto the market and used to feed workers their ration of *posho* and to supply the region's mushrooming urban population. Maize was priced preferentially to encourage its production, and newspaper advertisements, pamphlets, posters and films presented it as the quick-maturing, high-yielding 'wonder crop' of the modern farmer.[19] By paying higher prices for the new crops, the government ensured their take-up, as the Africans grew them in order to raise cash to pay the poll tax.

The traditional practice of planting a number of crops mixed in together was discouraged by most British agricultural officials, who regarded African farming methods with contempt. The jumbled fields offended British sensibilities, just as the messy fields with beans and squash straggling around the maize plants had affronted the early colonists in America. The canning companies did not want bags of mixed beans, and the practice of 'pure planting' was im-

244

... and the African countryside as it might be. A. R. Paterson's vision of rural Africa
after it had been 'improved' by the introduction of the plough.

posed by agricultural officers, who would inspect the fields to ensure that the
plants were organised in an orderly fashion. The archaeologist Louis Leakey
'had heard it argued again and again that if a Kikuyu would only divide up the
plot of ground that he happens to have available, and would plant his maize in
one part of it, his bean in another and his sweet potatoes in another and so on,
he would get a bigger yield of each of these crops, and moreover, a better one.
But would he?'[20] The answer was that he would not. Intercropping with beans
was a protective measure because they fixed nitrogen in the soil. The maize
monoculture the British advocated became known as 'maize mining' because it
stripped the soil of its fertility.[21]

In 1935, the agricultural officer for Kenya's Central Province,
W. L. Watt, noted with satisfaction that njahi 'has lost its supreme position
in the Kikuyu districts'.[22] It was replaced by *Phaseolus* beans, which were both
a subsistence and a cash crop, as any surplus could be sold to the canning factories. His triumph was misplaced. With the disappearance of njahi from their
diet, the Kikuyu lost one of their richest sources of protein. In the case of maize,
East Africans took a little more persuading before they accepted that it really
was a superior food.[23] After all, reality did not bear out the inflated claims of the
government. Maize requires just the right amount of rain at a precise moment
in its growing cycle in order to achieve its potential. If all goes well, yields can

be phenomenal, and between 1927 and 1947 Tanganyika's government statistics show that in some years maize yields were very high. But if the figures are
averaged out for all 20 years, then overall maize performed worse than millet
and sorghum. It did have the advantage that it matured in about half the time
of the traditional crops and it could be eaten as a vegetable as well as a grain, but
it was not quite the wonder crop it was made out to be.[24]

Nevertheless, the relentless campaign to impose maize eventually took
effect and it became the dominant dietary grain, even for the women and children living on the reserves.[25] Today East Africans regard maize as a quintessentially African food and find millet or sorghum porridge bitter and unpalatable.[26]
As the recipe at the beginning of the chapter shows, for Kenyans maize is now
an essential ingredient in irio. Claims once recognised as propaganda, that
maize is tastier, more nutritious and higher-yielding, have now come to be regarded as common sense. But the men who found cornmeal porridge disap-
pointingly light and insubstantial were intuitively correct. As we saw in Chapter
Five, the transference of the maize plant to Africa without the Mesoamerican
knowledge of how to prepare corn by boiling the kernels in lime water, has
resulted in dependence on a food that is deficient in both protein and vitamin
B. The crop's reliance on a specific pattern of rainfall in a region with unpredictable precipitation makes it a 'false icon of … food security'.[27] The East Africans
would have been better off if they had continued to grow millet, sorghum, njahi
and plantain, using traditional farming methods.

One positive consequence of the Kenyan nutritional study was that it brought
the problem of malnutrition in the colonies to light and led to the setting-up
in 1936 of a Committee on Nutrition in the Colonial Empire. The committee
commissioned reports on the nutritional health of the colonies and the findings were damning. Jamaica, Antigua, West Africa, the Far East, Mauritius
and Ceylon all returned evidence that malnutrition was an Empire-wide problem. Mauritians were reported to be smaller and unfit, and the Ceylonese were
thought to be suffering from lack of food due to overpopulation. The governors
of Jamaica and Antigua concluded that poverty was the cause of underfeeding.
'Parents cannot afford to buy food', stated the senior medical officer on
Antigua. On the Gold Coast the director of the medical department identified

the attention devoted to mining and cocoa as detrimental to subsistence farming and forest conservation. Besides poverty, low wages, poor yields and the lack of food crops, the ignorance of 'Government officials and those who have power over the nutrition of others' was identified as one of the primary causes of malnutrition.[28]

The Second World War diverted attention from the problem of colonial malnutrition, but after 1945, the authorities returned to their old plan of improving indigenous nutrition by commercialising the colonies' agricultural economies. A number of misguided schemes sought to transfer the farming techniques then currently effecting a revolution on British farms to Africa, where they were wholly inappropriate. Ironically, given that it was the slave trade that had led to the disappearance of West African mangrove rice farming, the Gambia Field Working Party attempted to 'introduce' rice farming to the region's swamp lands. Two tractors were dispatched in 1947, but when they sank into the silt on the rice fields, the experiment was abandoned.[29] In 1948, the Colonial Development Corporation was set up to organise the production of agricultural commodities such as sugar, rice, cocoa, eggs, meat and vegetable oils, both to feed Britain, suffering in the grip of post-war austerity, and to sell to the United States in order to earn much-needed foreign exchange.[30] The corporation did manage to set up a successful palm oil plantation and two sugar estates, but most of its schemes failed. The abattoirs, fruit-packing plants and canneries, fishing projects and banana, citrus, coconut, palm oil, rice, sugar and cocoa plantations all folded. Most of the eggs shipped to Britain from the poultry farm it established in the Gambia were declared unfit for human consumption.[31]

The Tanganyika groundnut scheme was perhaps the most costly of the string of failures. Between 1946 and 1951, the project absorbed the equivalent of three years' worth of development funding for the entire Empire. It was the brainchild of the Ministry of Food, which sought a source of cheap vegetable oil for Britain's fat-hungry population. Machinery was shipped to Tanganyika to clear the land in order to create a huge peanut plantation. But the tractors either broke down or their equipment was not strong enough to tackle the stubborn tree roots and deal with the hardness of the sun-baked earth when workers attempted to harvest the crop from the small area they had succeeded in planting. This was hardly a demonstration of the superiority of mechanised farming. It cost more to clear the land than it was worth even once it had been planted with peanuts. The little groundnut oil that was gleaned from the plantation made a negligible contribution to Britain's requirements. The money would have been better spent on repairing northern Nigeria's railways, where there was a glut of groundnuts but no infrastructure to take them to the ports.[32]

The colonial schemes did little to alleviate hunger or improve nutrition in the colonies. Rather than bringing to light the negative impact of colonial policy on indigenous diets, investigations into colonial malnutrition began to construct the still persistent notion that hunger and poverty were endemic to the colonies.[33] The various post-war 'development' schemes failed even to produce food for Britain.[34] More lamentably, the string of development failures did not sufficiently discredit the belief that Africa would be best served if it were transformed into a version of south-eastern England. This misguided way of thinking continued to colour post-colonial development policy even into the 1980s. East Africa was left with a less nutritious staple, which reduced the interest and variety of the indigenous diet while also making the population more vulnerable to food scarcity. When the world demand for dried *Phaseolus* beans fell in the 1970s, Kenyan dried bean cultivation also declined as women switched to growing green beans for the European market.[35] Hence the complaints in the *Daily Nation* in 1971 that the bean content in irio was falling and the eventual disappearance of beans altogether from the dish, to be replaced by European white potatoes. When contemporary Kenyans at a kiosk restaurant contemplate a volcano-shaped mound of potato–pea–maize irio, it should bring home to them the cry of Thomas Sankara, former president of Burkina Faso: 'Do you not know where imperialism is to be found? … Just look at your plate!'[36]

19

In which infantryman R. L. Crimp eats bully beef and sweet potatoes in a forward camp in the North African desert (September 1941)

How the Empire supported Britain during the Second World War

In September 1941, R. L. Crimp found himself in an 'austere and primitive' forward camp in the North African desert, a couple of hundred miles behind the front line. Life was led entirely in the open air, 'under the broiling sun by day, and by night in blanket beds made up on the hard desert surface, under the stars'.[1] Crimp had been assigned to a motorised infantry unit, and the focus of the camp was the section area where the company's thirty trucks were parked. His section's truck – called Mabel after the driver's wife – was surrounded by their gear and supplies: a Bren gun; a Boyes anti-tank rifle; several boxes of ammunition; a large Italian medical chest in which they stored their rations; a box full of tinned emergency rations and another for their plates, mess tins, mugs and cutlery; about half a dozen two-gallon water cans and another half a dozen supposedly 'untouchable' cans to be kept for an emergency; a tool box; a spare wheel and several spades. When they travelled, the brew pots and cut-down petrol tins that made the campfires were tied on to the side of the truck. In camp, these marked out the kitchen area next to the spaces where each man's bed roll was laid out on the hard ground, with his personal kit of a haversack, webbing equipment, overcoat, gas mask and tin hat neatly piled at its head.[2]

At six o'clock each evening, one man from each of the sections was called to accompany the corporal to platoon headquarters to collect their rations. Equipped with sacks, canisters and empty water cans, they made their way over to the quartermaster's sergeant, who had already laid out 'basic' piles on the ground consisting of four cans of bully for each six-man section, a tin of milk, a tin of cheese, and one orange per man. The men greeted him with the usual opening gambit, 'Wot, no fresh meat?' In fact, fresh meat only ever appeared 'once in a blue moon', but the men made it a habit to groan over their bully beef. This was the name sailors had given to those early cans produced by the pioneers of meat canning in imitation of Nicolas Appert's beef bouillon. But the bully beef the troops ate in North Africa was, in fact, that compacted form of canned beef invented by William Vestey in Chicago in the 1870s. The chances were that the cans had been shipped all the way to North Africa from the Fray Bentos canning factory in Argentina, which supplied Britain with most of its corned beef during the war. 'Anyone now for Cruft's Specials?' called out the sergeant.[3] This was the hardtack the troops compared to dog biscuits. No doubt the 28 lb tins had been packed in Carr's Carlisle biscuit factory, which churned out tons of hardtack for the army.

Corned beef, hardtack and, if they were fortunate, potatoes were the staple diet of the desert soldiers in this early part of the war. 'Here's two tins of spuds; you'll have to toss!' the sergeant continued.[4] The tins contained familiar white potatoes, which the men preferred. Those who lost the toss were given fresh yellow Egyptian sweet potatoes and cursed their luck. So unpopular with the troops were sweet potatoes that later in the war the British army set up a scheme to encourage the cultivation of white potatoes in the Middle East. The merchant seaman Roy Bayly recalled bringing a shipment of seed potatoes to Cairo, a troublesome cargo as they needed constant ventilation to ensure that they did not start to rot. In the post-war years, when he saw Egyptian white potatoes for sale in British supermarkets, he used to regard them proprietorially as 'descendants of "my" potatoes of 1943'.[5] Margarine and jam in 7 lb tins were distributed next, amid vociferous complaints that the jam was strawberry rather than the much-preferred gooseberry. There were also a few rude comments about the tins of fish the sergeant had spare. Last, but certainly not least, the sugar and tea were carefully measured out. The men virtually counted every leaf as the sergeant ladled each section's third of a mug of tea leaves out of his sack. The sugar was poured into German respirator cases. The British soldiers had adopted these as useful containers as they had hinged lids. Finally, two gallons of water were given out and, heavily laden, the men made their way back to camp.[6]

An open-air kitchen in the Western Desert much like the one set up by R. L. Crimp's
motorised infantry unit.

Here, Crimp suppressed his irritation with his NCO, who constantly
felt the need to demonstrate his authority by choosing which rations should
be cooked each day and allotting the men potato-peeling and tin-opening
duties. His interference made food preparation into an irksome exercise
when, in fact, left to their own devices they would have taken pleasure in
the performance of these small domestic chores.[7] As darkness fell, Crimp's
section prepared themselves a simple dinner of bully beef and sweet potatoes,
followed by rice pudding with a dollop of jam and an orange. Oranges were
virtually the only fresh fruit available in the desert. Cyprus, cut off from its
peacetime markets by U-boats in the Mediterranean, had a glut and these
were fed to the troops.

Crimp was glad to eat in the darkness, as during the day it was 'the
devil's own job' to keep the hordes of flies that plagued them with 'malign
persistence' from landing on their food. It was only at sunset that the flies all
simultaneously disappeared, 'as at some secret signal'.[8] With their dinner eaten,
the men began the serious business of brewing tea. The brew can was filled with
water and set over a cut-down biscuit tin with a few inches of petrol-soaked

sand in the bottom. When the water had come to a rolling boil, a couple of handfuls of tea leaves were thrown in and the brew was set aside to strengthen. Meanwhile tinned milk and sugar were distributed among the mugs gathered on the ground next to the fire. Hot, sweet tea was as much of a comfort to the soldiers in the desert as it was to the working classes at home. 'As long as there's no lack of char or fags everyone's happy', wrote Crimp. 'When there's a shortage of either, morale slumps.'[9]

Before the war John Tonkin worked for the New Zealand Shipping Company in charge of their stores department, and as a consequence he acquired 'an elementary knowledge of cooking'. Having originally been posted to an anti-aircraft battery that served in Norway, he retrained as a cook and was posted to Egypt and Crete, where he must have been one of the British army's most inventive chefs.

HOW TO USE UP AN EXCESS OF MARROWS

'Soldiers by and large will not eat vegetable marrow, with white sauce or without it.' Have the butcher make up two hundred pounds of mince from fresh beef, onions and herbs ('really hard graft in a hot climate'). Hollow out the excess numbers of vegetable marrows delivered to the unit. Fill said marrows with the mince mixture. Bake in Aldershot ovens. 'A great success with the troops.'

THE FAVOURITE METHOD FOR COOKING CORNED BEEF ON CRETE

'Cut the meat into slices and deep fry them in flour and egg batter.'

WELSH RAREBIT THE CRETAN WAY

First assign a fatigue party to undo multiple quantities
of the miniature cheese segments enclosed in foil which
the troops refuse to eat. 'Prepare onions by slicing
across them very thinly.' Make a 'quantity of thickening
with flour and plenty of splendid Cretan eggs'. Evaporated milk makes an especially good addition. Place this
and the cheese segments in Sawyer boilers and season.
Detail cooks to stir the mixture while it bubbles over the
fire. Finish with Worcester sauce. In the meantime have
cook's assistants line baking trays with slices of bread.
Brown this bread off lightly in the ovens and butter
the resulting toast. Cover generously with the cheese
mixture and return to the ovens and brown. Serve to the
eager troops.[10]

The British soldiers in North Africa were given the same ration that had fed the Empire's sailors, explorers, cowboys, indentured labourers and pioneer settlers. As we have seen, over the centuries the British had become expert in processing and packaging durable foods and transporting them great distances to feed their colonists and settlers as they spread to virtually every corner of the globe. When war broke out in 1939, the British Isles sat at the centre of a complex trading web. Every day between 15 and 20 ships docked at British ports bringing the wheat, frozen and chilled meat, sugar, tea and canned milk that fed the nation's working classes. At the same time, intercolonial trade took countless goods from one colony to another. After Britain, Australia was India's biggest customer for tea, while Burmese rice fed colonial subjects not only in Bengal and Ceylon but as far away as East and southern Africa, the Gambia, Mauritius, Zanzibar and Fiji.[11] This reliance on imports and dependence on sea trade could have been Britain's Achilles heel if Hitler had decided to prioritise the building of U-boats as the head of the submarine arm of the German navy, Admiral Karl Dönitz, recommended. Although U-boats were a menace, however, and thousands of

Empire seamen lost their lives when their ships were torpedoed, the German blockade never seriously threatened to bring Britain to its knees.[12]

The Empire was, in fact, the source of Britain's strength. Britain was not a tiny island standing alone on the edge of Europe but the centre of a powerful network on which it drew for supplies of men, arms and ammunition, raw materials and, above all, food. As an Englishman, Crimp was in a minority in the Eighth Army that fought Erwin Rommel in North Africa. He was joined in the desert by troops from all over the Empire: Australia, New Zealand, South Africa, Southern Rhodesia, India, Basutoland, Bechuanaland, Ceylon, Cyprus, the Gambia, the Gold Coast, Kenya, Mauritius, Nigeria, Palestine, Rodrigues, Sierra Leone, the Seychelles, Swaziland, Tanganyika and Uganda.[13] It was a similar picture in the other theatres of war. Australian warships fought in the Mediterranean; South Africa supplied mine sweepers, bombers and fighter air-craft; the Indian air force fought the Japanese; and British airmen received their training in Australia, Canada, South Africa and Southern Rhodesia.[14] Nigeria's supplies of tin and Ceylon's provisions of rubber were vital after the fall of Ma-laya to the Japanese, while Cyprus produced silk for parachutes.[15]

In 1939, Britain imported from Canada virtually all the wheat it used to make bread. It also imported large quantities of grain as fodder for livestock, as British farms still produced almost half of the country's meat supplies and all of its milk. However, the loss of calories involved in converting grain into meat meant that in wartime it made no sense to use scarce shipping space for bulky feed grains. And as the calorific value of wheat was also poor in comparison to that of meat, it made more sense to grow wheat and import meat.[16] The war-time ploughing-up campaign, which turned pastureland into fields of ripening corn, would have warmed the heart of Robert Cecil, who had in 1601 identi-fied the plough as the foundation of England's stable society.[17] As a result, in 1943, half of the wheat in the National Loaf was grown by British farmers.[18]

The farmers out on Canada's western prairies adapted by cultivating coarse feed grains instead of wheat. These were fed to pigs on the east coast to make into bacon for Britain. New Zealand responded to Britain's request for cheese, thereby packing twice as much energy and protein into a cubic foot of shipping space than was provided by frozen lamb. But when in 1942 the British discovered they were running short of cooking fat, due to the Japanese invasion of South East Asia, the New Zealanders obligingly introduced butter rationing and converted their cheese-making factories back to making butter. At the same time, Argentina supplied corned beef, which the British stored in warehouses as a reserve against meat shortages, and the United States provided deboned and telescoped beef – so as to fit as much as possible into ships' holds – canned Spam and sausages, cheese and dried egg.[19]

It was not only the settler colonies and the United States that came to Britain's rescue. 'Crack for Victory' became a slogan in West Africa, and schoolchildren throughout the region cheerfully broke open palm fruit stones while singing about winning the war by knocking Hitler on the head.[20] They produced over 400,000 tons of feather-light palm kernels to be processed into margarine to supply British housewives with their ration of 2–3 oz a week.[21] The tropical colonies mainly supplied goods that at the beginning of the war no one wanted. It appeared to be an act of benevolence when the British organised control boards to buy up West African cocoa and Mauritian sugar at low fixed prices. But as the war progressed, worldwide demand for food escalated and Britain found a market for cocoa beans in America, where they were turned into emergency K-rations for US troops. It was Britain that profited from the upturn in the fortunes of these commodities, not the colonial farmers.[22] And if British civilians were well fed as a result of the policy of importing condensed, high-energy foods, this was because the country was able to draw on farms in the settler colonies, which extended the nation's agricultural estate over vast tracts of the world's land.

In order to reach North Africa, Crimp's ship had sailed from England to Durban – where the infantryman spent a week ridding his nostrils of the cloying smell of the rotting vegetables kept in the store below his berth – before continuing up the east coast of Africa and into the Suez Canal.[23] German U-boats had effectively closed the Mediterranean to Allied shipping, and all troops and supplies for the North African campaign were forced to make the long journey around the Cape. This caused chaos in the Red Sea ports, as they did not have the capacity to cope with the more than five million tons of imported goods that were needed for the military campaign alone. Matters were made worse by American businessmen, not yet in the war, trying to capitalise on the wartime shortage of consumer goods in the Middle East; incongruous piles of crates of stockings and underwear imported from the United States began to build up on the docks alongside tanks and military supplies.[24]

The Middle East was saved from chaos by the talented young Australian, Robert Jackson, who headed the Middle East Supply Centre. The Centre successfully co-ordinated the harvest collection, food stocks, industrial production and import needs of the region so that it remained stable despite the wartime disruption.[25] Meanwhile, the military campaign was not going well, and in the summer of 1942, the Allies were driven back across the desert towards Cairo. On their diet of bully beef and biscuit, the troops fell sick with jaundice, dysentery, vitamin deficiency diseases and battle fatigue. Crimp displayed the symptoms of all these afflictions. He felt as though the barren desert had saturated his consciousness, making his 'mind as sterile as itself', and his whole being was so overwhelmed by apathy that he felt a 'vast aversion to exertion in every form'.[26] Large consignments of tinned fruit were brought up from South Africa in an effort to supply the men with vitamins, fibre and the will to fight.

The German advance was finally halted by the Second Battle of El Alamein in the autumn of 1942. At the other end of the desert the pressure on the Germans intensified with Allied landings in Morocco. Winston Churchill was determined to prioritise the needs of the troops fighting to push the Germans off the African continent, but at the same time the demands on British shipping were increasing. The United States was supplying less meat to Britain than it had promised, and the Ministry of Food was lobbying hard for extra ships to be sent to Argentina and Australia to replenish Britain's depleted meat reserves. Preparations for an assault on continental Europe meant that yet more ships had to be allocated to the build-up of American forces in Britain.[27] Churchill therefore decided to safeguard the supply of food imports into Britain, and cut the number of ships sailing to the Indian Ocean by 60 per cent.[28] The consequences for the subjects of the Empire were severe.

The effects were immediately felt in Mauritius. The sugar-producing island had done its best to replace its usual imports of Burmese rice and Indian lentils with home-grown manioc, maize and peanuts. But drought, a cyclone, and the sinking of a ship bringing peanut-processing machinery confounded the population's best efforts. When Indian Ocean shipping was cut, so was their lifeline of wheat imports. They only just managed to scrape through the war, malnourished but largely saved from starvation by mercy shipments of Australian wheat and manioc starch from Madagascar.[29]

In East Africa, forced conscription took many men off the reserves and into the army. Others were recruited to work as labourers in the ports and railways, on sisal plantations in Tanganyika, and as hands on white settlers' farms in the Rhodesias and Kenya. When the short rains of September to November failed in some areas in 1942, the elderly, women and children left behind on the reserves struggled to break new ground so as to plant extensively in time for when the long rains began in February. Added to this, the colonial administrations were pressing for the peasants to sell as much maize as possible to the government; they needed it to provide the men working outside the reserves with their daily ration of 2 lb of *posho* a day. That this left poorer households without food reserves and vulnerable to famine simply did not enter into their calculations.[30] When in some regions the long rains, which should have lasted until June, stuttered to a halt in March 1943, food scarcity led to a thriving black market. Maize brought in from areas where the rains had continued sold for four times the usual price. Wealthy families used their savings to get them through, but the poor were priced out of the market. They resorted to stealing green unripened cobs from their neighbours' fields. And in many areas they began to starve. In mid February 1943, two ships scheduled for India were diverted to take grain to East Africa to ease the situation.[31]

The Viceroy of India, Lord Linlithgow, protested against these diversions, for in Bengal in 1943, the need for outside assistance was pressing. When in January 1943 the British government announced that they would cut shipping to the Indian Ocean, they were aware that a food crisis was brewing in India. Linlithgow had asked for 600,000 tons of grain in the coming year. But Churchill and his scientific adviser, Lord Cherwell, were unsympathetic. Churchill regarded Eastern colonial governments as improvident, and pronounced that there was 'no reason why all parts of the British Empire should not feel the pinch in the same way as the Mother Country has done'.[32] The cut in shipping did not cause the Bengal famine, but it meant that there was no hope of staving it off or, when famine did strike, of alleviating it. A mixture of a poor rice harvest, wartime measures that hampered the movement of rice from surplus to deficit areas, and the government's incompetence when they fixed rice prices too low – causing what supplies there were to be channelled onto the black market – led to spiralling food price inflation. The poor and the wage-dependent – landless labourers and artisans, office clerks and teachers – who bought their food on a daily basis were priced out of the market.[33]

During the Durga Puja holidays in 1943, Bisewar Chakrabati, head-master of a secondary school in the north, visited his home village of Munsiganj in the Ganges delta. He was shocked to find that the 'whole population seems to be moving silently towards death'.[34] When the villagers could no longer find the strength to walk to the community kitchen, they simply lay down on the cold ground and died.[35] Desperate skeletons began drifting into Calcutta in the summer. Ian Stephens, editor of the Calcutta newspaper *The Statesman*, was struck by how quietly 'famine comes ... There was no shouting, no violence, no looting of shops.' The starving simply wandered about 'bewildered [and] finding no help ... squatted in the by-ways and grew feebler and lay down and after a while died'.[36]

It took an eight-week campaign on the part of Stephens, who ran edi-torials attacking government indifference to the plight of the Bengalis, and published letters and testimonials and photographs of the dead and dying on the streets of Calcutta, before the British government in London finally ac-knowledged in October 1943 that Bengal had been struck by famine.[37] And it was only when Lord Wavell replaced the incompetent Linlithgow as viceroy in September 1943 that any decisive action was taken to remedy the appalling situation. The military now escorted deliveries of rice to rural areas; boats that had been removed in order to deny their use to possible Japanese invaders were repaired and put back into service; price controls were enforced and ra-tioning was introduced.[38] People continued to die, but the starving and the destitute on Calcutta's streets were rounded up to perish out of sight in spe-cial camps.[39] While just over 31,000 Allied infantry died in the North Africa campaign, around three million Bengalis died from starvation and the effects of malnutrition.[40]

More than anything, India needed shipments of grain to stave off in-cipient famine in the rest of the country. There were reports of tensions among starving rubber estate workers in Mysore and Travancore. Wavell repeatedly asked London for shipments of food to be diverted to India, but a government committee set up to look into the question of Indian requirements decided that the priority for the limited shipping should continue to be British civilian food supplies. A Canadian offer of 100,000 tons of wheat was turned down for this reason. The Indian legislative assembly was prevented from applying to the United Nations Relief and Rehabilitation Administration, as the British feared the judgement of its officers. It was only when Wavell was able to persuade the South East Asia Command that the troops could withstand a reduction in supplies that he was able to secure a shipment of 200,000 tons of grain. Incompetence in India certainly exacerbated the situation, but Churchill and his War Cabinet deliberately chose to sacrifice India's population to hunger.[41] When Wavell heard of the airlifts of supplies to the Netherlands in March 1945, he remarked that they demonstrated 'a very different attitude towards feeding a starving population when the starvation is in Europe'.[42]

The decision to divert shipping away from the Empire enabled the British to rebuild their stocks of food. While Churchill's henchman, Lord Cherwell, was quite happy for India to 'tighten its belt', he became mildly hysterical when in March 1943 British food reserves fell below 50 per cent of their supposed minimum.[43] In fact, the cut in Indian Ocean shipping had allowed an extra two million tons of supplies to reach the British Isles.[44] Moreover, by 1942, the Ministry of Food had established a stable and satisfactory food distribution system that, to the great benefit of British civilian morale, the population perceived to be fair. The growth in war industries had also solved the scourge of unemployment. High wartime wages meant that the working classes could afford to buy enough food for their families, and the introduction of rationing ensured that everyone had equal access to the country's supplies.[45]

The British civilian's wartime ration was similar to the nineteenth-century working-class industrial diet, in that it was heavily dependent on bread and potatoes, both of which were unrationed. To the nutritionists' satisfaction, however, from 1942, the National Loaf was wholemeal. The scarcity of shipping forced the government to use as much home-grown wheat as possible, and the extraction rate for milled flour was raised from 70 to 80 per cent. This meant that it retained the nutritious wheatgerm and produced a much-loathed beige loaf.[46] In addition, British farmers produced so many potatoes that the public could not consume them all, and large amounts ended up as pig feed. In the inter-war years there had still been poor families in Britain for whom meat was a rare treat. Now rationing guaranteed every working-class person a shilling's worth of meat per week, as well as 4 oz of bacon, 2 oz each of cheese and butter, 4 oz of margarine, three pints of milk, an egg or its equivalent in dried egg powder, 8 oz of sugar and 2 oz of tea. Apart from the fact that tea supplies were constricted, this was a luxurious version of the industrial ration. Sugar, once seen as a profligate working-class indulgence, had become so integral a part of the British diet and so essential a source of energy that even though it was nutrionally deficient it was included on the ration.[47] In addition, the nutritionists on the sub-committee on food policy managed, with the co-operation of Lord Woolton, the Minister of Food, to ensure a programme of free school meals, priority supplies of milk for pregnant women and nursing mothers, as well as milk, orange juice and cod liver oil for under-fives. Rickets and vitamin deficiency diseases all but disappeared in Britain, and maternal and infant mortality rates improved. The stubborn pocket of working-class deprivation was at last removed.[48]

During the war, the hierarchy of priorities that had always operated within the Empire became glaringly obvious. British citizens were prioritised; below them were the white settlers in the dominions; and last, and definitely least, came Britain's colonial subjects. The Bengalis who died of famine in their millions, the East Africans forced to sell their reserves of maize and robbed of food security, the poor in Bechuanaland who were reduced to foraging for roots and berries, and the Gambians who ate the seed nuts intended for next year's planting of peanuts were not simply suffering from unrelated wartime shortages.[49] They were the other side of the coin that ensured that the British were well fed and maintained their health and energy throughout the war.[50] The trading rules of the Empire had always been rigged in favour of Britain – the war both intensified the exploitation of colonialism and exposed the hollowness of its rhetoric.

In which Mr Oldknow dreams of making an Empire plum pudding (24 December 1850) and Bridget Jones attends Una Alconbury's New Year's Day Turkey Curry Buffet Lunch (1 January 1996)

How Christmas fare took the Empire into British homes

On Christmas Eve 1850, Mr Oldknow sat before the kitchen fire smoking a cigar. He had spent the afternoon 'romping with his children' who now 'at last had gone to bed with flushed faces and disordered curls'. He followed his wife into the kitchen, where she read him the recipe for 'A Pound Christmas Pudding' from the family receipt book and showed him the 'rich, semi-liquefied mass, speckled with plums and currants' sitting in a 'vast earthen pan' waiting to be spooned into pudding cloths 'at the peep of dawn' the next morning. He was tempted to sit a while in the warmth and muse while his wife went off to bed. A keen armchair traveller, as he gazed upon the 'vast pudding dish' his thoughts turned to 'the mercantile history of the various substances of which th[e] pudding was composed'. Worn out 'after all the polking and blind man's buff' he fell into a doze and in his dreams the smoke from his cigar took on the form of a succession of ghostly figures, each one bearing the ingredients to make a plum pudding.[1]

The first figure to appear in Mr Oldknow's kitchen was the Genius of the Raisin from the sun-drenched hillsides of Andalusia, who complained that the British arrived at Mediterranean ports 'every year … with … linens and … woollens … glass and … pottery' to exchange for dried grapes that would have been better made into wine. Mr Oldknow patiently explained to his disgruntled interlocutor that the availability of 'the products of our looms

261

and our furnaces' would encourage industriousness among his people. 'For we induce a taste for comforts that will become a habit. When our glass and our porcelain shall find its way into your peasant's hut, then will your olives be better tended and your grapes more carefully dried. Man only worthily labours when he labours for exchange with other labour.'² Mr Oldknow's next visitor was, in contrast, a cheerful advocate of free trade. The Greek Genius of the Currant thought it more efficient to grow vines on his native soil where the climate suited them and then exchange currants for wheat, sugar and coffee. 'Welcome is your Christmas', he declared, for the laws of supply and demand meant that as long as Englishmen continued to want currants for their plum puddings, Greece would be sure of its bread.³

The currant genie was quickly replaced by the smock-frocked Genius of Bread in a straw hat and laced boots, slow of speech and muttering about 'Protection'. 'Who taught you that song?' asked Mr Oldknow, becoming agitated. 'Do *you* want protection against cheap bread … against warm and clean clothing; against a sound roof with glazed windows; against a coal fire; against your tea, your sugar, your butter, your cheese, your bacon, and your Christmas pudding?' The Corn Laws had been repealed only four years earlier and Mr Oldknow was clearly convinced of the benefits to Britain's labouring classes of cheap foreign food imports. The Genius of Suet had only a walk-on part, driving a tired ox to its end in Smithfield market, and was quickly replaced by a forest scene from the Banda Islands in the Indian Archipelago and the 'fantastic figure' of the Genius of Nutmeg. A strange creature, with the head of a Dutchman on the body of a wood pigeon, he delivered a speech on the shortcomings of his East India Company's attempts to monopolise the European spice trade. Having observed the thriving British colony of Ceylon, which sold cinnamon to all comers, he claimed to have learned that the 'end of commerce … is not to make [a few] individuals rich … but to diffuse all the productions of nature and art, amongst all the inhabitants of the globe'.⁴

It was more difficult to feel triumphant on the appearance of the Genius of Sugar in the guise of a freed West Indian slave who, although he was no longer in chains, had lost the security of an assured home market. 'The nation that demanded cheap corn would not be content with dear sugar', he complained, and now bought its annual 700 million lb of sugar from whatever was the cheapest source. Shying away from the complicated politics of slavery and sugar, Mr Oldknow was beguiled by the cloaked figure of the Egg-Collector of Cork, with laughing grey eyes and long black lashes, miraculously recovered from the effects of famine.

Next appeared the gnomic figure of Salt, who berated Mr Oldknow for depriving the Hindoo of fiscal justice, in a reference to the salt tax the British administration imposed on its Indian subjects. The Milky Genius took his place, a combination of a dairymaid and a water nymph. Finally a power-loom weaver 'stepped forth, with a pudding-cloth in hand. "The water boils," said he; "the ingredients are mixed. Be it mine to bind them together!"'[5] A giant pudding arose out of the bowl and swelled into 'an enormous globe' and a Frenchman emerged out of a bunch of holly to pour a flask of brandy over the pudding, announcing, 'It is the genius of our nation to flare up!' As the pudding burst into flames, the genii danced around it and Mr Oldknow broke into a song to celebrate Britain's bringing together of the 'league of mankind'.[6]

This was the scene conjured up in a piece entitled 'A Christmas pudding' published in Charles Dickens' periodical *Household Words* in December 1850. From the late 1830s, specially written Christmas books, short stories and periodical pieces were published every December; in them, the Victorians reinvented Christmas as a cosy celebration of Englishness. Families were portrayed gathered together to overindulge in roast beef and most particularly in plum pudding. Mr Oldknow declared it 'our England's annual luxury'.[7] Enriched with dried fruit and spices, plum pudding was a version of the plain pudding that had been a favourite with the English since they began boiling dough mixtures in a cloth in the seventeenth century. Although in the eighteenth and nineteenth centuries it was eaten on celebratory occasions throughout the year, Victorian seasonal literature's persistent association of plum pudding with Christmas meant that over time people began to think of it as Christmas pudding.

As Mr Oldknow's dream showed, the milk, wheat and beef suet needed to make a plum pudding were home-produced, although, with the repeal of the Corn Laws, an American pioneer farmer could just as well have replaced the Kentish ploughman as the Genius of Bread. However, the sugar, spices and dried fruit that made it special were foreign. The author of *The Book of Christmas* (1836) personified the plum pudding as a 'blackamoor who derives his extraction from the spice lands'. He went on to explain that 'his Oriental

One of several *Punch* cartoons which used a plum pudding to represent
the globe. Here Britannia is bountifully offering to share some plum
pudding with American Jonathan as a gesture of thanks after the United
States discovered and returned the exploration vessel the *Resolute*, abandoned
during a British expedition to the North Pole.

properties have, however, received an English education and taken an English
form'.[8] In the book's illustrations, the pudding appeared as a portly black man
whose rotund figure was clothed in archaic medieval English dress.

The plum pudding was thought of as 'a truly national dish' not in spite
of but because of its foreign ingredients.[9] These made it into an 'emblem of
our commercial eminence'.[10] *Punch* cartoons showing John Bull poised with his
knife and fork over the globe represented as a plum pudding are a powerful illustration of just how central the commercial empire was to the British sense of
self.[11] To be a Victorian Englishman was to possess the power to eat the world.

In the seventeenth and eighteenth centuries, the influx of large quantities
of tobacco, sugar, tea, spices and calicoes from the Empire meant that all levels
of society acquired new tastes and Britain was transformed into a nation of con-

sumers. Ordinary labourers like Nany Latham and her daughters were drawn into the commercial economy, taking up spinning in order to earn the cash to buy gingham dresses, china plates and sugar candy. People from all walks of life – not just the elite – could now be judged by the furnishings in their homes, the pretty ribbon in their hair, the quality of the tea they served their guests. These standards were used to assess the status of others, but in an important psychological shift people also applied them when judging themselves. This change in sensibilities gave rise to a new, recognisably modern sense of self. Thus the Empire played an important part in the creation of the modern capitalist consumer.[12]

In the Second Empire's era of free trade, the British saw it as their duty to bring about a similar industrious revolution in the rest of the world. Colonial Americans, from the Carolina rice planter with his fine mahogany dining table to the New England farmer who drank his rum out of a pewter goblet, had already been transformed into enthusiastic consumers in the eighteenth century.[13] But central to the ideology of the British civilising mission was the notion that even wayward Pacific islanders and nomadic Aborigines could be brought into the fold of respectable Christian civilisation if they were educated in the delights of British habits such as drinking sugared tea from china cups.

By the mid nineteenth century there could be nothing more British than a cup of sweet tea. And yet the drink was an infusion of a Chinese plant acquired in exchange for opium grown in Bengal. In the early years of its consumption it was drunk out of porcelain imported from China, although potteries in Britain's industrial heartland had by now begun to make china teapots and cups. The sugar to sweeten it was originally grown by African slaves on West Indian plantations, and was now cultivated by Indian indentured labourers transported around the globe to suit the needs of British capital. There was barely anything at all that was British about a cup of tea, and yet it became a symbol of national identity.

Mr Oldknow reminded the grumbling Genius of Bread that since the repeal of the Corn Laws, his wages went twice as far and now afforded him the basic comforts of life. First on Mr Oldknow's list of the labourer's staple foodstuffs were sugar and tea. By the 1850s, these foreign substances were intrinsic to the diet of the British industrial working classes. Sweet tea, and treacle poured on a pudding or spread on a slice of bread, fitted into the constraints of factory life when wages were too low to buy sufficient fuel to keep a pottage simmering over the fire; and a slice of bread and treacle could easily be handed to a hungry child to eat in the street. Even though it was lacking in nutritional value, sugar had been transmuted from an ephemeral luxury into a basic food-stuff. It was no longer a flavouring added to make food more palatable but in-stead had become an essential source of energy.[14] This recategorisation of sugar is one of the Empire's enduring legacies and has allowed sugar to take its central place within the modern diet.

In the nineteenth century, sugar and tea gave the workman the energy to spin and weave the cotton and forge the steel to make the British manufactures that were used to acquire more colonial foodstuffs.[15] Mr Oldknow argued that 'the artisan of Birmingham and Manchester – the seamen of London and Liver-pool – whose festive board will be made joyous, tomorrow, with that national dish [the plum pudding], has contributed by his labour, to make the raisins of Malaga and the currants of Zante – the oranges of Algarve, the cinnamon of Ceylon and the nutmegs of the Moluccas – of commercial value; and he has thus called them into existence as effectually as the labour of the native cultivator'.[16]

On the early Irish and American plantations the English applied the Tudor con-viction that the basis of a stable society was a well-ordered countryside where tenants tilled the soil while living in nuclear villages clustered around a church and a manor house. They felt entitled to appropriate Irish and American land as the indigenous inhabitants were judged unable to realise its full potential. The idea that they were rescuing territory from the wasteful negligence of its original owners continued to be a powerful strand of British imperial ideology. 'What a settlement one could have in this valley!' declared the explorer Henry Stanley in 1871 as he gazed out over open country near Lake Tanganyika. 'Fancy a church spire rising where that tamarind rears its dark crown of foliage, and think how well a score or so of pretty cottages would look instead of those thorn clumps and gum trees! Fancy this lovely valley teeming with herds of cattle and fields of corn, spreading to the right and left of this stream! How much better would such a state become this valley, rather than its wild and deserted aspect.'[17]

As Britain's impoverished rural population migrated to the United States and the Empire, they took with them the unshakeable British belief in land as 'an article to be measured, allocated, traded, and improved' and spread the notion of transferable, individual property rights across the globe.[18] By 1850, the feudal peasantry of Tudor times had disappeared from the countryside and Britain was in the process of acquiring a vast agricultural estate overseas.[19] In the last quarter of the nineteenth century, the reduction in transport costs brought about by railways and steamships, as well as the technological innovations of canning and refrigeration, meant that the white-dominated settler colonies were able to supply the industrial working classes with sufficient quantities of cheap bread and meat to distract them from thoughts of concerted political protest or revolution.

The import of wheat and meat from the settler colonies eradicated starvation among the British industrial population. Nevertheless, the problem of hidden malnutrition remained. The Empire supplied the working classes with enough calories to work hard throughout their short lives but their diminutive stature in comparison to the well-fed middle class revealed the poverty of their diets.[20] It was not until the 1930s that the existence of hidden malnutrition – deficiencies in calcium, iron and an array of vitamins – among the majority of Britain's population was identified.

The other half of Britain's imperial estate was populated by a non-white tributary peasantry in the tropics, where they grew cocoa, sugar and tea.[21] While Mr Oldknow spoke in self-congratulatory terms of encouraging industriousness among Britain's trading partners, in fact, while Britain had learned its lesson in America and allowed the white settler colonies a measure of self-government and eventually to grow into industrial nations in their own right, the development of manufacturing and industry was discouraged in the non-white world. The tropics were expected to supply Britain with raw materials and in turn to absorb British manufactures. The long-term impact of this policy was to retard the development of these countries. After independence they were trapped in the role of primary producers, often with economies based precariously on one or two products at the mercy of price fluctuations in the world market.

If Empire products helped to maintain social inequality within Britain, in the Empire ecosystems and traditional diets were destroyed by the arrival of the white man. Well-intentioned outreach officers forced 'proper' farming techniques on indigenous peasants, leaving them with drought-prone, less nourishing replacement crops; and those who worked for the British as porters, navvies or farm hands were fed the same innutritious industrial ration as the working classes at home, with the same depressing effect that they became malnourished and prone to disease. As remote villagers were drawn into the imperial commercial world, a new type of famine appeared, caused when food shortages led to such severe inflation that the poor were priced out of the market. Unable to afford to buy food, they starved.

Romanticised advertising showing colourfully dressed women picking tea on picturesque Indian hillsides diverted the attention of the metropolitan consumer away from the squalid reality of the labourers' lives on the plantations. British imperial ideology was caught in a contradiction. While the Empire was based on economic exploitation, Pax Britannica was supposed to bring peace and the impartial rule of British law to the colonies, freeing people from the auto-cratic decrees of Eastern despots and liberating them from the slave trade, which remained active on the African continent. The Quaker firm of Cadbury's was caught within this imperial contradiction when William Cadbury became aware in 1901 that more than half the high-quality cocoa the company sourced from Portuguese São Tomé and Príncipe was produced by slaves.[22] At the same time they took pride in assuring their customers that they never knowingly bought slave-harvested cocoa to make their drinking powder and confectionery. William solved the dilemma in a characteristically imperial fashion by safeguarding his business interests before acting on his moral principles. He immediately began looking for other sources of cocoa but it took him nine years before he was able to secure an alternative supply from the Gold Coast. Only then, when they no longer needed it, did Cadbury's boycott cocoa from Portuguese Africa.[23]

At the turn of the twentieth century the British held up their cheap white wheaten loaf made from imported grain as 'a symbol of national greatness and freedom', a visible demonstration of the benefits of liberalism and the empire of free trade.[24] In contrast, they pointed to the heavy black rye bread of Germany to demonstrate the shortcomings of autocracy and protectionism. German social commentators, on the other hand, saw black bread as a symbol of their tradi-tional values and collective strength. They warned German citizens, who showed clear signs of liking white wheaten bread, that the integrity of the nation would be undermined if Germany were to follow Britain's example and become de-pendent on foreign farmers for its food.[25] German anxieties were comparable to those of the Chinese in the early nineteenth century, who were dismayed by the flow of silver out of their country to buy opium. Importing wheat used precious foreign currency, and just as the Chinese projected social anxieties about the weakening of the nation onto the practice of opium smoking, so the Germans were told that white bread would turn them into anaemic weaklings.[26]

In the 1920s post-war world of depression, when many countries withdrew into nationalist policies of protection, Britain no longer felt like the cheerful Genius of the Currant who embraced free trade safe in the knowledge that commerce would secure his food supply. In a lecture delivered at Nottingham University in 1926, the agriculturalist Daniel Hall argued that while Britain could not hope to achieve food self-sufficiency within the confines of the island, it could look to its empire and source more of its food from 'our friends, our relatives and our own folk' in order to become 'a self-contained unit'.[27] Hall's definition of empire was much narrower than Mr Oldknow's commercial one and encompassed only those countries under the umbrella of the British Crown. He suggested expanding cattle ranching in central and southern Africa to replace Argentina as the nation's source of chilled beef, and argued for greater investment in farming in the colonies.[28] Food choices were politicised. Just as German housewives' associations campaigned for women to buy home-grown apples rather than imported oranges, the British Women's Patriotic League tried to persuade consumers to buy Australian rather than Californian currants and sultanas. (California had switched from growing wheat to market gardening.) As part of the campaign in 1924 the League published a recipe for an Empire Christmas pudding, which sourced the dried fruit from Australia and the rest of the ingredients from other British colonies.[29]

On 20 December 1926, Lord Meath, the organiser of the Empire Day movement, invited representatives from various colonies to make just such an Empire Christmas pudding in the grounds of Vernon House, the headquarters of the Overseas League in London. The ceremony was captured on film and was shown on cinema newsreels all over the country. As each ingredient was carried in by turbaned Indian servants it was formally announced as if it were a guest at a ball and was then added to an enormous mixing bowl. The ceremony finished with representatives from Canada, Australia, South Africa, British Guiana, Jamaica and India coming together to give the pudding a collective ritual stir.[30] Part of the invented tradition of the Victorian Christmas was Stir-up Sunday, the last Sunday before Advent, when the pudding was made to give it time to age and each member of the family gave the mixture a stir while making a wish. The Empire Day pudding ceremony created a powerful visual image of the Empire as Britain's family.

The event was given a further boost when the royal family agreed to eat the Empire Marketing Board's version of an Empire pudding that Christmas Day. The next year royal participation in the campaign went a step further when the king's chef supplied the Empire Marketing Board with the recipe for the Christmas pudding George V and his family would be eating at Sandringham; it was published with the name of a colony listed next to each ingredient. The Empire Christmas pudding revived the Victorian conflation of Englishness and Empire. Everyone in the country, from the king to the lowliest of his subjects in 'every household throughout the length and breadth of the British Empire', would be sitting down at the same time to eat exactly the same pudding made with ingredients from all over the Empire. This was a powerful ritual that consolidated the national and imperial into one community.[31]

The King's Chef, Mr Cédard, with Their Majesties'
gracious consent, has supplied to the Empire Marketing
Board the following recipe for

AN EMPIRE CHRISTMAS PUDDING

5 lbs of currants * AUSTRALIA

5 lbs of sultanas * AUSTRALIA

5 lbs of stoned raisins * SOUTH AFRICA

½ lb of minced apple * CANADA

5 lbs of breadcrumbs * UNITED KINGDOM

5 lbs of beef suet * NEW ZEALAND

2 lbs of cut candied peel * SOUTH AFRICA

2½ lbs of flour * UNITED KINGDOM

2½ lbs of demerara sugar * WEST INDIES

20 eggs * IRISH FREE STATE

2 oz ground cinnamon * CEYLON

1½ oz ground cloves * ZANZIBAR

1½ ground nutmegs * STRAITS SETTLEMENTS

1 teaspoonful pudding spice * INDIA

1 gill brandy * CYPRUS

2 gills rum * JAMAICA

2 quarts old beer * ENGLAND

When the National Socialists came to power in Germany in 1933, they regarded the British Empire with some envy. They wanted to spend foreign currency reserves on rearmament rather than on food imports and attempted to withdraw from the world market and achieve national self-sufficiency. In National Socialist rhetoric white bread was portrayed as the degenerate product of louche 'Anglo-American' – in the dog-whistle politics of the time, the audience heard or read 'Jewish' – democracy while wholemeal bread was the patriotic and wholesome food of a healthy Aryan race.[32] Hitler was convinced that in order to achieve wealth and prosperity and, most importantly, autonomy, Germany needed its own empire. In his (never published) sequel to *Mein Kampf,* the so-called 'Second Book' written in 1928, he identified the plains of fertile black earth in the Ukraine and Russia as the place where Germans would find sufficient *Lebensraum* or living space. The British tended to draw a veil over the brutal suppression of the indigenous people whose land they had appropriated. But in an analysis unfettered by moral scruples, Hitler took inspiration from the British and American examples. He wrote with admiration of the way the United States had exterminated the Native Americans and claimed that 'here in the East a similar process will repeat itself for a second time as in the conquest of America'.[33] In an uncanny echo of Elizabethan plans to relocate the Irish to a zone in the west beyond the River Shannon, the bureaucrats in the SS Department for the Settlement of the East devised a scheme to deport the Slav population to the Soviet Arctic zone, where they would join European Jews in working themselves to death.[34]

271

Britain's empire was a source of strength during the war that inevitably followed Hitler's rise to power. In the post-war years the revolution effected by wartime agricultural advances restored Britain's agricultural sector to productivity. Today British farmers provide the population with 84 per cent of their meat and nearly half their grain. With the gradual loss of its colonies Britain turned back to Europe as its main trading partner and the European Union is now the primary source of British food imports, supplying the United Kingdom with 28 per cent of its food.[35]

In 1601, Elizabeth I's Secretary of State, Robert Cecil, confidently asserted that 'whosoever doth not maintain the Plough, destroys this Kingdom'; in 1850, in contrast, Mr Oldknow proudly celebrated Britain's dependence on food imports.[36] Each held to their opposing view with conviction. Those days of certainty about agriculture have long since gone. We now worry about the ecological impact of the green revolution and whether we really want to eat vegetables liberally sprinkled with pesticides or meat impregnated with growth hormones. And if not, how would it be possible to make organic food affordable for all? Our concern about the carbon footprint of our meals leaves us weighing up whether it is better to eat tomatoes ripened in sunny climes and transported great distances by lorry or to opt for ones grown locally in heated greenhouses. Nowadays we find ourselves buying an array of foodstuffs in packaging emblazoned with Union Jacks in a celebration of local food production that smacks uncomfortably of 1930s nationalism. We no longer feel confident that we know the answer to the question of how we should grow or acquire our food.

The integration of foreign foods and cooking techniques into the culinary repertoire is a worldwide phenomenon. Often, all that was required for an imported food to be claimed by a people as their own was for them to eat it in sufficient quantity. West Indian molasses gave Newfoundland's lumberjacks and fishermen the energy they needed for hard physical work and they added it to virtually everything they ate, from brown bread to chicken and potato pie.[37] A large crock of molasses 'was always on the table' in the Newfoundland of the past and a local ditty claims that only if you pour molasses on your doughboys and your porridge, and even on your fish and brewis (a mix of salt cod and hardtack), are you 'a real true Newfie, remembering the way it used to be'.[38] In turn, as the food of the slaves, Newfoundland salt cod became so entrenched in the diets of Africans in the West Indies that on Jamaica, salt fish and ackee – a West African vegetable – is often cited as the national dish.[39] Southern Americans now claim distinctively West African dishes such as gumbo and Hoppin' John as their own regional foods. And if slavery firmly incorporated African foodstuffs and cookery into the foodscape of the Americas, in Africa, American maize has supplanted millet, sorghum and rice in the diets of the majority of the population. Indeed, many Africans refer to it as 'maize of the ancestors' and have no notion that it was introduced to the continent relatively recently by the Portuguese and British colonial officials.[40] To trace the history of the 'national' foods of former British colonies is to create a map of the web of connections the British Empire wove around the globe.

The ease with which foods travel the globe and reappear as 'national' foods in their new host countries should serve as a reminder that the notion is an illusion. French officials in Vietnam were as anxious as their counterparts in British India to recreate French food. However, they relied on British and American food imports, with the result that the 'French bread' consumed in the colony was often made by a Chinese baker with Australian wheat flour.[41] Shared food habits and tastes create the feeling that we belong to a larger group. When Scots eat haggis, neaps and tatties on Burns Night and American families gather at Thanksgiving to enjoy turkey and all the trimmings, including cranberries, corn and pumpkin pie, the entire population appears to be simultaneously putting on a performance of the nation.[42] Thanksgiving apparently connects Americans to the mythologised founding of the nation, and yet it was only in the nineteenth century that the Pilgrim Fathers were inserted into a celebration that had grown out of the English tradition of the harvest festival. Nor was Thanksgiving always seen in a positive light by all Americans. Some Southerners regarded it as a Yankee abolitionist holiday when in 1863, in an attempt to bring together a country riven by civil war, Abraham Lincoln declared that it would henceforward be a national holiday.[43] Although the British Empire has long since been dismantled, its legacy lives on in how Britain and its former colonies define their national identities.

In December 1985, an article in *The Times* used the Victorian device of depicting the globe as a plum pudding and on its surface traced the route that was taken by a Christmas pudding sent to the diplomats in the British embassy

The expatriate British went to great lengths to eat plum pudding on Christmas Day no matter where they were. In the 1870s Crosse & Blackwell exported more than a thousand tinned plum puddings to India, China and Australia. By the 1940s New Zealand canning companies were producing their own and capitalising on 'olde English' imagery of snow and Father Christmas on his sledge to sell them despite the fact that it was midsummer in New Zealand in December.

in Ulan Bator, Mongolia. The pudding was said to have sustained 'the morale … the indomitable Britishness of the group stranded in the cheerless waste'.[44] The tone was reminiscent of articles that appeared in Victorian periodicals recounting how intrepid colonials went to great lengths to keep up Christmas traditions in the wilds of the Empire, boiling their puddings by immersing them in springs of bubbling mud in New Guinea or concocting them out of biscuit, sugar and brandy in the Australian outback.[45] We still celebrate Christmas with an orgy of foods infused with sugar and spices – mince pies, Christmas cake and pudding, mulled wine – but nowadays it is the turkey, not the plum pudding, that is the centrepiece of our Christmas meal. Introduced to England from North America in the sixteenth century, these enormous birds remained out of reach of the pocket of the average working man until the 1950s, when factory farming made turkey affordable for the masses.[46]

In her fictional diary, Bridget Jones recorded that on August Bank Holiday her mother had rung her apparently to ask what she would like for Christmas. After a mystifying conversation discussing the merits of pull-along suitcases with wheels, Mrs Jones reverted to the real reason for the phone call.

'"Now darling," she suddenly hissed, "you will be coming to Geoffrey and Una's New Year's Day Turkey Curry Buffet this year, won't you?"' The 'rich, divorced-by-cruel-wife', 'top-notch lawyer' Mark Darcy would be there, and her mother was determined to set Bridget up with this suitable man.[47] On the day itself, Bridget, who obsessively records her overeating in her diary, noted that she ate a 'portion of Una Alconbury's turkey curry, peas and bananas' as well as a 'portion of Una Alconbury's Raspberry Surprise made with Bourbon biscuits, tinned raspberries, eight gallons of whipped cream, decorated with glacé cherries and angelica'.[48] She also met Mark, the man she was destined to marry, who was dressed in a tasteless diamond-patterned jumper.[49] What could be more British than a story based on a Jane Austen novel in which the hero and heroine fall in love at Christmas over an Indian-inspired dish of curried turkey?

RUTH'S LEFTOVER TURKEY CURRY

Ingredients

1 tbsp vegetable oil or butter

1 large onion, diced

2 sticks of celery, diced

2 cloves of garlic, crushed

1 inch of fresh ginger, grated

1 tbsp curry powder

1 tbsp plain flour

600 ml stock

Optional: finely diced vegetables of choice such as potatoes, carrots, swedes and beans

1 tbsp mango chutney

2 tbsp freshly grated coconut (can use desiccated
at a pinch)

salt and pepper

1 apple, diced

30 g sultanas

leftover turkey, diced

juice of half a lemon

Fry the onion and celery in the oil or butter until they
are really soft and beginning to brown at the edges. Add
the garlic and ginger and fry until they lose their raw
smell. Add the curry powder and flour and fry for a few
seconds. Add the stock, stirring continuously, and bring
to a simmer. Add the vegetables if using, the mango
chutney, grated coconut and salt and pepper. Simmer
gently on a low heat for twenty minutes. Add the apples
and sultanas and simmer for a further ten minutes.
Then add the turkey and lemon juice and simmer for a
further ten minutes to reheat the turkey. Serve with rice,
poppadums, chutney and pickle.[50]

Acknowledgements

I am grateful for the help I have received from the librarians at Cambridge University Library and for the library's policy of allowing past post-graduate students unfettered access to its collections. I would like to thank the archivists at Reading University Special Collections; Rachel Rowe of the Imperial and Commonwealth Collections, Cambridge; Jenni Skinner at the African Studies Library, Cambridge; and Christopher Dobbs at the *Mary Rose* museum, Portsmouth. And an extra hurrah for Kevin Greenbank at the Centre for South Asian Studies, Cambridge for his friendship and consistently good-humoured assistance. I am grateful to the History Department at Warwick University for making me an Associate Fellow and the Royal Literary Fund for providing me with a congenial means to earn a living when the number of years it took to write this book stretched into too many.

I am indebted to the many scholars whose work this book rests on, and in particular to Martin Jones whose book *Feast* inspired me to structure the book around meals. A number of people provided me with references, information and suggestions: thank you Yashaswini Chandra, Rebecca Earle, Vic Gatrell, David Nally, Kaori O'Connor, Emma Spary, Lesley Steinitz and David Zylberberg. I would like to thank Maxine Berg for not only providing me with helpful references but also lending me her lovely home; Peter and Irmgard Seidel for the regular 'Care Pakete'; Ruth and Philip Goodall for their encouragement, gin and tonics and cosy evenings by the fire; Sophie Gilmartin for her spirit-raising companionship at parallel desks and on windy beach walks on our writing holidays; Terry Roopnaraine for telling me stories about life with gold diggers and diamond miners and answering all my questions about Guyana as well as taking my photograph; John Hay and Sarah Burwood for giving my daughter Sophie a lovely holiday while I was busy writing.

In the final stages of revising the manuscript I sorely missed the late Mike O'Brien's propensity to catch my grammatical mistakes. I thank Tricia O'Brien for making me temporary custodian of his rug as it not only brightens my writing shed but acts as a salutary reminder of Mike and his high standards. I am also grateful to Tricia and Sue Belfrage for reading chapters and making helpful comments; Hiram Morgan for a friendly response to requests for help from a perfect stranger and for thereafter reading and commenting on the chapter on Ireland; Peter Garnsey for reading the entire manuscript and cheering me on and Lara Heimert for her careful reading and useful commentary. My sister Sarah I thank for finding Frank Swannell, reading and helping me revise numerous drafts and all her big-sisterly support. Jim and Anne Secord were both fantastically helpful and I thank them for their careful reading of the entire manuscript, constructive criticism, the loan of *Punch* and their boundless enthusiasm for the book. I am especially grateful to Jörg Hensgen who understood what I was trying to do and whose painstaking and skilful editing helped me turn a messy manuscript into a more readable book.

Indeed, I have been fortunate to have two lovely publishing teams and I am also grateful to Stuart Williams, Anna-Sophia Watts, Matt Broughton and Ceri Maxwell-Hughes at The Bodley Head; and to Alia Massoud, Nicole Capute and Betsy DeJesu at Basic Books. I am very fortunate to have Clare Alexander as my agent and I thank her for her continued encouragement and support and for chivvying me to hurry up when I needed a push.

I don't have the words to express how grateful I am to my neurosurgeon Mr Rikin Trivedi without whose skill I might not have been able to carry on writing. Thomas Seidel I thank for building me a beautiful writing shed and then not minding too much when I spent a lot of time there, reading and then re-reading drafts and always being willing to engage with my latest knotty problem and make helpful suggestions, ask difficult questions and challenge my arguments, and for bringing me endless cups of tea. To Sophie I promise to make more time for doing fun things from now on.

As an undergraduate I had the good fortune to be taught by the eminent art historian Partha Mitter who sparked my interest in the British Empire. Without Partha's encouragement I would never have applied to Cambridge where I had the privilege to be supervised by the late Chris Bayly, one of the leading historians of empire and a pioneering scholar of global history. It is to these two inspirational teachers and friends that this book is dedicated.

Notes

Introduction

1. Richards, *Land, Labour and Diet in Northern Rhodesia*, p.73.
2. Davis, 'English foreign trade, 1660–1700', p.300.
3. Price, 'The imperial economy, 1700–1776', p.79.
4. Bowen, 'British conceptions of global empire, 1756–83', pp.4–5.
5. Duffy, 'World-wide war and British expansion, 1793–1815', p.184.
6. Bayly, *The Birth of the Modern World 1780–1914*, p.136.
7. Cosgrove et al., 'Colonialism, international trade and the nation state', p. 226.

Chapter 1, in which it is fish day on the *Mary Rose*

1. Gardiner, *Before the Mast*, p.605; Hartman, *The true preserver and restorer of health*, p.59.
2. Gardiner, *Before the Mast*, p.604; Macdonald, *Feeding Nelson's Navy*, p.112.
3. Marsden, *Sealed by Time*, pp.97–8.
4. Gardiner, *Before the Mast*, p.449.
5. Laughton, *State Papers*, pp.108–9.
6. Marsden, *Sealed by Time*, p.18.
7. Ibid., pp.19–20.
8. Ibid., pp.20, 10, 107.
9. Ibid., pp.112–14.
10. Gardiner, *Before the Mast*, p.568.
11. Ibid., pp.572–7.
12. Hutchinson et al., 'The globalization of naval provisioning'.
13. Black, *The British Seaborne Empire*, pp.28, 56.
14. Fagan, *Fish on Friday*, pp.90–8.

15. Ibid., p.164.
16. Ibid., pp.183–4.
17. Ibid., p.230.
18. Ibid., p.195.
19. *A Brief Discourse on Wine*, p.39; Unwin, *Wine and the Vine*, pp.2–39.
20. Vickers, *Farmers and Fishermen*, p.86.
21. Fagan, *Fish on Friday*, p.xv.
22. Boyle, *Toward the Setting Sun*, pp.64–7, 178–9; Kurlansky, *Cod*, p.27; Andrews, *Trade, Plunder and Settlement*, p.47.
23. Kurlansky, *Cod*, p.27; Pope, *The Many Landfalls of John Cabot*, pp.13–16.
24. Pope, *The Many Landfalls of John Cabot*, p.22.
25. Kurlansky, *Cod*, pp.48–9.
26. Pope, *The Many Landfalls of John Cabot*, p.41.
27. Ibid., pp.41–2.
28. Fagan, *Fish on Friday*, p.229.
29. Ibid.
30. Kurlansky, *Cod*, p.51.
31. Hartman, *The true preserver and restorer of health*, p.59.
32. Fagan, *Fish on Friday*, p.230; Marsden, *Sealed by Time*, pp.1, 15.
33. Knighton and Loades, *The Anthony Roll of Henry VIII's Navy*.
34. Fagan, *Fish on Friday*, p.233.
35. Fury, *Tides in the Affairs of Men*, p.143.
36. Laughton, *State Papers*, pp.109–10.
37. Falls, *Elizabeth's Irish Wars*, p.262.
38. McGurk, *The Elizabethan Conquest of Ireland*, p.205.
39. Innis, *The Cod Fisheries*, pp.31–2.
40. The French continued to dominate offshore Newfoundland fishing. They preferred a wet salt cure for their cod and this meant that they did not need to come onto the land to dry their fish. Pope, *Fish into Wine*, p.17.
41. Ibid.
42. Ibid., p.144.
43. Poynter, *The Journal of James Yonge*, p.56.
44. Mason, *A briefe discourse of the Nevv found-land*.
45. Poynter, *The Journal of James Yonge*, p.57.
46. Cod livers were used to make 'train oil' to lubricate heavy machinery referred to as trains.
47. Poynter, *The Journal of James Yonge*, pp.56–7.
48. Ibid., pp.57–8.

49. Andrews, *Trade, Plunder and Settlement*, pp.6–9.
50. Williamson, *The Observations of Sir Richard Hawkins*, p.104.
51. Zahedieh, *The Capital and the Colonies*, p.192.
52. Fagan, *Fish on Friday*, pp.239, 244.
53. Ibid., p.240.
54. Black, *The British Seaborne Empire*, pp.28, 59.
55. In the 1680s, the sailor Edward Barlow recorded in his diary meeting various ships from Newfoundland laden with 'pore Jack', or dry salted cod: Lubbock, *Barlow's Journal of His Life at Sea*, I, p.268.
56. Poynter, *The Journal of James Yonge*, p.70.
57. Pope, *Fish into Wine*, p.116.
58. Innis, *The Cod Fisheries*, p.52.
59. Zahedieh, *The Capital and the Colonies*, p.184.
60. Collins, *Salt and Fishery*, p.95; Andrews, *Trade, Plunder and Settlement*, pp.3–4.
61. Davis, *The Rise of the English Shipping Industry*, p.389.
62. Andrews, *Trade, Plunder and Settlement*, p.9.

Chapter 2, in which John Dunton eats oatcake and hare boiled in butter

1. Dunton, *Teague Land or A Merry Ramble to the Wild Irish*, pp.17–20.
2. Ibid., p.16.
3. Ibid., p.18.
4. Glasse, *The Art of Cookery Made Plain and Easy*, pp.20–2.
5. Dunton, *Teague Land or A Merry Ramble to the Wild Irish*, p.17.
6. Glasse, *The Art of Cookery Made Plain and Easy*, p.298.
7. Pastore, 'The collapse of the Beothuk world', p.55.
8. Gillespie, 'Plantations in early modern Ireland', p.43.
9. Moryson, *An Itinerary*, p.244.
10. Foster, *Modern Ireland 1600–1972*, p.26.
11. Montaño, *The Roots of English Colonialism in Ireland*, pp.67–8, 79.
12. Gerald of Wales, *The History and Topography of Ireland*, pp.101–2.
13. Moryson, *An Itinerary*, p.261.
14. Shaw, 'Eaters of flesh, drinkers of milk', pp.22, 29; Garnsey, *Food and Society in Classical Antiquity*, pp.65–7.
15. Montaño, *The Roots of English Colonialism in Ireland*, pp.26–7, 44–7.
16. Derricke, *The Image of Irelande with a discoureie of vvoodkarne*; Foster, *Modern Ireland 1600–1972*, p.18.

17. Moryson, *An Itinerary*, pp.161–2; MacRae, *God Speed the Plough*, pp.13–19.

18. Dunton, *Teague Land or A Merry Ramble to the Wild Irish*, pp.21–2.

19. Moryson, *An Itinerary*, p.263.

20. Montaño, *The Roots of English Colonialism in Ireland*, p.9.

21. Pope, *The Many Landfalls of John Cabot*, p.165.

22. Montaño, *The Roots of English Colonialism in Ireland*, p.18.

23. Metcalfe, *Ideologies of the Raj*, pp.2–3.

24. MacRae, *God Speed the Plough*, p.8.

25. Clarkson and Crawford, *Feast and Famine*, p.13.

26. Montaño, *The Roots of English Colonialism in Ireland*, p.18.

27. Prominent among this group were Sir Thomas Smith, Secretary of State under Edward VI, who led a failed attempt under Elizabeth to establish an English plantation in Ulster in the 1570s; Lord Burghley, Sir William Cecil, Secretary of State and chief adviser to Elizabeth I, who drew up the plans for the Munster plantation in the 1580s; and Sir Henry Sidney, who served three times as Lord Deputy of Ireland under Elizabeth and planned and implemented a brutal and concerted military programme to bring Ireland under the control of the English crown: Montaño, *The Roots of English Colonialism in Ireland*, p.59; Bradshaw, 'The Elizabethans and the Irish', p.41.

28. Gaskill, *Between Two Worlds*, p.xvi.

29. Cited by Clarkson and Crawford, *Feast and Famine*, p.136.

30. This was about one fifteenth of Munster.

31. Montaño, *The Roots of English Colonialism in Ireland*, pp.387–8.

32. Foster, *Modern Ireland 1600–1972*, p.67; Canny, *Kingdom and Colony*, pp.50–1.

33. *A Direction for the plantation in Ulster* (1610), cited by Canny, 'Migration and opportunity', p.31; Canny, 'The origins of empire', pp.6–8.

34. Horning, 'On the banks of the Bann', p.97.

35. Ibid.

36. Gillespie, *Seventeenth-Century Ireland*, p.79.

37. Cullen, *Economy, Trade and Irish Merchants at Home and Abroad, 1600–1988*, p.29.

38. Lenihan, *Consolidating Conquest*, pp.231–3.

39. Cullen, *Economy, Trade and Irish Merchants at Home and Abroad, 1600–1988*, p.29.

40. Flavin, 'Consumption and material culture in sixteenth-century Ireland', pp.1147–8.

41. Ibid., p.1170.

42. Canny, 'Migration and opportunity', pp.9–11.

43. TCD, 1641 Depositions projects, online transcript January 1970, http://1641.tcd.ie/deposition.php?depID<?php echo 821025r011? (accessed 6 April 2016).

44. Ohlmeyer, 'Anatomy of Plantation', p.56.

45. Mac Cuarta, 'The plantation of Leitrim, 1620–41', p.317.
46. Nash, 'Irish Atlantic trade in the seventeenth and eighteenth centuries', p.343; Gillespie, *Seventeenth-Century Ireland*, p.79.
47. If the disturbingly brutal Grenville was typical of the English planters, this would account for the unpopularity of the plantation among the Irish. His party trick when carousing with Spanish captains was to crush wine glasses between his teeth until blood ran from his mouth.
48. Grant, *North Devon Pottery*, p.105.
49. Canny, 'Migration and opportunity', p.13.
50. Flavin, 'Consumption and material culture in sixteenth-century Ireland', p.1166.
51. Lenman, *England's Colonial Wars 1550–1688*, pp.1–2.
52. TCD, 1641 Depositions projects, online transcript January 1970, http://1641.tcd.ie/deposition.php?depID<?php echo 821025r011? (accessed 6 April 2016).
53. Parker, *Global Crisis*, p.24.
54. Ibid., p.25.
55. Barnard, *Improving Ireland?*, p.19.
56. Fox, 'Sir William Petty', p.6 (accessed 5 April 2016); Foster, *Modern Ireland 1600–1972*, p.14.
57. Barnard, 'Planters and policies in Cromwellian Ireland', p.32.
58. Schaffer, 'The earth's fertility as a social fact in early modern England', p.126; MacRae, *God Speed the Plough*, pp.159–62; Zahedieh, *The Capital and the Colonies*, pp.185–6.
59. Woodward, 'The Anglo-Irish livestock trade of the seventeenth century', p.490.
60. Ibid., pp.490–1, 497.
61. Pope, *Fish into Wine*, p.3.
62. See Pastore, 'The collapse of the Beothuk world', pp.52–67.
63. Grant, *North Devon Pottery*, pp.116–19. About three quarters of Irish exports went to England in the 1670s. The rest went to mainland France and the English colonies in the Americas.
64. Gillespie, *Seventeenth-Century Ireland*, p.249.
65. Woodward, 'A comparative study of the Irish and Scottish livestock trades in the seventeenth century', pp.150–4.
66. Mannion, 'Victualling a fishery', p.29.
67. Truxes, *Irish-American Trade, 1660–1783*, pp.158–9; Schaw, *Journal of a Lady of Quality*, p.80.
68. Mandelblatt, 'A transatlantic commodity', p. 20.
69. Truxes, *Irish-American Trade*, p.152.
70. Lenihan, *Consolidating Conquest*, pp.227–9.
71. Canny, *Kingdom and Colony*, p.132.

Chapter 3, in which the Holloway family eat maize bread and salt beef succotash

1. www.geni.com/people/Joseph-Holloway/6000000000688916384 (accessed 22 November 2013).
2. Rutman, *Husbandmen of Plymouth*, pp.45–6.
3. Russell, *Long, Deep Furrow*, p.93.
4. Rutman, *Husbandmen of Plymouth*, pp.66–9.
5. McWilliams, *A Revolution in Eating*, p.73.
6. Rutman, *Husbandmen of Plymouth*, pp.45–6.
7. Davidson, *The Oxford Companion to Food*, p.785.
8. Stavely and Fitzgerald, *America's Founding Food*, pp.40–1.
9. www.geni.com/people/Joseph-Holloway/6000000000688916384 (accessed 22 November, 2013).
10. See Gaskill, *Between Two Worlds*, pp.3–8.
11. Horn, 'Tobacco colonies', pp.173–4; Cronon, *Changes in the Land*, p.20.
12. Lacombe, '"A continuall and dayly table for Gentlemen of Fashion"', pp.669–97.
13. Horn, 'Tobacco colonies', p.179; Anderson, 'New England in the seventeenth century', p.196.
14. Taylor, *American Colonies*, p.169.
15. Ibid., p.164.
16. Clap, *Relating some of God's Remarkable Providence in Bringing Him into New England*, p.6.
17. Cressy, *Coming Over*, pp.96–8.
18. Kulikoff, *The Agrarian Origins of American Capitalism*, pp.190–2.
19. Taylor, *American Colonies*, pp.166–7; Cressy, *Coming Over*, pp.86–99.
20. MacRae, *God Speed the Plough*, p.165.
21. James Harrington, *The Oceana*: constitution.org/jh/oceana (accessed 20 January 2017); Schaffer, 'The earth's fertility as a social fact in early modern England', p.128.
22. www.geni.com/projects/Early-Families-of-Taunton-Massachusetts/3745 (accessed 22 November 2013).
23. Anderson, 'New England in the seventeenth century', pp.195–7.
24. Cited by Stavely and Fitzgerald, *America's Founding Food*, p.12; see also Cronon, *Changes in the Land*, pp.56–7; Kulikoff, *The Agrarian Origins of American Capitalism*, p.130.
25. Canny, 'The origins of empire', p.6; Zahedieh, *The Capital and the Colonies*, p.185.
26. Pluymers, 'Taming the wilderness in sixteenth- and seventeenth-century Ireland and Virginia', p.611.

27. Cronon, *Changes in the Land*, pp.43–4; McMahon, 'A comfortable subsistence', p.32.

28. Clap, *Relating some of God's Remarkable Providence in Bringing Him into New England*, p.7.

29. Ibid., p.14; Stavely and Fitzgerald, *America's Founding Food*, pp.88–9.

30. Cronon, *Changes in the Land*, pp.55–6.

31. Vickers, *Farmers and Fishermen*, pp.44–5.

32. Rutman, *Husbandmen of Plymouth*, pp.45–6.

33. Stavely and Fitzgerald, *America's Founding Food*, pp.12–19.

34. Clap, *Relating some of God's Remarkable Providence in Bringing Him into New England*, p.7.

35. Stavely and Fitzgerald, *America's Founding Food*, pp.31–2.

36. Ibid., p.182.

37. Horsman, *Feast or Famine*, p.16.

38. Emerson, *The New England Cookery*, pp.47, 59.

39. Rutman, *Husbandmen of Plymouth*, p.70.

40. Ogborn, *Global Lives*, p.63.

41. Anderson, *Creatures of Empire*, pp.6–8.

42. Valenze, *Milk*, p.143.

43. Rutman, *Husbandmen of Plymouth*, pp.66–9.

44. Mittelberger, *Journey to Pennsylvania*, p.49.

45. Shammas, *The Pre-industrial Consumer in England and America*, p.5.

46. Candee, 'Merchant and millwright', p.132; Russell, *Long, Deep Furrow*, p.91.

47. Kulikoff, *The Agrarian Origins of American Capitalism*, p.35.

48. McWilliams, *A Revolution in Eating*, pp.63–5.

49. Zahedieh, *The Capital and the Colonies*, p.275.

50. Hudgins, 'The "necessary calls of humanity and decency"', p.180.

51. Shammas, *The Pre-industrial Consumer in England and America*, pp.169, 181.

52. Carson, 'Consumption', pp.357–8.

53. Truxes, *Irish-American Trade*, p.148.

54. Ibid.

55. Vickers, *Farmers and Fishermen*, p.96.

56. Truxes, *Irish-American Trade*, p.148.

57. Taylor, *American Colonies*, p.177.

58. Parker, *The Sugar Barons*, p.125.

59. Stavely and Fitzgerald, *America's Founding Food*, p.124.

60. Kulikoff, *The Agrarian Origins of American Capitalism*, p.130.

61. McWilliams, *A Revolution in Eating*, p.16.

62. Drayton, 'The collaboration of labour', p.176.

Chapter 4, in which Colonel James Drax holds a feast at his sugar plantation

1. Ligon, *A True and Exact History of the Island of Barbados*, p.88.
2. Ibid.
3. Ibid.
4. Sloane, *A Voyage to the Islands Madera, Barbados, Nieves, St Christophers and Jamaica*, Vol. I, p.xxix.
5. Ligon, *A True and Exact History of the Island of Barbados*, p.89.
6. Ibid., p.40.
7. Ibid., p.67.
8. Ibid., pp.67, 156.
9. Gragg, *Englishmen Transplanted*, pp.19–20.
10. Zahedieh, *The Capital and the Colonies*, p.205.
11. Gragg, *Englishmen Transplanted*, pp.19–20; Parker, *The Sugar Barons*, pp.14–17
12. Ligon, *A True and Exact History of the Island of Barbados*, pp.67, 106.
13. Ward, 'A trip to Jamaica', p.89.
14. Mackie, *Life and Food in the Caribbean*, pp.34–5.
15. Paton, *Down the Islands*, pp.163–4.
16. Ligon, *A True and Exact History of the Island of Barbados*, pp.13–14.
17. Gragg, '"To procure negroes"', p.72.
18. Parker, *The Sugar Barons*, p.17.
19. Curtin, *The Rise and Fall of the Plantation Complex*, pp.3–5, 18–26.
20. Dalby, *An Historical Account of the Rise and Growth of the West-India Collonies*, pp.13–14.
21. Ligon, *A True and Exact History of the Island of Barbados*, p.147.
22. Ibid., p.148.
23. Ibid., p.160.
24. Craton, 'Reluctant creoles', p.331.
25. Ligon, *A True and Exact History of the Island of Barbados*, p.159.
26. Ibid., p.161.
27. Ibid., pp.161–3.
28. Mintz, *Sweetness and Power*, pp.47–55.
29. Bruce, *Three Journals of Stuart Times*, p.115.
30. Taylor, *American Colonies*, p.120.
31. Kulikoff, *The Agrarian Origins of American Capitalism*, pp.190–2.
32. Parker, *Global Crisis*, p.24; Beckles, 'The "hub of Empire"', p.223.
33. Beckles, 'The "hub of Empire"', p.230.

34. Ibid., p.230.
35. Ibid., p.231; Ligon, *A True and Exact History of the Island of Barbados*, p.23.
36. Beckles, '"Black men in white skins"', p.10.
37. Gragg, '"To procure negroes"', pp.68, 70. McCusker and Menard argue that planters used the money they made from tobacco and cotton to buy slaves, and that they were already buying them before sugar was introduced to the island. But this is contradicted by Gragg, who has looked at the ships bringing slaves to Barbados and times their arrival with that of sugar: McCusker and Menard, 'The sugar industry in the seventeenth century'.
38. Eltis and Richardson, *Atlas of the Transatlantic Slave Trade*, p.3; Beckles, 'The "hub of Empire"', p.232.
39. Gragg, '"To procure negroes"', p.65.
40. Amussen, *Caribbean Exchanges*, p.31.
41. Beckles, 'The "hub of Empire"', p.227; Thompson, 'Henry Drax's instructions on the management of a seventeenth-century Barbadian sugar plantation', p.575.
42. Ligon, *A True and Exact History of the Island of Barbados*, p.94.
43. Ibid., p.86.
44. Ibid., pp.78, 189.
45. Parker, *The Sugar Barons*, p.268.
46. Ligon, *A True and Exact History of the Island of Barbados*, pp.160–3.
47. Ibid., pp.66–8; Parker, *The Sugar Barons*, p.13.
48. Thompson, 'Henry Drax's instructions on the management of a seventeenth-century Barbadian sugar plantation', pp.571–3.
49. Gragg, 'A Puritan in the West Indies', p.775; Dunn, *Sugar and Slaves*, p.98.
50. Parker, *The Sugar Barons*, p.65.
51. Zahedieh, *The Capital and the Colonies*, p.219.
52. Walvin, *Fruits of Empire*, p.120.
53. Thompson, 'Henry Drax's instructions on the management of a seventeenth-century Barbadian sugar plantation', pp.571–3.
54. Walvin, *Fruits of Empire*, p.178; Dalby, *An Historical Account of the Rise and Growth of the West-India Collonies*, pp.10–11.
55. Ibid., p.11.
56. Nash, 'Irish Atlantic trade in the seventeenth and eighteenth centuries', p.330; Zahedieh, *The Capital and the Colonies*, p.263.
57. Ligon, *A True and Exact History of the Island of Barbados*, p.184.
58. Dalby, *An Historical Account of the Rise and Growth of the West-India Collonies*, pp.10–11; Walvin, *Fruits of Empire*, p.178.

59. O'Brien and Engerman, 'Exports and the growth of the British economy from the Glorious Revolution to the Peace of Amiens', p.182; Zacek, 'Rituals of rulership', p.117; Gragg, *Englishmen Transplanted*, p.107.

60. O'Brien and Engerman, 'Exports and the growth of the British economy from the Glorious Revolution to the Peace of Amiens', p.182; Price, 'The imperial economy, 1700–1776', p.86.

61. O'Brien, 'Inseparable connections', p.54; Mintz, 'Time, sugar and sweetness', p.363; Black, *The British Seaborne Empire*, p.60; Zahedieh, *The Capital and the Colonies*, p.10.

62. Davis, 'English foreign trade, 1660–1700', p.127; O'Brien and Engerman, 'Exports and the growth of the British economy from the Glorious Revolution to the Peace of Amiens', p.182; Price, 'The imperial economy, 1700–1776', p.86.

63. Mintz, *Sweetness and Power*, p.135.

64. Hall, 'Culinary spaces, colonial spaces', p.175.

65. Mintz, *Sweetness and Power*, pp.81, 221.

66. Ogborn, *Global Lives*, p.119; Brenner, *Merchants and Revolution*, pp.111–14, 669.

67. Brenner, *Merchants and Revolution*, pp.693, 706–8; Parker, *The Sugar Barons*, p.89.

68. Beckles, 'The "hub of Empire"', p.236.

69. Zahedieh, *The Capital and the Colonies*, pp.215–16.

70. Cited in ibid., p.2.

71. Ibid., pp.3, 5.

Chapter 5, in which la Belinguere entertains Sieur Michel Jajolet de la Courbe to an African-American meal

1. Ogborn, *Global Lives*, pp.126–8.

2. Wright, *The World and a Very Small Place in Africa*, p.105.

3. Cultru, *Premier Voyage du Sieur de la Courbe Fait à la Coste d'Afrique en 1685*, pp.195–6.

4. Ogborn, *Global Lives*, pp.126–7.

5. Cultru, *Premier Voyage du Sieur de la Courbe Fait à la Coste d'Afrique en 1685*, pp.197–8.

6. McCann, *Stirring the Pot*, p.115.

7. Cultru, *Premier Voyage du Sieur de la Courbe Fait à la Coste d'Afrique en 1685*, p.196. This elaborate tromple l'oiel dish known as Ashanti chicken became 'one of the classic dishes of West African settler cuisine'. See Sellick, *The Imperial African Cookery Book*, pp.176–7.

8. Ibid.

9.   Wright, *The World and a Very Small Place in Africa*, p.80.

10. Cultru, *Premier Voyage du Sieur de la Courbe Fait à la Coste d'Afrique en 1685*, pp.196–7.

11. Ibid., p.199.

12. Wright, *The World and a Very Small Place in Africa*, pp.28–9; Thornton, *Africa and the Africans in the Making of the Atlantic World, 1400–1800*, pp.28–9.

13. Parker, *Global Interactions in the Early Modern Age, 1400–1800*, p.229.

14. Corse, 'Introduction', p.7; Brooks, 'A Nhara of the Guinea-Bissau region', pp.305–8.

15. Cultru, *Premier Voyage du Sieur de la Courbe Fait à la Coste d'Afrique en 1685*, pp.195–6; Brooks, *Eurafricans in Western Africa*, p.151.

16. Brooks, *Eurafricans in Western Africa*, pp.128–9.

17. Brooks, 'The signares of Saint-Louis and Gorée', pp.22–6; Brooks, 'A Nhara of the Guinea-Bissau region', p.296.

18. Wright, *The World and a Very Small Place in Africa*, pp.74–6, 80.

19. Cited by Searing, *West African Slavery and Atlantic Commerce*, pp.98–9.

20. Ogborn, *Global Lives*, pp.127–8.

21. Thornton, *Africa and the Africans in the Making of the Atlantic World, 1400–1800*, pp.90, 93; Kea, *Settlements, Trade and Polities in the Seventeenth-Century Gold Coast*, p.49.

22. Searing, *West African Slavery and Atlantic Commerce*, p.50.

23. Thomas, *The Slave Trade*, p.792.

24. Searing, *West African Slavery and Atlantic Commerce*, p.46.

25. Richards, *The Unending Frontier*, p.81; Brooks, *Landlords and Strangers*, p.319; Brooks, *Eurafricans in Western Africa*, p.103.

26. Searing, *West African Slavery and Atlantic Commerce*, p.81.

27. Ibid.

28. Thornton, 'Sexual demography', pp.39–40.

29. See Meillassoux, 'Female slavery', pp.49–66, and Klein, 'Women in slavery in the Western Sudan', pp.67–92.

30. Searing, *West African Slavery and Atlantic Commerce*, p.54.

31. Ibid., p.28.

32. Ibid., p.56.

33. Wright, *The World and a Very Small Place in Africa*, p.80.

34. Searing, *West African Slavery and Atlantic Commerce*, pp.51, 87.

35. Ibid., p.79.

36. See Alpern, 'The European introduction of crops into West Africa in precolonial times'.

37. Ibid., p.68.

38. Carney and Rosomoff, *In the Shadow of Slavery*, pp.55–7.

39. Searing, *West African Slavery and Atlantic Commerce*, p.80; McCann, *Maize and Grace*, p.91.

40. McCann, *Maize and Grace*, pp.31–4.

41. Alpern, 'Exotic plants of western Africa', p.68.

42. O'Connor, 'Beyond "exotic groceries"', p.231.

43. Harms, 'Sustaining the system', p.100.

44. La Fleur, *Fusion Foodways of Africa's Gold Coast in the Atlantic Era*, p.155.

45. Searing, *West African Slavery and Atlantic Commerce*, p.79.

46. O'Connor, 'Beyond "exotic groceries"', p.232.

47. Harms, 'Sustaining the system', pp.95–110.

48. La Fleur, *Fusion Foodways of Africa's Gold Coast in the Atlantic Era*, pp.123–4.

49. Carney and Rosomoff, *In the Shadow of Slavery*, p.57.

50. Kea, *Settlements, Trade and Polities in the Seventeenth-Century Gold Coast*, p.12.

51. La Fleur, *Fusion Foodways of Africa's Gold Coast in the Atlantic Era*, pp.148–52.

Chapter 6, in which Samuel and Elizabeth Pepys dine on *pigeons à l'esteuvé* and *boeuf à la mode*

1. Latham and Matthews, *The Diary of Samuel Pepys*, VIII, p.211.

2. Ibid.

3. Scully, *La Varenne's Cookery*, p.98.

4. From Mr La Varenne, Kitchen Clerk of the Marquis of Uxelles, *The French Cook: Instructing on the Manner of Preparing and Seasoning All Sorts of Lean and Meat-Day Foods, Legumes, Pastries etc.* (Pierre David, Paris, 1652); reproduced in Scully, *La Varenne's Cookery*, pp.136–7, 158.

5. Pinkard, *A Revolution in Taste*, pp.86–94.

6. Latham and Matthews, *The Diary of Samuel Pepys*, I, p.78.

7. Scully, *La Varenne's Cookery*, p.11.

8. Pinkard, *A Revolution in Taste*, p.110.

9. Scully, *La Varenne's Cookery*, p.95.

10. Ibid., pp.91, 158.

11. Pinkard, *A Revolution in Taste*, p.46; Latham and Matthews, *The Diary of Samuel Pepys*, IV, p.400.

12. Latham and Matthews, *The Diary of Samuel Pepys*, IV, p.95.

13. For example, ibid., IV, p.341; VI, p.2.

14. Lehmann, *The British Housewife*, p.46.

15. Latham and Matthews, *The Diary of Samuel Pepys*, IX, pp.423–4.

16. Ibid., VI, p.300.
17. Ibid., VI, p.240; Chaudhuri, *The Trading World of Asia and the English East India Company 1660–1760*, p.321.
18. Chaudhuri, *The Trading World of Asia and the English East India Company 1660–1760*, p. 321.
19. Keay, *The Spice Route*, p.170.
20. Ibid., p.225.
21. McFadden, *Pepper*, p.17.
22. Pinkard, *A Revolution in Taste*, p.73.
23. Atkins, 'Vinegar and sugar', p.44.
24. Latham and Matthews, *The Diary of Samuel Pepys*, IX, p.261.
25. Peterson, *Acquired Taste*, pp.171–2.
26. Laudan, 'The birth of the modern diet', p.66.
27. Pinkard, *A Revolution in Taste*, pp.70–1.
28. Scully, *La Varenne's Cookery*, p.82; Peterson, *Acquired Taste*, p.40.
29. Pinkard, *A Revolution in Taste*, p.11.
30. Peterson, *Acquired Taste*, p.189.
31. Ibid., pp.186–9.
32. Ibid., pp.199, 201; Lawson, *The East India Company*, p.25; Pinkard, *A Revolution in Taste*, p.712.
33. Chaudhuri, *The Trading World of Asia and the English East India Company 1660–1760*, p.9.
34. Parker, *Global Interactions in the Early Modern Age, 1400–1800*, p.72.
35. Zahedieh, *The Capital and the Colonies*, pp.27–8.
36. Erikson, *Between Monopoly and Free Trade*, p.134.
37. Prakash, 'The English East India Company and India', pp.7–8.
38. Erikson, *Between Monopoly and Free Trade*, pp.12–25.
39. Riello, *Cotton*, pp.113–14.
40. Ibid.
41. Ibid., p.126.
42. Chaudhuri, *The Trading World of Asia and the English East India Company 1660–1760*, pp.97, 313; Erikson, *Between Monopoly and Free Trade*, pp.51–2.
43. Wills, 'European consumption and Asian production in the seventeenth and eighteenth centuries', p.136.
44. Riello, *Cotton*, p.130.
45. Latham and Matthews, *The Diary of Samuel Pepys*, I, p.178; III, p.226; IV, p.5; V, pp.64, 77, 105, 139, 329.
46. Ibid., I, p. 253; Burnett, *Plenty and Want*, p.61.

47. Latham and Matthews, *The Diary of Samuel Pepys*, VIII, p.302.

48. Smith, 'Complications of the commonplace', pp.263–4.

49. Stobart, *Sugar and Spice*, p.237; Vickery, 'Women and the world of goods', p.289.

50. Smith, *Consumption and the Making of Respectability, 1600–1800*, pp.270–1.

51. Mintz, *Sweetness and Power*, p.67; Zahedieh, *The Capital and the Colonies*, pp.221, 223.

52. Black, *The British Seaborne Empire*, p.5.

53. Ogborn, *Global Lives*, p.119; Brenner, *Merchants and Revolution*, pp.111–14, 669.

54. Bayly, *The Birth of the Modern World 1780–1914*, p.136.

55. Davis, 'English foreign trade, 1660–1700', p.139; Zacek, *Settler Society in the Leeward Islands, 1670–1776*, p.118.

56. Richardson, 'The slave trade, sugar and British economic growth, 1748–1776', pp.126–30.

57. Chaudhuri, *The Trading World of Asia and the English East India Company 1660–1760*, p.9.

Chapter 7, in which the Latham family eat beef and potato stew, pudding and treacle

1. In Britain molasses was known as treacle. There was black treacle and the more refined, and more popular, sweeter golden syrup.

2. Weatherill, *The Account Book of Richard Latham 1724–1767*, pp.69–70.

3. Misson, *Memoirs and Observations in His Travels over England*, p.315; Muldrew, *Food, Energy and the Creation of Industriousness*, p.42.

4. Weatherill, *The Account Book of Richard Latham 1724–1767*, p.70.

5. Thirsk, *Food in Early Modern England*, p.9.

6. Weatherill, *The Account Book of Richard Latham 1724–1767*, pp.xviii.

7. Zylberberg, 'Fuel prices, regional diets and cooking habits in the English industrial revolution (1750–1830)', p.118.

8. Glasse, *The Art of Cookery Made Plain and Easy*, pp.111, 22.

9. Weatherill, *The Account Book of Richard Latham 1724–1767*, p.xix.

10. Muldrew, *Food, Energy and the Creation of Industriousness*, pp.241–6.

11. Weatherill, *The Account Book of Richard Latham 1724–1767*, pp.40–2.

12. Ashton, *An Economic History of England*, pp.215–16.

13. Muldrew, *Food, Energy and the Creation of Industriousness*, pp.193–207; Pope, *Fish into Wine*, p.353; Shammas, *The Pre-industrial Consumer in England and America*, pp.169, 181; McKendrick et al., *The Birth of a Consumer Society*, p.23.

14. Weatherill, *The Account Book of Richard Latham 1724–1767*, pp.xxvii, 3–6.
15. Ibid., p.xxv.
16. Riello, *Cotton*, pp.123–6.
17. Weatherill, *The Account Book of Richard Latham 1724–1767*, pp.66–9.
18. Bickham, 'Eating the empire', pp.76–7.
19. Mintz, *Sweetness and Power*, p.67.
20. Muldrew, *Food, Energy and the Creation of Industriousness*, pp.51–7.
21. Cox, '"Beggary of the nation"'; Cox and Dannehl, *Perceptions of Retailing in Early Modern England*; Stobart, 'Gentlemen and shopkeepers'; Stobart, *Sugar and Spice*; Mui and Mui, *Shops and Shopkeeping in Eighteenth-Century England*.
22. Mui and Mui, *Shops and Shopkeeping in Eighteenth-Century England*, p.47.
23. Ibid., pp.211–16.
24. Ibid., p.148; Shammas, *The Pre-industrial Consumer in England and America*, p.260; Zahedieh, *The Capital and the Colonies*, p.235.
25. Mui and Mui, *Shops and Shopkeeping in Eighteenth-Century England*, pp.47, 211–16.
26. Ibid., pp.204–5.
27. Stobart, *Sugar and Spice*, p.144.
28. Mui and Mui, *Shops and Shopkeeping in Eighteenth-Century England*, pp.218–19.
29. Mintz, *Sweetness and Power*, p.117.
30. Shammas, *The Pre-industrial Consumer in England and America*, p.83; Lawson, 'Tea, vice and the English state', p.xiv.
31. Erikson, *Between Monopoly and Free Trade*, p.140; Burnett, *Liquid Pleasures*, p.53.
32. Cited by Mintz, *Sweetness and Power*, p.172.
33. Ibid.
34. Bickham, 'Eating the empire', pp.82–5.
35. Ibid., pp.86–9.
36. Lenman, *England's Colonial Wars 1550–1688*, pp.160–3.
37. Black, *The British Seaborne Empire*, p.11; Metcalfe, *Ideologies of the Raj*, p.4.
38. Bickham, 'Eating the empire', p.72.
39. Datta, 'The commercial economy of eastern India under early British rule', pp.341–2; Erikson, *Between Monopoly and Free Trade*, pp.41–2.
40. Bowen, 'British conceptions of global empire, 1756–83', p.10.
41. Bickham, 'Eating the empire', pp.89–92.
42. Mui and Mui, *Shops and Shopkeeping in Eighteenth-Century England*, pp.204–5.
43. Muldrew, *Food, Energy and the Creation of Industriousness*, pp.80–2.
44. Burnett, *Liquid Pleasures*, p.53.

45. Shammas, *The Pre-industrial Consumer in England and America*, p.147.
46. Brinley, 'Feeding England during the industrial revolution', p.333.
47. Zylberberg, 'Fuel prices, regional diets and cooking habits in the English industrial revolution (1750–1830)', p.109.
48. Muldrew, *Food, Energy and the Creation of Industriousness*, p.80.
49. Ibid., pp.81–2.
50. Zylberberg, 'Fuel prices, regional diets and cooking habits in the English industrial revolution (1750–1830)', p.106.
51. Coal did not replace wood in the south as transport costs increased the price to the point where it was beyond the reach of labourers' wages.
52. Walvin, *Fruits of Empire*, p.120; Muldrew, *Food, Energy and the Creation of Industriousness*, pp.101–2.
53. Eden, *The State of the Poor*, pp.264–5, 280.
54. Cited by Burnett, *Liquid Pleasures*, p.57.
55. Muldrew, *Food, Energy and the Creation of Industriousness*, p.255.
56. Shammas, *The Pre-industrial Consumer in England and America*, pp.147, 299.
57. Cited by Burnett, *Plenty and Want*, p.150.

Chapter 8, in which a slave family eat maize mush and possum

1. Henson, *The Life of Josiah Henson*, p.85.
2. Ball, *Fifty Years in Chains*; Crader, 'The zooarchaeology of the storehouse and the dry well at Monticello'; Crader, 'Slave diet at Monticello'; Reitz et al., 'Archaeological evidence for subsistence on coastal plantations'; Samford, 'The archaeology of African-American slavery and material culture'; Singleton, 'Introduction'.
3. Carney and Rosomoff, *In the Shadow of Slavery*, p.178.
4. Joyner, *Down by the Riverside*, p.280.
5. Ibid., pp.128, 174–6.
6. Ferguson, *Uncommon Ground*, p.xxi.
7. Ibid., pp.63–4, 72, 80–1; Joyner, *Down by the Riverside*, p.197; Butler, 'Greens', p.170.
8. Ferguson, *Uncommon Ground*, pp.xxxv–vi.
9. Ibid., p.24.
10. Ibid., p.97.
11. Ibid., p.10.
12. Ibid., p.84.
13. Ibid., pp.103–5.
14. Cited by ibid., p.90.

15. Rutledge, *The Carolina Housewife*, p.43.

16. Asare et al., *A Ghana Cook-Book for Schools*, p.30.

17. www.milliganfamily.org/middleburg.htm (accessed 18 October 2013).

18. Weir, *Colonial South Carolina*, p.64.

19. Rutledge, *The Carolina Housewife*, p.xviii.

20. It still stands, the oldest surviving wooden frame house in South Carolina: http://south-carolina-plantations.com/berkeley/middleburg.html (accessed 18 October 2013).

21. Catesby, *The Natural History of Carolina, Florida, and the Bahama Islands*, p.xvi.

22. Lawson, *A New Voyage to Carolina*, pp.66, 121; Catesby, *The Natural History of Carolina, Florida, and the Bahama Islands*, p.xxvi.

23. Lawson, *A New Voyage to Carolina*, p.20.

24. Ibid., p.66; Catesby, *The Natural History of Carolina, Florida, and the Bahama Islands*, p.xxvi.

25. McWilliams, *A Revolution in Eating*, p.152.

26. Ibid., pp.146, 149.

27. Ibid., p.133.

28. Catesby, *The Natural History of Carolina, Florida, and the Bahama Islands*, p.xxiv.

29. Russell Cross, 'Middleburg Plantation and the Benjamin Simons Family', www.rootsweb.ancestry.com/~scbchs/middle.html (accessed 18 October 2013).

30. Carney, *Black Rice*, p.51.

31. McWilliams, *A Revolution in Eating*, p.134; Littlefield, *Rice and Slaves*, pp.20–1.

32. Otto, *The Southern Frontiers, 1607–1860*, p.29.

33. Carney, *Black Rice*, pp.38–9.

34. Ibid., pp.145–6.

35. Clifton, 'The rice industry in colonial America', p.268.

36. Ibid., p.269; 'History of rice in Charleston and Georgetown', www.ricehope.com/history/Ricehistory.htm (accessed 18 October 2013).

37. Lawson, *A New Voyage to Carolina*, p.16.

38. Pinckney, *The Letterbook of Eliza Lucas Pinckney 1739–1762*, p.97.

39. Rutledge, *The Carolina Housewife*; Hooker, *A Colonial Plantation Cookbook*, p.25.

40. Hooker, *A Colonial Plantation Cookbook*, p.32.

41. Butler, 'Greens', p.171.

42. Carney, *Black Rice*, p.22.

43. Clifton, 'The rice industry in colonial America', p.268.

44. Otto, *The Southern Frontiers, 1607–1860*, p.34.

45. Ray Timmons, 'Brief history of Middleburg Plantation'; www.rootsweb.ancestry.com/~scbchs/middle.html (accessed 18 October 2013).

46. Carney, 'Rice, slaves and landscapes of cultural memory', p.56 (accessed 18 October 2013).

47. Tuten, *Lowcountry Time and Tide*, pp.14, 16 (accessed 18 October 2013).

48. Joyner, *Down by the Riverside*, p.132.

49. Clifton, 'The rice industry in colonial America', p.269.

50. Carney, 'Rice, slaves and landscapes of cultural memory' (accessed 18 October 2013).

51. Cited by Carney, *Black Rice*, pp.18–19.

52. Russell Cross, 'Middleburg Plantation and the Benjamin Simons Family', www.rootsweb.ancestry.com/~scbchs/middle.html (accessed 18 October 2013).

53. Carney, *Black Rice*, p.18.

54. Ray Timmons, 'Brief history of Middleburg Plantation'; Russell Cross, 'Middleburg Plantation and the Benjamin Simons Family', www.rootsweb.ancestry.com/~scbchs/middle.html (accessed 18 October 2013).

55. Ferguson, *Uncommon Ground*, p.xxiv.

56. Clifton, 'The rice industry in colonial America', p.275.

57. Ibid., p.279.

58. Carney, *Black Rice*, p.29.

59. Tuten, *Lowcountry Time and Tide*, p.13.

60. Olmsted, *A Journey in the Seaboard Slave States in the Years 1853–1854*, II, p.66–7.

61. Joyner, *Down by the Riverside*, p.43.

62. Park Ethnography Program, 'Gender, work and culture: South Carolina gold', www.nps.gov/ethnography/aah/aaheritage/lowCountryD.htm (accessed 18 October 2013).

63. http://south-carolina-plantations.com/berkeley/middleburg.html (accessed 18 October 2013); Ray Timmons, 'Brief history of Middleburg Plantation'; Russell Cross, 'Middleburg Plantation and the Benjamin Simons Family', www.rootsweb.ancestry.com/~scbchs/middle.html (accessed 18 October 2013).

64. Nicolson, *Gentry*, pp.252–4; Clifton, 'The rice industry in colonial America', p.279; Price, 'The imperial economy, 1700–1776', p.87.

65. 'History of rice in Charleston and Georgetown', www.ricehope.com/history/Rice-history.htm (accessed 18 October 2013).

66. Davis, 'English foreign trade, 1660–1700', p.155; Price, 'The imperial economy, 1700–1776', p.82.

67. Nash, 'Domestic material culture and consumer demand in the British Atlantic world', p.237.

68. Ibid., p.248.

69. Ibid., p.234.

Chapter 9, in which Lady Anne Barnard enjoys fine cabin dinners

1. Barnard, *South Africa a Century Ago*, pp.46–7.
2. Fairbridge, *Lady Anne Barnard at the Cape of Good Hope 1797–1802*, p.12.
3. Barnard, *South Africa a Century Ago*, p.47.
4. Fairbridge, *Lady Anne Barnard at the Cape of Good Hope 1797–1802*, p.12.
5. Rodger, *The Wooden World*, p.71.
6. Stobart, *Sugar and Spice*, pp.62, 217–18, 233; Jones, 'London mustard bottles', p.80.
7. Macdonald, *Feeding Nelson's Navy*, pp.128–9.
8. Gosnell, *Before the Mast in the Clippers*, pp.40–1.
9. Black, *The British Seaborne Empire*, p.125.
10. Barnard, *South Africa a Century Ago*, p.47.
11. Black, *The British Seaborne Empire*, pp.89, 143; Macdonald, *The British Navy's Victualling Board, 1793–1815*, p.1.
12. Davey, 'Within hostile shores', p.254.
13. Knight and Wilcox, *Sustaining the Fleet, 1793–1815*, p.56.
14. Davey, 'Within hostile shores', p.254.
15. Falconer, *A New Universal Dictionary of the Marine*, p.40.
16. Wilk, *Home Cooking in the Global Village*, p.35.
17. Knight and Wilcox, *Sustaining the Fleet, 1793–1815*, pp.61–2; Swinburne, 'Dancing with the mermaids', p.317.
18. Baugh, *British Naval Administration in the Age of Walpole*, pp.41, 422; Thompson and Cowan, 'Durable food production and consumption in the world economy', p.39.
19. Busteed, 'Identity and economy on an Anglo-Irish estate', pp.177, 191; Donnelly, 'Cork market', p.132.
20. Mannion, 'Victualling a fishery', pp.36–7.
21. Truxes, *Irish-American Trade*, p.165.
22. Rodger, *The Wooden World*, p.101.
23. Glasse, *The Art of Cookery Made Plain and Easy*, p.240.
24. Coad, *The Royal Dockyards 1690–1850*, p.272; Swinburne, 'Dancing with the mermaids,' p.316; Jones, 'Commercial foods, 1740–1820', p.30.
25. Cited by Newton, *Trademarked*, p.117.
26. Atkins, 'Vinegar and sugar', p.43.
27. Price, 'The imperial economy, 1700–1776', pp.87–8.
28. Shammas, *The Pre-industrial Consumer in England and America*, pp.65, 68; Black, *The British Seaborne Empire*, p.60.

29. Jones, 'Commercial foods, 1740–1820', p.36.

30. 6 January 1774 in the *New Hampshire Gazette*, cited by Penderey, 'The archaeology of urban foodways in Portsmouth, New Hampshire', p.12.

31. Davis, 'English foreign trade, 1700–1774', p.151.

32. Ibid.

33. Roberts, *Scenes and Characteristics of Hindoostan*, II, pp.101–2.

34. Erikson, *Between Monopoly and Free Trade*, p.103.

35. Cited by Cotton, *East Indiamen*, pp.32–6.

36. Ibid.

37. Worthington, *Coopers and Customs Cutters*, p.7.

38. Jones, 'Commercial foods, 1740–1820', pp.27, 38.

39. Cornell, *Amber Gold and Black*, pp.101–2.

40. Pryor, 'Indian pale ale', p.40.

41. Cornell, *Amber Gold and Black*, p.106.

42. Mayhew, *The Shops and Companies of London and the Trades and Manufactories of Great Britain*, I, p.24.

43. Cornell, *Amber Gold and Black*, p.106.

44. Pryor, 'Indian pale ale', pp.45–53.

45. Cited by ibid., pp.52–3.

46. Mayhew, *The Shops and Companies of London and the Trades and Manufactories of Great Britain*, I, p.24.

47. Hancock, *Oceans of Wine*, pp.87–92, 155.

48. Ibid., p.xxii.

49. Spelling corrected. Thompson, 'Henry Drax's instructions on the management of a seventeenth-century Barbadian sugar plantation', p.601.

50. Mackie, *Life and Food in the Caribbean*, pp.73–4.

51. Wood, 'The letters of Simon Taylor of Jamaica to Chaloner Arcedekne, 1765–1775', p.10.

52. Lehmann, *The British Housewife*, p.259.

53. Mandelkern, 'The politics of the turtle feast' (accessed 16 January 2017).

54. Schaw, *Journal of a Lady of Quality*, p.95.

55. Mandelkern, 'The politics of the turtle feast' (accessed 16 January 2017).

56. Although from 1707 I generally refer to the British, contemporary discussions about identity spoke of 'Englishness' not 'Britishness'.

57. Bickham, 'Eating the empire', section III.

58. Cole, *The Lady's Complete Guide*, pp.183–9.

59. Ibid., pp.187–8.

60. Edmunds, *Curries*, p.30.

61. Skeat, *The Art of Cookery and Pastery*, p. 41.

62. Mason, *The Lady's Assistant for Regulating and Supplying the Table*, p.245.
63. 'Reminiscences of a returning Indian', p.18.
64. Cited by Zlotnick, 'Domesticating imperialism', p.52.
65. Collingham, *Curry*, p.133.
66. Hancock, *Oceans of Wine*, p.271.
67. Wilk, *Home Cooking in the Global Village*, p.213.
68. Jones, 'Commercial foods, 1740–1820', p.38.
69. Eedle, *Albion Restored*, p.124; Maidment, *Reading Popular Prints 1790–1829*, pp.27–52.

Chapter 10, in which Sons of Liberty drink rum punch

1. From the papers of William Russel (accessed 25 August 2016).
2. Information on 'An alphabetical list of the Sons of Liberty who din'd at the Liberty Tree' (accessed 24 August 2016).
3. Thompson, 'The "friendly glass"', p.561.
4. Stevens, *The Silver Punch Bowl Made by Paul Revere*.
5. Sons of Liberty Bowl, 1768.
6. Ammerman, 'The tea crisis and its consequences, through 1775', p.196.
7. Gollanek, *Empire Follows Art*, p.348.
8. Sons of Liberty Bowl, 1768.
9. Stevens, *The Silver Punch Bowl Made by Paul Revere*, pp.16–18.
10. http://cdm.bostonathenaeum.org/cdm/landingpage/collection/p16057coll32 (accessed 26 August 2016).
11. Ibid.; Wikitree.com/wiki/Homer-114 (accessed 25 August 2016).
12. Thompson, 'Henry Drax's instructions on the management of a seventeenth-century Barbadian sugar plantation', p.595.
13. Ibid., p.587.
14. Ibid., p.595.
15. Talburt, *Rum, Rivalry and Resistance Fighting for the Caribbean Spirit*, p.40.
16. Sloane, *A Voyage to the Islands Madera, Barbados, Nieves, St Christophers and Jamaica*, Vol. I, p.xxix.
17. Cullen, *Economy, Trade and Irish Merchants at Home and Abroad, 1600–1988*, pp.107–9.
18. Goodwin, *An Archaeology of Manners*, pp.68–71.
19. McCusker, *Rum and the American Revolution*, p.536.
20. It used to be thought that the Sugar Act of 1764 was so incendiary because the extra-American trade in rum balanced American trade. But in fact, rum did not raise sufficient money to balance the colonies' trading books. Rum revenues only

ever covered about 11 per cent of the American import bill for British manufactures: McCusker, *Rum and the American Revolution*, pp.537–8.

21. Ibid., p.68.
22. Ibid., pp.478, 141.
23. Talburt, *Rum, Rivalry and Resistance Fighting for the Caribbean Spirit*, p.39.
24. Conroy, *In Public Houses*, p.97.
25. Ibid., p.154.
26. McWilliams, *A Revolution in Eating*, pp.245–6, 264–5, 285–6, 569.
27. Cited by Rothschild and Rockman, 'City tavern, country tavern', p.113.
28. Thompson, 'The "friendly glass"', p.562; Conroy, *In Public Houses*, p.76.
29. Conroy, *In Public Houses*, p.39.
30. Ibid., p.196.
31. Ibid., p.241.
32. Ibid., pp.34–5.
33. Rice, *Early American Taverns*, p.79.
34. Thompson, 'The "friendly glass"', p.556.
35. Rice, *Early American Taverns*, p.98.
36. McWilliams, *A Revolution in Eating*, pp.245, 263.
37. Gollanek, *Empire Follows Art*, p.350.
38. Conroy, *In Public Houses*, p.244.
39. Ibid., p.176.
40. Sons of Liberty Bowl, 1768.
41. McWilliams, *A Revolution in Eating*, pp.287–8; Parker, *The Sugar Barons*, pp.241–2, 320.
42. Parker, *The Sugar Barons*, p.307.
43. Ibid., pp.320–2.
44. Simmons, 'Trade legislation and its enforcement', p. 170
45. Sons of Liberty Bowl, 1768.
46. http://oldnorth.com/2015/02/26/this-old-pew-4-and-25-captain-daniel-malcolm-merchant-and-enemy-to-oppression/ (accessed 27 August 2016).
47. Ibid.
48. Parker, *The Sugar Barons*, p.322.
49. Cited by ibid., p.241.
50. Conroy, *In Public Houses*, pp.276–7.
51. O'Brien and Engerman, 'Exports and the growth of the British economy from the Glorious Revolution to the Peace of Amiens', p.182.
52. O'Brien, 'Inseparable connections', p.54.
53. Black, *The British Seaborne Empire*, p.42; Belich, *Replenishing the Earth*, p.50.

Chapter 11, in which Kamala prepares a meal for her family

1. Khare, *Hindu Hearth and Home*, p.97.
2. Montgomery, *The History, Antiquities, Topography, and Statistics of Eastern India*, I, p.207; O'Brien, *The Penguin Food Guide to India*, pp.110–11.
3. O'Brien, *The Penguin Food Guide to India*, p.287.
4. Khare, *Hindu Hearth and Home*, p.97.
5. James, *Raj*, p.42.
6. Metcalfe, *Ideologies of the Raj*, pp.4–21.
7. Keay, *The Honourable Company*, p.430; Bayly, *Imperial Meridian*, p.220.
8. Montgomery, *The History, Antiquities, Topography, and Statistics of Eastern India*, I, pp.278–9; Mazumdar, 'The impact of New World food crops on the diet and economy of China and India, 1600–1900', p.72; Watt, *The Commercial Products of India*, p.351.
9. Montgomery, *The History, Antiquities, Topography, and Statistics of Eastern India*, II, p.207.
10. Ibid., I, pp.278–9.
11. Richards, 'The Indian empire and peasant production of opium in the nineteenth century', pp.75, 78.
12. Price, 'The imperial economy, 1700–1776', p.83.
13. Bayly, *The Birth of the Modern World 1780–1914*, pp.94–5.
14. Shineberg, *They Came for Sandalwood*, p.3.
15. In 1761–70, British silver paid for 53 per cent of the bill for tea, British goods 23.4 per cent and Indian goods 24.3 per cent: Chung, 'The British–China–India trade triangle, 1771–1840', p.413.
16. Richards, 'The Indian empire and peasant production of opium in the nineteenth century', p.60.
17. Dikötter et al., 'China, British imperialism and the myth of the "opium plague"', pp.23–4.
18. Richards, 'The Indian empire and peasant production of opium in the nineteenth century', p.67.
19. Ibid.
20. Chowdhury, *Growth of Commercial Agriculture in Bengal*, p.56.
21. Richards, 'The Indian empire and peasant production of opium in the nineteenth century', pp.71, 80.
22. Chowdhury, *Growth of Commercial Agriculture in Bengal*, p.49.
23. Ibid., p.51.
24. Richards, '"Cannot we induce the people of England to eat opium?"', p.76.

25. Richards, 'The Indian empire and peasant production of opium in the nineteenth century', p.76.
26. Hunt, *The India–China Opium Trade in the Nineteenth Century*, pp.67, 92.
27. Polacheck, *The Inner Opium War*, p.110.
28. Siddiqi, 'Pathways of the poppy', p.25.
29. Chung, The British–China–India trade triangle, 1771–1840', pp.416–17.
30. Siddiqi, 'Pathways of the poppy', pp.24–5.
31. Chowdhury, *Growth of Commercial Agriculture in Bengal*, p.5.
32. Ibid., pp.4–5; Chung, 'The British–China–India trade triangle, 1771–1840', p.413.
33. Richards, 'The Indian empire and peasant production of opium in the nineteenth century', p.66; Richards, 'The opium industry in British India', p.153.
34. Richards, 'The opium industry in British India', p.155.
35. Richards, 'The Indian empire and peasant production of opium in the nineteenth century', p.71.
36. Watt, *The Commercial Products of India*, p.860.
37. The legal sales of opium in poppy-growing districts were so much lower than for the rest of the region that it is clear that an illicit trade existed. Richards, '"Cannot we induce the people of England to eat opium?"', p.76.
38. Richards, 'The Indian empire and peasant production of opium in the nineteenth century', p.82.
39. Cited in ibid., pp.72, 77.
40. Chung, 'The British–China–India trade triangle, 1771–1840', pp.419–20.
41. Dikötter et al., 'China, British imperialism and the myth of the "opium plague"', p.19.
42. Ibid.
43. Calculated at a rate of consumption of 17 g a day: Richards, 'The opium industry in British India', p.164.
44. Newman, 'Opium smoking in late imperial China', p.783.
45. Dikötter et al., 'China, British imperialism and the myth of the "opium plague"', p.21.
46. Smith, *The Compleat Housewife*, p.262.
47. Fairbank and Twitchett, *The Cambridge History of China*, p.179.
48. Gray, *Rebellions and Revolutions*, p.28; Richards 'The opium industry in British India', p.168.
49. Von Glahn, *Fountain of Fortune*, p.256; Fairbank and Twitchett, *The Cambridge History of China*, p.178; Kuhn, *Soulstealers*, p.39; Gray, *Rebellions and Revolutions*, p.28.

50. Deng, 'Miracle or mirage? Foreign silver, China's economy and globalisation from the sixteenth to the nineteenth centuries', p.353.

51. Polacheck, *The Inner Opium War*, p.105.

52. Ibid., p.2.

53. Fairbank and Twitchett, *The Cambridge History of China*, p.164.

54. Polacheck, *The Inner Opium* War, p.110.

55. Ibid., p.102.

56. Dikötter et al., *Narcotic Culture*, p.16.

57. Polacheck, *The Inner Opium War*, p.123.

58. Ibid., pp.134–5.

59. Bayly, *The Birth of the Modern World*, pp.136–8.

60. Chung, 'The British–China–India trade triangle, 1771–1840', p.416.

61. Brendon, *The Decline and Fall of the British Empire 1781–1997*, p.104.

62. Gray, *Rebellions and Revolutions*, pp.36, 50.

63. Dikötter et al., *Narcotic Culture*, p.109.

64. Ammerman, 'The tea crisis and its consequences, through 1775', p.204.

65. Dikötter et al., 'China, British imperialism and the myth of the "opium plague"', p.28.

66. Ibid., pp.26–7.

67. Newman, 'Opium smoking in late imperial China', p.779.

68. Ibid., p.765.

Chapter 12, in which Sarah Harding and her family grow fat eating plenty of good food

1. Arch, *From Ploughtail to Parliament*, pp.126–7.

2. Cited by Arnold, *The Farthest Promised Land*, p.127.

3. Ibid.

4. Ibid., p.112.

5. Ibid., p.109.

6. Arch, *From Ploughtail to Parliament*, p.100.

7. Ibid., p.101.

8. Burnett, *Plenty and Want*, p.25.

9. Ibid., p.133.

10. Ibid., pp.26–7.

11. Arch, *From Ploughtail to Parliament*, p.73.

12. Arnold, *The Farthest Promised Land*, p.35.

13. Ibid., p.5.

14. Ibid., p.116.

15. Ibid., pp.117–18.

16. Ibid., p.126.

17. Ibid., p.127.

18. Nally, '"That coming storm"', p.715.

19. Hoerder, 'From dreams to possibilities', p.11.

20. Richter, '"Could you not turn your back on this hunger country"', pp.19–20.

21. Belich, *Replenishing the Earth*, p.158.

22. Cameron et al., *English Immigrant Voices*, p.85.

23. Arnold, *The Farthest Promised Land*, p.243.

24. Ibid., pp.127–8.

25. Friedmann, 'Beyond "voting with their feet"', p.558; Richards, *Britannia's Children*, p.119; Burnett, *Plenty and Want*, p.3.

26. Tosh, 'Jeremiah Goldswain's farewell', p.34.

27. Ibid., p.28.

28. Errington, 'British migration and British America, 1783–1867', pp.140–6.

29. Tosh, 'Jeremiah Goldswain's farewell', p.35.

30. Long, *The Chronicle of Jeremiah Goldswain*, pp.1–4. The account of his departure is heart-rending. His parents watched the party of would-be emigrants depart. His mother had asked him when he reached the turn in the road 'to hold up my hankershift as this wold be probley the Last time she wold see me for ever, I lost site of them and went on with a hevey hart' (pp.5–6).

31. Belich, 'The rise of the Anglo-world', p.49.

32. The number of available passenger berths for crossing the Atlantic tripled.

33. Stephenson, *Recollections of a Long Life 1829–1915*, p.23.

34. Richards, *Britannia's Children*, p.118.

35. Nally, '"That coming storm"', pp.723–31.

36. Richards, *Britannia's Children*, p.118.

37. Ibid., p.152.

38. Erikson, *Leaving England*, p.57.

39. Rössler, 'The dream of independence', p.138.

40. Ibid., p.130.

41. Ibid., p.139.

42. Dublin, *Immigrant Voices*, p.69.

43. Rössler, 'The dream of independence', p.151.

44. Arnold, *The Farthest Promised Land*, p.325.

45. Ibid., p.11.

46. Kennaway, *Crusts*, p.21.

47. Burnett, *Plenty and Want*, p.30.

48. Horsman, *Feast or Famine*, p.13.

49. Diner, *Hungering for America*, p.16.

50. Dale, *The Cross Timbers*, p.35.

51. Arch, *From Ploughtail to Parliament*, p.207.

52. Dale, *The Cross Timbers*, p.41.

53. Barker, *Station Life in New Zealand*, pp.107–8.

54. Arnold, *The Farthest Promised Land*, p.172.

55. Ibid., pp.156–7.

56. Barker, *Station Life in New Zealand*, p.41.

57. Dublin, *Immigrant Voices*, p.80.

58. Belich, *Making Peoples*, p.281.

59. Bickersteth, *The Land of Open Doors*, pp.25–6.

60. Arnold, *The Farthest Promised Land*, p.314.

61. Ibid., p.127.

62. Ibid., p.313.

63. Ibid., pp.318–19.

64. See Goldswain (ed.), 'Introduction'.

65. Weaver, *The Great Land Rush and the Making of the Modern World, 1650–1900*, p.88.

Chapter 13, in which Frank Swannell eats bean stew, bannock and prune pie

1. Sherwood, *Surveying Southern British Columbia*, p.41.

2. Ibid., p.43.

3. Ibid.

4. Ibid.

5. See for example, Kelsey, 'Food for the Lewis and Clark expedition', p.201.

6. Wilk, *Home Cooking in the Global Village*, pp.63–4; Wilk, 'The extractive economy', p.288.

7. Horsman, *Feast or Famine*, p.42.

8. Sellick, *The Imperial African Cookery Book*, p.28.

9. Sherwood, *Surveying Southern British Columbia*, pp.21–4, 68.

10. Wilk, *Home Cooking in the Global Village*, pp.26–7.

11. Tye, '"A poor man's meal"', pp.38–40; Stephenson, *Recollections of a Long Life 1829–1915*, p.43.

12. See Murgatroyd, *The Dig Tree*.

13.   Macdonald, *Feeding Nelson's Navy*, pp.9–10.

14.   Rodger, *The Wooden World*, pp.100–1.

15.   Wynter, *Our Social Bees*, p.199.

16.   Farrer, *A Settlement Amply Supplied*, pp.36–9; Geoghegan, 'The story of how the tin nearly wasn't' (accessed 11 September 2016).

17.   Drummond and Lewis, *Historic Tinned Food*, p.14.

18.   Ibid., pp.13–17.

19.   Farrer, *A Settlement Amply Supplied*, pp.42–3.

20.   Robertson, '"Mariners' mealtimes"', p.156.

21.   Ibid., pp.152–3; Goody, 'Industrial food', p.341.

22.   Drummond and Lewis, *Historic Tinned Food*, p.15.

23.   Robertson, '"Mariners' mealtimes"', p.155.

24.   Wynter, *Our Social Bees*, p.194.

25.   Geoghegan, 'The story of how the tin nearly wasn't' (accessed 11 September 2016).

26.   Farrer, *A Settlement Amply Supplied*, pp.45–6.

27.   Ibid., pp.83–6.

28.   Drummond and Lewis, *Historic Tinned Food*, p.13.

29.   Muller, 'Industrial food preservation in the nineteenth and twentieth centuries', p.128; Hughes, *Victorians Undone*, pp.364–5.

30.   Burnett, *Plenty and Want*, p.116.

31.   Goody, 'Industrial food', p.343.

32.   Parks, *Wanderings of a Pilgrim in Search of the Picturesque during Four-and-Twenty Years in the East*, p.230.

33.   Roberts, *Scenes and Characteristics of Hindoostan*, I, p.75.

34.   Horsman, *Feast or Famine*, p.2.

35.   Shepherd, *Pickled, Potted and Canned*, p.245.

36.   Mayhew, *The Shops and Companies of London and the Trades and Manufactories of Great Britain*, V, p.177; Atkins, 'Vinegar and sugar', pp.44–6; Cowen, *Relish*, p.154.

37.   Mayhew, *The Shops and Companies of London and the Trades and Manufactories of Great Britain*, V, p.183.

38.   Ibid., p.185.

39.   Hull and Mair, *The European in India*, p.93.

40.   Mayhew, *The Shops and Companies of London and the Trades and Manufactories of Great Britain*, I, p.13.

41.   Ibid.

42.   In 1874, the Reading biscuit maker Huntley & Palmers manufactured 3,200 tons of biscuits, while J. D. Carr's of Carlisle produced 950 tons of 128 different varieties:

Corley, *Quaker Enterprise in Biscuits*, p.77; Forster, *Rich Desserts and Captain's Thin*, p.136.

43. Mayhew, *The Shops and Companies of London and the Trades and Manufactories of Great Britain*, V, pp.15–16.

44. Corley, 'Nutrition, technology and the growth of the British biscuit industry 1820–1900', p.22.

45. Corley, *Quaker Enterprise in Biscuits*, pp.74–5; *Annual Statement of the Trade and Navigation of the United Kingdom with Foreign Countries and British Possessions in the Year 1870*, p.115.

46. Forster, *Rich Desserts and Captain's Thin*, p.139.

47. Corley, *Quaker Enterprise in Biscuits*, p.94.

48. Muller, *Baking and Bakeries*, p.24.

49. Corley, *Quaker Enterprise in Biscuits*, p.94.

50. Wenzel, *House Decoration in Nubia*, pp.3, 150–1.

51. Collingham, *Imperial Bodies*, pp. 60–1.

52. Ibid., pp.50–3.

53. Johnson, *The Stranger in India, or Three Years in Calcutta*, I, p.164.

54. Lawrence, *Genteel Women*, p.193.

55. 'Culinary jottings for Madras by Wyvern', p.xiv.

56. Dutton, *Life in India*, p.100.

57. Lawrence, *Genteel Women*, pp.213–16.

58. Wyvern, *Culinary Jottings*, p.28.

59. Boyle, *Diary of a Colonial Officer's Wife*, p.17.

60. Ibid., pp.3, 67.

61. Hall, 'And the Nights were more terrible than the days', Ch. X, p.5.

62. Ibid., Ch. X, pp.4, 10.

63. Ibid.

64. Ibid., Ch. X, p.43.

65. Ibid., Ch. X, pp.36–7.

66. Ibid., Ch. X, p.37.

67. Wilk, *Home Cooking in the Global Village*, pp.48–9; Wilk, 'Anchovy sauce', p.93.

68. Goody, 'Industrial food', p.342.

69. Wyvern, *Culinary Jottings*, p.28.

70. Raphael, 'Steam power and hand technology', p.24.

71. Black, *The British Seaborne Empire*, p.62.

72. Mayhew, *The Shops and Companies of London and the Trades and Manufactories of Great Britain*, V, p.181.

73. Corley, *Quaker Enterprise in Biscuits*, pp.36–7, 45; Atkins, 'Vinegar and sugar', p.47.

74. Correspondence between H&P and Col. A. J. Palmer regarding his fact-finding mission to South America, the West Indies and New York in 1938.

75. 0.095 per cent of total UK industrial production, or £919,000 out of an estimated £968 million. Corley, *Quaker Enterprise in Biscuits*, p.125; Payne, 'The emergence of the large-scale company in Great Britain, 1879–1914', p.540.

76. Atkins, 'Vinegar and sugar', p.47; Mayhew, *The Shops and Companies of London and the Trades and Manufactories of Great Britain*, V, p.177.

Chapter 14, in which the Reverend Daniel Tyerman and Mr George Bennet attend a tea party

1. Montgomery, *Journal of Voyages and Travels by the Rev. Daniel Tyerman and George Bennet, Esq.*, pp.530–1.

2. Ibid.

3. Ibid., pp.516–17.

4. Ibid., p.531.

5. Ibid., p.533.

6. Smith, *Consumption and the Making of Respectability, 1600–1800*, pp.189–90.

7. 'Respectability heavily emphasized an image of the family as an entity devoted primarily to educating its members in moral behaviour and to sustaining their virtue … A respectable home and its inhabitants were clean. Respectable people were properly dressed, modestly … fashionably … in *public*': ibid., pp.210–11.

8. Montgomery, *Journal of Voyages and Travels by the Rev. Daniel Tyerman and George Bennet, Esq.*, pp.533–4.

9. Ibid.

10. Ibid., p.535.

11. Daws, *A Dream of Islands*, p.32.

12. Ibid., p.39.

13. Smith, *Consumption and the Making of Respectability, 1600–1800*, pp.241–2.

14. Sivasundaram, *Nature and the Godly Empire*, pp.163–6.

15. Curr, *Recollections of Squatting in Victoria*, p.170.

16. McDonald, 'Encounters at "Bushman Station"'; Reynolds, 'The other side of the frontier', p.61.

17. Nettelbeck and Foster, 'Food and governance on the frontiers of colonial Australia and Canada's North West Territories', p.22.

18. Hallam, 'Aboriginal women as providers', pp.38, 43–51.

19. Foster, 'Rations, coexistence, and the colonisation of Aboriginal labour in the South Australian pastoral industry, 1860–1911', p.12.
20. Ibid., p.11.
21. Nettelbeck and Foster, 'Food and governance on the frontiers of colonial Australia and Canada's North West Territories', pp.26–8.
22. Foster, 'Rations, coexistence, and the colonisation of Aboriginal labour in the South Australian pastoral industry, 1860–1911', p.19.
23. Reynolds, 'The other side of the frontier', p.54.
24. Smith, 'Station camps', p.80.
25. Siochrú and Brown, 'The Down Survey of Ireland project', p.6.
26. Bayly, *The Birth of the Modern World, 1780–1914*, p.443.
27. Weaver, *The Great Land Rush and the Making of the Modern World, 1650–1900*, pp.229–30.
28. Nettelbeck and Foster, 'Food and governance on the frontiers of colonial Australia and Canada's North West Territories', pp.25, 33–4.
29. Foster, 'Rations, coexistence, and the colonisation of Aboriginal labour in the South Australian pastoral industry, 1860–1911', p.16.
30. Coutts, 'Merger or takeover', p.513.
31. Hallam, 'Aboriginal women as providers', pp.38, 43–51.
32. Cronon, *Changes in the Land*; Shawcross, 'Fern-root and the total scheme of eighteenth century Maori food production in agricultural areas'.
33. Wilk, *Home Cooking in the Global Village*, pp.63–4.
34. Hall, 'And the Nights were more terrible than the days', Ch. X, p.32.
35. Ibid.
36. Collingham, *Imperial Bodies*, pp.57, 186.
37. Wilk, *Home Cooking in the Global Village*, pp.80–2, 94.
38. Ibid., p.91.
39. Tandon, *Beyond Punjab 1937–1960*, p.67.
40. Collingham, *Around India's First Table*, pp.93, 127.
41. Sellick, *The Imperial African Cookery Book*, p.11.
42. Cusack, 'African cuisines', p.210.
43. Richards, *Land, Labour and Diet in Northern Rhodesia*, p.61.
44. Ibid., p.3.

Chapter 15, in which diamond miners cook up an iguana curry

1. Terry Roopnaraine in conversation with the author, August 2016.
2. Pagrach-Chandra, 'Damra bound', pp.177–8.

3. Terry Roopnaraine in conversation with the author, August 2016; Bahadur, *Coolie Woman*, pp.5–6.

4. Bayly, *The Birth of the Modern World, 1780–1914*, pp.300–1.

5. Cain, 'Economics and empire', pp.38–40.

6. Shineberg, *They Came for Sandalwood*, p.3.

7. Rodney, *History of the Guyanese Working People*, p.61–2.

8. Lai, *Indentured Labor, Caribbean Sugar*, pp.5–9.

9. Allen, 'Slaves, convicts, abolitionism and the global origins of the post-emancipation indentured labor system', p.334.

10. Ibid., p.332.

11. St John, *The Making of the Raj*, pp.72–3.

12. Ramdin, *Arising from Bondage*, p.12; Sharma, '"Lazy" natives, coolie labour and the Assam tea industry', p.1311.

13. Carter, *Voices from Indenture*, pp.65–6; Lai, *Indentured Labor, Caribbean Sugar*, pp.20–3.

14. Havinden and Meredith, *Colonialism and Development*, p.41; Tomlinson, 'Economics and empire', p.61; Osterhammel, *The Transformation of the World*, p.159.

15. Lai, *Indentured Labor, Caribbean Sugar*, p.12.

16. Carter, *Voices from Indenture*, p.21.

17. Havinden and Meredith, *Colonialism and Development*, p.42.

18. Carter, *Voices from Indenture*, p.94.

19. Ibid.; Eltis and Richardson, *Atlas of the Transatlantic Slave Trade*, pp.167–8.

20. Carter, *Voices from Indenture*, p.103.

21. Graves, 'Colonialism and indentured labour migration in the Western Pacific, 1840–1915', p.225.

22. Pagrach-Chandra, 'Damra bound', p.173.

23. Osterhammel, *The Transformation of the World*, p.159.

24. Pagrach-Chandra, 'Damra bound', p.174; Pillai, 'Food culture of Indo Caribbean', p.2.

25. Pillai, 'Food culture of Indo Caribbean', p.5.

26. Pagrach-Chandra, 'Damra bound', p.176.

27. Dods, *The Cook and Housewife's Manual*, p.192.

28. Pagrach-Chandra, 'Damra bound', pp.176–7; Pillai, 'Food culture of Indo Caribbean', pp.4–5.

29. Adapted from The Inner Gourmet with thanks to Terry Roopnaraine for his grandmother's recipe.

30. Rodney, *History of the Guyanese Working People*, p. 99.

31. Wills, 'European consumption and Asian production in the seventeenth and eighteenth centuries', p.145.

32. Antrobus, *A History of the Assam Tea Company, 1839–1953*, p.22; Liu, 'The birth of a noble tea country', pp.77, 80.

33. Antrobus, *A History of the Assam Tea Company, 1839–1953*, p. 30.

34. Liu, 'The birth of a noble tea country', p.82.

35. Collingham, *Curry*, p.194.

36. Antrobus, *A History of the Assam Tea Company, 1839–1953*, p.99.

37. Gardella, *Harvesting Mountains*, p.46.

38. Sharma, '"Lazy" natives, coolie labour and the Assam tea industry', p.1308.

39. Ibid., pp.1303–8; Macfarlane and Macfarlane, *Green Gold*, pp.215–16.

40. Collingham, *Imperial Bodies*, pp.143–4.

41. Allen, 'Slaves, convicts, abolitionism and the global origins of the post-emancipation indentured labor system', p.328.

42. Rappaport, 'Packaging China', pp.125–35.

43. Gardella, *Harvesting Mountains*, p.110; Collingham, *Curry*, p.194.

44. Mintz, *Sweetness and Power*, p.71.

45. The four counties were Taishan, Kaiping, Xinhui, Enping: Li, *The Chinese in Canada*, p.20; Hsu, *Dreaming of Gold, Dreaming of Home*, p.28.

46. Hsu, *Dreaming of Gold, Dreaming of Home*, p.30.

47. Ibid., p.29.

48. Friday, *Organizing Asian American Labour*, p.25.

49. Hsu, *Dreaming of Gold, Dreaming of Home*, p.35.

50. Ross, 'Factors influencing the dining habits of Japanese and Chinese migrants at a British Columbia salmon cannery', p.71.

51. Graves, 'Colonialism and indentured labour migration in the Western Pacific, 1840–1915', pp.243–54; Graves, *Cane and Labour*, pp.74–101.

52. Brooks, 'Peanuts and colonialism', pp.43–6.

53. Ibid., p.41.

54. Clarence-Smith, *Cocoa and Chocolate, 1765–1914*, pp.158–9; Iliffe, *Africans*, p.203.

55. Cited in Mintz, *Sweetness and Power*, p.42.

Chapter 16, in which the Bartons entertain the Wilsons to tea

1. Gaskell, *Mary Barton*, pp.1–17.

2. Broomfield, *Food and Cooking in Victorian England*, pp.78–9.

3. Osterhammel, *The Transformation of the World*, pp.245–9, 259.

4. Engels, *The Condition of the Working Class in England*, pp.18–20.

5. Burnett, *Plenty and Want*, pp.56–7.

6. Bell, *At the Works*, p.47.

7. The worst recessions were in 1816, 1826–7, 1841–3, 1848–9 and 1861.

8. Burnett, *Plenty and Want*, p.41; Oddy, 'Urban famine in nineteenth-century Britain', p.74.

9. Foster, 'Introduction', p.x.

10. Engels, *The Condition of the Working Class in England*, p.17.

11. Dickens, 'Hard Times', p.5.

12. Zylberberg, 'Fuel prices, regional diets and cooking habits in the English industrial revolution (1750–1830)', p.106.

13. Burnett, *Plenty and Want*, pp.56–7.

14. Engels, *The Condition of the Working Class in England*, p.84.

15. Thompson, *The Empire Strikes Back?*, p.267.

16. Bell, *At the Works*, p.62.

17. Oddy, 'A nutritional analysis of historical evidence', p.225.

18. Oddy, 'Urban famine in nineteenth-century Britain', p.80.

19. Sharpe, 'Explaining the short stature of the poor', pp.1477–9.

20. Ibid., pp.1475–6.

21. Szreter and Mooney, 'Urbanization, mortality, and the standard of living debate', pp.88, 96.

22. Gaskell, *Mary Barton*, pp.10–11.

23. Engels, *The Condition of the Working Class in England*, p.31.

24. McLean and Bustani, 'Irish potatoes and British politics', p.819.

25. Ibid., p.820.

26. Nally, '"That coming storm"', p.728.

27. McLean and Bustani, 'Irish potatoes and British politics', pp.822–5.

28. Vugt, 'Running from ruin?', p.418.

29. Belich, *Replenishing the Earth*, p.343.

30. Ibid., p.344.

31. Ibid., p.340; Cronon, *Nature's Metropolis*, pp.102–3, 110.

32. Ibid., p.113–14; Sharp and Weisdorf, 'Globalization revisited', p.90.

33. Paul, 'The wheat trade between California and the United Kingdom', pp.391–3.

34. Ibid., p.397.

35. West, 'Grain kings, rubber dreams and stock exchanges', p.110.

36. Paul, 'The wheat trade between California and the United Kingdom,' p.411.

37. Ibid., p.399.

38. Fremdling, 'European foreign trade policies, freight rates and the world markets of grain and coal during the nineteenth century', p.91.

39. Perren, *Agriculture in Depression, 1870–1914*, pp.2–3.

40. Burnett, *Plenty and Want*, p.116; Hobsbawm, *The Age of Capital 1848–1875*, p.175.

41. Perren, *Agriculture in Depression, 1870–1914*, pp.6, 17.

42. Spring, 'Land and politics in Edwardian England', pp.18–20.

43. Ibid., pp.21–6; Cain and Hopkins, *British Imperialism 1688–2000*, pp.109–10. See also Blackwell, '"An undoubted jewel"'.

44. Rothstein, 'Rivalry for the British wheat market, 1860–1914', p.402.

45. Ibid., p.407.

46. Ibid., p.415.

47. Andrabi and Kuehlwein, 'Railways and price convergence in British India', pp.354–74.

48. Osterhammel, *The Transformation of the World*, pp.199, 207.

49. Srivastava, *The History of Indian Famines and Development of Famine Policy 1858–1918*, pp.331–2.

50. Sweeney, 'Indian railways and famine 1875–1914', p.146. Famine struck in 1860–1, 1865–7, 1868–70, 1873–4, 1876–9, 1899–1900, 1907–8, 1913–14 and 1918–19.

51. Cosgrove et al., 'Colonialism, international trade and the nation-state', p.234.

52. Hall-Matthews, *Peasants, Famine and the State in Colonial Western India*, p.8.

53. St John, *The Making of the Raj*, p.64.

54. Belich, *Replenishing the Earth*, pp.364–5.

55. Solberg, *The Prairies and the Pampas*, p.28.

56. Ibid., p.1.

57. Asteris, 'The rise and decline of South Wales coal exports, 1870–1930', p.40.

58. Jones, *Empire of Dust*, p.88.

59. Weaver, *The Great Land Rush and the Making of the Modern World, 1650–1900*, p.267; Solberg, *The Prairies and the Pampas*, pp.39, 56, 79.

60. Smith, *The People's Health, 1830–1910*, pp.209–10.

61. Thompson, *The Empire Strikes Back?*, p.46.

62. Perren, *Agriculture in Depression, 1870–1914*, p.13.

63. Ibid., p.14; Hobsbawm, *The Age of Empire 1875–1914*, p.36; Thirsk, *Alternative Agriculture*, p.177.

64. Hoffmann, *British Industry 1700–1950*, pp.204–5; Torode, 'Trends in fruit consumption', p.123. The Caribbean sugar planters survived by amalgamating their plantations and diverting their sugar to America and Canada: Heuman, 'The British West Indies', p.490–1.

65. Paterson, *Across the Bridges, or, Life by the South London River-side*, p.36.

66. Burnett, *Plenty and Want*, p.115.

67. Smith, *The People's Health, 1830–1910*, pp.214–15.

68. Szreter and Mooney, 'Urbanization, mortality, and the standard of living debate', p.88.

Chapter 17, in which Prakash Tandon enjoys a Sunday roast

1. Tandon, *Punjabi Century 1857–1947*, p.214.
2. Ibid.
3. Ibid., pp.214–15.
4. Ibid.
5. The pancreas and the testicles: ibid., p.205.
6. Ibid., p.211.
7. Perren, *Taste, Trade and Technology*, pp.8–9.
8. Ibid., p.40.
9. Smith, *Practical Dietary for Families, Schools, and the Labouring Classes*, pp.79–80.
10. Belich, *Replenishing the Earth*, p.449.
11. Smith, *Practical Dietary for Families, Schools, and the Labouring Classes*, p.269.
12. Ibid., pp.268–9.
13. Ibid., pp.79–80.
14. Wynter, *Our Social Bees*, p.204.
15. Plummer, *New British Industries in the Twentieth Century*, p.229; Farrer, *A Settlement Amply Supplied*, pp.69, 76.
16. Farrer, *A Settlement Amply Supplied*, pp.134–5.
17. Ibid., p.139.
18. Ibid., pp.145–6.
19. Knightley, *The Rise and Fall of the House of Vestey*, p.10.
20. Wade, *Chicago's Pride*, p.103.
21. Goody, 'Industrial food', p.347; Farrer, *A Settlement Amply Supplied*, p.152; Thompson, *The Empire Strikes Back?*, p.43.
22. Perren, *Taste, Trade and Technology*, pp.45, 60; Farrer, *A Settlement Amply Supplied*, p.149; Burnett, *Plenty and Want*, pp.116–17.
23. Freidberg, *Fresh*, p.56; Whitten and Whitten, *The Birth of Big Business in the United States, 1860–1914*, p.168.
24. Shannon, *The Farmer's Last Frontier*, p.194.
25. Dale, *Frontier Ways*, pp.14–16; Cronon, *Nature's Metropolis*, pp.219–21.
26. Perren, *Taste, Trade and Technology*, pp.68–9; Freidberg, *Fresh*, pp.68–9.
27. Whitten and Whitten, *The Birth of Big Business in the United States, 1860–1914*, pp.170–1; Cronon, *Nature's Metropolis*, pp.212–13.
28. Belich, *Replenishing the Earth*, pp.344–5; Perren, *Taste, Trade and Technology*, pp.1, 68, 73.
29. Perren, 'The North American beef and cattle trade with Great Britain, 1870–1914', p.432; Dale, *Frontier Ways*, p.14.

30. Woods, 'Breed, culture, and economy', p.295.
31. Moore, 'National identity and Victorian Christmas foods', p.149.
32. Farrer, *A Settlement Amply Supplied*, p.189.
33. Ibid., pp.192–3.
34. Ibid., p.196.
35. Ibid., p.192.
36. Woods, 'Breed, culture and economy,' p.297.
37. Ibid., p.288.
38. Farrer, *A Settlement Amply Supplied*, pp.192–4; Perren, *Taste, Trade and Technology*, p.49.
39. Critchell and Raymond, *A History of the Frozen Meat Trade*, pp.285–6.
40. Ibid., pp.33, 76.
41. Ibid., pp.65, 78.
42. Ibid., p.78; Solberg, *The Prairies and the Pampas*, p.5.
43. Smith, *Practical Dietary for Families, Schools, and the Labouring Classes*, pp.79–80.
44. Perren, *Taste, Trade and Technology*, p.49.
45. Freidberg, *Fresh*, p.75; Dingle, 'Drink and working-class living standards in Britain, 1870–1914', p.129.
46. Burnett, *Plenty and Want*, p.155.
47. Cited by Keating, *Into Unknown England, 1866–1913*, pp.130–1.
48. Othick, 'The cocoa and chocolate industry in the 19th century', pp.81–2.
49. Clarence-Smith, *Cocoa and Chocolate, 1765–1914*, p.24.
50. Ibid., p.27; Othick, 'The cocoa and chocolate industry in the 19th century', p.86.
51. Othick, 'The cocoa and chocolate industry in the 19th century', p.84; Clarence-Smith, *Cocoa and Chocolate*, pp.71–4.
52. Cited by Steinitz, 'The tales they told'.
53. Ibid.
54. Goody, 'Industrial food,' p.343; den Hartog, 'The discovery of vitamins and its impact on the food industry', pp.131–4.
55. Steel, 'New Zealand is butterland', p.182.
56. Whitten and Whitten, *The Birth of Big Business in the United States, 1860–1914*, p.169.
57. Perren, *Taste, Trade and Technology*, pp.72, 76.
58. Winstanley, *The Shopkeeper's World 1830–1914*, p.38.
59. Steel, 'New Zealand is butterland', p.185.
60. Blackman, 'The corner shop: the development of the grocery and general provisions trade', p.154.
61. Mathias, *Retailing Revolution*, p.175.
62. Ibid., pp.107–9.

63. Mathias, 'The British tea trade in the nineteenth century', p.96.

64. Ibid., p.97.

65. Dingle, 'Drink and working-class living standards in Britain, 1870–1914', p.128; Kennedy, *The Merchant Princes*, p.211.

66. Corley, 'Nutrition, technology and the growth of the British biscuit industry 1820–1900', p.24; Corley, *Quaker Enterprise in Biscuits*, pp.137, 256.

67. Aucamp, 'The establishment and development of the Cape fresh fruit industry 1886–1910', pp.86–7.

68. Torode, 'Trends in fruit consumption', p.118.

69. Hawkins, 'The pineapple canning industry during the world depression of the 1930s', pp.49, 55.

70. Tandon, *Punjabi Century 1857–1947*, p.215; Imperial Economic Committee, 'Canned and dried fruit notes'.

71. Offer, 'The working classes, British naval plans and the coming of the Great War', p.206.

72. *Empire Marketing Board Posters.*

73. Perren, *Agriculture in Depression, 1870–1914*, p.61.

74. Ibid.

75. Hobsbawm, *The Age of Empire 1875–1914*, p.39.

Chapter 18, in which the recipe for irio changes

1. Sellick, *The Imperial African Cookery Book*, pp.253–4.

2. Robertson, 'Black, white, and red all over', p.269.

3. Ibid., pp.267–8.

4. Ibid., p.269.

5. Brantley, 'Kikuyu-Maasai nutrition and colonial science', pp.55–7.

6. Ibid., p.49.

7. Burnett, *Plenty and Want*, p.281; Orr, *As I Recall*, p.115; Mayhew, 'The 1930s nutrition controversy', pp.457–8.

8. Brantley, 'Kikuyu-Maasai nutrition and colonial science', pp.57–66.

9. Robertson, 'Black, white, and red all over', pp.264–6.

10. Ibid., p.270.

11. Richards, *Land, Labour and Diet in Northern Rhodesia*, p.52.

12. Brantley, 'Kikuyu-Maasai nutrition and colonial science', p.74.

13. Ibid.

14. Ibid.

15. Ibid., p.51.

16. Ibid., pp.83–4.
17. Fourshey, '"The remedy for hunger is bending the back"', p.236.
18. Robertson, 'Black, white, and red all over', pp.274–9.
19. Fourshey, '"The remedy for hunger is bending the back"', p.238.
20. Cited by Robertson, 'Black, white, and red all over', p.286.
21. Ibid., pp.286–8.
22. Ibid., p.281.
23. Fourshey, '"The remedy for hunger is bending the back"', p.257.
24. Ibid., pp.250–1.
25. Robertson, 'Black, white, and red all over', pp.270–4.
26. Fourshey, '"The remedy for hunger is bending the back"', p.225.
27. Ibid.
28. Worboys, 'The discovery of colonial malnutrition between the wars', pp.217–19.
29. Brantley, *Feeding Families*, p.150.
30. Havinden and Meredith, *Colonialism and Development*, p.284.
31. Ibid., p.292.
32. Ibid., p.283.
33. Destombes, 'From long-term patterns of seasonal hunger to changing experiences of everyday poverty', p.202.
34. Havinden and Meredith, *Colonialism and Development*, p.289.
35. Robertson, 'Black, white, and red all over,' pp.291–2; see also Freidberg, 'Freshness from afar'; Freidberg, 'Postcolonial paradoxes'.
36. *'Vous ne savez pas où est l'imperialisme? … Regardez dans votre assiette!'* Cited by Cusack, 'African cuisines', p.207.

Chapter 19, in which infantryman R. L. Crimp eats bully beef and sweet potatoes

1. Crimp, *The Diary of a Desert Rat*, p.23.
2. Ibid., p.24.
3. Ibid., pp.20–1.
4. Ibid., p.21.
5. Bayly, 'Spunyarns', p.33.
6. Crimp, *The Diary of a Desert Rat*, pp.20–1.
7. Ibid., p.22.
8. Ibid., p.30.
9. Ibid., pp.38–9.
10. Tonkin, 'No Tunnels – No Wooden Horses', pp.37, 48–9.

11. Collingham, *The Taste of War*, p.67–8.
12. Overy, *Why the Allies Won*, p.31.
13. Jackson, *The British Empire and the Second World War*, p.2.
14. Ibid., p.4.
15. Ibid., p.44.
16. Adams, *Farm Problems in Meeting Food Needs*, p.12; Smith, *Conflict over Convoys*, pp.45–6.
17. MacRae, *God Speed the Plough*, p.8.
18. Martin, 'The structural transformation of British agriculture', p.34.
19. Collingham, *The Taste of War*, pp.96–100.
20. Swinton, *I Remember*, p.97.
21. Collingham, *The Taste of War*, p.140.
22. Ibid., p.141.
23. Crimp, *The Diary of a Desert Rat*, p.11.
24. Wilmington, *The Middle East Supply Centre*, p.50.
25. Ibid., pp.43–50.
26. Crimp, *The Diary of a Desert Rat*, p.30.
27. Collingham, *The Taste of War*, p.125.
28. Tunzelmann, *Indian Summer*, p.138.
29. *The Production of Food Crops in Mauritius during the War*.
30. Maxon, '"Fantastic prices" in the midst of an "acute food shortage"', pp.36–9.
31. Smith, *Conflict Over Convoys*, p.159.
32. Ibid.
33. Sen, *Poverty and Famines*, pp.71–2.
34. Greenough, *Prosperity and Misery in Modern Bengal*, p.168.
35. Ibid.
36. Stephens, *Monsoon Morning*, pp.169–70.
37. Ibid., pp.185–7.
38. Greenough, *Prosperity and Misery in Modern Bengal*, pp.136–7.
39. Stevenson, *Bengal Tiger and British Lion*, pp.153–4.
40. Greenough, *Prosperity and Misery in Modern Bengal*, p.140; Ellis, *The World War II Databook*, p.255.
41. Collingham, *The Taste of War*, p.151.
42. Sarkar, *Modern India 1885–1947*, p.406.
43. Smith, *Conflict Over Convoys*, p.152.
44. Ibid., p.156.
45. Mackay, *Half the Battle*, p.201.
46. Collingham, *The Taste of War*, pp.387–9.

47. Oddy, *From Plain Fare to Fusion Food*, p.134.
48. Ibid., pp.165, 209.
49. Jackson, *Botswana 1939–1945*, p.156; Wright, *The World and a Very Small Place in Africa*, p.195.
50. Collingham, *The Taste of War*, p.126.

Chapter 20, in which Mr Oldknow dreams of making an Empire plum pudding

1. 'A Christmas pudding', pp.300–301.
2. Ibid., p.301.
3. Ibid., p.302.
4. Ibid., p.302–3.
5. Ibid., p.303.
6. Ibid., p.303–4.
7. 'A Christmas pudding', p.301.
8. Hervey, *The Book of Christmas*, pp.106–7.
9. Ibid., p.277.
10. 'A Christmas pudding', p.301.
11. Moore, *Victorian Christmas in Print*, pp.66–7.
12. Mintz, 'The changing roles of food', pp.267, 271–2.
13. Breen, 'Empire of goods', pp. 491–6.
14. Oddy, *From Plain Fare to Fusion Food*, p.134.
15. Mintz, 'Time, sugar and sweetness', p.366.
16. 'A Christmas pudding', p.301.
17. Cited by Weaver, *The Great Land Rush and the Making of the Modern World, 1650–1900*, p.4.
18. Ibid., p.5.
19. O'Brien and Engerman, 'Exports and the growth of the British economy from the Glorious Revolution to the Peace of Amiens', p.179; Hobsbawm, *The Age of Extremes*, p.289.
20. Cosgrove et al., 'Colonialism, international trade and the nation-state', p.234.
21. Bayly, *The Birth of the Modern World, 1780–1914*, p.418.
22. Higgs, *Cocoa, Slavery and Colonial Africa*, p.3.
23. Higgs, 'Happiness and work', pp.58, 68.
24. Trentmann, 'Coping with shortage', p.17.
25. Ibid., pp.20–1.
26. Spiekermann, 'Vollkorn für die Führer', p.95.

27. Hall, 'The food supply of the Empire', p.5.

28. Ibid., pp.20, 30.

29. Day, 'One family and Empire Christmas pudding'.

30. Ibid.; O'Connor, 'The King's Christmas pudding', p.146.

31. O'Connor, 'The King's Christmas pudding', p.127.

32. Spiekermann, 'Brown bread for victory', pp.144–9.

33. Tooze, *The Wages of Destruction*, p.469.

34. Carey, 'John Derricke's *Image of Irelande*', p.306; Madajzyk, 'Vom "Generalplan Ost" zum "Generalsiedlungsplan"', p.16; Roth, '"Generalplan Ost" – "Gesamtplan Ost"', pp.40–1.

35. *Food Statistics Pocket Book 2014*, p.26.

36. MacRae, *God Speed the Plough*, p.9.

37. Tye, '"A poor man's meal"', p.344.

38. Ibid., p.335.

39. Goucher, *Congotay! Congotay!*, p.129; McWilliams, *A Revolution in Eating*, pp.45–7.

40. McCann, *Maize and Grace*, p.viii.

41. Peters, 'National preferences and colonial cuisine', pp.152–3.

42. Ichijo and Ranta, *Food, National Identity and Nationalism*, pp.9–10.

43. Kirkpatrick, 'A uniquely American holiday' (accessed 23 March 2017).

44. Moore, *Victorian Christmas in Print*, p.142.

45. O'Connor, 'The King's Christmas pudding', p.133.

46. 'The turkey at Christmas' (accessed 17 March 2017).

47. Fielding, *Bridget Jones's Diary*, pp.8–9, 13.

48. Ibid., p.7.

49. Ibid., p.13.

50. With thanks to Ruth Goodall for supplying me with her post-Christmas turkey curry recipe.

Bibliography

Online sources

1641 Depositions, Trinity College Library, Dublin: http://1641.tcd.ie/deposition.php?depID<?php echo 821025r011?> (accessed 6 April 2016).

'An alphabetical list of the Sons of Liberty who din'd at the Liberty Tree, Dorchester, 14 August 1769', Massachusetts Historical Society, collections online, masshist.org/database/viewer.php?item_id=8.

Candee, Richard M., 'Merchant and millwright: the water powered sawmills of the Piscataqua': www.historicnewengland.org.

Carney, Judith, 'Rice, slaves and landscapes of cultural memory', www.cr.nps.gov/crdi/conferences/AFR_43-62_Carney.pdf (accessed 18 October 2013).

Cross, Russell, 'Middleburg plantation and the Benjamin Simons Family', www.rootsweb.ancestry.com/~scbhs/middle.html (accessed 18 October 2013).

Day, Ivan, 'One family and Empire Christmas pudding', Food History Jottings, Thursday 30 August 2012, foodhistorjottings.blogspot.co.uk/2012/08/one-family-and-empire-christmas-pudding.html (accessed 19 March 2017).

Deng, Kent, 'Miracle or mirage? Foreign silver, China's economy and globalisation from the sixteenth to the nineteenth centuries' (January 2007), www.geocities.jp/akitashigeru/PDF/DiscussionPaper2007_01_13Deng.pdf, p.353.

Drummond, J. C., and W. R. Lewis, *Historic Tinned Food*: itri.co.uk/index.php?option=com_mtree&task=att_download&link_id=47511&cf_id=24.

Fox, 'Sir William Petty: Ireland, and the making of a political economist, 1653–1687', scha.ed.ac.uk/staff/supporting_files/apfox/fox-publ.pdf (accessed 5 April 2016).

Geoghegan, Tom, 'The story of how the tin nearly wasn't', BBC News Magazine, 21 April 2013, http://www.bbc.co.uk/news/magazine-21689069 (accessed 11 September 2016).

Harrington, James, *The Oceana*, constitution.orgjh/oceana (accessed 20 January 2017).

'History of Rice in Charleston and Georgetown', www.ricehope.com/history/Ricehistory.htm (accessed 18 October 2013).

http://cdm.bostonathenaeum.org/cdm/landingpage/collection/p16057coll32.

http://founders.archives.gov/documents/Adams/01–03-02- (accessed 27 August 2016).

http://oldnorth.com/2015/02/26/this-old-pew-4-and-25-captain-daniel-malcolm-merchant-and-enemy-to-oppression/.

http://south-carolina-plantations.com/berkeley/middleburg.html (accessed 18 October 2013).

Kirkpatrick, Melanie, 'A uniquely American holiday', Hudson Institute, 23 November 2016, Hudson.org/research/13067-a-uniquely-american-holiday-thanksgiving (accessed 23 March 2017).

Mandelkern, India, 'The politics of the turtle feast', 20 November 2013: theappendix.net/issues/2013/10/the-politics-of-the-turtle-feast (accessed 16 January 2017).

Park Ethnography Program, Gender, work and culture, South Carolina Gold, www.nps.gov/ethnography/aah/aaheritage/lowCountryD.htm (accessed 18 October 2013).

Pillai, Suresh Kumar, 'Food culture of Indo Caribbean', academic.edu.

Russel, William, from the papers of, a Boston school teacher and Son of Liberty, for sale at https://www.sethkaller.com/item/1418-%E2%80%9CLiberty-without-End.-Amen.%E2%80%9D-Incredibly-Rare-Toasts-from-Boston%E2%80%99s-Sons-of-Liberty,-1769.

Sons of Liberty Bowl, 1768, Paul Revere Jr. (1734–1818), Museum of Fine Arts, Boston, bowl-39072, mfa.org/collections/object/sons-of-liberty-bowl-39072.

Stephenson, Isaac, *Recollections of a Long Life 1829–1915* (R. R. Donelley & Sons, Chicago, 1915), on the website of American Memory, Library of Congress: http://memory.loc.gov/cgi-bik/query/r?ar (accessed 11 November 2014).

Stevens, Benjamin Franklin, *The Silver Punch Bowl Made by Paul Revere* (1903): http://archive.org/stream/silverpunchbowlm00ste/silverpunchbowl00ste_djvu.txt.

Tate and Lyle: www.tateandlyle.com/AboutUs/History.aspx (accessed 4–5 June 2015).

'The turkey at Christmas', oakden.co.uk/the-history-of-the-turkey-at-christmas (accessed 17 March 2017).

Timmons, Ray, 'Brief history of Middleburg Plantation', www.rootsweb.ancestry.com/~scbhs/middle.html (accessed 18 October 2013).

Wikitree.com/wiki/Homer-114 (accessed 25 August 2016).

www.geni.com/people/Joseph-Holloway/6000000000688916384 (accessed 22 November 2013).

www.geni.com/projects/Early-Families-of-Taunton-Massachusetts/3745 (accessed 22 November 2013).

www.milliganfamily.org/middleburg.htm (accessed 18 October 2013).

Centre for South Asian Studies, Cambridge

Margery Hall, 'And the Nights were more terrible than the days', Hall Papers.

Imperial War Museum, London

John Tonkin, 'No Tunnels – No Wooden Horses: A factual account of Prisoner of War life in Crete, Greece and Germany', P461.

Reading University Special Collections

Correspondence between H&P and Col. A. J. Palmer regarding his fact-finding mission to South America, the West Indies and New York in 1938, Huntley and Palmer Collections, MS 1490, HP 77.

Books and articles

A Brief Discourse on Wine; Embracing an historical and descriptive account of the vine its culture and produce in all countries, ancient and modern. Drawn from the best authorities (J. L. Denman, London, 1861).

'A Christmas pudding', *Household Words* 39/2 (21 Dec. 1850), 300–304.

Adams, R. L., *Farm Problems in Meeting Food Needs* (University of California Press, Berkeley, 1942).

Allen, Richard B., 'Slaves, convicts, abolitionism and the global origins of the post-emancipation indentured labor system', *Slavery and Abolition* 35/2 (2014), 328–48.

Alpern, Stanley B., 'The European introduction of crops into West Africa in precolonial times', *History in Africa* 19 (1992), 13–43.

Alpern, Stanley B., 'Exotic plants of western Africa: where they came from and when', *History in Africa* 35 (2008), 63–102.

Ammerman, David L., 'The tea crisis and its consequences, through 1775', in Jack P. Greene and J. R. Pole (eds), *A Companion to the American Revolution* (Blackwell, Oxford, 2000), 195–205.

Amussen, Susan Dwyer, *Caribbean Exchanges: Slavery and the Transformation of English Society, 1640–1700* (University of North Carolina Press, Chapel Hill, 2007).

Anderson, Virginia De John, 'New England in the seventeenth century', in Nicholas Canny (ed.), *The Origins of Empire: British Overseas Enterprise to the Close of the Seventeenth Century, Vol. I The Oxford History of the British Empire* (Oxford University Press, Oxford, 1998), 193–217.

Anderson, Virginia De John, *Creatures of Empire: How Domestic Animals Transformed Early America* (Oxford University Press, New York, 2004).

Andrabi, Tahir, and Michael Kuehlwein, 'Railways and price convergence in British India', *Journal of Economic History* 70/2 (2010), 351–77.

Andrews, Kenneth R., *Trade, Plunder and Settlement: Maritime Enterprise and the Genesis of the British Empire, 1480–1630* (Cambridge University Press, Cambridge, 1984).

Annual Statement of the Trade and Navigation of the United Kingdom with Foreign Countries and British Possessions in the Year 1870 (Her Majesty's Stationery Office, London, 1871).

Antrobus, H. A., *A History of the Assam Tea Company, 1839–1953* (T. & A. Constable, Edinburgh, 1957).

Arch, Joseph, *From Ploughtail to Parliament: An Autobiography* (The Cresset Library, London, 1986).

Arnold, Rollo, *The Farthest Promised Land: English Villagers, New Zealand Immigrants of the 1870s* (Victoria University Press with Price Milburn, Wellington, 1981).

Asare, J., A. Addo, E. Chapman and E. Amarteifio, *A Ghana Cook-Book for Schools* (London, Macmillan & Co., 1963).

Ashton, T. S., *An Economic History of England: The Eighteenth Century* (Methuen & Co., London, 1955).

Asteris, Michael, 'The rise and decline of South Wales coal exports, 1870–1930', *Welsh History Review* 13/1 (1986), 24–43.

Atkins, Peter, J., 'Vinegar and sugar: the early history of factory-made jams, pickles and sauces in Britain', in Derek J. Oddy and Alain Drouard (eds), *The Food Industries of Europe in the Nineteenth and Twentieth Centuries* (Ashgate, Farnham, Surrey, 2013), 41–54.

Aucamp, Chris, 'The establishment and development of the Cape fresh fruit industry 1886–1910', *South African Journal of Economic History* 2/1 (1987), 68–91.

Bahadur, Gaiutra, *Coolie Woman: The Odyssey of Indenture* (C. Hurst & Co., London, 2013).

Ball, Charles, *Fifty Years in Chains* (Dover Publications, New York, 1970).

Barker, Lady, *Station Life in New Zealand* (first published 1870; Virago, London, 1984).

Barnard, Lady Anne, *South Africa a Century Ago: Letters Written from the Cape of Good Hope (1797–1801)*, ed. W. H. Wilkins (Smith, Elder & Co., London, 1901).

Barnard, T. C., 'Planters and policies in Cromwellian Ireland', *Past and Present* 61 (1973), 31–69.

Barnard, T. C., *Improving Ireland? Projectors, Prophets and Profiteers, 1641–1786* (Four Courts Press, Dublin, 2008).

Baugh, Daniel A., *British Naval Administration in the Age of Walpole* (Princeton University Press, Princeton, NJ, 2015).

Bayly, C. A., *Imperial Meridian: The British Empire and the World, 1780–1830* (Longman, London, 1989).

Bayly, C. A., *The Birth of the Modern World, 1780–1914: Global Connections and Comparisons* (Blackwell, Oxford, 2004).

Bayly, Roy E., 'Spunyarns: Some Impressions of My Years at Sea' (by the Bayly family for the Bayly family, July 1993).

Beckles, Hilary, 'The "hub of Empire": the Caribbean and Britain in the 17th century', in Nicholas Canny (ed.), *The Origins of Empire: British Overseas Enterprise to the Close of the Seventeenth Century, Vol. I The Oxford History of the British Empire* (Oxford University Press, Oxford, 1998), 218–40.

Beckles, Hilary, '"Black men in white skins": the formation of a white proletariat in West Indian slave society', *Journal of Imperial and Commonwealth History* 15/1 (1986), 5–21.

Belich, J., *Making Peoples: A History of the New Zealanders from Polynesian Settlement to the End of the Nineteenth Century* (Allen Lane, London, 1996).

Belich, James, 'The rise of the Anglo-world: settlement in North America and Australasia, 1784–1918', in Phillip Buckner and R. Douglas Francis (eds), *Rediscovering the British World* (University of Calgary Press, Calgary, 2005).

Belich, James, *Replenishing the Earth: The Settler Revolution and the Rise of the Anglo-World, 1783–1939* (Oxford University Press, Oxford, 2009).

Bell, Florence, *At the Works: A Study of a Manufacturing Town* (Edward Arnold, London, 1907).

Bickersteth, J. Burgon, *The Land of Open Doors: Being Letters from Western Canada* (Wells, Gardner, Darton & Co., London, 1914).

Bickham, Troy, 'Eating the empire: intersections of food, cookery and imperialism in eighteenth-century Britain', *Past and Present* 198 (2008), 71–109.

Black, Jeremy, *The British Seaborne Empire* (Yale University Press, London, 2004).

Blackman, Janet, 'The corner shop: the development of the grocery and general provisions trade', in Derek Oddy and Derek Miller (eds), *The Making of the Modern British Diet* (Croom Helm, London, 1976), 148–60.

Blackwell, P., '"An undoubted jewel": a case study of five Sussex country houses, 1880–1914', *Southern History* 3 (1981), 183–200.

Bowen, H. V., 'British conceptions of global empire, 1756–83', *Journal of Imperial and Commonwealth History* 26/3 (1998), 1–27.

Boyle, David, *Toward the Setting Sun: Columbus, Cabot, Vespucci, and the Race for America* (Walker & Company, New York, 2008).

Boyle, Laura, *Diary of a Colonial Officer's Wife* (Alden Press, Oxford, 1968).

Bradshaw, Brendan, 'The Elizabethans and the Irish' (review of Nicholas P. Canny, *The Elizabethan Conquest of Ireland: A Pattern Established 1565–1756*), *Studies: An Irish Quarterly Review* 66/261 (1977), 38–50.

Brantley, Cynthia, 'Kikuyu-Maasai nutrition and colonial science: the Orr and Gilks study in late 1920s Kenya revisited', *International Journal of African Historical Studies* 30/1 (1997), 48–96.

Brantley, Cynthia, *Feeding Families: African Realities and British Ideas of Nutrition and Development in Early Colonial Africa* (Heinemann, Portsmouth, NH, 2002).

Breen, T. H., 'An empire of goods: the Anglicization of colonial America, 1690–1776', *Journal of British Studies* 25 (1986), 467–99.

Brendon, Piers, *The Decline and Fall of the British Empire 1781–1997* (Jonathan Cape, London, 2007).

Brenner, Robert, *Merchants and Revolution: Commercial Change, Political Conflict, and London's Overseas Traders, 1550–1653* (Cambridge University Press, Cambridge, 1993).

Brinley, Thomas, 'Feeding England during the industrial revolution: a view from the Celtic fringe', *Agricultural History* 56/1 (1982), 328–42.

Brooks, George E., 'Peanuts and colonialism: consequences of the commercialization of peanuts in West Africa, 1830–70', *Journal of African History* 16/1 (1975), 29–54.

Brooks, George E., 'The signares of Saint-Louis and Gorée: women entrepreneurs in eighteenth century Senegal', *in* N. J. Hafkin and E. G. Bay (eds), *Women in Africa: Studies in Social and Economic Change* (Stanford University Press, Stanford, CA, 1976), 20–44.

Brooks, George E., 'A Nhara of the Guinea-Bissau region: Mãe Aurélia Correia', in Claire C. Robertson and Martin A. Klein (eds), *Women and Slavery in Africa* (University of Wisconsin Press, Madison, 1983), 295–319.

Brooks, George E., *Landlords and Strangers: Ecology, Society, and Trade in Western Africa, 1000–1630* (Westview Press, Oxford, 1993).

Brooks, George E., *Eurafricans in Western Africa: Commerce, Social Status, Gender, and Religious Observance from the Sixteenth to the Eighteenth Century* (James Currey, Oxford, 2003).

Broomfield, Andrea, *Food and Cooking in Victorian England* (Praeger, London, 2007).

Bruce, S. Ingram (ed.), *Three Journals of Stuart Times* (Constable & Co., London, 1936).

Burnett, John, *Plenty and Want: A Social History of Food in England from 1815 to the Present Day* (Routledge, London, 1989).

Burnett, John, *Liquid Pleasures: A Social History of Drinks in Modern Britain* (Routledge, London, 1999).

Busteed, Mervyn, 'Identity and economy on an Anglo-Irish estate: Castle Caldwell, Co. Fermanagh, c.1750–1793', *Journal of Historical Geography* 26/2 (2000), 174–202.

Butler, Brooke, 'Greens', in John T. Edge (ed.), *Foodways: The New Encyclopaedia of Southern Culture*, Vol. 7 (University of North Carolina Press, Chapel Hill, 2007).

Cain, P. J., 'Economics and empire: the metropolitan context', in Andrew Porter (ed.), *The Nineteenth Century, Vol. III The Oxford History of the British Empire* (Oxford University Press, Oxford, 1999), 31–52.

Cain, P. J., and A. G. Hopkins, *British Imperialism 1688–2000* (2nd edn, Longman, London, 2002).

Cameron, Wendy, Sheila Haines and Mary McDougall Maude (eds), *English Immigrant Voices: Labourers' Letters from Upper Canada in the 1830s* (McGill-Queen's University Press, Montreal, 2000).

Canny, Nicholas, 'Migration and opportunity: Britain, Ireland and the New World', *Irish Economic and Social History* 12 (1985), 7–32.

Canny, Nicholas, *Kingdom and Colony: Ireland in the Atlantic World 1560–1800* (Johns Hopkins University Press, London, 1988).

Canny, Nicholas, 'The origins of empire', in Nicholas Canny (ed.), *The Origins of Empire: British Overseas Enterprise to the Close of the Seventeenth Century, Vol. I The Oxford History of the British Empire* (Oxford University Press, Oxford, 1998), 1–33.

Canny, Nicholas (ed.), *The Origins of Empire: British Overseas Enterprise to the Close of the Seventeenth Century, Vol. I The Oxford History of the British Empire* (Oxford University Press, Oxford, 1998).

Carey, Vincent P., 'John Derricke's *Image of Irelande*, Sir Henry Sidney, and the massacre at Mullaghmast, 1578', *Irish Historical Studies* XXXI/123 (1999), 305–27.

Carney, Judith A., *Black Rice: The African Origins of Rice Cultivation in the Americas* (Harvard University Press, London, 2001).

Carney, Judith A., and Richard Nicholas Rosomoff, *In the Shadow of Slavery: Africa's Botanical Legacy in the Atlantic World* (University of California Press, London, 2009).

Carson, Cary, 'Consumption', in Daniel Vickers (ed.), *A Companion to Colonial America* (Blackwell, Oxford, 2003), 334–65.

Carter, Marina, *Voices from Indenture: Experiences of Indian Migrants in the British Empire* (Leicester University Press, Leicester, 1996).

Catesby, Mark, *The Natural History of Carolina, Florida, and the Bahama Islands* (2 vols, London, 1754).

Chaudhuri, K. N., *The Trading World of Asia and the English East India Company 1660–1760* (Cambridge University Press, Cambridge, 1978).

Chowdhury, Benoy, *Growth of Commercial Agriculture in Bengal (1757–1900)*, vol. I (Indian Studies Past & Present, Calcutta, 1964).

Chung, Tan, 'The British–China–India trade triangle, 1771–1840', *Indian Economic and Social History Review* 11/4 (1974) 411–31.

Clap, Roger, *Relating Some of God's Remarkable Providence in Bringing Him into New England* (T. Prince, Boston, 1731).

Clarence-Smith, William Gervase, *Cocoa and Chocolate, 1765–1914* (Routledge, London, 2000).

Clarkson, L. A., and E. Margaret Crawford, *Feast and Famine: Food and Nutrition in Ireland 1500–1920* (Oxford University Press, Oxford, 2001).

Clifton, James R., 'The rice industry in colonial America', *Agricultural History* 55 (1981), 266–83.

Coad, Jonathan G., *The Royal Dockyards 1690–1850: Architecture and Engineering Works of the Sailing Navy* (Scolar Press, Aldershot, 1989).

Cole, Mary, *The Lady's Complete Guide; or Cookery in all its Branches* (3rd edn, London, 1791).

Collingham, E. M., *Imperial Bodies: The Physical Experience of the Raj c.1800–1947* (Polity Press, Cambridge, 2001).

Collingham, Lizzie, *Curry: A Tale of Cooks and Conquerors* (Vintage, London, 2006).

Collingham, Lizzie, *The Taste of War: World War II and the Battle for Food* (Allen Lane, London, 2011).

Collingham, Lizzie, *Around India's First Table: A History of Dining and Entertaining at the Rashtrapati Bhavan* (Additional Director General Publications Division, Ministry of Information & Broadcasting, Government of India, New Delhi, 2016).

Collins, John, *Salt and Fishery: A discourse* (A. Godbid and J. Playford, London, 1682).

Conroy, David W., *In Public Houses: Drink and the Revolution of Authority in Colonial Massachusetts* (University of North Carolina Press, London, 1995).

Corley, T. A. B., *Quaker Enterprise in Biscuits: Huntley and Palmers of Reading 1822–1972* (Hutchinson, London, 1972).

Corley, T. A. B., 'Nutrition, technology and the growth of the British biscuit industry 1820–1900', in Derek Oddy and Derek Miller (eds), *The Making of the Modern British Diet* (Croom Helm, London, 1976).

Cornell, Martyn, *Amber Gold and Black: The History of Britain's Great Beers* (History Press, Stroud, 2010).

Corse, Christopher R. de, 'Introduction', in Christopher R. de Corse (ed.), *West Africa during the Atlantic Slave Trade: Archaeological Perspectives* (Leicester University Press, London, 2001), 1–13.

Cosgrove, William, David Egilman, Peter Heywood, Jeanne X. Kasperson, Ellen Messer and Albert Wessen, 'Colonialism, international trade and the nation-state', in Lucil F. Newman (ed.), *Hunger in History: Food Shortage, Poverty and Deprivation* (Basil Blackwell, Oxford, 1990), 215–40.

Cotton, Sir Evan, *East Indiamen: The East India Company's Maritime Service* (Batchworth Press, London, 1949).

Coutts, P. F. J., 'Merger or takeover: a survey of the effects of contact between Europeans and Maori in the Fovaux Strait region', *Journal of the Polynesian Society* 78/4 (1969), 495–516.

Cowen, Ruth, *Relish: The Extraordinary Life of Alexis Soyer, Victorian Celebrity Chef* (Weidenfeld & Nicolson, London, 2006).

Cox, Nancy, '"Beggary of the nation": moral, economic and political attitudes to the retail sector in the early modern period', in John Benson and Laura Ugolini (eds), *A Nation of Shopkeepers: Five Centuries of British Retailing* (I. B. Tauris, London, 2003), 26–51.

Cox, Nancy, and Karin Dannehl, *Perceptions of Retailing in Early Modern England* (Ashgate, Aldershot, 2007).

Crader, Diana C., 'The zooarchaeology of the storehouse and the dry well at Monticello', *American Antiquity* 49/3 (1984), 542–88.

Crader, Diana C., 'Slave diet at Monticello', *American Antiquity* 55/4 (1990), 690–717.

Craton, Michael, 'Reluctant creoles: the planters' world in the British West Indies', in Bernard Bailyn and Philip D. Morgan (eds), *Strangers within the Realm: Cultural Margins of the First British Empire* (University of North Carolina Press, Chapel Hill, 1991), 314–62.

Cressy, David, *Coming Over: Migration and Communication between England and New England in the Seventeenth Century* (Cambridge University Press, Cambridge, 1987).

Crimp, R. L., *The Diary of a Desert Rat* (Leo Cooper, London, 1971).

Critchell, James Troubridge, and Joseph Raymond, *A History of the Frozen Meat Trade: An Account of the Development and Present Day Methods of Preparation, Transport, and Marketing of Frozen and Chilled Meats* (Constable and Company, London, 1912).

Cronon, William, *Changes in the Land: Indians, Colonists, and the Ecology of New England* (Hill and Wang, New York, 1983).

Cronon, William, *Nature's Metropolis: Chicago and the Great West* (W. W. Norton & Company, London, 1991).

Cullen, L. M., *Economy, Trade and Irish Merchants at Home and Abroad, 1600–1988* (Four Courts Press, Dublin, 2012).

Cultru, P., *Premier Voyage du Sieur de la Courbe Fait à la Coste d'Afrique en 1685* (Édouard Champion, Paris, 1913).

Curr, Edward M., *Recollections of Squatting in Victoria Then Called the Port Phillip District (from 1841 to 1851)* (George Robertson, Melbourne, 1853).

Curtin, Philip D., *The Rise and Fall of the Plantation Complex* (Cambridge University Press, Cambridge, 1990).

Cusack, Igor, 'African cuisines: recipes for nation-building?', *Journal of African Cultural Studies* 13/2 (2000), 207–25.

Dalby, Thomas, *An Historical Account of the Rise and Growth of the West-India Collonies* (first published 1690; Arno Press, New York, 1972).

Dale, Edward Everett, *The Cross Timbers: Memories of a North Texas Boyhood* (University of Texas Press, London, 1966).

Dale, Edward Everett, *Frontier Ways: Sketches of Life in the Old West* (University of Texas Press, Austin, TX 1959).

Datta, Rajat, 'The commercial economy of eastern India under early British rule', in H. V. Bowen and E. Mancke (eds), *Britain's Oceanic Empire: Atlantic and Indian Ocean Worlds, c.1500–1850* (Cambridge University Press, Cambridge, 2012).

Davey, James, 'Within hostile shores: victualling the Royal Navy in European waters during the French Revolutionary and Napoleonic wars', *International Journal of Maritime History* 21/2 (December 2009), 241–60.

Davidson, Alan, *The Oxford Companion to Food*, ed. Tom Jaine (Oxford University Press, Oxford, 2014).

Davis, Ralph, *The Rise of the English Shipping Industry in the Seventeenth and Eighteenth Centuries* (David & Charles, Newton Abbot, 1962).

Davis, Ralph, 'English foreign trade, 1660–1700', *Economic History Review* 7/2 (1954), 150–66, in Susan Socolow (ed.), *The Atlantic Staple Trade, Vol. I: Commerce and Politics (An Expanding World: The European Impact on World History, 1450–1800)* (Variorum, Ashgate, Aldershot, 1996), 127–43.

Davis, Ralph, 'English foreign trade, 1700-1774', *Economic History Review* 15/2 (1962), 285–303, in Susan Socolow (ed.), *The Atlantic Staple Trade, Vol. I: Commerce and Politics (An Expanding World: The European Impact on World History, 1450–1800)* (Variorum, Ashgate Aldershot, 1996), 145–63.

Daws, Gavan, *A Dream of Islands: Voyages of Self-Discovery in the South Seas* (W. W. Norton & Company, London, 1980).

den Hartog, Adel P., 'The discovery of vitamins and its impact on the food industry: the issue of tinned sweetened condensed skim milk, 1890–1940', in Peter J. Atkins, Peter Lummel and Derek J. Oddy (eds), *Food and the City in Europe since 1800* (Ashgate, Aldershot, 2007), 131–42.

Derricke, John, *The Image of Irelande with a discoureie of vvoodkarne* (J. Kingston for Ihon Daie, London, 1581).

Destombes, Jérome, 'From long-term patterns of seasonal hunger to changing experiences of everyday poverty: Northeastern Ghana, c.1930–2000', *Journal of African History* 47/2 (2006), 181–205.

Dickens, Charles, 'Hard Times', in *Household Words* 26 (1854).

Dikötter, Frank, Lars Laamann and Xun Zhou, 'China, British imperialism and the myth of the "opium plague"', in James H. Mills and Patricia Barton (eds), *Drugs and Empires: Essays in Modern Imperialism and Intoxication, c.1500–1930* (Palgrave Macmillan, Basingstoke, 2007), 19–38.

Dikötter, Frank, Lars Laamann and Xun Zhou, *Narcotic Culture: A History of Drugs in China* (Hurst & Company, London, 2004).

Diner, Hasia R., *Hungering for America: Italian, Irish and Jewish Foodways in the Age of Migration* (Harvard University Press, Cambridge, MA, 2001).

Dingle, A. E., 'Drink and working-class living standards in Britain, 1870–1914', in Derek Oddy and Derek Miller (eds), *The Making of the Modern British Diet* (Croom Helm, London, 1976), 117–34.

Dods, Margaret, *The Cook and Housewife's Manual* (Edinburgh, 1827).

Donnelly, James S., 'Cork market: its role in the nineteenth century Irish butter trade', *Studia Hibernica* 11 (1971), 130–63.

Drayton, Richard, 'The collaboration of labour: slaves, empires, and globalizations in the Atlantic world, *c.* 1600–1850', in A. G. Hopkins (ed.), *Globalization in World History* (Pimlico, London, 2002), 98–114.

Dublin, Thomas (ed.), *Immigrant Voices: New Lives in America, 1773–1986* (University of Illinois Press, Chicago, 1993).

Duffy, Michael, 'World-wide war and British expansion, 1793–1815', in P. J. Marshall (ed.), *The Oxford History of the British Empire, Vol. II: The Eighteenth Century* (Oxford University Press, Oxford, 1998), 184–207.

Dunn, Richard S., *Sugar and Slaves: The Rise of the Planter Class in the English West Indies, 1624–1713* (Jonathan Cape, London, 1972).

Dunton, John, *Teague Land or A Merry Ramble to the Wild Irish: Letters from Ireland, 1698*, ed. Edward MacLysaght (Irish Academic Press, Dublin, 1982).

C. Dutton, *Life in India* (1882).

Eden, Frederick Morton, *The State of the Poor, or, A History of the Labouring Classes in England, with parochial reports*, abridged and ed. A. G. L. Rogers (George Routledge & Sons, London, 1928).

Edmunds, Joseph, *Curries: and How to Prepare Them* (The Food & Cookery Publishing Agency, London, n.d.).

Eedle, Arthur and Rosalind, *Albion Restored: A Detective Journey to Discover the Birth of Christianity in England* (Lulu, Lincs., 2013).

Ellis, John, *The World War II Databook: The Essential Facts and Figures for All the Combatants* (Aurum Press, London, 1993).

Eltis, David, and David Richardson, *Atlas of the Transatlantic Slave Trade* (Yale University Press, London, 2010).

Emerson, Lucy, *The New England Cookery, or the Art of Dressing All Kinds of Flesh, Fish and Vegetables and the Best Modes of Making Pastes, Puffs, Pies, Tarts, Pudding, Custards and Preserves, and all kind of Cakes ... Particularly adapted to this part of our Country* (Josiah Parks, Montpelier, 1808).

Empire Marketing Board Posters (Manchester Art Gallery, Manchester, 2011).

Engels, Friedrich, *The Condition of the Working Class in England* (first published 1846; Oxford University Press, Oxford, 1993).

Erikson, Charlotte, *Leaving England: Essays on British Emigration in the Nineteenth Century* (Cornell University Press, Ithaca, 1994).

Erikson, Emily, *Between Monopoly and Free Trade: The English East India Company, 1600–1757* (Princeton University Press, Princeton, 2014).

Errington, Elizabeth Jane, 'British migration and British America, 1783–1867', in Philip Buckner (ed.), *Canada and the British Empire* (Oxford University Press, Oxford, 2010), 140–59.

Fagan, Brian, *Fish on Friday: Feasting, Fasting and the Discovery of the New World* (Basic Books, New York, 2006).

Fairbank, J. K., and D. Twitchett (eds), *The Cambridge History of China, Vol. 10.1: The Late Ch'ing* (Cambridge University Press, Cambridge, 1978).

Fairbridge, Dorothea, *Lady Anne Barnard at the Cape of Good Hope, 1797–1802* (Clarendon Press, Oxford, 1924).

Falconer, William, *A New Universal Dictionary of the Marine, now modernised and much enlarged by William Burney* (T. Cadell, London, 1815).

Falls, Cyril, *Elizabeth's Irish Wars* (Barnes and Noble, New York, 1970).

Farrer K. T. H., *A Settlement Amply Supplied: Food Technology in Nineteenth Century Australia* (Melbourne University Press, Melbourne, 1980).

Ferguson, Leland, *Uncommon Ground: Archaeology and Early African America, 1650–1800* (Smithsonian Institution Press, London, 1992).

Fielding, Helen, *Bridget Jones's Diary* (Picador, London, 1996).

Flavin, Susan, 'Consumption and material culture in sixteenth-century Ireland', *Economic History Review* 64/4 (2011), 1144–74.

Food Statistics Pocket Book 2014 (Department for Environment, Food and Rural Affairs, 2014).

Forster, Margaret, *Rich Desserts and Captain's Thin: A Family and their Times* (Chatto & Windus, London, 1997).

Foster, Robert, 'Rations, coexistence, and the colonisation of Aboriginal labour in the South Australian pastoral industry, 1860–1911', *Aboriginal History* 24 (2000), 1–26.

Foster, R. F., *Modern Ireland 1600–1972* (Allen Lane, London, 1988).

Foster, Shirley, 'Introduction', in Elizabeth Gaskell, *Mary Barton* (Oxford World Classics, Oxford University Press, Oxford, 2006).

Fourshey, Catherine Cymone, '"The remedy for hunger is bending the back": maize and British agricultural policy in southwestern Tanzania, 1920–1960', *International Journal of African Historical Studies* 41/2 (2008), 223–61.

Freidberg, Susanne, 'Postcolonial paradoxes: the cultural economy of African export horti-culture', in Alexander Nützenadel and Frank Trentmann (eds), *Food and Globalization: Consumption, Markets and Politics in the Modern World* (Berg, Oxford, 2008), 215–33.

Freidberg, Susanne, *Fresh: A Perishable History* (Belknap Press, London, 2009).

Freidberg, Susanne, 'Freshness from afar: the colonial roots of contemporary fresh foods', *Food & History* 8/1 (2010), 257–78.

Fremdling, R., 'European foreign trade policies, freight rates and the world markets of grain and coal during the nineteenth century', *Jahrbuch für Wirtschaftsgeschichte* 2 (2003), 83–98.

Friday, Chris, *Organizing Asian American Labour: The Pacific Coast Canned-Salmon Industry, 1870–1942* (Temple University Press, Philadelphia, 1994).

Friedmann, Max Paul, 'Beyond "voting with their feet": toward a conceptual history of "America" in European migrant sending communities, 1860s to 1914', *Journal of Social History* 40/3 (2007), 557–75.

Fury, Cheryl A., *Tides in the Affairs of Men: The Social History of Elizabethan Seamen, 1580–1603* (Greenwood Press, London, 2002).

Gardella, Robert, *Harvesting Mountains: Fujian and the China Tea Trade, 1757–1937* (University of California Press, London, 1994).

Gardiner, Julie (ed.), *Before the Mast: Life and Death Aboard the Mary Rose* (*The Archae-ology of the Mary Rose, Vol. 4*) (Mary Rose Trust, Portsmouth, 2005).

Garnsey, Peter, *Food and Society in Classical Antiquity* (Cambridge University Press, Cambridge, 1999).

Gaskell, Elizabeth, *Mary Barton*, 2 vols (Chapman & Hall, London, 1850).

Gaskill, Malcolm, *Between Two Worlds: How the English Became American* (Oxford University Press, Oxford, 2014).

Gerald of Wales, *The History and Topography of Ireland* (Penguin Books, London, 1982).

Gillespie, Raymond, 'Plantations in early modern Ireland', *History Ireland* 1/4 (1993), 43–7.

Gillespie, Raymond, *Seventeenth-Century Ireland: Making Ireland Modern* (Gill & Macmillan, London, 2006).

Glasse, Hannah, *The Art of Cookery Made Plain and Easy; which far exceeds anything of the kind ever yet published* (3rd edn, printed for the author, London, 1748).

Goldswain, Ralph, 'Introduction', in Ralph Goldswain (ed.), *The Chronicle of Jeremiah Goldswain, 1820 Settler* (30° South Publishers, Pinetown, South Africa, 2014).

Gollanek, Eric Frederick, *Empire Follows Art: Exchange and the Sensory Worlds of Empire in Britain and its Colonies, 1740–1775* (ProQuest, 2008).

Goodwin, Lorinda B. R., *An Archaeology of Manners: The Polite World of the Merchant Elite of Colonial Massachusetts* (Kluwer Academic/Plenum Publishers, New York, 1999).

Goody, Jack, 'Industrial food: towards the development of a world cuisine', in Carole Counihan and Penny van Esterik (eds), *Food and Culture: A Reader* (Routledge, London, 1997), 338–56.

Gosnell, Harpur Allen (ed.), *Before the Mast in the Clippers: The Diaries of Charles A. Abbey, 1856 to 1860* (first published Derrydale Press, New York, 1937; Dover Publications, New York, 1989).

Goucher, Candice, *Congotay! Congotay! A Global History of Caribbean Food* (Routledge, Abingdon, 2014).

Gragg, Larry, 'A Puritan in the West Indies: the career of Samuel Winthrop', *William and Mary Quarterly* 4 (1993), 768–86.

Gragg, Larry, '"To procure negroes": the English slave trade to Barbados, 1627–60', *Slavery and Abolition* 16/1 (1995), 65–84.

Gragg, Larry, *Englishmen Transplanted: The English Colonization of Barbados, 1627–1660* (Oxford University Press, Oxford, 2003).

Grant, Alison, *North Devon Pottery: The Seventeenth Century* (University of Exeter, Exeter, 1983).

Graves, Adrian, 'Colonialism and indentured labour migration in the Western Pacific, 1840–1915', in P. C. Emmer (ed.), *Colonialism and Migration: Indentured Labour Before and After Slavery* (Matinus Nijhoff Publishers, Dordrecht, 1986), 237–59.

Graves, Adrian, *Cane and Labour: The Political Economy of the Queensland Sugar Industry, 1862–1906* (Edinburgh University Press, Edinburgh, 1993).

Gray, Jack, *Rebellions and Revolutions: China from the 1800s to 2000* (Oxford University Press, Oxford, 2002).

Greenough, Paul R., *Prosperity and Misery in Modern Bengal: The Famine of 1943–1944* (Oxford University Press, Oxford, 1982).

Hall, Daniel, 'The food supply of the Empire', Cust Foundation Lecture, University of Nottingham, 1926.

Hall, Kim F., 'Culinary spaces, colonial spaces: the gendering of sugar in the seventeenth century', in Valerie Traub, Lindsay M. Kaplan and Dympna Callaghan (eds), *Feminist Readings of Early Modern Culture: Emerging Subjects* (Cambridge University Press, Cambridge, 1996), 168–90.

Hallam, Sylvia, 'Aboriginal women as providers: the 1830s on the Swan', *Aboriginal History* 15/1–2 (1991), 38–53.

Hall-Matthews, David, *Peasants, Famine and the State in Colonial Western India* (Palgrave Macmillan, London, 2005).

Hancock, David, *Oceans of Wine: Madeira and the Emergence of American Trade and Taste* (Yale University Press, New Haven, 2009).

Harms, Robert, 'Sustaining the system: trading towns along the middle Zaire', in Claire C. Robertson and Martin A. Klein (eds), *Women and Slavery in Africa* (University of Wisconsin Press, Madison, 1983), 95–110.

Hartman, G., *The true preserver and restorer of health being a choice collection of select and experienced remedies for all distempers incident to men, women, and children: selected from and experienced by the most famous physicians and chyrugeons in Europe: together with Excellent directions for cookery … with the description of an ingenious and useful engine for dressing of meat and for distilling th[e] choicest cordial water with-out wood coals, candle or oyl: published for the publick good* (1682).

Havinden, Michael, and David Meredith, *Colonialism and Development: Britain and its Tropical Colonies, 1850–1960* (Routledge, London, 1993).

Hawkins, Richard A., 'The pineapple canning industry during the world depression of the 1930s', *Business History* 1 (1989), 48–66.

Henson, Josiah, *The Life of Josiah Henson, formerly a slave, now an inhabitant of Canada, as narrated by himself* (electronic edition, University of North Carolina, Chapel Hill, 2001).

Hervey, Thomas K., *The Book of Christmas* (William Spooner, London, 1836).

Heuman, Gad, 'The British West Indies', in Andrew Porter (ed.), *The Nineteenth Century, Vol. III The Oxford History of the British Empire* (Oxford University Press, Oxford, 1999), 470–94.

Higgs, Catherine, *Cocoa, Slavery and Colonial Africa* (Ohio University Press, Athens, 2012).

Higgs, Catherine, 'Happiness and work: Portuguese peasants, British labourers, African contract workers and the case of São Tomé and Príncipe, 1901–1909', *International Labour and Working-Class History* 86 (2014), 55–71.

Hobsbawm, Eric, *The Age of Capital 1848–1875* (first published 1962; Weidenfeld & Nicolson, London, 1995).

Hobsbawm, Eric, *The Age of Empire 1875–1914* (first published 1987; Weidenfeld & Nicolson, London, 1995).

Hobsbawm, Eric, *The Age of Extremes: The Short Twentieth Century 1914–1991* (Michael Joseph, London, 1994).

Hoerder, Dirk, 'From dreams to possibilities: the secularization of hope and the quest for independence', in Dirk Hoerder and Horst Rössler (eds), *Distant Magnets: Expectations and Realities in the Immigrant Experience, 1840–1930* (Homes and Meier, London, 1993), 1–32.

Hoffmann, Walther, *British Industry, 1700–1950*, trans. W. O. Henderson and W. H. Chaloner (Basil Blackwell, Oxford, 1955).

Hooker, Richard J. (ed.), *A Colonial Plantation Cookbook: The Receipt Book of Harriet Pinckney Horry, 1770* (University of South Carolina Press, Columbia, 1984).

Horn, James, 'Tobacco colonies: the shaping of English society in the seventeenth-century Chesapeake', in Nicholas Canny (ed.), *The Origins of Empire: British Overseas Enterprise to the Close of the Seventeenth Century, Vol. I The Oxford History of the British Empire* (Oxford University Press, Oxford, 1998), 170–92.

Horning, Audrey J., 'On the banks of the Bann: the riverine economy of an Ulster plantation village', *Historical Archaeology* 41/3 (2007), 94–114.

Horsman, Reginald, *Feast or Famine: Food and Drink in American Westward Expansion* (University of Missouri Press, London, 2010).

Hsu, Madeline Yuan-yin, *Dreaming of Gold, Dreaming of Home: Transnationalism and Migration between the United States and South China, 1882–1943* (Stanford University Press, Stanford, 2000).

Hudgins, Carter L., 'The "necessary calls of humanity and decency": the archaeology of Robert "King" Carter and the material life of Virginia, 1680–1740', in Eric Klingelhofer (ed.), *A Glorious Empire: Archaeology and the Tudor–Stuart Atlantic World. Essays in Honour of Ivor Noël Hume* (Oxbow Books, Oxford, 2013), 173–89.

Hughes, Kathryn, *Victorians Undone: Tales of Flesh in the Age of Decorum* (4th Estate, London, 2017).

Hull, C. P., and Edmund Mair, *The European in India; or Anglo-Indian's Vade Mecum* (1871).

Hutchinson, William F., Mark Culling, David C. Orton, Bernd Hänfling, Lori Lawson Handley, Sheila Hamilton-Dyer, Tamsin C. O'Connell, Michael P. Richards and James H. Barrett, 'The globalization of naval provisioning: ancient DNA and stable isotope analyses of stored cod from the wreck of the *Mary Rose,* AD 1545', *Royal Society Open Science* (9 September 2015).

Ichijo, Atsuko, and Ronald Ranta, *Food, National Identity and Nationalism: From Everyday to Global Politics* (Palgrave Macmillan, London, 2016).

Iliffe, John, *Africans: The History of a Continent* (Cambridge University Press, Cambridge, 1996).

Imperial Economic Committee, 'Canned and dried fruit notes', Vol. VII, No. 1 (May 1937).

Innis, Harold A., *The Cod Fisheries: The History of an International Economy* (University of Toronto Press, Toronto, 1954).

Jackson, Ashley, *Botswana 1939–1945: An African Country at War* (Clarendon Press, Oxford, 1999).

Jackson, Ashley, *The British Empire and the Second World War* (Hambledon Continuum, London, 2006).

James, Lawrence, *Raj: The Making and Unmaking of British India* (Abacus, London, 1997).

Janin, Hunt, *The India–China Opium Trade in the Nineteenth Century* (McFarland & Co., London, 1999).

Johnson, G. W., *The Stranger in India, or Three Years in Calcutta*, 2 vols (1843).

Jones, David C., *Empire of Dust: Settling and Abandoning the Prairie Dry Belt* (University of Alberta Press, Edmonton, 1987).

Jones, Martin, *Feast: Why Humans Share Food* (Oxford University Press, Oxford, 2007).

Jones, Olive, 'London mustard bottles', *Historical Archaeology* 17/1 (1983), 69–84.

Jones, Olive, 'Commercial foods, 1740–1820', *Historical Archaeology* 27/2 (1993), 25–41.

Joyner, Charles, *Down by the Riverside: A South Carolina Slave Community* (University of Illinois Press, Urbana and Chicago, 1984).

Kea, Ray A., *Settlements, Trade and Polities in the Seventeenth-Century Gold Coast* (Johns Hopkins University Press, London, 1982).

Keating, P. (ed.), *Into Unknown England, 1866–1913: Selections from the Social Explorers* (Manchester University Press, Manchester, 1976).

Keay, John, *The Spice Route: A History* (John Murray, London, 2005).

Keay, John, *The Honourable Company: A History of the English East India Company* (HarperCollins, London, 1993).

Kelsey, Mary Wallace, 'Food for the Lewis and Clark Expedition: exploring North West America, 1804–06', in Harlan Walker (ed.), *Food on the Move*, Proceedings of the Oxford Symposium on Food and Cookery (Prospect Books, Devon, 1997), 200–207.

Kennaway, Laurence J., *Crusts: A Settler's Fare due South* (London, 1874).

Kennedy, Carol, *The Merchant Princes: Family, Fortune and Philanthropy: Cadbury, Sainsbury and John Lewis* (Hutchinson, London, 2000).

Khare, R. S., *Hindu Hearth and Home* (Vikas, New Delhi, 1976).

Klein, Martin A., 'Women in slavery in the Western Sudan', in Claire C. Robertson and Martin A. Klein (eds), *Women and Slavery in Africa* (University of Wisconsin Press, Madison, 1983), 67–92.

Knight, R. J. B., and Martin Howard Wilcox, *Sustaining the Fleet, 1793–1815: War, the British Navy and the Contractor State* (Boydell & Brewer, Woodbridge, 2010).

Knightley, Philip, *The Rise and Fall of the House of Vestey: The True Story of How Britain's Richest Family Beat the Taxman – and Came to Grief* (Warner Books, London, 1993).

Knighton, S., and D. M. Loades, *The Anthony Roll of Henry VIII's Navy: Pepys Library 2991 and British Library MS 22047 with related documents* (Ashgate for the Royal Naval Records Society in Association with the British Library and Magdalene College, Cambridge, 2000).

Kuhn, P., *Soulstealers: The Chinese Sorcery Scare of 1768* (Harvard University Press, Cambridge, MA, 1990).

Kulikoff, Allan, *The Agrarian Origins of American Capitalism* (University Press of Virginia, London, 1992).

Kurlansky, Mark, *Cod: A Biography of the Fish that Changed the World* (Jonathan Cape, London, 1998).

Lacombe, Michael, '"A continuall and dayly table for Gentlemen of Fashion": humanism, food and authority at Jamestown 1607–09', *American Historical Review* 115/3 (June 2010), 669–87.

La Fleur, J. D., *Fusion Foodways of Africa's Gold Coast in the Atlantic Era* (Brill, Leiden, 2012).

Lai, Walton Look, *Indentured Labor, Caribbean Sugar: Chinese and Indian Migrants to the British West Indies, 1838–1918* (Johns Hopkins University Press, Baltimore, 1993).

Latham, Robert, and William Matthews (eds), *The Diary of Samuel Pepys*, 10 vols (G. Bell & Sons, London, 1974).

Laudan, Rachel, 'The birth of the modern diet', *Scientific American* (August 2000), 62–7.

Laughton, John Knox, *State Papers Relating to the Defeat of the Spanish Armada Anno 1558* Vol. I (reprinted 1894; Temple Smith for the Navy Records Society, London, 1987).

Lawrence, Dianne, *Genteel Women: Empire and Domestic Material Culture, 1840–1910* (Manchester University Press, Manchester, 2012).

Lawson, John, *A New Voyage to Carolina* (University of North Carolina Press, Chapel Hill, 1967).

Lawson, P., 'Tea, vice and the English state', in Philip Lawson, *A Taste for Empire and Glory: Studies in British Overseas Expansion, 1660–1800* (Variorum, Ashgate, Aldershot, 1997).

Lawson, Philip, *The East India Company: A History* (Longman, Harlow, 1993).

Lehmann, Gilly, *The British Housewife: Cookery Books, Cooking and Society in Eighteenth-Century Britain* (Prospect Books, Devon, 2003).

Lenihan, Pádraig, *Consolidating Conquest: Ireland, 1603–1727* (Pearson, Longman, Harlow, 2008).

Lenman, Bruce P., *England's Colonial Wars, 1550–1688: Conflicts, Empire and National Identity* (Longman, Harlow, 2001).

Li, Peter S., *The Chinese in Canada* (Oxford University Press, Toronto, 1998).

Ligon, Richard, *A True and Exact History of the Island of Barbados*, ed. Karen Ordahl Kupperman (first published 1673; Hackett Publishing Company, Indianapolis, 2011).

Littlefield, Daniel C., *Rice and Slaves: Ethnicity and the Slave Trade in Colonial South Carolina* (Louisiana State University Press, London, 1981).

Liu, Andrew B., 'The birth of a noble tea country: on the geography of colonial capital and the origins of Indian tea', *Journal of Historical Sociology* 23/1 (2010), 73–100.

Lloyd Evans, Dyfed, *The Big Book of Christmas Recipes* (self-published, October 2011).

Long, Una (ed.), *The Chronicle of Jeremiah Goldswain: Albany Settler of 1820* (Van Riebeeck Society, Cape Town, 1946).

Lubbock, Basil (ed.), *Barlow's Journal of His Life at Sea in King's Ships, East and West Indiamen and Other Merchantmen from 1659 to 1703*, 2 vols (Hurst & Blackett, London, 1934).

McCann, James, *Maize and Grace: Africa's Encounter with a New World Crop, 1500–2000* (Harvard University Press, Cambridge, MA, 2005).

McCann, James C., *Stirring the Pot: A History of African Cuisine* (Ohio University Press, Athens, 2009).

Mac Cuarta, Brian, 'The plantation of Leitrim, 1620–41', *Irish Historical Studies* 32/127 (2001), 297–320.

McCusker, John, *Rum and the American Revolution: The Rum Trade and the Balance of Payments of the Thirteen Continental Colonies*, 2 vols (Garland Publishing, London, 1989).

McCusker, John J., and Russell R. Menard, 'The sugar industry in the seventeenth century: A new perspective on the Barbadian "Sugar Revolution"', in Stuart B. Schwartz (ed.), *Tropical Babylons: Sugar and the Making of the Atlantic World, 1450–1680* (University of North Carolina Press, Chapel Hill, 2004), 289–330.

Macdonald, Janet, *Feeding Nelson's Navy: The True Story of Food at Sea in the Georgian Era* (Chatham Publishing, London, 2006).

Macdonald, Janet, *The British Navy's Victualling Board, 1793–1815: Management, Competence and Incompetence* (Boydell Press, Woodbridge, 2010).

McDonald, Jared, 'Encounters at "Bushman Station": reflections on the fate of the San of the Transgariep Frontier, 1828–1833', *South African Historical Journal* 61/2 (2009), 372–88.

McFadden, Christine, *Pepper: The Spice that Changed the World* (Absolute Press, Bath, 2007).

Macfarlane, Alan, and Iris Macfarlane, *Green Gold: The Empire of Tea. A Remarkable History of the Plant that Took Over the World* (Ebury Press, London, 2003).

McGurk, John, *The Elizabethan Conquest of Ireland: The 1590s Crisis* (Manchester University Press, Manchester, 1997).

Mackay, Robert, *Half the Battle: Civilian Morale in Britain During the Second World War* (Manchester University Press, Manchester, 2002).

McKendrick, Neil, John Brewer and J. H. Plumb, *The Birth of a Consumer Society: The Commercialization of Eighteenth-Century England* (Europa Publications, London, 1982).

Mackie, Cristine, *Life and Food in the Caribbean* (Weidenfeld & Nicolson, London, 1991).

McLean, Iain, and Camilla Bustani, 'Irish potatoes and British politics: interests, ideology, heresthetic and the repeal of the Corn Laws', *Political Studies* 47/5 (1999), 817–36.

McMahon, Sarah F., 'A comfortable subsistence: the changing composition of diet in rural New England, 1620–1840', *William and Mary Quarterly* 42/1 (1985), 26–65.

MacRae, Andrew, *God Speed the Plough: The Representation of Agrarian England, 1500–1660* (Cambridge University Press, Cambridge, 1996).

McWilliams, James E., *A Revolution in Eating: How the Quest for Food Shaped America* (Columbia University Press, New York, 2005).

Madajzyk, Czeslaw, 'Vom "Generalplan Ost" zum "Generalsiedlungsplan"', in Mechtild Rössler and Sabine Schleiermacher, with Cordula Tollmien (eds), *Der 'Generalplan Ost': Hauptlinien der nationalsozialistischen Planungs- und Vernichtungspolitik* (Akademie Verlag, Berlin, 1993), 12–17.

Maidment, Brian, *Reading Popular Prints, 1790–1829* (Manchester University Press, Manchester, 2001).

Mandelblatt, Bertie, 'A transatlantic commodity: Irish salt beef in the French Atlantic world' *History Workshop Journal* 63 (Spring 2007), 18–47.

Mannion, John, 'Victualling a fishery: Newfoundland diet and the origins of the Irish provisions trade, 1675–1700', *International Journal of Maritime History* 12/1 (June 2000), 1–60.

Marsden, Peter, *Sealed by Time: The Loss and Recovery of the* Mary Rose: *The Archaeology of the* Mary Rose *Vol. I* (Mary Rose Trust, Portsmouth, 2003).

Martin, John, 'The structural transformation of British agriculture: the resurgence of progressive high-input arable farming', in Brian Short, Charles Watkins and John Martin (eds), *The Front Line of Freedom: British Farming in the Second World War* (British Agricultural Society, Exeter, 2006), 16–35.

Martin, Robert Montgomery, *The History, Antiquities, Topography, and Statistics of Eastern India: comprising the districts of Behar, Shahabad, Bhagulpoor, Goruckpoor, Dinajepoor, Puraniya, Rungpoor, & Assam, in Relation to their Geology, Mineralogy, Botany, Agriculture, Commerce, Manufactures, Fine Arts, Population, Religion, Education, Statistics, etc. surveyed under the orders of the Supreme Government, and collated from the original documents at the E. I. House, with the permission of the Honourable Court of Directors,* 3 vols (W. H. Allen, London, 1838).

Mason, Charlotte, *The Lady's Assistant for Regulating and Supplying the Table, being a complete system of cookery* (C. Whittingham for J. Walter, London, 1801).

Mason, John, *A briefe discourse of the Nevv found-land with the situation, temperature, and commodities thereof, inciting our Nation to go forward in that hopefull plantation begunne* (Andro Hart, Edinburgh, 1620; consulted at EEBO – Early English Books Online).

Mathias, P., 'The British tea trade in the nineteenth century', in Derek Oddy and Derek Miller (eds), *The Making of the Modern British Diet* (Croom Helm, London, 1976), 91–100.

Mathias, Peter, *Retailing Revolution: A History of Multiple Retailing in the Food Trades Based Upon the Allied Suppliers Group of Companies* (Longmans, London, 1967).

Maxon, Robert M., '"Fantastic prices" in the midst of an "acute food shortage": market, environment, and the colonial state in the 1943 Vihiga (western Kenya) famine', *African Economic History* 28 (2000), 27–52.

Mayhew, Henry (ed.), *The Shops and Companies of London and the Trades and Manufactories of Great Britain*, Parts I–V (March 1865).

Mayhew, Madeline, 'The 1930s nutrition controversy', *Journal of Contemporary History* 23/3 (1988), 445–64.

Mazumdar, Sucheta, 'The impact of New World food crops on the diet and economy of China and India, 1600–1900', in Raymond Grew (ed.), *Food in Global History* (Westview, Boulder, Colorado, 1999), 58–78.

Meillassoux, Claude, 'Female slavery', in Claire C. Robertson and Martin A. Klein (eds), *Women and Slavery in Africa* (University of Wisconsin Press, Madison, 1983), 49–66.

Metcalfe, Thomas, *Ideologies of the Raj* (Cambridge University Press, Cambridge, 1995).

Mintz, Sydney, *Sweetness and Power: The Place of Sugar in Modern History* (Penguin, New York, 1985).

Mintz, Sidney, 'The changing roles of food in the study of consumption', in John Brewer and Roy Porter (eds), *Consumption and the World of Goods* (Routledge, London, 1993), 261–73.

Mintz, Sidney, 'Time, sugar and sweetness', in Carole Counihan and Penny van Esterik (eds), *Food and Culture: A Reader* (Routledge, London, 1997), 357–69.

Misson, M., *Memoirs and Observations in His Travels over England*, trans. Mr Ozell (printed for D. Brown and others, London, 1719).

Mittelberger, Gottlieb, *Journey to Pennsylvania* (Belknap Press, Cambridge, MA, 1960).

Montaño, John Patrick, *The Roots of English Colonialism in Ireland* (Cambridge, 2011).

Montgomery, James, *Journal of Voyages and Travels by the Rev. Daniel Tyerman and George Bennet, Esq. Deputed from the London Missionary Society, to visit their various stations in the South Sea Islands, China, India, &c., between the years 1821 and 1829*, 2 vols (Frederick Westley and A. H. Davis, London, 1831).

Moore, Tara, 'National identity and Victorian Christmas foods', in Tamara S. Wagner and Narin Hassan (eds), *Consuming Culture in the Long Nineteenth Century, 1700–1900* (Lexington Books, Plymouth, 2007), 141–54.

Moore, Tara, *Victorian Christmas in Print* (Palgrave Macmillan, Basingstoke, 2009).

Moryson, Fynes, *An Itinerary*, trans. Charles Hughes (CELT – Corpus of Electronic Texts: a project of the History Department, University College, Cork, 2010).

Mui, Hoh-Cheung, and Lorna H. Mui, *Shops and Shopkeeping in Eighteenth-Century England* (Routledge, London, 1989).

Muldrew, Craig, *Food, Energy and the Creation of Industriousness: Work and Material Culture in Agrarian England, 1550–1780* (Cambridge University Press, Cambridge, 2011).

Muller, H. G., *Baking and Bakeries* (Shire Publications, Princes Risborough, 1986).

Muller, H. G., 'Industrial food preservation in the nineteenth and twentieth centuries', in C. Anne Wilson (ed.), *Waste Not, Want Not: Food Preservation from Early Times to the Present Day* (Edinburgh University Press, Edinburgh, 1991), 104–58.

Murgatroyd, Sarah, *The Dig Tree: The Extraordinary Story of the Ill-Fated Burke and Wills Expedition* (Bloomsbury, London, 2002).

Nally, David, '"That coming storm": the Irish poor law, colonial biopolitics and the Great Famine', *Annals of the Association of American Geographers* (2008), 714–41.

Nash, R. C., 'Irish Atlantic trade in the seventeenth and eighteenth centuries', *William and Mary Quarterly* 42/3 (1985), 329–56.

Nash, R. C., 'Domestic material culture and consumer demand in the British Atlantic world: colonial South Carolina, 1670–1770', in David S. Shields (ed.), *Material Culture in Anglo-America: Regional Identity and Urbanity in the Tidewater, Lowcountry, and Caribbean* (University of South Carolina Press, Columbia, 2009), 221–66.

Nettelbeck, Amanda, and Robert Foster, 'Food and governance on the frontiers of colonial Australia and Canada's North West Territories', *Aboriginal History* 36 (2012), 21–41.

Newman, R. K., 'Opium smoking in late imperial China: a reconsideration', *Modern Asian Studies* 29/4 (1995), 765–94.

Newton, David, *Trademarked: A History of Well-known Brands from Aertex to Wright's Coal Tar* (Sutton Publishing, Stroud, 2008).

Nicolson, Adam, *Gentry: Six Hundred Years of a Peculiarly English Class* (Harper Press, London, 2011).

O'Brien, Charmaine, *The Penguin Food Guide to India* (Penguin, New Delhi, 2013).

O'Brien, P. K., and S. L. Engerman, 'Exports and the growth of the British economy from the Glorious Revolution to the Peace of Amiens', in Barbara Solow (ed.), *Slavery and the Rise of the Atlantic System* (Cambridge University Press, Cambridge, 1991).

O'Brien, Patrick, 'Inseparable connections: trade, economy, fiscal state, and the expansion of empire, 1688–1815', in P. J. Marshall (ed.), *The Oxford History of the British Empire, Vol. II: The Eighteenth Century* (Oxford University Press, Oxford, 1998), 53–77.

O'Connor, Kaori, 'The King's Christmas pudding: globalization, recipes, and the commodities of empire', *Journal of Global History* 4/1 (2009), 127–55.

O'Connor, Kaori, 'Beyond "exotic groceries": tapioca/cassava/manioc, a hidden commodity of empires and globalisation', in Jonathan Curry-Machado (ed.), *Global Histories, Imperial Commodities, Local Interactions* (Palgrave Macmillan, Basingstoke, 2013), 224–47.

Oddy, D. J., 'A nutritional analysis of historical evidence: the working-class diet, 1880–1914', in Derek Oddy and Derek Miller (eds), *The Making of the Modern British Diet* (Croom Helm, London, 1976), 214–31.

Oddy, D. J., 'Urban famine in nineteenth-century Britain: the effect of the Lancashire cotton famine on working-class diet and health', *Economic History Review* 36/1 (1983), 68–86.

Oddy, Derek J., *From Plain Fare to Fusion Food: British Diet from the 1890s to the 1990s* (Boydell Press, Woodbridge, 2003).

Oddy, Derek J., and Alain Drouard (eds), *The Food Industries of Europe in the Nineteenth and Twentieth Centuries* (Ashgate, Farnham, Surrey, 2013).

Offer, Avner, 'The working classes, British naval plans and the coming of the Great War', *Past and Present* 107 (1985), 204–26.

Ogborn, Miles, *Global Lives: Britain and the World, 1550–1800* (Cambridge University Press, Cambridge, 2008).

Ohlmeyer, Jane H., 'A laboratory for empire? Early modern Ireland and English imperialism', in Kevin Kenny (ed.), *Ireland and the British Empire: The Oxford History of the British Empire* (Oxford University Press, Oxford, 2004), 26–60.

Ohlmeyer, Jane H., 'Anatomy of plantation: the 1641 Depositions', *History Ireland* 17/6 (2009), 54–6.

Olmsted, Frederick Law, *A Journey in the Seaboard Slave States in the Years 1853–1854 with remarks on their economy*, 2 vols (Knickerbocker Press, London, 1904).

Orr, John Boyd, *As I Recall* (MacGibbon & Kee, London, 1966).

Osterhammel, Jürgen, *The Transformation of the World: A Global History of the Nineteenth Century* (Princeton University Press, Princeton, 2014).

Othick, J., 'The cocoa and chocolate industry in the 19th century', in Derek Oddy and Derek Miller (eds), *The Making of the Modern British Diet* (Croom Helm, London, 1976), 77–90.

Otto, John Solomon, *Cannon's Point Plantation, 1794–1860: Living Conditions and Status Patterns in the Old South* (Academic Press, London, 1984).

Otto, John Solomon, *The Southern Frontiers, 1607–1860: The Agricultural Evolution of the Colonial and Antebellum South* (Greenwood Press, London, 1989).

Overy, Richard, *Why the Allies Won* (Pimlico, London, 1995).

Pagrach-Chandra, Gaitri, 'Damra bound: Indian echoes in Guyanese foodways', in Harlan Walker (ed.), *Food and Memory: Proceedings of the Oxford Symposium on Food and Cookery* (Prospect Books, Devon, 2001).

Parker, Charles H., *Global Interactions in the Early Modern Age, 1400–1800* (Cambridge University Press, Cambridge, 2010).

Parker, Geoffrey, *Global Crisis: War, Climate Change and Catastrophe in the Seventeenth Century* (Yale University Press, New Haven, 2013).

Parker, Matthew, *The Sugar Barons: Family, Corruption, Empire and War* (Windmill Books, London, 2012).

Parks, Fanny, *Wanderings of a Pilgrim in Search of the Picturesque during Four-and-Twenty Years in the East; with Revelations of Life in the Zenana*, 2 vols (Pelham Richardson, London, 1850).

Pasley, Thomas, *Private Sea Journals, 1778–1782*, ed. Rodney M. S. Pasley (J. M. Dent and Sons, London, 1931).

Pastore, Ralph, 'The collapse of the Beothuk world', *Acadiensis* 1/19 (1989), 52–71.

Paterson, Alexander, *Across the Bridges, or, Life by the South London River-side* (Edward Arnold, London, 1912).

Paton, William Agnew, *Down the Islands: A Voyage to the Caribees* (Charles Scribner's Sons, New York, 1890).

Paul, Rodman W., 'The wheat trade between California and the United Kingdom', *Mississippi Valley Historical Review* 45/3 (1958), 391–412.

Payne, P. L., 'The emergence of the large-scale company in Great Britain, 1879–1914', *Economic History Review* 3/20 (1967), 519–42.

Penderey, Steven R., 'The archaeology of urban foodways in Portsmouth, New Hampshire', in Peter Benes (ed.), *Foodways in the Northeast: The Dublin Seminar for New England Folklife, Annual Proceedings 1982* (Boston University, Boston, 1984), 9–27.

Perren, R., 'The North American beef and battle trade with Great Britain, 1870–1914', *Economic History Review* 24/3 (1971), 430–44.

Perren, Richard, *Agriculture in Depression, 1870–1914* (Cambridge University Press, Cambridge, 1995).

Perren, Richard, *Taste, Trade and Technology: The Development of the International Meat Industry since 1840* (Ashgate, Aldershot, 2006).

Peters, Erica J., 'National preferences and colonial cuisine: seeking the familiar in French Vietnam', *Proceedings of the Western Society for French History* 27 (2001), 150–9.

Peterson, T. Sarah, *Acquired Taste: The French Origins of Modern Cooking* (Cornell University Press, Ithaca, 1994).

Pinckney, Elise (ed.), *The Letterbook of Eliza Lucas Pinckney, 1739–1762* (University of North Carolina Press, Chapel Hill, 1972).

Pinkard, Susan, *A Revolution in Taste: The Rise of French Cuisine, 1650–1800* (Cambridge University Press, Cambridge, 2009).

Plummer, Alfred, *New British Industries in the Twentieth Century: A Survey of Development and Structure* (Sir Isaac Pitman & Sons, London, 1937).

Pluymers, Keith, 'Taming the wilderness in sixteenth- and seventeenth-century Ireland and Virginia', *Environmental History* 16/4 (2011), 610–32.

Polacheck, James, *The Inner Opium War* (Harvard University Press, Cambridge, MA, 1992).

Pope, Peter E., *The Many Landfalls of John Cabot* (University of Toronto Press, Toronto, 1997).

Pope, Peter E., *Fish into Wine: The Newfoundland Plantation in the Seventeenth Century* (University of North Carolina Press, Chapel Hill, 2004).

Poynter, F. N. L., *The Journal of James Yonge [1647–1721], Plymouth Surgeon* (Longmans, London, 1963).

Prakash, Om, 'The English East India Company and India', in H. V. Bowen, Margarette Lincoln and Nigel Rigby (eds), *The Worlds of the East India Company* (Boydell Press, Woodbridge, 2002), 1–18.

Price, Jacob M., 'The imperial economy, 1700–1776', in P. J. Marshall (ed.), *The Oxford History of the British Empire, Vol. II: The Eighteenth Century* (Oxford University Press, Oxford, 1998), 77–104.

Pryor, Alan, 'Indian pale ale: an icon of empire', in Jonathan Curry-Machado (ed.), *Global Histories, Imperial Commodities, Local Interactions* (Palgrave Macmillan, Basingstoke, 2013), 38–57.

Ramdin, Ron, *Arising from Bondage: A History of the Indo-Caribbean People* (I. B. Tauris, London, 2000).

Raphael, Samuel, 'Steam power and hand technology', *History Workshop* 3 (1977).

Rappaport, Erika, 'Packaging China: foreign articles and dangerous tastes in the mid-Victorian tea party', in Frank Trentmann (ed.), *The Making of the Consumer: Knowledge, Power and Identity in the Modern World* (Berg, Oxford, 2006), 125–46.

Reitz, Elizabeth J., Tyson Gibbs and Ted A. Rathbun, 'Archaeological evidence for subsistence on coastal plantations', in Theresa A. Singleton (ed.), *The Archaeology of Slavery and Plantation Life* (Academic Press, London, 1985), 163–91.

'Reminiscences of a returning Indian', *The Asiatic Journal* (September–December 1835), 17–29.

Reynolds, Henry, 'The other side of the frontier: early aboriginal reactions to pastoral settlement in Queensland and Northern New South Wales', *Historical Studies* 17/66 (1976), 50–63.

Rice, Kym S., *Early American Taverns: For the Entertainment of Friends and Strangers* (Fraunces Tavern Museum, Regnery Gateway, Chicago, 1983).

Richards, Audrey I., *Land, Labour and Diet in Northern Rhodesia: An Economic Study of the Bemba Tribe* (International Institute of African Languages and Cultures, Oxford University Press, London, 1939).

Richards, Eric, *Britannia's Children: Emigration from England, Scotland, Wales and Ireland since 1600* (Hambledon and London, London, 2004).

Richards, J. F., 'The Indian empire and peasant production of opium in the nineteenth century', *Modern Asian Studies* 15/1 (1981), 59–82.

Richards, J. F., 'The opium industry in British India', *Indian Economic and Social History Review* 39/2–3 (2002), 149–80.

Richards, John F, '"Cannot we induce the people of England to eat opium?" The moral economy of opium in colonial India', in James H. Mills and Patricia Barton (eds), *Drugs and Empires: Essays in Modern Imperialism and Intoxication, c.1500–1930* (Palgrave Macmillan, Basingstoke, 2007), 73–80.

Richards, John F., *The Unending Frontier: An Environmental History of the Early Modern World* (University of California Press, Berkeley, 2003).

Richardson, David, 'The slave trade, sugar and British economic growth, 1748–1776', in Barbara Solow and Stanley L. Engerman (eds), *British Capitalism and Caribbean Slavery: The Legacy of Eric Williams* (Cambridge University Press, Cambridge, 1987), 103–34.

Richter, Linda, '"Could you not turn your back on this hunger country": food in the migration process of German emigrants, 1816-1856', *Aspeers* 5 (2012), 19-40.

Riello, Giorgio, *Cotton: The Fabric that Made the Modern World* (Cambridge University Press, Cambridge, 2013).

Roberts, Emma, *Scenes and Characteristics of Hindoostan, with Sketches of Anglo-Indian Society*, 2 vols (London, 1837).

Robertson, Claire C., 'Black, white, and red all over: beans, women, and agricultural imperialism in twentieth-century Kenya', *Agricultural History* 71/3 (1997), 259–99.

Robertson, Una A., '"Mariners' mealtimes": the introduction of tinned food into the diet of the Royal Navy', in Astrid Riddervold and Andreas Ropeid (eds), *Food Conservation* (Prospect Books, London, 1988), 147–57.

Rodger, N. A. M., *The Wooden World: An Anatomy of the Georgian Navy* (Fontana Press, London, 1986).

Ross, Douglas, E., 'Factors influencing the dining habits of Japanese and Chinese migrants at a British Columbia salmon cannery', *Historical Archaeology* 45/2 (2011), 68–96.

Rössler, Horst, 'The dream of independence: the "America" of England's North Staffordshire potters', in Dirk Hoerder and Horst Rössler (eds), *Distant Magnets:*

Expectations and Realities in the Immigrant Experience, 1840–1930 (Homes and Meier, London, 1993), 128–59.

Roth, Karl Heinz, '"Generalplan Ost" – "Gesamtplan Ost". Forschungsstand, Quellenprobleme, neue Ergebnisse', in Mechtild Rössler and Sabine Schleiermacher, with Cordula Tollmien (eds), *Der "Generalplan Ost". Hauptlinien der nationalsozialistischen Planungs- und Vernichtungspolitik* (Akademie Verlag, Berlin, 1993), 25–95.

Rothschild, Nan, and Diana Rockman, 'City tavern, country tavern: analysis of four colonial sites', *Historical Archaeology* 18 (1984), 112–21.

Rothstein, Morton, 'Rivalry for the British wheat market, 1860–1914', *Mississippi Valley Historical Review* 47/3 (1960), 401–18.

Russell, Howard S., *Long, Deep Furrow: Three Centuries of Farming in New England* (University Press of New England, Hanover, NH, 1976).

Rutledge, Sarah, *The Carolina Housewife* (facsimile of the 1847 edition: University of South Carolina Press, Columbia, 1979).

Rutman, Darrett B., *Husbandmen of Plymouth: Farms and Villages in the Old Colony 1620–1692* (Beacon Press, Boston, 1967).

St John, Ian, *The Making of the Raj: India under the East India Company* (Praeger, Oxford, 2012).

Samford, Patricia, 'The archaeology of African-American slavery and material culture', *William and Mary Quarterly* 53/1 (1996), 87–114.

Sarkar, Sumit, *Modern India, 1885–1947* (Macmillan, London, 1989).

Schaffer, Simon, 'The earth's fertility as a social fact in early modern England', in Mikulas Teich, Roy Porter and Bo Gustafson (eds), *Nature and Society in Historical Context* (Cambridge University Press, Cambridge, 1997), 124–47.

Schaw, Janet, *Journal of a Lady of Quality: Being the Narrative of a Journey from Scotland to the West Indies, North Carolina, and Portugal, in the Years 1774 to 1776*, ed. Evangeline Walker Andrews in collaboration with Charles McLean Andrews (University of Nebraska Press, London, 2005).

Scully, Terence, *La Varenne's Cookery* (Prospect Books, Totnes, 2006).

Searing, James F., *West African Slavery and Atlantic Commerce: The Senegal River Valley, 1700–1860* (Cambridge University Press, Cambridge, 1993).

Sellick, Will, *The Imperial African Cookery Book: Recipes from English-Speaking Africa* (Jeppestown Press, London, 2010).

Sen, Amartya, *Poverty and Famines: An Essay on Entitlement and Deprivation* (Clarendon Press, Oxford, 1981).

Shammas, Carole, *The Pre-industrial Consumer in England and America* (Clarendon Press, Oxford, 1990).

Shannon, Fred A., *The Farmer's Last Frontier: Agriculture, 1860–1897. The Economic History of the United States, Vol. V* (M. E. Sharpe, London, 1945).

Sharma, Jayeeta, '"Lazy" natives, coolie labour and the Assam tea industry', *Modern Asian Studies* 43/6 (November 2009), 1287–324.

Sharpe, Pamela, 'Explaining the short stature of the poor: chronic childhood disease and growth in nineteenth-century England', *Economic History Review* 65/4 (2012), 1475–94.

Sharp, Paul, and Jacob Weisdorf, 'Globalization revisited: market integration and the wheat trade between North America and Britain from the eighteenth century', *Explorations in Economic History* 50/1 (2013), 88–98.

Shaw, Brent, 'Eaters of flesh, drinkers of milk: the ancient Mediterranean ideology of the pastoral nomad', *Ancient Society* 13–14 (1982/83), 6–31.

Shawcross, Kathleen, 'Fern-root and the total scheme of eighteenth century Maori food production in agricultural areas', *Journal of the Polynesian Society* 76/3 (1967), 330–52.

Shepherd, Sue, *Pickled, Potted and Canned: The Story of Food Preserving* (Headline, London, 2000).

Sherwood, Jay, *Surveying Southern British Columbia: A Photojournal of Frank Swannell, 1901–1907* (Caitlin Press, Halfmoon Bay, BC, 2014).

Shineberg, Dorothy, *They Came for Sandalwood: A Study of the Sandalwood Trade in the South-West Pacific, 1830–1865* (Melbourne University Press, London, 1967).

Siddiqi, Asiya, 'Pathways of the poppy: India's opium trade in the nineteenth century', in Madhavi Thampi (ed.), *India and China in the Colonial World* (Social Science Press, New Delhi, 2005), 21–32.

Simmons, R. C., 'Trade legislation and its enforcement, 1748–1776', in Jack P. Greene and J. R. Pole (eds), *A Companion to the American Revolution* (Blackwell, Oxford, 2000), 165– 72.

Singleton, Theresa A., 'Introduction', in Theresa A. Singleton (ed.), *The Archaeology of Slavery and Plantation Life* (Academic Press, London, 1985), 1–14.

Siochrú, Michael, and David Brown, 'The Down Survey of Ireland project', *History Ireland* 21/2 (2013), 6–7.

Sivasundaram, Sujit, *Nature and the Godly Empire: Science and Evangelical Mission in the Pacific, 1795–1850* (Cambridge University Press, Cambridge, 2005).

Skeat, J., *The Art of Cookery and Pastery made easy and familiar* (Norwich, 1769).

Sloane, Hans, *A Voyage to the Islands Madera, Barbados, Nieves, St Christophers and Jamaica*, 2 vols. (BM for the author, London, 1707).

Smith, Edward, *Practical Dietary for Families, Schools, and the Labouring Classes* (Walton and Maberley, London, 1865).

Smith, Eliza, *The Compleat Housewife* (London, 1742).

Smith, F. B., *The People's Health, 1830–1910* (Croom Helm, London, 1979).

Smith, Kevin, *Conflict over Convoys: Anglo-American Logistics Diplomacy in the Second World War* (Cambridge University Press, Cambridge, 1996).

Smith, Pamela, 'Station camps: legislation, labour relations and rations on pastoral leases in the Kimberley region, Western Australia', *Aboriginal History* 24 (2000), 75–97.

Smith, Woodruff D., 'Complications of the Commonplace', *Journal of Interdisciplinary History* 23/2 (1992), 259–78.

Smith, Woodruff D., *Consumption and the Making of Respectability, 1600–1800* (Routledge, London, 2002).

Solberg, Carl E., *The Prairies and the Pampas: Agrarian Policy in Canada and Argentina, 1880–1930* (Stanford University Press, Stanford, 1987).

Spiekermann, Uwe, 'Vollkorn für die Führer. Zur Geschichte der Vollkornbrotpolitik im "Dritten Reich"', *Zeitschrift für Sozialgeschichte des 20 & 21 Jahrhunderts* 16/1 (2001), 91–128.

Spiekermann, Uwe, 'Brown bread for victory: German and British wholemeal politics in the inter-war period', in Frank Trentmann and Flemming Just (eds), *Food and Conflict in Europe in the Age of the Two World Wars* (Palgrave Macmillan, Basingstoke, 2006), 143–71.

Spring, David, 'Land and politics in Edwardian England', *Agricultural History* 58/1 (January 1984), 17–42.

Srivastava, Hari Shanker, *The History of Indian Famines and Development of Famine Policy, 1858–1918* (Sri Ram Mehra Co., Agra, 1968).

Stavely, Keith, and Kathleen Fitzgerald, *America's Founding Food: The Story of New England Cooking* (University of North Carolina Press, London, 2004).

Steel, Frances, 'New Zealand is butterland: interpreting the historical significance of a daily spread', *New Zealand Journal of History* 39/2 (2005), 179–94.

Steinitz, Lesley, 'The tales they told: the creation of a healthy ideal through branded health food advertising, 1895–1918', paper delivered at 'Devouring: Food, Drink and the Written Word, 1800–1945', Warwick University, 8 March 2014.

Stephens, Ian, *Monsoon Morning* (Ernest Benn, London, 1966).

Stevenson, Richard, *Bengal Tiger and British Lion: An Account of the Bengal Famine of 1943* (XLibris Corporation, 2005).

Stobart, Jon, 'Gentlemen and shopkeepers: supplying the country house in 18th century England', *Economic History Review* 64/3 (2011), 885–904.

Stobart, Jon, *Sugar and Spice: Grocers and Groceries in Provincial England, 1650–1830* (Oxford University Press, Oxford, 2013).

Sweeney, Stuart, 'Indian railways and famine, 1875–1914: magic wheels and empty stomachs', *Essays in Economic and Business History* 26 (2008), 147–57.

Swinburne, Layinka, 'Dancing with the mermaids: ship's biscuit and portable soup', in Harlan Walker (ed.), *Food on the Move: Proceedings of the Oxford Symposium on Food and Cookery 1996* (Prospect Books, Devon, 1997), 309–21.

Swinton, Viscount, *I Remember* (Hutchinson & Co., London, n.d.).

Szreter, Simon, and Graham Mooney, 'Urbanization, mortality, and the standard of living debate: new estimates of the expectation of life at birth in nineteenth-century British cities', *Economic History Review* 51/1 (1998), 84–112.

Talburt, Tony, *Rum, Rivalry and Resistance Fighting for the Caribbean Spirit* (Hansib, London, 2010).

Tandon, Prakash, *Punjabi Century, 1857–1947* (Chatto & Windus, London, 1961).

Tandon, Prakash, *Beyond Punjab, 1937–1960* (Chatto & Windus, London, 1961).

Taylor, Alan, *American Colonies: The Settlement of North America to 1800. The Penguin History of the United States* (Allen Lane, London, 2001).

The Australasian Cookery Book: Specially Compiled for the Requirements of Australian and New Zealand Homes (Ward, Lock & Co., Melbourne, 1913).

The Production of Food Crops in Mauritius during the War (J. Eliel Felix, Acting Government Printer, Port Louis, Mauritius, 1947).

Thirsk, Joan, *Alternative Agriculture: A History – From the Black Death to the Present Day* (Oxford University Press, Oxford, 1997).

Thirsk, Joan, *Food in Early Modern England: Phases, Fads, Fashions, 1500–1760* (Hambledon Continuum, London, 2007).

Thomas, Hugh, *The Slave Trade: The History of the Atlantic Slave Trade, 1440–1870* (Picador, London, 1997).

Thompson, Andrew, *The Empire Strikes Back? The Impact of Imperialism on Britain from the Mid-Nineteenth Century* (Pearson Longman, Harlow, 2005).

Thompson, Peter, 'Henry Drax's instructions on the management of a seventeenth-century Barbadian sugar plantation', *William and Mary Quarterly* 66/3 (July 2009), 565–604.

Thompson, Peter J., 'The "friendly glass": drink and gentility in Colonial Philadelphia', *Pennsylvania Magazine of History and Biography* 113 (1989), 549–73.

Thompson, Susan J., and J. Tadlock Cowan, 'Durable food production and consumption in the world economy', in Philip McMichael (ed.), *Food and Agrarian Orders in the World-Economy* (Greenwood Press, London, 1995), 35–52.

Thornton, John, 'Sexual demography: the impact of the slave trade on family structure', in Claire C. Robertson and Martin A. Klein (eds), *Women and Slavery in Africa* (University of Wisconsin Press, Madison, 1983), 39–48.

Thornton, John, *Africa and the Africans in the Making of the Atlantic World, 1400–1800* (Cambridge University Press, Cambridge, 1999).

Tomlinson, B. R., 'Economics and Empire: the periphery and the imperial economy', in Andrew Porter (ed.), *The Nineteenth Century, Vol. III The Oxford History of the British Empire* (Oxford University Press, Oxford, 1999), 53–74.

Tooze, Adam, *The Wages of Destruction: The Making and Breaking of the Nazi Economy* (Allen Lane, London, 2006).

Torode, Angeliki, 'Trends in fruit consumption', in T. C. Barker, J. C. McKenzie and J. Yudkin (eds), *Our Changing Fare: Two Hundred Years of British Food Habits* (MacGibbon & Kee, London, 1966).

Tosh, John, 'Jeremiah Goldswain's farewell: family and fortune in early nineteenth-century English emigration', *History Workshop Journal* 77/1 (2014), 26–44.

Trentmann, Frank, 'Coping with shortage: the problem of food security and global visions of coordination, *c.*1902– 1950', in Frank Trentmann and Flemming Just (eds), *Food and Conflict in Europe in the Age of the Two World Wars* (Palgrave Macmillan, Basingstoke, 2006), 13–48.

Truxes, Thomas R., *Irish-American Trade, 1660–1783* (Cambridge University Press, Cambridge, 1988).

Tunzelmann, Alex von, *Indian Summer: The Secret History of the End of Empire* (Simon & Schuster, London, 2007).

Tuten, James H., *Lowcountry Time and Tide: The Fall of the South Carolina Rice Kingdom* (Mobius, Columbia, SC, 2010; accessed on the web, 18 October 2013, at www.sc.edu/uscpress/books/2010/3926x.pdf).

Tye, Diane, '"A poor man's meal": molasses in Atlantic Canada', *Food, Culture and Society* 11/3 (September 2008), 335–53.

Unwin, Tim, *Wine and the Vine: An Historical Geography of Viticulture and the Wine Trade* (Routledge, London, 1991).

Valenze, Deborah M., *Milk: A Local and Global History* (Yale University Press, London, 2011).

Vickers, Daniel, *Farmers and Fishermen: Two Centuries of Work in Essex County, Massachusetts, 1630–1850* (University of North Carolina Press, Chapel Hill, 1994).

Vickery, Amanda, 'Women and the world of goods: a Lancashire consumer and her possessions, 1751–81', in John Brewer and Roy Porter (eds), *Consumption and the World of Goods* (Routledge, London, 1993).

von Glahn, Richard, *Fountain of Fortune: Money and Monetary Policy in China, 1000–1700* (University of California Press, London, 1996).

Vugt, William E. van, 'Running from ruin? The emigration of British farmers to the USA in the wake of the repeal of the Corn Laws', *Economic History Review* 43 (1988), 411–28.

Wade, Louise Carroll, *Chicago's Pride: The Stockyards, Packingtown and Environs in the Nineteenth Century* (University of Illinois Press, Urbana, 2003).

Walvin, James, *Fruits of Empire: Exotic Produce and British Taste, 1660–1800* (Macmillan, London, 1997).

Ward, Edward, 'A Trip to Jamaica' (1698), in Thomas W. Krise (ed.), *Caribbeana: An Anthology of English Literature of the West Indies, 1657–1777* (University of Chicago Press, Chicago, 1999), 78–92.

Watt, George, *The Commercial Products of India Being an Abridgement of 'The Dictionary of the Economic Products of India'* (John Murray, London, 1908).

Weatherill, Lorna (ed.), *The Account Book of Richard Latham, 1724–1767* (Oxford University Press, Oxford, 1990).

Weaver, John C., *The Great Land Rush and the Making of the Modern World, 1650–1900* (McGill-Queen's University Press, Montreal and Kingston, 2003).

Weir, Robert M., *Colonial South Carolina: A History* (KTO Press, New York, 1983).

Wenzel, Marion, *House Decoration in Nubia* (Duckworth, London, 1972).

West, Elliott, 'Grain kings, rubber dreams and stock exchanges: how transportation and communication changed frontier cities', in Jay Gitlin, Barbara Berglund and Adam Arenson (eds), *Frontier Cities: Encounters at the Crossroads of Empire* (University of Pennsylvania Press, Philadelphia, 2013), 107–20.

Whitten, David O., and Bessie E. Whitten, *The Birth of Big Business in the United States, 1860–1914: Commercial, Extractive, and Industrial Enterprise* (Praeger, London, 2006).

Wilk, Richard, *Home Cooking in the Global Village: Caribbean Food from Buccaneers to Ecotourists* (Berg, Oxford, 2006).

Wilk, Richard R., 'Anchovy sauce and pickled tripe: exporting civilized food in the colonial Atlantic world', in Warren Belasco and Roger Horowitz (eds), *Food Chains: From Farmyard to Shopping Cart* (University of Pennsylvania Press, Philadelphia, 2009), 87–107.

Wilk, Richard, 'The extractive economy: an early phase of the globalization of diet', *Review. A Journal of the Fernand Braudel Center* 27/4 (2004), 285–305.

Williamson, James A. (ed.), *The Observations of Sir Richard Hawkins* (Argonaut Press, London, 1933).

Wills, John E., 'European consumption and Asian production in the seventeenth and eighteenth centuries', in John Brewer and Roy Porter (eds), *Consumption and the World of Goods* (Routledge, London, 1993), 131–47.

Wilmington, Martin, *The Middle East Supply Centre* (University of London Press, London, 1972).

Winstanley, M. J., *The Shopkeeper's World, 1830–1914* (Manchester University Press, Manchester, 1983).

Wood, Betty, with the assistance of T. R. Clayton and W. A. Speck, 'The letters of Simon Taylor of Jamaica to Chaloner Arcedekne, 1765–1775', in *Travel, Trade and Power in the Atlantic, 1765–1884*, Camden Miscellany Vol. XXXV, Camden Fifth Series, Vol. 19 (Cambridge University Press, Cambridge, 2002).

Woods, Rebecca, 'Breed, culture, and economy: the New Zealand frozen meat trade, 1880–1914', *Agricultural History Review*, 60/2 (2012), 288–308.

Woodward, Donald, 'A comparative study of the Irish and Scottish livestock trades in the seventeenth century', in L. M. Cullen and T. C. Smout (eds), *Comparative Aspects of Scottish and Irish Economic and Social History, 1600–1900* (John Donald Publishers, Edinburgh, n.d.), 147–64.

Woodward, Donald, 'The Anglo-Irish livestock trade of the seventeenth century', *Irish Historical Studies* 17/72 (1973), 489–523.

Worboys, M., 'The discovery of colonial malnutrition between the wars', in David Arnold (ed.), *Imperial Medicine and Indigenous Societies: Studies in Imperialism* (Manchester University Press, Manchester, 1988).

Worthington, Janet Robyn, *Coopers and Customs Cutters: Worthingtons of Dover and Related Families 1560–1906* (Phillimore & Co., Chichester, 1997).

Wright, Donald R., *The World and a Very Small Place in Africa: A History of Globalization in Niumi, The Gambia* (3rd edition, M. E. Sharpe, Armonk, NY, 2010).

Wynter, Andrew, *Our Social Bees: Pictures of Town and Country Life and Other Papers* (Robert Hardwicke, London, 1861).

Wyvern, 'Culinary Jottings for Madras', *The Calcutta Review* 68 (1879).

Wyvern, *Culinary Jottings: A Treatise in Thirty Chapters on Reformed Cookery for Anglo-Indian Exiles, based upon Modern English and Continental Principles* (Higginbotham & Co., Madras, 1885).

Zacek, Natalie, 'Rituals of rulership: the material culture of West Indian politics', in David S. Shields (ed.), *Material Culture in Anglo-America: Regional Identity and Urbanity in the Tidewater, Lowcountry, and Caribbean* (University of South Carolina Press, Columbia, 2009), 115–26.

Zacek, Natalie, *Settler Society in the Leeward Islands, 1670–1776* (Cambridge University Press, Cambridge, 2010).

Zahedieh, Nuala, *The Capital and the Colonies: London and the Atlantic Economy, 1660–1700* (Cambridge University Press, Cambridge, 2010).

Zlotnick, Susan, 'Domesticating imperialism: curry and cookbooks in Victorian England', *Frontiers: A Journal of Women Studies* 16/2–3 (1996), 51–68.

Zylberberg, David, 'Fuel prices, regional diets and cooking habits in the English industrial revolution (1750–1830)', *Past & Present* 229 (November 2015), 91–122.

Index